Social Media Data Mining and Analytics

Gabor Szabo
Gungor Polatkan
Oscar Boykin
Antonios Chalkiopoulos

WILEY

Social Media Data Mining and Analytics

Published by
John Wiley & Sons, Inc.
10475 Crosspoint Boulevard
Indianapolis, IN 46256
www.wiley.com

Copyright © 2019 by John Wiley & Sons, Inc., Indianapolis, Indiana Published simultaneously in Canada

ISBN: 978-1-118-82485-6
ISBN: 978-1-118-82490-0 (ebk)
ISBN: 978-1-118-82489-4 (ebk)

Manufactured in the United States of America

C10004500_091218

For general information on our other products and services please contact our Customer Care Department within the United States at (877) 762-2974, outside the United States at (317) 572-3993 or fax (317) 572-4002.

Wiley publishes in a variety of print and electronic formats and by print-on-demand. Some material included with standard print versions of this book may not be included in e-books or in print-on-demand. If this book refers to media such as a CD or DVD that is not included in the version you purchased, you may download this material at http://booksupport.wiley.com. For more information about Wiley products, visit www.wiley.com.

Library of Congress Control Number: 2018956702

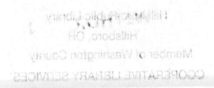

About the Authors

Gabor Szabo works on large-scale data analysis and modeling problems in social networks, self-organized online ecosystems, transportation systems, and autonomous driving. Previously, his research focus was on the description of randomly organized networks in online communities and biological systems at Harvard Medical School, the University of Notre Dame, and HP Labs. After that he built distributed algorithms to understand and predict user behavior at Twitter. He has created models for resource allocation in Lyft's ride-sharing network, and most recently he led a team at Tesla's Autopilot.

Gungor Polatkan is a machine learning expert and engineering leader with experience in building massive-scale distributed data pipelines serving personalized content at LinkedIn and Twitter. Most recently, he led the design and implementation of the AI backend for LinkedIn Learning and ramped the recommendation engine from scratch to hyper-personalized models learning billions of coefficients for 500M+ users. He deployed some of the first deep ranking models for search verticals at LinkedIn improving Talent Search. He enjoys leading teams, mentoring engineers, and fostering a culture of technical rigor and craftsmanship while iterating fast. He has worked in several notable applied research groups in Twitter, Princeton, Google, MERL and UC Berkeley before joining LinkedIn. He published and refereed papers at top-tier ML & AI venues such as UAI, ICML, and PAMI.

Oscar Boykin works on machine learning infrastructure at Stripe, building systems to predict fraud at scale. Prior to Stripe, Oscar spent more than 4 years at Twitter, first working on modeling and prediction for ads, and later on data infrastructure systems. At Twitter, Oscar co-developed many open-source scala libraries including Scalding, Algebird, Summingbird, and Chill. Before

Twitter, Oscar was an assistant professor of electrical and computer engineering at the University of Florida. Oscar has a Ph.D. in physics from the University of California, Los Angeles and is the coauthor of dozens of academic papers in top journals and conferences.

Antonios Chalkiopoulos is a fast/big data distributed system specialist with experience in delivering production-grade data pipelines in the media, IoT, retail, and finance industries. Antonios is a published author in big data, an open source contributor, and the co-founder and CEO of Landoop LTD. Landoop LTD builds the innovative and award winning Lenses platform for data in motion, which provides visibility and control over streaming data, data discovery via an intuitive web interface, and is a comprehensive SQL experience for data in motion, monitoring, alerting, data governance, multi-tenancy, and security. Lenses is a complete user experience for building and managing real-time data pipelines and micro-services.

About the Technical Editors

Sriram Krishnan is a senior director of the Einstein Platform team at Salesforce, where he is responsible for the foundational services that bring machine learning capabilities to Salesforce. Prior to Salesforce, Sriram was head of the Data Platform team at Twitter, and a tech lead on the Big Data Platform team at Twitter. He holds a Ph.D. in Computer Science from Indiana University, and spent several years as a researcher and group lead at the San Diego Supercomputer Center enabling scientific applications to use grid and cloud technologies. Sriram has co-authored more than 50 publications in the area of data, grid, and cloud computing, and his work has been cited more than 1700 times. Sriram has contributed to several influential open source projects that are being used widely in industry and academia.

Ben Peirce is director of XR Analytics at Samsung, which he joined on the acquisition of Vrtigo, a virtual reality analytics startup he co-founded. Previously, Ben built analytics systems at early stage startups in healthcare and advertising technology for over a decade. He holds a Ph.D. from Harvard, where he studied control systems and robotics.

Dashun Wang is an associate professor of management and organizations at the Kellogg School of Management, (by courtesy) industrial engineering and management sciences at the McCormick School of Engineering, and a core faculty at NICO, the Northwestern Institute on Complex Systems. Dashun received his Ph.D. in physics in 2013 from Northeastern University, where he was a member of the Center for Complex Network Research. From 2009 to 2013, he had also held an affiliation with Dana-Farber Cancer Institute, Harvard University as a research associate. He is a recipient of the AFOSR Young Investigator Award (2016).

Dr. Jian Wu is an assistant professor in the Department of Computer Science at the Old Dominion University. Dr. Wu obtained his Ph.D. in 2011 from Pennsylvania State University and then worked with Dr. C. Lee Giles on the CiteSeerX project as a tech leader. Dr. Wu's research interest is text mining and knowledge extraction on scholarly big data using machine learning, deep learning, and natural language processing. He has published nearly 30 peer-reviewed papers in ACM, IEEE, and AAAI conferences and magazines with best papers and nominations. He was the best reviewer in the ACM/IEEE Joint Conference on Digital Libraries (JCDL) 2018. As a tech leader, Dr. Wu made critical improvements to the architecture, web crawling, and extraction modules of CiteSeerX, increasing the collection to 10 million by 2017.

Credits

Project Editor
Tom Dinse

Technical Editors
Sriram Krishnan
Ben Peirce
Dashun Wang
Dr. Jian Wu

Production Editor
Athiyappan Lalith Kumar

Copy Editor
San Dee Phillips

Production Manager
Kathleen Wisor

**Content Enablement and
Operations Manager**
Pete Gaughan

Marketing Manager
Christie Hilbrich

Associate Publisher
Jim Minatel

Project Coordinator, Cover
Brent Savage

Proofreader
Evelyn Wellborn

Indexer
Johnna VanHoose Dinse

Cover Designer
Wiley

*To our families who supported us even though
we missed a lot of time from them to write this book.*

Acknowledgments

We would like to send our gratitude to our friends and colleagues at Twitter. With them invaluable discussions and collaborations have opened new perspectives for us to be able to look at social media data in unexpected ways, and allowed us to work on tools and approaches that let us expand our understanding of social media users. Their open-minded support throughout has always been greatly appreciated.

A very special thank you to Prof. David Blei, who provided the innovative research on topic modeling and a proper methodology for teaching machine learning through his Princeton class "Interacting with Data." In this book we followed his examples to cover the topics on representation learning and the applications in recommendations problems.

We would like to thank Jonathan Chang, the author of the R LDA package, for providing a machine learning tool for efficient and easy-to-use topic modeling techniques.

We would also like to thank Tom Dinse, Robert Elliott, and Jim Minatel, our editors at Wiley, who have been leading us down the path of publishing this book since the beginning for their great project management and editorial review of the content, as well as our team of technical editors for their review and insightful suggestions throughout the process. Moreover we would like to thank all the people who worked behind the scenes to help get this book together.

As for the rest of the authors, we would like to thank one of us, Gabor Szabo, who patiently shepherded the entire book writing process while we were working on it.

Contents

Introduction

This book is about using data to understand how social media services are used. Since the advent of Web 2.0, sites and services that give their users the power to actively change and contribute to the services' content have exploded in popularity. Social media finds its roots in early social networking and community communication services, including the bulletin board systems (BBS) of the 1980s, then the Usenet newsgroups, and Geocities in the '90s, whose communities organized around topical interests and provided their users with either email or chat room communications. The worldwide information communication network known as the Internet gave rise to a higher-level networking: a global web of connections among like-minded individuals and groups. Although the basic idea of connecting people across the globe has changed little since then, the scope and influence of social media services have attained never-before seen proportions. Although it's natural that a large part of the conversation is still happening in the "real world," the shift toward electronic information exchange on the level of human interactions has been getting stronger. The proliferation of mobile devices and connectivity puts the "Internet in our pockets," and with it the possibility to get in touch with our friends, families, and preferred businesses, anytime, anywhere.

No wonder that a myriad of services has popped up and started serving our needs for communication and sharing, which led to a transformation of public and private life. Through these services, we can immediately know what others think about politics, brands, products, and each other. By sharing their ideas privately or anonymously, people have the choice to speak their minds more freely than they would in traditional media. Everybody can be heard if they choose, so it's also become the responsibility of these services to find the needle in the haystack of people's contributions, so to speak, in delivering relevant and interesting content to us.

What's common to all these services? They are dependent on us, as they're only the mediators between humans. This means that in a way the mathematical regularities that we may discover through analyzing their usage data reflect our own behavior, so we can expect to see similar insights and challenges when we work with these datasets. The purpose of this book is to highlight these regularities and the technical approaches that lead to an understanding of how users of these services attend to them through the lens of the data these services collect.

Human Interactions Measured

Social media, as its name suggests, is driven by social interactions around the content that the online service provides. Social networking, for instance, makes it easy for individuals to connect with each other and share pictures and multimedia, news articles, Web content, and various other bits of information. In the most common usage scenario of these services, people go to Facebook to get updates about their friends, relatives, and acquaintances, and to share something about their lives with them. For example, on Twitter, because the follow relationship doesn't have to be reciprocated, users can learn about what any other user thinks, shares, or communicates with others. With LinkedIn, a professional social network, the goal is to connect like-minded professionals to each other through its network and its groups, and to serve as an interface between job seekers and companies looking to hire.

There are other social media services where the networking aspect of social interactions is used more as a facilitator rather than an end to co-create or enjoy shared content (for instance on Wikipedia, YouTube, or Instagram). Although the connections among users can be present, their purpose there is to make content discovery manageable for the users and to make the creation of content—for instance, Wikipedia articles—more efficient.

Of course, there are many other social media sites and services, usually targeting a specific interest or domain (art, music, photography, academic institutions, geographical locations, religions, hobbies, and the list could go on), which just shows that online users have the deepest desire to connect to people based on their shared interests or commonalities.

One thing among these services, their vastly different areas of focus notwithstanding, is common: They exist only because their *users* and *audience* are there. This is what makes them different from "pre-created" or static Internet locations such as traditional media news sites, company home pages, directories, and just about any Web resource that is created centrally by a relatively small group of authorized content creators ("small" at least in comparison to the crowds of people that use social media services with numbers generally in the millions). The result of the collective dynamics of these millions of social media users is what we can observe when we dig deep into the usage patterns of these services, and this is what we're interested in understanding in this book.

Online Behavior Through Data Collection

When we collect usage log data from social media services, we have a glimpse into the statistical behavior of many human beings coming together who have similar motivations or expectations or act toward the same goal. Naturally, the way the given service is organized and how it highlights its content has a great influence on what we'll see in the logs about the users' activities. The access and usage logs are stored in the databases of the service, and, therefore, the statistical patterns by which we all interact with others and the content the service hosts are bound to show up in these traces. (Provided there *are* such patterns, and we don't just carry out our daily activities in a completely inconsistent and random way! We'll see that—as perhaps expected by common sense—statistical regularities are abundant everywhere.)

Fortunately, the services (in most cases) don't differ so radically from each other in their designs that they would give rise to completely different user behavior characteristics. What do we mean by this? Let's say, for example, that we want to measure a simple thing: how frequently users come back to our service within a week and take part in some activity. This would be just a number, ranging from 0 to (in theory) infinity, for every user. Of course, we won't see anyone undertake an infinite number of actions on our service within a limited amount of time, but it may still be a large number. So, having set our mind to measuring the number of activities, can we expect to have different *statistical* results for two different systems: users posting videos to their YouTube channels and users uploading photos to their Flickr accounts?

The answer, obviously, is a resounding yes. If we looked at the distributions of the number of times people used either YouTube or Flickr, respectively, we would, of course, see that the fraction of YouTube users who upload *one* video per week *is* different from the fraction of Flickr users who upload *one* image per week. This is natural, as these two different services attract different demographics with different usage scenarios, so the exact distributions, consequently, will be different. However, what is not perhaps straightforward is that in most online systems that researchers have looked at we find *a similar qualitative statistical behavior* for these distributions.

By "qualitative" we mean that although the exact parameters of the usage model may be different for the two respective services, the model itself, through which we can best describe user behavior in both systems, is still the same or very similar between the services (with perhaps slight variations).

The good news about this is that we can be reasonably confident that what we're measuring with the data in the activity logs is indeed the underlying human behavior that drives the content creation, diffusion, sharing, and more, on these sites. The other piece of good news is that from this we can extrapolate and if we encounter a new service operating on user-generated content, we can make educated guesses about what we can measure in it. Therefore, if we see something unexpected in the graphs that's different from the general pattern we have seen before, we should look for a service-specific reason for it that we can be inclined to explore further.

So, in a way, the methods and the results that we highlight in this book may well apply to a completely new service if it's also governed by the same underlying human behavior. With few exceptions, this is true of the social media services for which we're aware research exists, and therefore we like to think of these systems as providing insight into human behavior. The opportunity, then, to observe and describe many people acting loosely together is unprecedented; this is because of the digital footprints they leave behind in the services' logs. (Privacy issues are, of course, a valid practical concern, but here we're interested only in the large picture and not how specific individuals behave.) The next sections look at what kinds of data can be of interest in various social media services and which public datasets we'll be using for examples in this book.

What Types of Data Are Essential to Collect?

The questions we would like to ultimately answer with data determine the types of data you need to collect, but in general, the more data you have at your disposal, the better you can answer those and future questions as well. You never know when you want to refine or expand the data analysis, so if you design a service, it's better to think ahead and log all or almost all the interactions users have with the service and each other. These days, storage is inexpensive, so it's wise to cater to as many future data needs as possible by not trying to optimize too early for storage space. Naturally, as the service evolves and it becomes clear what the focus areas are, it's possible to trim the data collection back and refactor the existing data sources, if necessary.

To better understand the user activity data we generally require, let's look at some typical questions around social media usage that we could be interested in answering:

- Who are the most active/inactive users? How many of them do we have?
- How does usage evolve over time? Can we predict usage per user segment (by geography, demographics, type of usage) ahead of time?
- How do we match users to content? Users to users? How do we surface content of interest to the user in a timely manner?
- What do users' networks look like? Do more engaged users form different kinds of networks?

- Why do people leave the service, if they do (*churn*)? Are there precursors to this churn, and can we predict it?

- What brings new users to the service to join? Do they like it, and if not, what makes happy users different from dissatisfied ones?

- Are there users who exploit our service in any way? Is there any spamming, unscrupulous usage, and deceptive behavior going on among the users?

- What are the most "interesting" or "trending" pieces of content at any given time? Who are attending to it from among our users, how can we find it, and what is it about?

- Can we find specific content of interest to us among the sheer amounts of streaming or historical data that the users produce? For instance, can we find users who mentioned a specific word or subject recently?

- What pieces of content are "popular" among the users? Are there big differences among their popularities, and if so, how big?

The chapters in this book address some of these questions and offer answers for specific services. As may be apparent, some of these can be best answered by doing active experiments with our users, in particular A/B testing experiments. (In an A/B testing experiment we show one feature or use one algorithm for one set of users *A*, and another for another set of users *B*. By measuring the differences in user activities between the *A* and *B* groups we can decide what influence the change in the feature had on users.) However, because we focus more on analyzing data that has been collected previously and learning as much about it as possible, we won't cover this powerful technique generally used to optimize the user experience on the service.

What kind of data should we collect either from the service we run or from other social media services we have access to, then? Guided by the previous questions, a few aspects of log data should be required for our analysis:

1. As users come to our service, they carry out specific actions: reading articles, viewing pictures, tagging photos, and sharing status updates. The (anonymized) identity of the users is what we want to know when we ask ourselves about what they are doing, along with a description of the actions.

2. We also need to know *when* they are taking the actions. Sub-second resolution for data collection (milli- or microseconds) usually suffices.

3. Obviously, for each action there could be a multitude of different kinds of metadata pieces that go along with it. If, for instance, the user favors or likes a post, we obviously want to store the unique identifier of that post together with the action.

As any of the users may have many actions over a period, the raw data logged in such a way may ultimately take a large amount of backend storage to save. This could take a long time to process for even simple questions; also, we don't always need *all* the information for the most common questions. Therefore, we normally create snapshots of *aggregated* data through automated ETL (extract, transform, load) processes in a production environment, for instance about the current state of the social graph with all the relationships among the users, the number of Tweets, posts, and photos that they have created or shared, and so on. When we want to analyze the data to gain certain insights, these aggregations are frequently the first source of information to turn to.

Although we need to think about how to best store all this data in appropriate databases, the design and implementation of such schemas is a science and is beyond the scope of this book. Also, we would like to rather focus on the way insights can be derived from the data and will use publicly available data from social media services to illustrate how we proceed with the different types of analyses.

Asking and Answering Questions with Data

Our goal is to expose you to several common situations you will encounter while making sense of data generated by social media services. The usual way of studying empirical phenomena (not necessarily just related to social media) has been following the centuries-long tradition of the scientific method:

1. Asking the question comes first, in generic terms. This doesn't yet have to involve any further assumptions about the data; we're just formalizing what we'd like to know about a specific behavior. For instance, "What are the temporal dynamics of users coming back to the service so that we can predict how long their session on the service will last?"

2. Optionally formulate a hypothesis about the expected outcome. This is useful for verifying whether your preconceptions make sense. Also, if you have a model in mind that you think best describes the quantitative outcome, you can check this. After you have formulated a hypothesis, predict what the result should be if the hypothesis holds. This step is optional because, if you don't want to build a model around the question and your goal is to use the result only to gain insights, you can skip this step. A hypothesis to the question in step 1, for instance, can be that "users come back to the service in a random manner, independently of whether they used it recently." (Whether this actual hypothesis is true in real services, you'll see later in Chapter 3.)

3. Determine the procedure to follow and what input data to collect to answer the question asked in step 1. Although the procedure is usually

straightforward given the computational tools and existing techniques you have, you usually have a lot of freedom in social media to select the test data set. Do you want to take samples from among the users or use everyone? What date range will you use? Do you filter out certain actions you consider undesirable? You obviously want to be thorough and explore as much about the data as possible to gain confidence about the results, for instance by taking different periods for the dataset or looking at different user cohorts. For the question you want to answer (see step 1), you may want to take the timestamps of any action generated by the users for a given month, for instance, and then take time differences between subsequent timestamps and analyze their temporal correlations.

4. Perform the data analysis! Ideally, the data collection has been already done by you or for you so that you don't have to wait for that. If your goal is to test your hypothesis, you also want to perform statistical testing. If you just want to gain insights, your numerical results are the answer to the question you asked.

The Datasets Used in This Book

To elucidate the processes and regularities that you can observe in social media due to human interactions, you naturally want to use some existing data coming from such systems, downloadable from various places on the Internet. Although most of the social media services keep their data private (privacy concerns being the paramount reason but also because these datasets can become huge), some services, most notably Wikipedia, make *all* their data available to the public. In other cases, academic researchers have collected data from these services through crawling or data sharing. The following sections list the data sources that we used throughout the book. We encourage you to try (and expand on) the examples for which having these datasets at hand is a prerequisite.

We selected a few services that have public, widely available, and easily obtainable datasets about their users and their content, to show what results we can expect in actual social media services for the questions we'll be asking. The names of these services should be familiar, and we also wanted to ensure that the datasets are at least medium-sized for users and the time range they span, and thus are amenable to analysis to draw meaningful conclusions. Follow the practical examples showcased throughout the book; to this end, the following sections describe the datasets used. As a summary, Table I.1 provides short descriptions of the example datasets we use.

Table I.1: Descriptions and Locations of the Datasets Used in This Book

SERVICE	MAIN PAGE	DATASET
Wikipedia	`wikipedia.org`	Revision and page meta information, no actual text
Twitter	`twitter.com`	Tweets created
Stack Exchange	`scifi.stackexchange.com`	Questions and answers from Stack Exchange's Science Fiction & Fantasy category
LiveJournal	`livejournal.com`	Directed social network connections
Cora dataset		Scientific documents from an academic search engine
MovieLens	`movielens.org`	Sample of movie ratings
Amazon Fine Food Reviews		Historical reviews on Amazon for "Fine Foods"

> **NOTE** Wikipedia and Stack Exchange content are licensed under the Creative Commons Attribution-ShareAlike 3.0 License, `https://creativecommons.org/licenses/by-sa/3.0/`; Livejournal data collected are due to Mislove et al., "Measurement and Analysis of Online Social Networks," IMC 2007, `http://social-networks.mpi-sws.org/data-imc2007.html`; the MovieLens dataset is from GroupLens Research, `http://grouplens.org/datasets/movielens/`; and Cora appeared in McCallum et al., "Automating the Construction of Internet Portals with Machine Learning," Information Retrieval vol 3, issue 2, 2000.

We made it easier for you to obtain these datasets: run `data/download_all.sh`, available from the book's downloads to get all the data files that the examples build on. (Note that due to the large size of the datasets, especially the Wikipedia dataset, at 50-60 GB the downloads take some time to complete). The location of the source code is given at the end of this Introduction.

Wikipedia

The biggest dataset we use is the English-language Wikipedia's revision histories of the several million articles it hosts. Wikipedia is a collaboratively edited encyclopedia, and the English version has approximately 5.7 million articles in 2018, with approximately 300,000 monthly active editors (`http://en.wikipedia.org/wiki/Wikipedia:Statistics`). A screen shot of the article "Wikipedia" can be seen in Figure I.1.

Twitter

On Twitter (Figure I.2), users can send out status updates of at most 140 characters in length (until 2017, when the service increased the maximum length of updates). Other users, who "follow" the sender, will receive these short messages

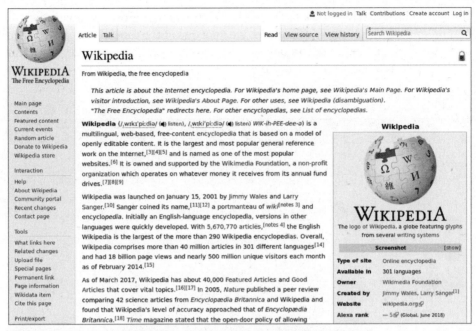

Figure I.1: An entry from the online encyclopedia Wikipedia about Wikipedia

in their so-called timeline. Pictures and short videos can also be attached to the status update. Many users follow news sources, celebrities, or their friends and family. Often, Twitter is considered an "information network" where users can follow anyone who they're interested in getting updates from, and those users do not have to follow them back.

We will collect Tweets using Twitter's API to analyze the activity of a sample of the users in Chapter 1.

Stack Exchange

Stack Exchange (Figure I.3) is a federated network of websites following the model of question answering, where users ask a question on a variety of different topics, and other users can answer these questions and vote both on questions and answers. This way high-quality content (at least in the eyes of the users) rises to the top. As of 2018, the Stack Exchange network consists of more than 350 sites covering different topics from software programming to astronomy to poker. The most well-known of these sites is the one that the network started with in 2008, Stack Overflow, focusing on various topics in computer programming. In Chapter 4, we take one of the topical Stack Exchange sites, the Science Fiction & Fantasy category, and look at the various properties of the posts that users submit there.

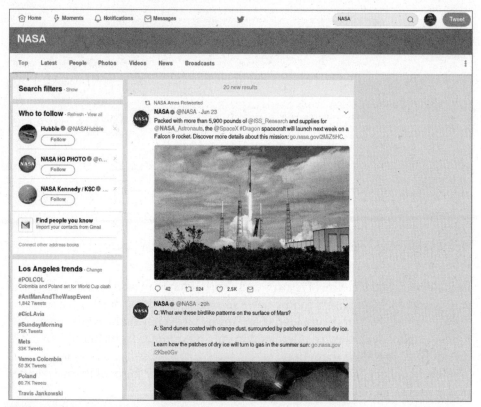

Figure I.2: A screen shot of a typical Twitter search timeline. Tweets appear in the main section, whereas trending topics and "who to follow" recommendations are shown on the side.

LiveJournal

LiveJournal (Figure I.4) is an online journal keeping and blogging service, in which users can make either mutual or unilateral connections to other users. Friends of users can read their protected entries, and conversely, the blog posts of friends show up on their "friends page." We'll use this dataset to study the directed connection structure of a social network in Chapter 2.

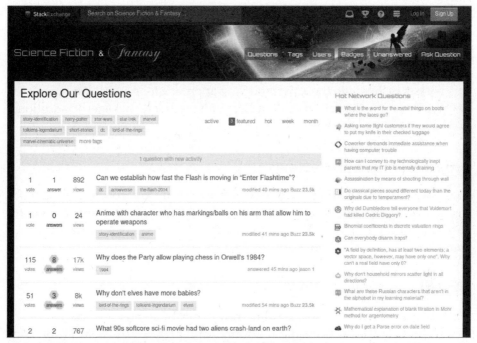

Figure I.3: Stack Exchange is a question answering service with a lot of topical sub-sites. We chose the Science Fiction & Fantasy category as it is not overly technical in nature (compared to computer-related categories or those focused on mathematics, for instance), yet has a decent number of users and amount of content.

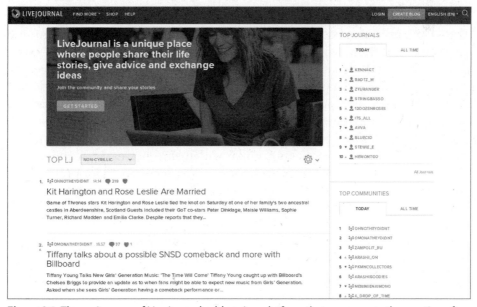

Figure I.4: The main page of LiveJournal, a blogging platform that encourages the creation of communities as well

Scientific Documents from Cora

This is a smaller dataset, containing the texts of 2,410 scientific documents from the Cora search engine. (This search engine has been deprecated; it was a proof-of-concept search engine for academic publications in computer science.) We use this dataset to illustrate the topic modeling approach for natural language texts in Chapter 4. The dataset comes bundled with the `lda` R package; no additional download will be necessary.

Amazon Fine Food Reviews

This is a dataset containing "Fine Food" reviews from Amazon, including product review summaries, scores, and some user details. The dataset has data for 10 years, through October 2012. For more details, see `https://snap.stanford.edu/data/web-FineFoods.html`.

MovieLens Movie Ratings

This dataset contains movie ratings from the MovieLens service (`https://movielens.org/`) on a scale ranging from 1 through 5, left by 938 users on 1,682 movies. Chapter 6 uses this dataset in the examples to predict how users would likely rate a movie that they haven't seen yet, given how other users like them have rated the movie before.

The Languages and Frameworks Used in This Book

The examples in this book are predominantly written in three programming languages and frameworks: R, Python, and Scalding. We use R for its excellent capabilities in statistics, machine learning, and graphics; Python because preprocessing large datasets and interfacing with service APIs is easy and fast in this language; and Scalding because it's a flexible and robust framework for carrying out distributed computations on MapReduce.

In general, we also believe these tools are great to know for data mining; therefore, we assume that you are familiar with them, or at least can understand code written in them. They provide a rapid development path for prototyping algorithms and writing quick tests around data, and through the extensive community support available for them, answers to almost any common technical challenge are readily available on online forums.

The titles of the code examples in this book reference the example's source code file (unless the code snippet is very short). The source files are in the `src/chapterX` subfolder of the book's code repository, where *x* refers to the chapter where the code example appears.

> **NOTE** See the "Source Code" section at the end of this Introduction for information about downloading the files.

The scripts are supposed to be executed from the folder where you have extracted the repository to, no need to change the default directory to where they reside: For instance, to download the Wikipedia dataset only, you can execute `src/chapter1/wikipedia/get_data.sh`; to pre-process the Stack Exchange dataset, you can run `python src/chapter4/process_stackexchange_xml.py` (we'll explain what these particular scripts do later in the appropriate chapters).

R

R is a statistical programming language that is popular not only among statisticians, but also among professionals from other disciplines wanting to perform data analysis. This is largely because of the vast set of libraries that the community has developed for it: When you look at the CRAN Task Views page (`http://cran.r-project.org/web/views/`) about available libraries categorized by discipline, you find econometrics, finance, genetics, the social sciences, and Web technologies in the list, among many others. Because R is free and open source, the culture of code sharing has resulted in this burgeoning ecosystem of community-developed libraries from all over the world. The community around R is active as well, and it's easy to find answers to at least the more common issues. (However, Web searches are sometimes a challenge, as the letter "R" is such a common occurrence in other documents as well—try `rseek.org`!)

For those not intimately familiar with the language yet, the syntax may seem slightly intimidating: R straddles the functional and the imperative programming styles, drawing on both paradigms. Its learning curve is steep but it's well worth it to learn the language. The official R tutorial, available at `http://cran.r-project.org/doc/manuals/R-intro.pdf`, is a good way to become familiar with the language and enough to understand the examples used in this book. A powerful asset that R offers is its essential data storage mechanism, called data frames, where related records of data can be stored in named columns of a matrix (with the exception that the columns can hold vectors of arbitrary types, not only numerical values).

Downloading and installing the base R system is a straightforward process. R is available for Linux, Mac OS X, and Windows at `http://cran.r-project.org/`. The documentation on the project's installation page is good, so we don't feel it's necessary to repeat the steps here, although if you follow our steps in the "System Requirements to Run the Examples" section later in this Introduction, you won't even need to install it manually. One thing we do note, however, is that using an Integrated Development Environment (IDE) for R pays dividends: Although R does have a command line, it's much easier to use a graphical interface. The two major options here are RStudio (`http://www.rstudio.com/`) and the

StatET plugin for Eclipse (`http://www.walware.de/goto/statet`). The former provides a one-click installation and a straightforward interface, whereas the latter provides more flexibility and better integration for working with other programming languages for existing Eclipse users.

You also need to install a couple of packages on top of the basic R installation to run the code examples. Table I.2 lists these R packages. The following section, "System Requirements to Run the Examples," has information about how to easily install these packages.

Table I.2: The R Packages Used in This Book's Code Examples

R PACKAGE	FUNCTIONALITY WE USE
ggplot2 scales	Creates pretty plots using an intuitive syntax for building up the graphs from layers
reshape2	Restructures data frames and switches between long and wide tabular data representations
plyr	Groups data by column values, performs some aggregations on the chunks, and puts the results back together
forecast	Time series forecasting
Matrix	Package for sparse matrices
NMF	Non-negative matrix factorization functions for matrix completion
glmnet	Efficiently solves the logistic regression problem
ROCR	Visualizes performance metrics for prediction tasks
tm	Creates term-document matrices from natural text
ggdendro	Plots dendrograms
Wordcloud dendextend	Create word clouds to visualize frequent terms in documents
entropy	Calculates the entropies of distributions
lda	Implements the Latent Dirichlet Allocation model for topic detection in texts
rPython	Calls Python functions from R—the best of both worlds

Python

Although R is an immensely powerful and versatile tool given the multitude of libraries that it can be extended with, it's not the optimal choice for certain tasks that are also commonplace when analyzing social media use. We often need to clean, filter down, or transform the datasets that we collect from the service we're looking at. In this case, R would prove suboptimal as its focus is on operating on in-memory structures, so, for instance, if we wanted to work only with one week of a year's worth of timestamped user engagement data in R, traditionally we would read the whole dataset first and then apply some filter to restrict the scope. Many times, given the usually large amounts of data we encounter, this is not even possible in a personal computer's RAM.

For preprocessing and aggregating medium- to large-sized data sets for further analysis, better choices exist. The other programming language we use for code examples is Python, which is an efficient programming language in terms of how long it takes to develop the scripts. It's also one of the most widespread programming languages in the world, with an incredibly active community around it as well. Again, similarly to R, there exists a huge collection of modules for it, naturally all open source such that the workings of the code can be easily examined. The modules we use in this book are shown in Table I.3.

Table I.3: The Python Packages Used in This Book's Code Examples

PYTHON MODULE	FUNCTIONALITY WE USE
`matplotlib`	Plots from Python
`networkx` `python-igraph`	Store, traverse, and plot graphs
`nltk`	Tokenizes documents and finds the stems of words
`beautifulsoup4`	Preprocesses text containing HTML tags
`tweepy`	Fetches tweets from the Twitter API
`scipy` `numpy`	Generic-purpose scientific & numeric libraries

Python is a capable machine learning and analytics platform with the help of libraries such as `SciPy`, `NumPy`, `matplotlib`, and `pandas`, among others. However, because we cover most of this functionality with R, we'll mostly use the core functionalities of the language and a few additional modules only. As mentioned, Python is great for stream-processing medium-sized datasets when we want to perform simple transformations on them. Also, if the task is more "lower level," closer to a traditional procedural programming problem, Python is often a better tool than R. Its syntax is pseudocode-like, so we believe that even in the absence of a deep Python experience, the code examples are readable if you know the basic concepts of lists and dictionaries in Python. (Otherwise, the official Python tutorial, available at `https://docs.python.org/2/tutorial/`, is a great start.) Python version 2.7 is required to run the code examples. The following section, "System Requirements to Run the Examples," describes how to set up Python as well.

In data analysis, you often have several stages of computation that build on top of each other. Let's take a short example: You want to determine the distribution of shortest path lengths in a small social network among all nodes whose degree (number of neighbors) is greater than 1. In this case, the stages would be load the network; filter for nodes with degrees greater than 1; calculate all shortest paths; and create a histogram from the results. If you have a largish network, the shortest path calculations may take a long time, as will also perhaps reading and building the network from a file. The easiest way is to write a Python script with all the steps, and run it once. However, often we make a mistake or forget about something during the analysis that we wanted to include. For instance, after building the histogram, we decide we also want to write the results into an output file, not only on the screen. In this case, we'd have to change the script and rerun it, again performing all the costly computations.

Because of this it's almost always better to use an interactive Python console where you can issue Python commands while keeping all variables in memory. The built-in Python console is good for this (launched by running `python`). However, a more powerful version of it is `ipython` (`https://ipython.org/`) and the Jupyter Notebook (`http://jupyter.org/`), which provide a host of additional helper functions such as variable name completion, command history search, embedded and interactive plotting, and parallel computing (`http://ipython.org/ipython-doc/dev/parallel/`). Although we don't make use of it in this book, the latter is useful for computations that would take a long time on one CPU core.

There's also a large selection of IDEs to choose from for Python—for a list see `https://wiki.python.org/moin/IntegratedDevelopmentEnvironments`. Figure I.5 shows a simple console-based IPython session at work.

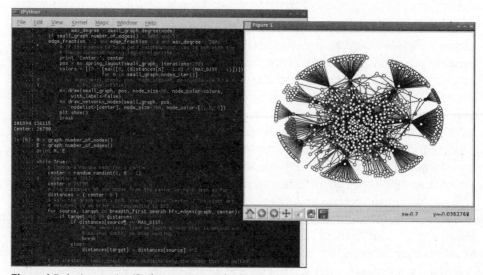

Figure I.5: An interactive IPython session with plotting

Scalding

Chapter 5 of this book highlights the algorithmic approaches to processing large datasets that we're almost always confronted with when analyzing logs from social media services. For most of the example questions in this book, it suffices to run code on a single processor of a single computer, but in some cases the processing can take several hours. In practice, we almost always turn to distributed computing solutions when we work with activity data generated by a few million users.

We've been witnessing an unprecedented pace of progress in the development of toolsets and frameworks for large-scale data processing these days, where new frameworks, tools, and databases make the previous generations obsolete, often within a few years. The MapReduce paradigm, however, has emerged as a dominant model for batch processing large datasets on hundreds or thousands of computers, due to its ability to scale to large data centers and its resiliency against individual server failures, which necessarily happen when so many computers are utilized all at the same time, round-the-clock (the open-source world has embraced its Java-based implementation, Hadoop). This technology has been the reliable workhorse of distributed data processing for long enough now that mature solutions have been developed for it. Knowing how to think in terms of these solutions can help cope with the large amounts of user-generated data that you routinely need to process.

Although MapReduce is the "engine" that sits atop the clustered computers, in its purest form it's not convenient for writing analytical jobs. Although many operations on social media data could be directly written for the most basic MapReduce framework, we're better served by moving to higher-level execution planners, where expressing these operations is more natural and closer to our everyday thinking. One of these frameworks is Scalding (available at `https://github.com/twitter/scalding`), which enables you to use the Scala programming language to build data processing pipelines for analyzing social media log data. With Scalding, we would like to present the underlying ideas and design patterns that enable us to make accurate, but approximative, calculations on large datasets coming from social media services.

System Requirements to Run the Examples

We developed and ran the examples showcased in this book on the Ubuntu Linux operating system, release 18.04 LTS. If you use any other operating system, especially Windows, we recommend setting up a development environment either in a virtual machine with Ubuntu 18.04 LTS as the guest, or to explore one of the popular online cloud hosting services to provision an instance initialized with Ubuntu 18.04 LTS.

After obtaining the source code repository we provide with this book (see "Online Repository for the Book" at the end of this chapter), you can extract it into a folder of your choice, and run `setup/setup.sh` in that folder to install the required system, R, and Python packages to be able to run the source code we present in the book.

Additionally, as previously mentioned, executing the `data/download_all.sh` script is also necessary to have the data files available for the examples to operate on; please run it once before executing any of the examples. As mentioned, the downloads take about 60 GB of disk space.

Overview of the Chapters

We organized this book around exploring and understanding the essential building blocks of social media systems, which we simplified as the *who, how, when,* and *what* of social media processes. Because social media is essentially about people flocking together on various sites to discuss, to be entertained, and to share, we're looking at these topics from the perspective of the users. Who are they? How do they connect? When is it in time that they become engaged? And, finally, what is the content like that they create and consume as a collective?

Chapter 1: Users: The *Who* of Social Media. Chapter 1 looks at one of the most important questions we usually ask about users of a service: How active are its users? You explore the universal aspects of human activities that are characteristic of these services, and why such vast differences among some users occur, supported by metrics from Wikipedia and Twitter.

Chapter 2: Networks: The *How* of Social Media. This chapter describes another important facility that social media services provide: the social network. Sometimes, the term is used by itself to encompass the service as a whole; however, here the focus is on the directed connection graph (as witnessed on Wikipedia, Twitter, and LiveJournal) and what kinds of regularities you can discover in it.

Chapter 3: Temporal Processes: The *When* of Social Media. This is a chapter about when things happen. We collect temporal data on Tweets and Wikipedia edits, and see what the timestamps tell us about user behavior on these sites. We also compare the results to baseline expectations that are generally assumed to hold in dynamic systems and introduce basic techniques to make time series forecasts.

Chapter 4: Content: The *What* of Social Media. Chapter 4 reviews the low-level and high-level approaches to help you understand what people are talking about in their textual posts using common natural language processing techniques. Beyond basic text data preparation, we describe the statistical properties of text and move on to find topics in the posts using multiple algorithms, in posts collected from Stack Exchange questions and answers, and in texts of published articles on Cora.

Chapter 5: Processing Large Datasets. In this chapter, you are introduced to the challenges of analyzing large datasets prevalent in social media studies. After a review of MapReduce, you see code examples using the Scalding framework to highlight generic programming patterns while working with large human behavior-induced datasets. As an extension, you see how to use approximation algorithms when your goal is to have results quickly, but only within known error bounds around the exact result. We also briefly cover the procedure for setting up clusters of computers on a cloud service to execute the parallel frameworks.

Chapter 6: Learn, Map, and Recommend. This chapter is about making recommendations to users and showcases machine learning techniques to predict whether people will like movies and to evaluate the result of the prediction. You also examine the model to see whether it tells something about how to categorize the items (the movie titles).

Chapter 7: Conclusions. The final chapter takes a slightly deeper look at the generic statistical patterns that you have seen emerge across the different problems throughout the book, and how to use similar analytical techniques to understand them.

Online Repository for the Book

The book's website at Wiley.com has the full source code files for the examples, support material, and updates. To locate these, search for either this book's title or its ISBN (this book's ISBN is 978-1-118-82485-6) on Wiley.com, then, once on the book's main page, scroll down to the Downloads tab.

Users: The *Who* of Social Media

Social media revolves around users, and their activities and interactions. Users create the content, communicate with each other, and ultimately keep the service alive and growing. This chapter looks at the typical user's behavior on social media services and the universal similarities you can see across the different services.

First, we focus on the most basic questions about the *overall activity* of those using the service: Are there some regularities in their aggregate statistics? If regularities exist in one service, can they be generalized to other systems? A few very basic conditions affecting usage give rise to measured activity distributions, and we quantify the differences among users in terms of overall activity with the help of observed regularities. Because activity distributions have a specific analytical form, we discuss why it's hard to take and interpret averages in actual social media systems in the presence of such distributions.

Throughout, we support our conclusions with data collected from Wikipedia and Twitter.

Measuring Variations in User Behavior in Wikipedia

One of the most important questions in terms of user activities is: How much do users contribute to, or use, the service? You can look at this question from many different points of view, but certainly one of the most straightforward ways to characterize users is to describe how frequently they come back and are present on the service. You can certainly expect that some users are more "active" than others—but how do you exactly quantify user activity in relation to the service?

User activity can be characterized in the most obvious manner by *how many times* a user performed a certain action such as leaving a comment, sharing a picture, creating or removing social network connections, and so on—in other words, using any facility that the service provides to its users. To determine this, the first thing to do is to define the time period for collecting the data needed to make the measurements.

Figure 1.1 shows two possible scenarios for choosing periods from which we can collect user activity data. In scenario (a), we chose more or less random, non-consecutive periods for the data collection. Although this choice may be valid under specific requirements, we generally prefer consecutive, closed-time ranges for data collection, like those that we can see in case (b). General user behavior may change over time (for instance new users might have different characteristics than older ones), so we prefer to sample user activity within as short a time range as possible. For this reason, case (b) is the natural choice, in which we select a continuous time interval and count the number of times a user has been active within this interval. This is the *frequency* of usage in the given time window.

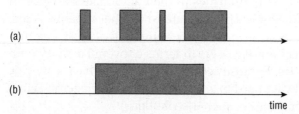

Figure 1.1: Possible choices for sampling time windows to measure aggregate user activity. In scenario (a), we pick non-consecutive time windows randomly. In (b), we choose a continuous time window between two given points in time.

The Diversity of User Activities

We can reasonably assume that users will differ in how likely they are to use a service: some will be very active, whereas others will use the service only once in a while. How large are these differences, and how can we characterize them? These are the questions you look at in this section.

This section uses the Wikipedia edit history logs. First, we look at how often Wikipedia editors contribute to articles: The question is how many times a given user makes a change to any Wikipedia article in each time period. A Wikipedia "editor" is anyone with a registered user name, and in the broader sense anyone who makes a smaller or larger change to any Wikipedia article. Luckily, the Wikimedia foundation makes the edit history of all articles and users available on its web site (`http://en.wikipedia.org/wiki/Wikipedia:Database_download#English-language_Wikipedia`). The dataset used in this chapter describes all revisions (edits) of the English-language Wikipedia. We chose the English Wikipedia because it is the oldest and most comprehensive among Wikipedias in various languages. (For statistics on the different Wikipedias, see `http://en.wikipedia.org/wiki/Wikipedia:Size_of_Wikipedia#Comparisons_with_other_Wikipedias`).

You can find the revisions metadata (without actual page content) in the file named `enwiki-*-stub-meta-history.xml.gz` for the latest dump date. At the beginning of 2018, the compressed file measured approximately 54GB. The data is in XML format, and for each page the file contains the full edit history with the name and ID of the user, and the timestamp of the edit. To measure users' frequencies of usage in a time window, it's only these fields that are of interest to us. You can download the latest Wikipedia data dump by running the shell script `src/chapter1/wikipedia/get_data.sh` from the book's online repository.

Generally, in data analysis you spend a significant amount of effort on just preprocessing and cleaning up data in a database or flat file. To illustrate the typical workflow, we'll walk you through this step with the downloaded Wikipedia file. Because XML is a rather verbose way to describe structured data, the first task is to transform this file into a format that you can easily work with later because you'll want to read through it multiple times as you experiment with the data. Transforming data files into a format that you feel comfortable with improves development and running times. To that end, in this example you first preprocess the downloaded file with the `src/chapter1/wikipedia/process_revisions_xml.py` Python script, which generates a flat text file with the edit records in rows and the user IDs and timestamps in tab-separated columns (this may take a long time, given the large size of the input file). Alternatively, we could have chosen to store the data in a relational (SQL) database, which in many cases is a preferable solution. However, for simplicity, we use a plain text file in this example.

PROCESSING LARGE XML FILES: DOM VERSUS SAX

For processing large XML files, you have a choice between the Document Object Model (DOM) or the Simple API for XML (SAX) approach. In both cases, there is a variety of high-quality libraries at your disposal in every major programming language, including Python, so the toolset available to you with either approach is essentially equivalent. The difference is, however, that the DOM model represents the XML file after reading it in its entirety as a *tree in memory*, mapping the XML nodes to nodes of the tree. On the other hand, SAX takes an event-driven approach: As the SAX parser reads the XML input, events are fired as callbacks to your main program, and you can decide what to do and how to process the nodes and data read. Obviously, for this example, only SAX parsing works, as you cannot reasonably hope to store this much data in RAM. (Nor should you want to, as you need only one pass through the file to distill the relevant information about the revisions, writing the fields of every revision out as you finish with a record.) In Python, the SAX library is in the package `xml.sax`, and you can see how XML nodes are handled in `process_revisions_xml.py` in the `startElement` and `endElement` methods that are called when an XML node is opened and closed, respectively.

The result of parsing the Wikipedia revision database with our script is a flat tab-separated text file as mentioned, with the following columns:

- Name of the page edited
- "Namespace" of the page (which is the "type" of the page, `https://en.wikipedia.org/wiki/Wikipedia:Namespace`)
- ID of the page
- Revision ID
- Timestamp of the revision
- ID of the editing user
- Editing user's account name
- IP address of the user (only for anonymous editors)

Although Wikipedia pages are categorized into *namespaces*, such as normal articles, user pages, and help pages, among others, we did not restrict ourselves to any specific namespace and considered all edits. With this distilled file, we can easily calculate how many edits any user made in a given time frame by simply iterating through the file and recording the user ID of a revision that falls within a specific time range. In Listing 1.1, we specify three date ranges (the first one, two, and three months of 2013, respectively) for counting the times a user made an edit within each of the date ranges. The number of times a user edited an article will then be written into the output file, where every line is for a user and three columns are for the number of edits by that user for the given date range, respectively.

Listing 1.1: This script takes all Wikipedia revisions and outputs the number of edits made by any user between the date periods defined in DATE_RANGES. (user_edits_in_timeframes.py)

```
'''
Count the number of times particular users made edit in the given time
frames.
'''

import gzip
from collections import defaultdict


INPUT_FILE = 'data/wikipedia/revisions.tsv.gz'
OUTPUT_FILE = 'data/wikipedia/user_edits_in_timeframes.tsv.gz'

DATE_RANGES = [('2013-01-01T00:00:00', '2013-02-01T00:00:00'),
               ('2013-01-01T00:00:00', '2013-03-01T00:00:00'),
               ('2013-01-01T00:00:00', '2013-04-01T00:00:00')]

# The number of times a user made a revision in a given date range.
user_frequencies = defaultdict(lambda: defaultdict(int))

user_names = dict()
with gzip.open(INPUT_FILE, 'r') as input_file:
    for line in input_file:
        title, namespace, page_id, rev_id, timestamp, user_id, \
        user_name, ip = line[:-1].split('\t')
        # We only keep registered users, and need to strip user ID 0
        # due to a logging bug (http://en.wikipedia.org/wiki/User:0).
        if user_id != '' and user_id != '0':
            for range_id in xrange(0, len(DATE_RANGES)):
                if timestamp >= DATE_RANGES[range_id][0] and \
                timestamp < DATE_RANGES[range_id][1]:
                    user_frequencies[user_id][range_id] += 1
                    user_names[user_id] = user_name

with gzip.open(OUTPUT_FILE, 'w') as output_file:
    for user_id in user_frequencies.iterkeys():
        output_file.write('\t'.join(
            [user_names[user_id]] + \
            [str(user_frequencies[user_id].get(range_id, 0)) \
            for range_id in xrange(0, len(DATE_RANGES))
            ]))
        output_file.write('\n')
```

The first step toward describing aggregate user activities is to calculate a histogram of the number of times a user made an edit within a date range.

Visualizing histograms is a common task carried out to understand the differences among users, and we'll frequently do this in this book. The R code snippet in Listing 1.2 reads in the output produced by the Python script in Listing 1.1 and plots the number of users with a given number of edits in the first time period (January 2013).

Listing 1.2: Read and plot a frequency histogram for the number of times a Wikipedia editor changed a page for January 2013. (`user_edits_in_timeframes.R`)

```
library(plyr)
library(ggplot2)

revs.in.periods = read.table(
        gzfile('data/wikipedia/user_edits_in_timeframes.tsv.gz'),
        sep='\t', col.names=c('account', 'range1', 'range2', 'range3'),
        comment.char='', quote='')

# Only users with > 0 edits in Jan 2013 are considered.
ggplot(subset(revs.in.periods, range1 > 0, select='range1'),
aes(range1)) +
        geom_histogram(binwidth=1, origin=-0.5) + xlim(0, 20) +
        xlab('Number of revisions made') + ylab('Number of users in
        period')
```

The result of this is shown in Figure 1.2, where you can see that as you consider a larger and larger number of revisions, the number of editors making that many edits quickly decreases. In fact, when you look at the distribution more in detail, you find that there were a handful of registered users (this may include so-called "bots", or robots, that are automated Wikipedia agents to carry out some bookkeeping task) that made tens of thousands of edits in just 1 month!

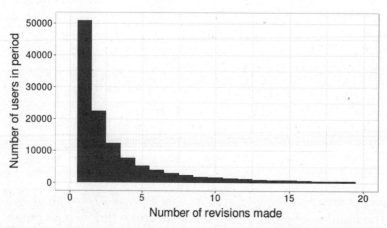

Figure 1.2: The number of editors who made a certain number of revisions to any Wikipedia article during January 2013. The horizontal axis has been truncated to show no more than 20 edits a month; however, the data shows that you can find users with tens of thousands of edits as well.

Nevertheless the number of such users is few; the average number of edits per user in January 2013 is approximately 30, and the median is 2. You can immediately see a big difference between the mean and the median: This is a sign of a highly *skewed* distribution, where a few of the high-end outliers can change the average, whereas the median will not be significantly affected by them. We discuss this in more detail a little later in this chapter.

You can consider the number of revisions made by a user as a random process because so many unknown factors determine a user's activity that it's impossible to account for all. Users may come and go, find something interesting and add some modifications to an article, or start a new article when they find that the topic of their interest does not exist yet. Indeed, when and how frequently users find the time to come back to the service varies as well, yet, as Figure 1.2 suggests, you can expect some regularities in this if you aggregate the behavior of many users: The histogram looks like a rather smooth function, so it wouldn't be surprising to find an explanation for why this is so.

Regarding user activity as a random process, then, you can also approximate the *probability density function* (PDF) of the process as just the normalization of the histogram displayed in Figure 1.2. This means that you need to divide the frequency counts for users by the total number of users, which of course is also the area under the histogram considered as a function. The probability that a user will have *n* edits is given by the following formula:

$$P(edits = n) = \frac{U(edits = n)}{\sum\limits_{i=1}^{\infty} U(edits = i)}.$$

(1.1)

In this formula, *P* gives the likelihood that a randomly chosen user will have made *n* edits in the period under consideration. *U(edits = n)* denotes the number of users who made *n* edits, so the denominator is just exactly the total number of users we have (because a user may not belong to two different activity buckets at the same time, and every user belongs to a bucket). This is the probability distribution function, yielding the likelihood of an event over the range of all possible events. (It is also sometimes called the *probability mass function* for discrete distributions, such as we have for the number of edits per time period). If we were to plot the probability distribution function, it would look just like Figure 1.2, with only the vertical axis rescaled because we have divided all values by the same constant, the total number of users.

Is there anything more we can say, though, about how many revisions we will expect to see from the users, in the future, or for any time period? The smooth decay of the frequencies we have seen from this limited example suggests that we may find some regularities for user behavior in a more general sense as well. After all, the whole purpose of this exercise is to learn from the past and to anticipate the user activity distribution in the future and detect any deviations from our expectations.

Now we'll see how the user activity distribution changes if we consider longer and longer periods for our observations. To this point in the example we've been discussing, we took the edits of all users who were active during 1 month. Now, we will extend this 1-month period to 2, and then to 3 months. We made provisions in Listing 1.1 for these measurements, where, to go through our distilled Wikipedia revisions file only once, we defined two other time periods aside from the 1 month we have been focusing on until now. These two additional date ranges, as the code example shows, are from the beginning of January until the end of February, and until the end of March 2013, respectively. To see how the user activity distributions relate to each other, we'll plot them together. It is, of course, expected that 2 or 3 months will naturally enable more users to participate, and this is exactly what you can see in Figure 1.3. Although the shapes of the functions for the number of users making a certain number of revisions are similar across the three different time ranges, a longer range allows for more users to make more edits.

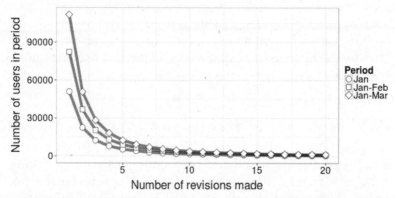

Figure 1.3: The number of revisions for three different time windows: for the first, the first 2, and first 3 months of 2013, respectively, as is also indicated by the figure's legend. The calculations were made the exact same way as for Figure 1.2.

Moving on from just absolute user counts, now look at the probability distribution functions for the number of revisions for all time periods: What is the likelihood that a given user will make a certain number of edits in the given period? For this we will calculate the probability that a randomly chosen user will make exactly r edits in period p. The corresponding equation follows the same formulation as Equation 1.1:

$$P_p(r) = \frac{U_p(r)}{\sum_{i=0}^{\infty} U_p(i)}.$$

(1.2)

Here and later in this section, $U_p(r)$ denotes the number of users making exactly r Wikipedia edits in the chosen period p (where p may be 1, 2, or 3 in our particular setup to denote the three date ranges of Figure 1.3, for instance). $p = 1$ for Jan 2013, $p = 2$ for Jan–Feb 2013, and $p = 3$ for Jan–Mar 2013. $P_p(r)$ is therefore the likelihood that a randomly chosen user has r revisions in period p.

The part of the R code that calculates $P_p(r)$ can be seen in Listing 1.3.

Listing 1.3: This R code snippet splits up `revs.in.periods.long` twice, first by time period, and then by revision count, and calculates the fraction of users in a time period who made a given number of edits, out of all the users in that time period. (`user_edits_in_timeframes.R`)

```
# Calculate the fraction of users separately for each date range who
# make a certain number of revisions, excluding all users who make zero
# edits in any of the time windows.

revs.in.periods.long = melt(revs.in.periods, 'account',
        variable.name='range', value.name='revisions')

normalized.revisions = ddply(subset(revs.in.periods.long,
                        revisions > 0),
        .(range), function(one.range) {
            user.count = nrow(one.range)
            ddply(one.range, .(revisions),
                    function(one.revision)
                        data.frame(user.fraction=
                        nrow(one.revision) / user.count)
            )
        })
```

We plotted the results of this for the normalized user counts in Figure 1.4. One thing that you can immediately notice is that the three probability distribution functions are similar to each other. (Actually, to prove this visual similarity with numbers, look at the code snippet under Calculation 1.1 in the `user_edits_in_timeframes.R` source file. This takes the three probability points for every single revision count and calculates the relative mean squared errors from their respective averages: They're all in the 6–8% range for the revision counts between 1 and 10.) Now take a leap of faith, and assume that for every possible revision count r the user fractions are the same for all three periods:

$$\frac{U_1(r)}{\sum_{i=1}^{\infty} U_1(i)} = \frac{U_2(r)}{\sum_{i=1}^{\infty} U_2(i)} = \frac{U_3(r)}{\sum_{i=1}^{\infty} U_3(i)}. \tag{1.3}$$

This assumption will help us a lot going forward, as we'd like to explain why this regularity may arise.

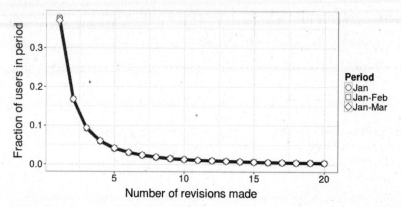

Figure 1.4: The probability that a user will make a given number of Wikipedia edits. Note that the functions for the three periods overlap to a large degree, and it is hard to see a difference for any but the first data point.

Because the denominators of Equation 1.3 are all constants (these are the total number of users making at least one edit in each of the periods), we also should express the detailed user counts $U_p(r)$ with each other in a simpler way by introducing the following ratios:

$$C_{21} = \frac{\sum_{i=1}^{\infty} U_2(i)}{\sum_{i=1}^{\infty} U_1(i)}$$

$$C_{31} = \frac{\sum_{i=1}^{\infty} U_3(i)}{\sum_{i=1}^{\infty} U_1(i)}. \tag{1.4}$$

Ostensibly, C_{21} is the total number of active users in Period 2, divided by the number of active users in Period 1 (and similarly for C_{31}). With these, we can express both $U_2(r)$ and $U_3(r)$ using $U_1(r)$, as follows:

$$U_2(r) = C_{21}U_1(r)$$

$$U_3(r) = C_{31}U_1(r). \tag{1.5}$$

Remember, though, that it was only our intuition that the normalized user counts should be equal at every r, and Equation 1.3 holds. To check this in a more direct way, we'll for a second relax our assumption that C_{p1} is independent of r because we can measure the $U_p(r)/U_1(r)$ fractions for every r, which we'll naturally call $C_{p1}(r)$. We can also check how C_{21} and C_{31} look in practice, and whether, by measuring them directly, we can still see them being constant. The R code example in Listing 1.4 calculates these ratios for both Periods 2 and 3.

Listing 1.4: Calculate the ratio of the number of edits between users in Periods 2 and 3 to those in Period 1, with the same number of revisions. See the figure below for the results. (user_edits_in_timeframes.R)

```
# Count the number of users in each period with a given number of > 0
# revisions.
user.counts.long = ddply(subset(revs.in.periods.long, revisions > 0),
                 .(range, revisions), nrow)

# Reformat the results into a wide table where the number of revisions
# are the rows and in three columns we have the user counts for each of
# the ranges.
user.counts.wide = dcast(user.counts, revisions ~ range)

# Calculate the pairwise ratios between the user frequencies in each
# revision bucket, with respect to those in range 1.
ratios = within(user.counts.wide, {
                ratio21 = range2 / range1
                ratio31 = range3 / range1
        })
```

Figure 1.5 displays $C_{21}(r)$ and $C_{31}(r)$ as a function of the number of revisions made. What we can immediately notice is that to a large degree, (the revision dependent) $C_{21}(r)$ and $C_{31}(r)$ appear to be constant, independent of the number of revisions, r. Now we can ask: What if we can indeed model these ratios as constants, and what consequences does this fact have on our understanding of user activities?

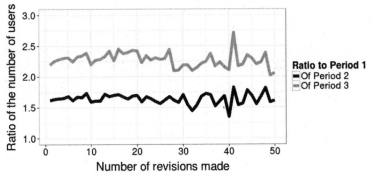

Figure 1.5: The number of active users were taken for the three periods we used before (Jan 2013 for Period 1, Jan–Feb 2013 for Period 2, and Jan–Mar 2013 for Period 3) for any given revision count. For this plot, we divided the number of editors with a given number of revisions in Period 2 with those in Period 1 with the same number of revisions, and plotted it in the dark line. Similarly, we also took the ratio of the user counts in Period 3 to those in Period 1 and plotted those with the lighter line.

First, let's estimate what the values of these constants are! Figure 1.5 suggests that the ratio between Periods 2 and 1 is approximately 1.6, and the ratio between Periods 3 and 1 is approximately 2.2–2.3. If we were thinking that these ratios are the same as the ratios between the lengths of the appropriate periods, assuming that a longer period gives rise to a proportionally larger number of active users, then we were wrong: If we divide the number of days in each period with each other, we will get (31 + 28) / 31 ≈ 1.9 and (31 + 28 + 31) / 31 ≈ 2.9, respectively. The differences between these pairs of numbers are large, so we cannot just assume that the longer periods we take, the more users we will see in the revision buckets, proportionately.

At any rate, what have we learned about user activity distributions up to now from Wikipedia's example? To summarize the main findings:

- A large diversity exists in the number of actions that users take in a given period. There are many users who have only a few actions, and the number of the active users decreases sharply as the number of actions we consider increases.

- If we take longer and longer time periods, we will naturally observe a larger number of actions from a larger number of users. However, the histograms for user activity counts appear to come from the same family of functions, as their functional forms are scaled with respect to each other.

- Considering the normalized probability distribution functions, no matter which period we are sampling users from, these functions will be the same. We have also seen that this is because the number of users with a certain number of actions is a constant multiple of a universal function that does not depend on the period. (This is what we expressed by the C_{p1} constants earlier.)

The Origin of the User Activity Distribution

Let's develop this last point further: Can we say something more about the user activity distributions, given that we found the regularities in the previous section? This section highlights some more measurements necessary to come to our conclusion, and also some analytical methods often useful in modeling the random nature of online user behavior. For this we can also make and verify one more assumption: If we observe *particular* users for longer, the number of times they are active will be also larger. This is an almost trivial assumption, as we can expect that the longer time ranges are available for the users, the more chances they will find to use the service. Also, we can reasonably think that their individual number of actions, on a large scale, will be proportional to the length of the time window for the observation. This expresses our belief that individual users can be characterized by an average activity rate *specific to them* that describes how many times they use the service in a unit of time, and we assume that this rate stays more or less constant over time. (At least if we take long enough time windows. We may expect that there are times when the user acts in "bursts," which are short periods of time when they are more active than at other times. More on this in Chapter 4.) Note that this proportionality assumption does not necessarily mean that a time window that is, for example, twice as long as another will necessarily result in twice as many actions for a given user. Overall user activity may seasonally fluctuate in time (for instance, with a yearly periodicity), and there could be periods when large-scale user activity goes down, and some other periods when it goes up.

To see how the number of user edits changes when you change the length of the observation window, you can look at how many more or fewer edits users made in Periods 2 or 3, *given* that they made a certain number of edits in Period 1. There are obviously a lot of users who make a given number of edits in Period 1, and they all individually have possibly different numbers of revisions in the other periods. Therefore, you can take the *average* of the number of edits in the other periods for all users with that same exact number of edits in Period 1. In other words, if $\overline{r}_2(r_1)$ denotes the average number of edits in Period 2 for all users who had r_1 number of edits in Period 1, then, more formally,

$$\overline{r}_2(r_1) = \frac{\sum_{i=1}^{N} I(r_{i,1} = r_1) r_{i,2}}{\sum_{i=1}^{N} I(r_{i,1} = r_1)}, \tag{1.6}$$

where the sums go over all users (their number we denoted here by N); $r_{i,1}$ and $r_{i,2}$ stand for the number of revisions made by the ith user in Periods 1 and 2, respectively; and $I(r_{i,1} = r_1)$ is the *indicator function* being 1 when its argument is true, and 0 when it is false. The numerator of this equation is therefore the sum of the revisions in Period 2 for users who had r_1 revisions in Period 1, and the denominator is the number of such users.

When you look at the average number of edits made by users calculated in this way, as shown by the Figure 1.6, you can notice that the edits in the longer periods are well approximated by linear functions of the edits made in the shorter period. Also, remember that Periods 2 and 3 run from January through the end of February and March, respectively, so they overlap with Period 1 (which is January only), and thus the edits made in those two periods are never fewer than the edits in Period 1.

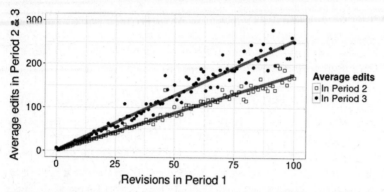

Figure 1.6: The average number of edits made by users in Periods 2 (and 3), given that they made a certain number of edits in Period 1. The average values seem to be in a linear relationship with the number of edits in Period 1, and the best fitting linear functions are shown with the straight lines.

According to the observations above, then, you can assume that a good model for the number of revisions in two different time frames, at least in the average sense, as shown by the equation below, is that

$$r_2 = R_{21}r_1, \tag{1.7}$$

such that if the user made r_1 revisions in Period 1, he will make *on average* r_2 revisions in Period 2, which is linearly proportional to r_1 with the constant R_{21}.

To recap, bear in mind the following two facts, which we will develop further:

1. The edits made by a user in two time periods of different lengths are linearly proportional to each other (Figure 1.6).

2. The probability distribution function of the activities does not depend on the time frame we performed the measurements in, as you saw in the previous section (Figure 1.4).

In the next few paragraphs we elaborate on both facts, starting with the first. Remember: Our goal is to explain the origin of the distribution functions that describe user activities.

Consider the number of edits that a user makes in a given time period as a random variable, R. We'll denote the probability distribution function (which is, recall, approximated by the normalized number of users making a certain number of edits as in Figure 1.4) by $f_R(r)$. R here stands for the random variable, and r is its particular value. This is, again, the probability that a random user will have r revisions. Although we know that r is a discrete random variable, we can proceed with the underlying assumption that it is continuous. The reason is that at this point we don't want to derive exact results, but instead understand the distributions that we have seen in a general sense that may be applicable to other systems as well.

If we multiply this continuous random variable by a constant c, its PDF $f_{cR}(r)$ will become, as expressed by its original PDF $f_R(r)$,

$$f_{cR}(r) = \frac{1}{|c|} f_R\left(\frac{r}{c}\right). \tag{1.8}$$

This is just a fact from probability theory for the resulting distribution function when we multiply the random variable by a constant. We should now consider how the PDF of the edit activity changes when we move from Period 1 to Period 2. Let's first write out the PDF for the random variable r, the number of revisions a user makes, because this is the PDF we're going to work with. If U_1 denotes the total number of users in Period 1 such that $U_1 = \sum_{i=1}^{\infty} U_1(i)$, then the PDF in Period 1 for instance is approximated by

$$f_R(r) = \frac{U_1(r)}{U_1}. \tag{1.9}$$

We know that according to our assumption (Equation 1.5) we need to multiply the number of revisions for every user by R_{21}, to arrive at the number of revisions r_2 they make in Period 2; our ultimate goal is to compare the product-distribution with the actual distribution that we can measure and see if they match up. Now when we multiply the random variable argument r of f_R by R_{21}, we should be able to deduce what the new PDF will be. Using Equation 1.8:

$$f_{R_{21}R}(r) = \frac{1}{R_{21}} \frac{U_1\left(\frac{r}{R_{21}}\right)}{U_1'}. \tag{1.10}$$

Notice that, more importantly, we did not simply write U_1 in the denominator of this equation. Instead, we have U_1' there. The reason we do this is that the normalization factor will also change when we multiply the random variable as in Equation 1.9: The proper sum for the normalization again runs through all integers from 1 to ∞ as

$$U_1' = \sum_{r=1}^{\infty} U_1\left(\frac{r}{R_{21}}\right). \tag{1.11}$$

We have a challenge now. The arguments of U_1 in the sum are not going to be integers, and also for $r < R_{21}$, the argument of U_1 is less than 1, which is not possible. This we can interpret, though, as referring to users who "did not show up" in Period 1 because their activity rate was so low that we could not observe even one revision from them. However, we can still think of them as having had a strictly positive, but less than 1, activity rate, which, after being multiplied by

R_{21}, became measurable in the longer Period 2. But because we could not count their numbers (given that they did not show up in Period 1!), how are we going to determine what U_1' has to be?

We can also have a different approach to calculating U_1': It must be the sum of all user counts over all possible activity buckets in Period 2, because it was exactly our purpose with multiplying the revision counts r_1 by R_{21} to arrive at the revision counts r_2 in Period 2. This sum, we know, is exactly U_2, the number of users who had any activity in Period 2; therefore $U_1' = U_2$. Seeing this we can finally complete the expression for the probability density function for the rescaled argument in Equation 1.10 as

$$f_{R_{21}R}(r) = \frac{1}{R_{21}} \frac{U_1\left(\dfrac{r}{R_{21}}\right)}{U_2}. \tag{1.12}$$

Why is it good, though, that we know this? We can use our other empirical observation now about the probability distribution functions being unchanged over observation periods, as described by Equation 1.3. What we recovered, then, when we multiplied the revision counts for all users in Period 1 by R_{21} (Equation 1.7), is the probability distribution of the number of revisions in Period 2. Combining this and Equation 1.12, we get

$$\frac{U_1(r)}{U_1} = \frac{U_2(r)}{U_2} = \frac{1}{R_{21}} \frac{U_1\left(\dfrac{r}{R_{21}}\right)}{U_2}. \tag{1.13}$$

Because we would like to say something about $U_1(r)$, let's just focus on the first and third terms in this equation. Slightly reorganizing the constants,

$$U_1\left(\frac{r}{R_{21}}\right) = \frac{U_2}{U_1} R_{21} U_1(r). \tag{1.14}$$

Remember though that our ultimate goal is to figure out why $U_1(r)$ (and $U_2(r)$, and $U_3(r)$) have the particular shape they have, which could help us understand several further properties of user behavior down the line. For this, let's simplify for a moment the notations in Equation 1.12 to see the problem more clearly. By pulling the constants together and using the simpler notation g, instead of $U_1(r)$ for the unknown function, we can say that what we're looking for is a function g that satisfies:

$$Ag(x) = g(Bx), \tag{1.15}$$

with A and B being constants. In other words, if we multiply the argument of the function by a given constant, we get back almost exactly the function value as we would otherwise have for the argument, except that this value is also multiplied by another, different constant. This looks simple, but what kind of functions will satisfy this condition? We can use a theorem called *Euler's homogeneous function theorem* to find a solution for *g*. Euler's theorem states that if the following is true for a given constant γ and *any* other constant C:

$$g(Cx) = C^{\gamma} g(x), \tag{1.16}$$

then *g* should also satisfy

$$xg'(x) = \gamma g(x). \tag{1.17}$$

g′, as usual, is the derivative of *g* with respect to *x*. It must be also true then that

$$\frac{g'(x)}{g(x)} = \frac{\gamma}{x}. \tag{1.18}$$

Because the left side is equal to $[\ln g(x) + a]'$, and the right side to $\left[\ln\left(kx^{\gamma}\right) + b\right]'$ with arbitrary, new constants *k*, *a*, and *b* (it's easy to see knowing the basic rules of derivation), we come to

$$[\ln g(x) + a]' = \left[\ln\left(kx^{\gamma}\right) + b\right]'$$

$$\ln g(x) + a = \ln\left(kx^{\gamma}\right) + b + c$$

$$g(x) = Kx^{\gamma}. \tag{1.19}$$

(We introduced *K*, which is just another constant, and could be expressed with *k*, *a*, *b*, and *c*.) This result is rather simple and elegant, and we used two facts only: (1) that the probability distribution functions for user activities over time are unchanged (Figure 1.4); and (2) that the number of user actions between two time frames changes proportionally, no matter how active the users were in the first place (Figure 1.6). With this we can go back and rename our variables again. Our final result is that the number of users *U* having a certain number of revisions, *r*, should follow a so-called *power law* (because we raise the variable in the formula to a constant power)

$$U(r) = Kr^{\gamma}, \tag{1.20}$$

with some constant γ and a scaling factor *K*. Seeing this, it's indeed surprising how compactly we can express our user activity distribution: Our hunch at the beginning of the chapter that the distribution could be some sort of a smooth function was indeed right. Now that we have a closed form for this, we can analyze some of its properties.

We can also check directly whether we can observe a power law for the user activities: Let's see if we can show that this is the case for Wikipedia editors as well! If our assumptions along the way were correct, we should find that the number of editors making a certain number of revisions follows Equation 1.20 to a large degree. The easiest way to proceed with this is by noticing that if we take the logarithms of both sides of this equation, we get

$$\ln U(r) = \ln\left(Kr^{\gamma}\right) = \gamma \ln r + \ln K. \tag{1.21}$$

In other words, the logarithm of the number of users with r revisions, $U(r)$, is a linear function of the logarithm of the number of revisions, r. $\ln K$ is just a constant, and so is γ, so we can see how the linearity arises between $\ln U$ and $\ln r$. We can now take the exact same data as we did for Figure 1.3, transform the variables both on the horizontal and vertical axes, and plot them against each other. The result is shown in Figure 1.7.

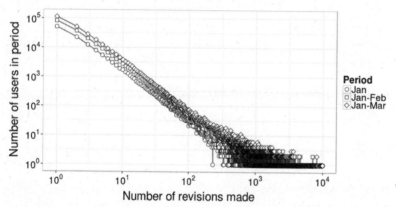

Figure 1.7: Similar to Figure 1.3, we show the number of users who made a certain number of revisions in the three time periods. However, in this figure, we rescaled both axes logarithmically, so we can now clearly observe the power law relationships.

We can notice a few things:

- Whereas the horizontal axis of Figure 1.3 shows a limited range only (it goes only up to 20 because otherwise we would not see anything interesting due to the fast decay of the power-law function), the logarithmic rescaling lets us see a much more detailed and complete picture of the relationships well beyond this restricted range. Although the distance between neighboring data points becomes shorter and shorter on paper as we go toward larger x values, it's exactly this gradual increase in density that allows us to also discern how the functions behave at the far ends of their ranges.

- The logarithmic axes also make comparisons between the three distributions easier. In this figure, we can clearly follow through the functions' differences across the entire horizontal domain, and we can discern both large differences (on the order of tens of thousands of revisions, on the left side) and small differences (on the order of 1–10, right side) in the same plot. This is because the vertical, y axis is logarithmically rescaled as well.

- What we can observe is that the functions seem to remain "parallel" with each other. What this means is that the *ratios* of their y values at every point are constant: A $\ln y_1 - \ln y_2 = C$ constant difference can be expressed as $y_1 / y_2 = e^C = const.$; therefore, a parallel shift on a logarithmic axis means a multiplication by a constant on the original scale. Alternatively, if we multiply a function by a constant, on a logarithmic y axis, it will appear as a shift upward or downward, depending on whether the multiplier constant was greater or less than 1, respectively.

- Now we can immediately see the linear relationships on the logarithmic scales between the log-transformed number of revisions and the log-transformed number of users, apparent from the fact that all three curves follow (approximate) straight lines on the log-log scales. Equation 1.21 already expressed this, and now we can see that it is indeed the case. In fact, if any function is a straight line on a double logarithmic plot, we can be assured that it's a power law of the form given by Equation 1.19.

- We can also observe a "fanning out" of the y values at the high end of the horizontal scale. This is a result of the higher variances at smaller sample sizes: You can see that at approximately 1,000 revisions per user, we find only a few users per revision bucket (fewer than 10). Although we still expect that a power-law model reasonably approximates the user counts, our observations, which can be considered a sample drawn with a small size from a random process, will have considerable variation around the expected mean (which is given by the power law). A remedy for this can be to use increasing bin sizes to pool several buckets into one, and average out the user counts, as we'll see in the "Logarithmic Binning" section of this chapter.

- In contrast to our usual experience with linear plots, moving one "unit" to the right or toward the top in the log-log plot means that we are stepping *decades* (in the case of base-10 logarithmic scales), or in other words we are multiplying our values by 10. So, as we move from the origin to the right, for example, we are moving on the x axis from 1, to 10, to 100, to 1,000, and so on, so making linearly displaced steps in the plot will result in exponential changes in the values on the axes they represent.

Furthermore, we can make one more prediction for the power-law exponent as a validation of our assumptions, realizing that Equation 1.14 for u_1 has the same shape as Equation 1.16. Comparing these two equations, we can see that $C = 1/R_{21}$, and so what we need to determine is, n, the exponent of C, on the right side of Equation 1.16. But this we can calculate easily:

$$C^{\gamma} = \frac{U_2}{U_1} R_{21}$$

$$\gamma = \log_C \left(\frac{U_2}{U_1} R_{21} \right) = \frac{\log\left(\frac{U_2}{U_1} R_{21} \right)}{\log \frac{1}{R_{21}}} = -\frac{\log \frac{U_2}{U_1}}{\log R_{21}} - 1. \qquad (1.22)$$

We know all the actual values in this expression for Periods 1 and 2: the measured total number of active users happens to be $U_1 = 134,804$ and $U_2 = 219,604$. R_{21} is the slope of the linear fit to the data points represented by the "square" symbols in Figure 1.6: $R_{21} = 1.75$. Substituting these for the exponent γ into Equation 1.22, we will get $\gamma = -1.87$. So, our expectation is that the number of users with a given number of revisions will go as

$$\frac{U_1(r)}{U_1} = \frac{U_2(r)}{U_2} = \frac{U_3(r)}{U_3} \propto r^{-1.87}. \qquad (1.23)$$

(We neglected the normalizing constant, and this proportionality is indicated by the commonly used "$\propto$" sign.) We obviously have the chance to check this statement for the exponent, using real data; we will do this momentarily, after inspecting some more properties of the power-law relationship found for user activities.

The Consequences of the Power Law

What are the further consequences of this law that we just found for the user activities? Let's first look at the *cumulative distribution function* of the probability distribution function that is shown in Figure 1.4. The cumulative distribution function gives the probability that the value of the random variable is *no greater* than a given threshold. In our specific case, it means that we are looking for the fraction of our users that make less than or equal to a certain number of revisions in the time period. Let's call this upper limit ρ.

$$CDF(\rho) = P(r \le \rho) = \frac{1}{U} \sum_{i=1}^{\rho} U(i). \qquad (1.24)$$

Here, as before, $U(i)$ is the number of users making i edits, and U is the total number of users. To calculate this, we can use Listing 1.5. (For Period 1, as we can see in the `subset` statement, however all periods have the same PDF so this should not matter.)

Listing 1.5: Approximate the cumulative distribution function of the user activities—the fraction of users who have no more than a certain number of edits in a given time period. (`user_edits_in_timeframes.R`)

```
rev.buckets = ddply(subset(revs.in.periods, range1 > 0,
                    select='range1'), .(range1), summarise,
          count=length(range1))
names(rev.buckets)[1] = 'revisions'

# Make sure we have an increasing ordering of the revision buckets.
rev.buckets = rev.buckets[order(rev.buckets$revisions),]
total.users = sum(rev.buckets$count)
rev.buckets = within(rev.buckets, {
          cdf = cumsum(count) / total.users
      })
```

The result of this simple calculation is shown in Figure 1.8. Again, we rescaled the horizontal axis, the number of edits, logarithmically. We have every reason to do so, as we by now know that this value spans a vast range, from 1 to 10,000; if we used linear scale, we could not have discerned the sharp rise of the function at the beginning of the scale. This lets us observe surprising facts about our activity distribution: 40% of the active users have only one edit for that one month, and approximately 85% or so have at most 10! Apparently, most of our users are not that active compared to the most frequent editors, and only a small fraction makes a large number of edits.

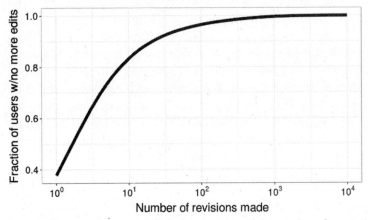

Figure 1.8: The cumulative distribution function of the number of users with a given number of edits. The CDF is the fraction of users with no greater than a specific number of edits. We rescaled the horizontal axis for better visibility.

We have now looked at what fraction of our users have made no more than a certain number of edits, or in other words what fraction of the users are making the least number of revisions. Can we also look at the inverse of the problem, the fraction of users who are making the *most* number of edits? This is certainly not much harder than what we just did, and this is called the *complementary cumulative distribution function* or the *tail distribution* of the activities:

$$CCDF(\rho) = P(r > \rho) = \frac{1}{U} \sum_{i=\rho+1}^{\infty} U(i) = 1 - CDF(\rho). \qquad (1.25)$$

Similar to Listing 1.5, we can also calculate the tail distribution of the user activities as shown in Listing 1.6. Note that we use a trick to calculate this using the built-in cumsum function: We reversed the frequency vector twice to simulate a cumulative sum from the end to the beginning of the vector.

Listing 1.6: Calculating the tail distribution of the fraction of users with more than a given number of edits. (user_edits_in_timeframes.R)

```
rev.buckets = within(rev.buckets, {
          # We reverse the vector twice since 'cumsum' adds up
          # from the beginning, and discard the very first bucket
          # since the CCDF is defined as a strict "greater". Finally,
          # we append a 0.0 value for the last element since there are
          # no users with more than the maximum number of edits.
          ccdf = c(rev(cumsum(rev(tail(count, -1)))) / total.users,
                   0.0)
     })
```

Figure 1.9 displays the tail distribution as we calculated it on Wikipedia edits. Again, we can notice a few consequences of the long-tailed distribution of the revisions: Only 15% of the users have more than 10 revisions in a month, and this drops to below 5% for 100 revisions. To inspect how many users have a large number of edits, it would make sense to also rescale the vertical axis so that we can see the smaller fractions as well, as we did in Figure 1.10.

When we perform this rescaling, we can notice something interesting: The tail distribution seems to follow a power law as well, just like the original probability distribution did (Figure 1.7). Can we find a reason for why this should be so? For this let's first recall that our power-law PDF for the number of revisions r can be described by the following relationship:

$$P(r) = Ar^{\gamma}, \qquad (1.26)$$

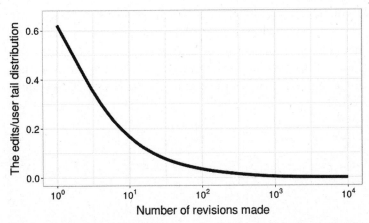

Figure 1.9: The tail distribution of the users' revisions: This shows what fraction of users had more revisions than a threshold. Comparing this with Figure 1.8, we can immediately see that the two functions add up to 1.

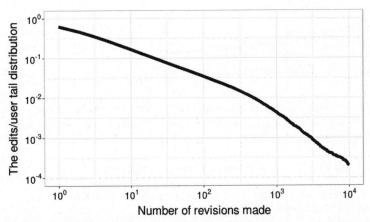

Figure 1.10: The tail distribution of the users' revisions again as in Figure 1.9, but this time on double-logarithmic axes. We can now see that, similar to the PDF, this tail distribution also follows a power law (or two power laws, given the slightly faster decay at the end as we can recognize by the steeper linear section of the plot starting at approximately $10^{2.5}$ revisions).

with an appropriate constant A that normalizes the area of the function to 1, and γ being the exponent of the power law. Then the tail distribution can be expressed as the tail sum over all values above the threshold: $CCDF(\rho) = \sum_{r>\rho}^{\infty} P(r)$.

Let's try to express this in a closed form by approximating this discrete sum with a continuous integral of the same function. This we can do assuming the function does not change *too* quickly because the integral is nothing else but an infinitely refined box covering of the integrand, and the discrete sum can be thought of as a rough covering of the continuous function. This trick is illustrated by Figure 1.11.

$$CCDF(r) = \sum_{i>r}^{\infty} P(i) \approx \int_{r}^{\infty} Az^{\gamma}\,dz = \frac{A}{\gamma+1}\left[z^{\gamma+1}\right]_{r}^{\infty} = \frac{A}{\gamma+1}(0 - r^{\gamma+1})$$

$$= -\frac{A}{\gamma+1}r^{\gamma+1}. \tag{1.27}$$

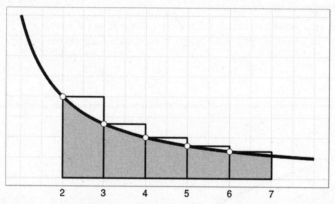

Figure 1.11: Imagine that we are summing up the values of a function indicated by the five white dots. This is the same as the sum of the areas of the white (unfilled) rectangles. However, we can approximate this area by taking the integral of the underlying continuous function as well (shaded by gray): $\sum_{i=2}^{6} f(i) \approx \int_{x=2}^{7} f(x)\,dx$. Although we cover a slightly smaller area as can be seen from the figure, the error we're making is negligible compared to the actual differences between our model and the actual social media system.

You may have noticed that there was one bold assumption in the previous calculation: that $\infty^{\gamma+1} = 0$. This is, however, true, as long as $\gamma < -1$ because in this case we raise ∞ (think of it as a very large number) to a negative power, which is the same as $1/\infty^{-(\gamma+1)}$. For this to converge to 0, $-(\gamma + 1) > 0$ is required, hence our stipulation that $\gamma < -1$. (Otherwise, if this is not the case, the theoretical power law would not have a finite area under it, and we could not have assumed the power law extends up to infinity. It must have been "truncated" so that we can have a finite area under the probability density function.)

To summarize Equation 1.27 in plain terms: If we can assume that our probability distribution function for user activities follows a power law with an exponent γ, then the tail distribution will also follow a power law, with an exponent $\gamma + 1$.

There is moreover one more thing we can read from Figure 1.10, which is that the tail end of the CCDF decays with a steeper exponent beyond approximately 2.5 decades ($10^{2.5} \approx 316$) than the earlier part of the distribution. This means that the original PDF of Figure 1.7 *also* drops faster at the end than earlier, but we could not really have seen this fact from that plot. This is immediately one benefit of transforming the PDF into a tail distribution: For a power law, we essentially "smoothed" out that function, as here we obviously do not observe the spreading out of the tail as happened for the original PDF due to the small sample sizes at the end.

However, we can discover a further non-obvious fact of the tail of the PDF. If we plot the tail distributions of Periods 2 and 3 separately, we notice that where this regime of faster decay starts is dependent on which period we are looking at: For this period, Period 1, it was $10^{2.5}$, whereas if we had taken Period 3, which is about three times longer than Period 1, we would have seen it begin later, at 10^3. (We leave it to the reader to check this.) The point of onset of this faster decay is sometimes called a *cutoff*, especially if it's even more pronounced than what we see in this example. This phenomenon is called the *finite size effect*, which arises because we can observe only a constrained snapshot, instead of an infinitely long period as it would be for the "ideal" system. However, as we noted, the threshold where the finite size starts to show up keeps shifting to higher activity values as we increase the length of the observation period.

The Long Tail in Human Activities

Over the last few pages we saw that the power-law distribution that describes users' activities reveals a large diversity among the users, showing that most of them are rather inactive, but there are a few who are immensely more active than the rest. Another question that comes up frequently for characterizing user contributions is the following: If we rank users by increasing activities, what percentage of actions comes from the most active users? Conversely, what percentage of contributions can be attributed to the least active users?

To answer these questions we'll order users by the number of revisions they have, and will look at what fraction of all edits have the most active 10% of users made. Obviously, we can look at any percentage of users, but for this example we've chosen 10%. What we need to do, therefore, is to order the revision counts of users from highest to lowest, so we will get the most active users in the beginning of the vector, and the least active ones at the end. We call the position of a user in this vector a user's *rank*, so the user ranked 1 is the user with the largest number of revisions, the user ranked 2 is the second most active user, and so on. Then we can calculate the cumulative sum over this vector, arriving at the number of edits users made up to a certain rank (Listing 1.7).

Listing 1.7: To calculate the number of edits that the most active users make, we first order the users by decreasing activity counts so that we can cumulatively sum up their number of revisions. (`user_edits_in_timeframes.R`)

```
range.considered = subset(revs.in.periods, range1 > 0, select='range1')
names(range.considered)[1] = 'revisions'
ordered.activities = range.considered[order(range.considered$revisions,
                decreasing=TRUE),]
total.revisions = sum(ordered.activities)
tail.fractions = data.frame(user.rank=(1 : length(ordered.activities)),
        fraction=cumsum(ordered.activities) / total.revisions)
```

The plot for the fraction of edits made by the most active users is shown in Figure 1.12: It's surprising that only a few of the users seem to be responsible for most of the edits. In fact, it looks like only 10 users make approximately 12% of all edits; and the top 100 users make approximately 29%. This is tremendous; of the 134.8k users active in this period, only 0.07% is making nearly one-third of all revisions!

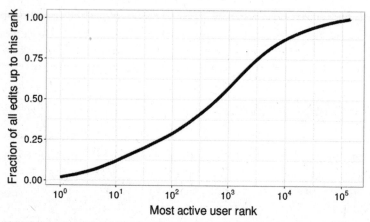

Figure 1.12: The fraction of all edits made by users up to a certain rank. We rescaled the axis for the user rank logarithmically.

At this point we should realize that it's humanly impossible to have as many edits in only one month as the top users have. For instance, Table 1.1 lists the heaviest "users" and their revision counts. It's apparent from this table that the users with the most edits are "bots" (an abbreviation for "robots"): Wikipedia agent programs that perform some automatic maintenance or fix on the encyclopedia pages. "CLueBot NG," the most active bot, is for instance a bot that tries to detect and prevent vandalism to pages, whereas "Addbot" is a bot that performs a diverse set of clean-up and maintenance tasks on pages. In the case of Wikipedia, we may have an idea which accounts are bots, but this is not always possible in every social media service. (A list of registered bots can be found here: `http://en.wikipedia.org/wiki/Wikipedia:Bots/Status`.) In many cases, automated accounts may appear as legitimate users; on Twitter, for instance, it's often the case that Internet-connected appliances, news headline relays, or algorithmic accounts replying to or quoting other users are also present on the service as legitimate (and useful) accounts. At other times, these active accounts belong to spammers, in which case it's doubtful we can call the account useful.

Table 1.1: The Most Active Wikipedia Accounts in Our Period 1, January 2013

ACCOUNT NAME	PERIOD 1 EDITS	AVERAGE SECONDS BETWEEN TWO EDITS
ClueBot NG	80003	33
EmausBot	79357	34
Addbot	63136	42
BG19bot	47897	56
WP 1.0 bot	46910	57
Cydebot	46067	58
Yobot	39489	68
Makecat-bot	31228	86
ZéroBot	30351	88
AnomieBOT	30122	89
Xqbot	30111	89
BD2412	25710	104

The list in Table 1.1 was generated by the (UNIX) shell command: `zcat data/wikipedia/user_edits_in_timeframes.tsv.gz | sort -n -r -k 2 -t "$(printf '\t ')" | head -12`. Often it saves time to run these "one-liners" in a terminal window.

There's usually no obvious way to know what accounts are automated, unless the service whose data we're analyzing provides a way to identify them. To see the effect of removing these bot accounts from Wikipedia, we can simply exclude all known accounts listed as bots from our activity data. Because even after this we found accounts that were apparently bots, we examined the top accounts by hand and also removed these from among the top 100 most active users (Listing 1.8).

Listing 1.8: This simple piece of code removes all known (and assumed) bot accounts from our data frame. (`user_edits_in_timeframes.R`)

```
bots = read.table(gzfile('wikipedia_robots.txt.gz'),
        col.names=c('account'))
revs.in.periods =
        revs.in.periods[!(revs.in.periods$account %in% bots$account), ]
```

We can also generate a plot similar to Figure 1.12 with the bot accounts removed; however, we will not repeat that in print because it looks similar to this figure. With the bots removed, the top 10 users have 6% of the edits, and the top 100 have 18% (cf. 12% and 29% before removing the bots, respectively). This is a significant change in the percentages, but the proportions are still huge for such a small number of users. Only a vanishingly small fraction of the users is responsible for a majority of all activities on the service. We can also describe this surprisingly unbalanced split more generally. What could we expect in other social media systems, for which the activity distribution is also a power law, similarly to Wikipedia?

Long Tails Everywhere: The 80/20 Rule (*p/q* Rule)

You have seen that there's a strong imbalance in the engagements of users: A few of them are very active, whereas the majority of them have relatively low engagement counts. Can we find a way to describe this observation quantitatively as well?

In 1906, the Italian economist Vilfredo Pareto recognized that (in his time) 80% of the land in Italy was owned by only 20% of the population: 20% seems to be a relatively low number, whereas 80% is high. Later, this observation was generalized and was called the *Pareto principle*. In the original incarnation of the Pareto principle it is posited that 80% of the consequences are attributable to 20% of the causes. (Note that the 80% and 20% in this phrasing don't have to add up to 100%, because they refer to different entities; it's just a slightly misleading "coincidence" that the principle was formulated in this way.) In a more general setting, you could say that a fraction p of the consequences are coming from a fraction q of the effects, where p is relatively close to 1, and q is relatively close to 0. We already know that applying it to the metrics we have considered for our social media services, this will certainly be the case. The question is now how large p and how small q will be for our typical cases.

What we would like to do, then, is find the relationship between the *fraction of the most active users* and the *fraction of activities they are responsible for*. The information we have available for each user, which should be enough for us, is how many activities they have for a given period. We already know that the number of users with r revisions follows a power law: $U(r) \propto r^{\gamma}$. The trick we will use, as before, is to approximate the sums of discrete variables by integrals over the functions of their expected values. Although strictly speaking the discrete sums are not equal to the integral of the approximating function (a graphical illustration can be seen in Figure 1.11), the difference is small, especially for ranges of a function where it changes slowly (such as at the tail end of the power law function). Also, these calculations are always going to be a well-informed model of reality, so as long as we can find a reasonably good description of online user behavior, we're fine with making good numerical approximations such as this as well.

So to repeat: We will express the total number of edits made by the most active users. The most active users are those whose number of revisions are the highest; let's say they have more than R number of revisions. Because the number of users having r revisions is $U(r) = U_0 r^\gamma$ (as before with a normalizing constant U_0), and because we can approximate the discrete distribution by a continuous one and the sum of users by an integral over the continuous distribution function, the number of users having more than R revisions will be $N_u(R)$ as shown in Equation 1.28:

$$N_u(R) = \int_{r=R}^{\infty} U_0 r^\gamma \, dr = \frac{U_0}{\gamma+1}\left[r^{\gamma+1}\right]_R^{\infty} = -\frac{U_0}{\gamma+1} R^{\gamma+1}. \tag{1.28}$$

We had to assume again that when we evaluate the antiderivative at ∞, we get 0. The condition for this, again, is that $\gamma < -1$, which holds for our case, and this is what we also see in practice for social media services in general.

Now, what can we say about the total number of edits that these most active users make? For one given revision count, r, the number of edits made by all the users who have exactly this many edits is $rU(r)$. To calculate the total number of edits made by users with more than R revisions is simple, and similar to the calculation we just performed. However, we will not immediately try to integrate up to infinity, but only up to a maximum revision count, R_m. The reason for this will become clear in a moment. $N_a(R)$ will be the total number of activities (revisions) by these users:

$$N_a(R) = \int_{r=R}^{R_m} r \cdot U_0 r^\gamma \, dr = \frac{U_0}{\gamma+2}\left[r^{\gamma+1}\right]_R^{R_m} = \frac{U_0}{\gamma+2}\left(R_m^{\gamma+2} - R^{\gamma+2}\right). \tag{1.29}$$

We can see why we couldn't automatically assume that we can integrate up to infinity: having $\gamma \approx -1.8$ for Wikipedia, $\gamma + 2 > 0$, so substituting R_m as the upper limit would make $N_a(R)$ grow without bounds if we did not stop at some point with it. However, how can we have a good model assumption for what R_m's reasonable value is? Note that at this point we are slightly at the mercy of our assumptions, and instead of getting back exactly what we can measure in an actual system (Wikipedia), what we would like to do is explain qualitatively *why* we are seeing such huge skews in the activities of the topmost users. Let's therefore do our best, and say that R_m is the revision count beyond which we do not expect to see more than *one* user altogether; at this point the power-law model would tell us that there is "fewer" than one user expected with more than so many edits, so we can conveniently stop counting. Therefore, when we plug R_m into $N_u(r)$, we expect to see 1 as the result:

$$N_u(R_m) = -\frac{U_0}{\gamma+1} R_m^{\gamma+1} = 1. \tag{1.30}$$

From this we can express R_m as

$$R_m = \left(-\frac{\gamma+1}{U_0}\right)^{\frac{1}{\gamma+1}}. \tag{1.31}$$

We are almost finished; we just need to put R_m back into Equation 1.29. Before we do that, let's revise our original goal: to express the number of edits made by the topmost users. This means that we need to get rid of R because this was just a "helper" parameter for us to express both N_u and N_a. We can then invert Equation 1.28 to get R:

$$R = \left(-\frac{\gamma+1}{U_0} N_u\right)^{\frac{1}{\gamma+1}} = \left(-\frac{\gamma+1}{U_0}\right)^{\frac{1}{\gamma+1}} N_u^{\frac{1}{\gamma+1}}. \tag{1.32}$$

This way we have now both R_m and R to complete Equation 1.29 so that we can get N_a as a function of N_u. In the end, what we'll get is the following:

$$N_a(N_u) = \frac{U_0}{\gamma+2} \left(-\frac{\gamma+1}{U_0}\right)^{\frac{1}{\gamma+1}} \left(1 - N_u^{\frac{\gamma+2}{\gamma+1}}\right). \tag{1.33}$$

This is the relationship we wanted to derive. We can see that the first terms are just a constant. This constant, according to this model, should be the *total number edits*, as setting $N_u = \infty$ guarantees that we get back all the activities. (Setting $N_u = \infty$ intuitively means that we're taking all the users.) $(\gamma + 2)/(\gamma + 1) < 0$, so raising a large number to a negative power will make it small. Therefore, for the sake of our discussion, we can simplify this expression to show only the salient term that depends on the variable N_u:

$$N_a(N_u) \propto 1 - N_u^{\frac{\gamma+2}{\gamma+1}}. \tag{1.34}$$

N_u is the exact same user rank that we used to plot Figure 1.12 because what we just calculated is the number of edits made altogether by the *most active N_u users*.

The reason we went through these lengthy calculations was to expose the reader to the oft-cited *long tail of human behavior*, where only a small fraction of the participants is responsible for most of the actions. To recap what you saw earlier in this chapter, we realize that this is the consequence of two simple factors in social media:

- That the user activity distribution is unchanged over time.

- That users make proportionally more edits by the same constant multiplier between two sampling windows, independently of how active they are.

We know that any time we observe similar regularities in any social media system (or for that matter, any other kind of a natural system whose statistical properties are similar to what we have seen in Wikipedia), the rules for the skewed activity distribution should apply.

What are the consequences of the relationship we discovered in Equation 1.34? To see this more clearly, we can plot this function for some choices of γ, as we did in Figure 1.13. One thing we can immediately see is that the function is rather sensitive to the value of γ. Slight changes in the exponent yield vastly different results, even when we consider the top 100 users or so only. γ, in reality, means the exponent that can be fitted to the *tail end* of the user–activity distribution: According to Figure 1.10, this exponent for Wikipedia is greater (by absolute value) at the end of the distribution than in the body. Remember, the tail distribution of Figure 1.10 is closely related to the original $U(r)$ distribution with a γ exponent: The slope of the locally fitted straight line to the function in Figure 1.10 yields γ + 1. So, as we include more and more users from among the most active ones, any small local change in the γ exponent will cause strong deviations from the pure model that assumed a constant for γ.

Figure 1.13 shows that none of the theoretical curves with a fixed γ is a great fit to the actual measurement (which for Wikipedia is shown by the line with a lighter shade). But it's expected that when we have so few users to fit a model to (we are talking about the top 100 or 1,000 most active users!), the changes in the "local value" (at a given user rank) of the γ exponent will be amplified by the $N_a(N_u)$ function, which is extremely sensitive to it. Actually, consider that just by removing the most active 10 (about 0.01% of all) users we could have erased *one-tenth* of all edit activities! It's hard to overstate this fact, and therefore it is understandable that at this minuscule scale any prediction will have large uncertainties. To put it in a different way, we are trying to predict how many edits only 10 or 100 users will have; although these are the most active users, any slight relative change in their individual production rates will show up in the total number of activities.

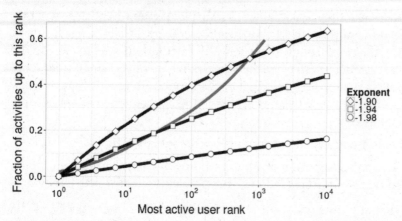

Figure 1.13: The expectation for the fraction of activities generated by the most active users, in a hypothetical system whose user activity distribution perfectly follows the $U(r) \propto r^\gamma$ law. The horizontal axis shows how many of the most active users we consider, and the vertical axis is the proportion of activities attributable to them. We show three examples with different γ exponents. The lighter unmarked line shows the real measurements for Wikipedia, which happens to be the initial part of the line in Figure 1.12.

The lesson we learned is far-reaching when we are designing or provisioning for a social media service. Due to this general characteristic that we can observe in systems affected by human behavior, it is always true that there will be vast differences in activity levels between individuals.

Online Behavior on Twitter

Do our conclusions hold more generally for other kinds of online social systems? What we have seen until now is strictly speaking only true for Wikipedia. However, you will learn shortly that, at least in terms of large-scale trends, you should expect to find similar behavior in most social media systems. It is nevertheless the users who generate activities on the online services, so it is the statistical properties of the underlying human behavior that you can measure with most of these metrics exhibited through the different services.

For this reason, let's turn to a different kind of social sharing service, Twitter. In Twitter, users can send out status updates of at most 280 characters in length, and other users, who "follow" the sender, will receive these short messages in their so-called timeline. The service provides an API (`https://developer .twitter.com/en/docs.html`) for third-party applications that can read and manipulate timelines and various Twitter objects on behalf of the user. Due to this easy extensibility and API access, we can also download example datasets that we can analyze for user activity.

Similarly, as the number of edits characterize the activity of Wikipedia users, we would like to measure the activity of Twitter users in the example in this section by the *number of Tweets* that they have sent in a given period of time. The API lets us download all the Tweets that a given user has sent in the recent past; therefore, if we have a list of valid IDs for users we can query the API in a loop to return all their most recent Tweets. Courtesy of Twitter, we have a list of *randomly chosen* user IDs belonging to normal users that we can continue working with in this chapter. (A normal account is one that has not been deleted by the user or has not been suspended for violating any terms of the service, such as spamming.)

Retrieving Tweets for Users

We need to iterate through the list of user IDs and ask the API for their most recent Tweets. We would like to work with 4 weeks of data, and because Twitter returns only a limited number of the most recent Tweets for each request to keep the response size under control (this count is 200), we may need to issue more than one request to retrieve all the Tweets for a user for the last 28 days. We also must watch out for *rate limiting*, which is the maximum number of requests in a service-specific time window. Rate limiting is employed by virtually every popular Web service's API to maintain a predictable quality of service level for everyone. Without this, we could reasonably expect that there would be a few API applications or users who would consume most of the bandwidth or server capacity. In fact, by now you might expect that the query activities of these apps could likely have a long tail, having learned about the presence of a strong skew in activity distributions from the previous sections, so a few of the most aggressive clients would dominate resource usage in the absence of such limits.

Since response throttling, retry fallbacks, and rate limiting are common notions in third-party API access patterns, we list the corresponding Python code in Listing 1.9 that implements these to download the Twitter data. This script fetches and records the Tweet IDs for the last 4 weeks for a predefined list of users. The longer we let the script run, the more users we will cover, and the more data we will have as well. This is a bare minimum example for how to connect to and download data from a Web service that provides API access and rate limiting. To simplify the OAuth authentication and response handling, we utilize the `tweepy` external library.

Listing 1.9: The Python code to consume the Twitter API to get the latest Tweets for a list of valid users. (`get_users_tweets.py`)

```
import sys, gzip, time, tweepyfrom datetime import datetime, timedelta

# The consumer and access keys & secrets for the Twitter application.
# See https://developer.twitter.com/en/docs/basics/authentication
```

```
# /overview/oauth
# on how to access these credentials.
CONSUMER_KEY = '<consumer key from the Twitter dev site>'
CONSUMER_SECRET = '<consumer secret from the Twitter dev site>'
ACCESS_KEY = '<access key from the Twitter dev site>'
ACCESS_SECRET = '<access secret from the Twitter dev site>'

# The maximum number of Tweets we can ask for in one request.
# See https://developer.twitter.com/en/docs/tweets/timelines
# /api-reference/get-statuses-user_timeline.html
MAX_ITEMS_PER_REQUEST = 200

# The file where we store a list of valid Twitter user IDs.
USER_LIST = 'data/twitter/user_handles_sample.gz'
# The result file
OUTPUT_FILE = 'data/twitter/tweets_per_user.tsv'

auth = tweepy.OAuthHandler(CONSUMER_KEY, CONSUMER_SECRET)
auth.set_access_token(ACCESS_KEY, ACCESS_SECRET)
api = tweepy.API(auth)

# The start date and time of our data collection; 28 days before now.
start_day = datetime.utcnow() - timedelta(days=28)

user_list_file = gzip.open(USER_LIST, 'r')
output_file = open(OUTPUT_FILE, 'w')
for user_id in user_list_file:
    user_id = user_id.rstrip()
    # The ID of the earliest Tweet in the result batch.
    earliest_tweet_id = None
    while True:
        try:
            if earliest_tweet_id is None:
                # The first request for the user
                timeline = api.user_timeline(
                    id=user_id, include_rts=True,
                    count=MAX_ITEMS_PER_REQUEST)
            else:
                # There are possibly more recent Tweets than
                # MAX_ITEMS_PER_REQUEST.
                timeline = api.user_timeline(
                    id=user_id, include_rts=True,
                    count=MAX_ITEMS_PER_REQUEST,
                    max_id=earliest_tweet_id)
```

```
        except Exception as e:
            if e.response.status == 429:
                # If we are rate limited, wait 60 seconds before
                # retrying. See https://developer.twitter.com/en/docs
                # /basics/response-codes.html
                time.sleep(60)
                continue
            else:
                # In any other case do not retry to load user data.
                # This may be changed to cover other error conditions.
                print 'Could not access', user_id
                break
    tweet_count = 0
    found_early_tweets = False
    for tweet in timeline:
        if tweet.created_at >= start_day:
            output_file.write('\t'.join( \
                [str(f) for f in [user_id, tweet.id,
                                    tweet.created_at]]))
            output_file.write('\n')
            output_file.flush()
        else:
            found_early_tweets = True
        if earliest_tweet_id is None or \
        tweet.id < earliest_tweet_id:
            earliest_tweet_id = tweet.id
        tweet_count += 1
    if tweet_count < MAX_ITEMS_PER_REQUEST or found_early_tweets:
        # Finished with this user's Tweets if no more to download
        # or we got back before start_day.
        break
user_list_file.close()
output_file.close()
```

When we have collected enough users, we can look at their activity distributions. We have retrieved the Tweet counts for the random set of users for a one-week (Period 1), a two-week (Period 2), and a three-week period (Period 3). Again, we chose overlapping periods starting on the same day, like we did for Wikipedia. Figure 1.14 shows the probability distribution functions for the number of users who tweeted a given number of times in the three periods.

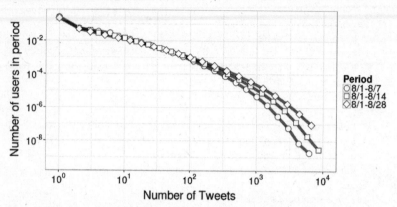

Figure 1.14: The probability distribution function for the number of users with a given number of Tweets sent, for a one-week, a two-week, and a three-week period, respectively.

Logarithmic Binning

Comparing Figure 1.14 to its Wikipedia counterpart in Figure 1.7, the first thing to notice is that the data points appear to be sparser, more spaced out, and positioned more equally from each other than in the previous plot. The reason for this is that in this case, to illustrate a common way of aggregating and smoothing a distribution that is being plotted on a logarithmically rescaled horizontal axis, we used *logarithmic binning*. Where previously our buckets were the naturally occurring integer activity counts (as in Figure 1.7), here we created buckets whose length is *not uniform* along the horizontal axis. However, if we carefully inspect any one of the three curves corresponding to a given period in Figure 1.14, we see that the data points (corresponding to buckets) are equally spaced from each other. What this means on the logarithmic scale is that their distance in the log-space is equal; therefore, on a linear scale the positions of the bucket boundaries are constant multiples of each other. In R, it's easy to create bucket boundaries that satisfy this condition: First, we create equidistant bins in log-space, and then transform them back to the natural scale with the exponential function (Listing 1.10).

Listing 1.10: Create bucket boundaries that we can use in `hist` **to create histograms with increasing bin sizes. The range is defined by** `from` **and** `to`, **and** `bucket.count` **is the number of bins we want to create.**

```
buckets = exp(seq(log(from), log(to), length.out=bucket.count + 1))
```

Figure 1.15 illustrates the relative sizes of these buckets on a linear scale. What this kind of binning means is that as we progress toward higher and higher activity counts, we will have buckets that are longer and longer, and therefore able to capture an ever-increasing range of activities. However, we also know that if the distribution we are plotting is approximately a power law, we will have fewer and fewer users in the high activity ranges, so increasing the bucket sizes counteracts the diluting statistics, to the effect that we will also have a substantial number of data points in the buckets in the upper range. In fact, the challenge with *not* increasing the bucket sizes for Figure 1.7 was exactly that the tail ends of the distributions became noisy because in many cases we found only one or two users with a given number of edits (in contrast to the head part of the distribution, where we have a large number of users with just one or two revisions).

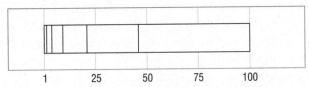

Figure 1.15: Logarithmic binning illustrated. In this example our original range is 1 … 100, and we split this range up into six buckets that increase exponentially in size: The length of every bucket is a constant multiple of the previous one. You can see that in the beginning the buckets are short, whereas their size is growing rapidly on this natural, linear scale.

However, we would like to calculate the probability that a randomly selected user will fall into a given bucket. Obviously, the larger buckets we take, the more chances we will have to capture users within this bucket. So to arrive at an approximation for the probability distribution of the underlying random process, we need to divide the number of users that we empirically count into one bucket by the *length* of the bucket (as the `hist` R command does this automatically when we consider the `density` field in the result).

User Activities on Twitter

Turning back to user behavior on Twitter, it's also apparent from Figure 1.14 that, in contrast to Wikipedia, for the three different time windows the probability distribution functions do not overlap, at least not on the higher end of Tweet scale. The consequence of this is that the relationships on log-log scales between the Tweet counts and the corresponding user counts are not linear, and the distributions *do not* exactly follow power laws. We have seen that the stability of the distribution functions over time was a requisite for us to see a power-law behavior—on Twitter, although our model *approximately* holds, there are also measurable deviations from it. In this case, as we take longer and longer observation periods, we are seeing more of the high activity users as well, and the high end of the activity distribution shifts up. On this note, the second benefit of the logarithmic binning is that it lets us actually discern the differences among the high activity users: We can see in Figure 1.14 that even beyond 10^3 Tweets we can meaningfully explore the tails of the probability distributions and see their differences. In the case of linear binning, the smallest number of users we might get per bucket is one, and as such that is the lower bound for our estimated probability in a bucket (refer to Figure 1.7). For logarithmic binning the bucket sizes themselves grow, so we can estimate the likelihood of progressively smaller probability events as well.

Furthermore, we can check one more property of user activities for Twitter users: how many more Tweets they send if we increase the length of our observation period. Figure 1.16 is the counterpart of Figure 1.6, and it essentially implies what we have found previously: that as we consider another time window (Period 2 and 3, respectively), the average number of Tweets sent by a user who sends q number of Tweets in Period 1 is a constant multiple of q. (Again, this is *almost* true; if we take a closer look, we can see that the data does have some curvature, and it is not increasing strictly monotonically for the first few data points.)

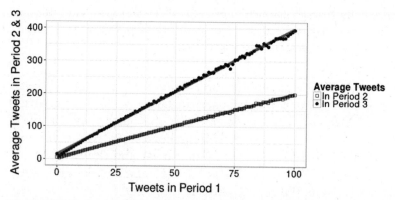

Figure 1.16: The average number of Tweets that Twitter users sent in Periods 2 and 3, as a function of the number of Tweets they sent in Period 1, respectively.

In summary, we have seen that our model and quantitative explanations that fit Wikipedia users well will not be unconditionally good descriptions for Twitter users with a high degree of accuracy; however, such idiosyncrasies are present in every kind of social media system. In fact, our point with the Twitter example was that while in general these model assumptions hold to a large degree, if we need more accurate descriptions, we need to refine the models. After all, certain product decisions or intentional limitations can very well change the user behavior that we can observe in the end. Think of for instance the upper bound on the number of social connections that certain social networks impose: In this case, obviously, we will not see anyone with more than that many connections. However, the principles we have studied are general enough that notwithstanding these system-specific constraints, we will normally observe large variations among user activity levels that can be well described by the laws and regularities that we discovered in the previous sections of this chapter.

Summary

In this chapter, we have talked about the large degree of diversity that we can observe in the activities of users. Understanding that they can be characterized by general statistical laws across different types of social media systems suggests that these are the consequences of more universal human behavioral traits. Specifically, this chapter discussed the following:

- You saw that although most users use online social media rather infrequently, a few are very avid users. The counts of activities within a given time frame follow power-law distributions.

- When we consider the distributions across different time windows, they are similar to each other in the head of the distributions (characterized by the exponent of the power law). The cutoff where they diverge depends on the length of the time window. This is, of course, only true if there're no major changes to how users use the service over time (no major site redesigns, competing service, or rapidly increasing growth).

- The long-tail activity distributions give rise to surprising facts for the user metrics. We cannot say that there's an "average" or "typical" user behavior: The averages of the activity metrics are subject to large variances whenever we measure them, and we must be mindful about the strong effect on the means of the outliers in the distributions that are always present.

- In practice, a small fraction of the most active users can influence our averages strongly. If for some reason these users don't come back, we could see a significant drop in our metrics, even though the behavior of most of the users may stay unchanged, for example.

- Therefore, if our goal is concentrated on measuring total activities, we should focus on understanding how our most active users behave. Because there are relatively few of these, even going through them "by hand" can give insights.

- If we want to focus on describing how active user counts change for a time window, it's most useful to understand the behavior of the least active users. Namely, these are the users who are likely to be the most numerous in our social media service.

The focus of this chapter is to understand and describe the most important features of the user activity statistics. We did this by thinking of the users in isolation from each other, as if each individual acts independently of each other. This is certainly true to a large degree; however, the next chapter explores another defining function of social media systems: The networks that users create to express their interest in each other's activities.

## CHAPTER 2

Networks: The *How* of Social Media

Social networks are one of the most important, if not *the* defining feature, of many social media services. It is hard to imagine any Web-scale service nowadays without a feature that enables users to connect with other users or groups of users, based on shared interests, real-world friendships, or organizational hierarchy. Networks enable users to stay up-to-date on the activities of other users and see what content they change, share, and contribute to. In general, we can consider social networks as a strong filter that only lets events generated by users reach other users who are interested in them. This is obvious in social networks modeled after actual friendships or relationships: The online social network is an extension of and reflects the real-world connections that users have, therefore enabling easier communication and sharing. In this sense, users don't think of the online social network very differently than they would think of their existing social connections. The online network is the same as the network they would otherwise have through face-to-face, telephone, email, chat, or letter conversations and interactions. However, social networks are also used by many services to enable users to connect to other individuals based on shared personal or professional interests, as a way for the users to keep track of others' activities or, again, to make communication between them easier. In contrast to social networks that mirror users' real-life connections, these interest-based networks are many times created only online without the participants ever meeting each other in person as a result of the users discovering the service and other users.

The networks that users of these services create also often serve another important purpose: They impose certain privacy restrictions on who can see or change the content that individuals share. The expectation from networks where users must acknowledge connection requests, such as Facebook or LinkedIn, is that no one else but the connected individuals or their close friends can see most communications. Services such as Twitter and Tumblr, however, exist to make information (by default) publicly available, providing a way for individuals to share their experiences with anyone who follows them or browses their profiles. The modes of operation of these two types of networks are fundamentally different: In private networks, creating a connection requires acknowledgment and intent from both parties, whereas in a public social network, usually only the user wanting to follow another one must do so, and the person being followed does not have to authorize the link. Therefore, following, in a sense, is expressing interest in another user's updates or newly created content and about letting the user know that we are indeed interested in what they are posting.

Facilitating communication and sharing, and allowing users to follow each other, are the most important use cases of social networks from the users' points of view. However, they also play a role as a tremendous resource for the operators of social media sites. Because it is the users who express their interest in or relationships with other users, the structure of their personal social networks will be a strong signal about their preferences and social circles. Using this information for the benefit of their users, the operator of the service may give them recommendations about other participants they should be interested in following, or discover further acquaintances they are not yet connected to. This kind of "guided serendipity" is important in making the network denser and, therefore, is essential in bootstrapping a fledgling social media service in the beginning.

This chapter explores the most important large-scale properties of social networks that we can observe in several services. Fortunately, these properties do not vary fundamentally across the services, and if you understand one network, you can use this knowledge when working with other social networks as well. We'll explain why they look the way they do, and how their statistical description shares several commonalities with the properties of the user activities. We'll also consider interesting features in social networks, such as the high degree of triangle formation that we can witness.

Types and Properties of Social Networks

Since social networks can exist in many shapes and forms, modeling them in the simplest way possible will help us understand their basic properties better. For this, in the next few sections we'll revisit how we can represent them, and how we can describe their additional attributes.

When Users Create the Connections: Explicit Networks

Most of the time when we talk about social networks, we think about two things: the users of the service and the connections that they created among each other. In this sense, the network captures one moment in time, the time when we observe its users and links, but obviously, networks are usually the result of a possibly long-term process that created them in the first place.

Thus, before we go more deeply into the details about how we can measure and model social networks, let's take a step back and consider how these networks came into existence and why they have achieved the popularity we can certainly witness today. No social network was born the way they are today: They all started with a handful of individuals (the founders of the services, most likely), possibly together with a few others from their existing close-knit social circle, using the service. The millions of registered users of these services, in most cases, all joined later in an organic way, by hearing about the service from their friends and mass media either through online or offline channels. Certainly, a large part of why they were all motivated to join the service is because it held some value to them, by letting them find their interests or connect with their acquaintances in an easy way. Another draw social networks have exploited many times during their early years has been an air of exclusivity that was associated with being part of them, which happens when users can join the service only if another existing user invites them to participate. Although this necessarily slows down the growth of the networks initially, the early adopters of the service will likely be active users who create many connections later, thus building a healthy core network that can potentially sustain the network later.

In any case, the value these networks provide to their users is the network itself, and the connections they can make to other users and the content they create. Consider the first individual in a "social network": There is not much to do, in the absence of any other activity going on but theirs. The second person joining this simple network composed of our single individual already adds some value to both. They now both can interact with each other, even if there is nobody else around yet. The third person who joins the network, and links to both the first two users, at that point, may be quite a bit happier with the decision to join than either of the first two: There are already two people using the service, so if we just go by the numbers, this is twice as many as the first two members had when they connected. There is, however, an additional benefit provided to not only the third person, but also the first two. They also increased the number of their respective communication partners by one, making the social network more valuable to them than it used to be.

We don't have to repeat this procedure ad infinitum to see that each additional person joining the network not only benefits proportionately more from an ever-increasing network size, but so does the whole of the network itself. Consider the general case: If we have n users in the network, what is the value of the network provided to its users? We must proceed without quantifying what *value* means to the users, as it's in most cases intangible and not easy to put a number on. We can reasonably assume as a first approximation, however, that the value that one single user among the n users derives from being part of the network is proportional to the number of possible connections he can make to other members of the network, which is $n - 1$. (It's conceivable in some cases that the marginal value of each user decreases as the network grows, in which case this value will be less than $n - 1$.) In reality, of course, it's not possible for users to make all these connections due to the constraints in time and resources they can devote to the network, but the social media service can still help surface interesting or relevant content to its users. When looked at in this way, these possible but unexploited connections do exist between virtually all users, and it's the responsibility of well-designed recommendation algorithms to highlight these links. Because each link (or potential link) provides some additional value to the whole network, we can count the total number of possible links among the network participants. Again, if there are n users in the network, the value of the network will scale as $n \times (n - 1) / 2$, where this expression gives the number of all possible links among users. (Each of the n users can connect with $n - 1$ others, but this way we are double-counting links, hence the division by 2.) The observation we just made about how the network's value grows with the number of participants is called *Metcalfe's Law*, and it originates back to around 1980 when it was first pronounced in terms of communication devices linked together in a network (fax machines, at that time, but the reasoning also works for Internet-connected appliances, telephones, and users of a social network).

Social networks are generally structurally simple in the sense that we can think of them as having two kinds of constituents: users and their connections. A branch of mathematics, graph theory, describes these kinds of structures as graphs, where the objects that are connected to each other are called *nodes* or *vertices*, and the links connecting them are called *edges*. In our case, users would be the nodes, and the relationships between them would be the edges. Many times, it makes sense to think of social networks in this way, even more so because this way we can develop generic algorithms and measurements that operate on the abstract concept of graphs. This has the additional benefit that we can map several other problems to graphs as well. For instance, even if users do not have an explicit follower or friendship link between them, but they did communicate in the past in any way (for example, they mentioned each other in a post), we can immediately see a place for this action in the graphical framework. Instead of only friendship or follower links, we would also capture with edges the past act of mentioning each other. Although explicitly created links are very valuable, we can see that modeling different kinds of interrelations with graphs opens up a lot of possibilities, where we can transform our problem into a similar problem that can be described by graphs, and use the tools and insights that we have developed for social networks. We will explore this more in the next sections.

We don't have to stop at describing connections as simple edges between nodes, however. Although many times such a model suffices, sometimes it is unavoidable to amend this simple model with further properties. Let's discuss the most important additional features that graphs may possess, as some are necessary for us to characterize social networks properly.

Directed Versus Undirected Graphs

One of the most obvious additions we can make to the graph model is making the edges directed. This means that the edge has a head and a tail, or in other words points from one node to another (or even back to itself). The head of the edge is where it originates, and the tail is the node it is pointing to. In an undirected graph, no such distinction exists: All edges go both ways, the nodes have back and forth connections. When visualizing a graph, we usually use arrows in the conventional way to show the direction of a directed edge and just a simple line to denote an undirected edge.

An immediate application of directed edges to social networks is where creating a link to a user does not require the target user to confirm the connection. These kinds of relationships are usually provided by services where sharing content is by default public, such as Twitter, Pinterest, and Tumblr, where you can follow another user without that user having to give you permission to do so. (There exists, of course, "private" accounts on these services as well, where this rule does not hold, but this practice is commonplace enough.) However, social media services built around more private or personal connections, such as Facebook, are better modeled by undirected graphs, where a friendship link must be confirmed by both the receiving and requesting ends.

Node and Edge Properties

Although directed or undirected edges describe the fact that there exists a relationship between the nodes, we usually would also like to store some properties together with the nodes and edges. What if we need to know the account ID, user name, or country of signup of a node corresponding to a user? What if we would like to store the last time user A sent user B a message, or the number of times a user tagged content created by another user? Questions such as these come up frequently, and we can immediately see that they could be solved by assigning certain properties to either the nodes, the edges, or both.

As a practical consideration, these properties may be objects of any kind, and because we usually do not know beforehand what kinds of objects we would like to store together with the nodes or edges, it is best to store them separately from the nodes or edges and provide only an indexed lookup between the entities in the graph and the objects. This way the set of properties can be extended indefinitely, without regard to how well we design the graph storage in the first place. Consider the alternative, when for instance we store nodes in a relational database, indexed by a unique node ID and pre-allocate columns also for certain properties: This is a good solution if these properties are stable and are not expected to change in the future, such as an account name or signup time and date. If the property in question is less commonly used, however, it may well be worth having a normalized database design for these tables and store the property separately in a related table. Even if we believe such properties will be used often, but not in all tasks, it is worth assigning them to different tables so that the retrieval of data from the table storing only the most essential properties is faster and easier.

Node and edge property objects, as usual, may take any form: from scalars and categorical variables to vectors to images to sets of IDs and user profile settings. When we start talking about complicated objects, however, it is better to start thinking about these properties just in a way that they are loosely related to the nodes and edges of the graph, instead of being always assigned to them. We may, for example, be interested in finding connected neighborhoods where users are all interested in the same topic of photography; in this case, the property we need to work with is a vector of ranked interests of the users, so we need to consider that in unison with the graph structure in our search algorithm. Because of this isolated task, however, we do not have to store the interest vectors together with the graph; they are best kept separately and indexed only by a user ID to provide the relation to the original graph.

Weighted Graphs

A specific and most likely the simplest possible property frequently used by graph algorithms is a *weight* associated with an edge in the graph. This is just a real number attached to the directed or undirected edge, and its meaning varies depending on the interpretation we have for the weight. It may mean the number of times users communicated with each other within a certain time window, the degree of belief or certainty we have that a link should exist if we are to make a recommendation to a user to create a connection with someone else, or the social strength of the link that we devised in some other manner. Specifically, the last interpretation in this list, the strength of the link, is useful to have in practical setups. We can hardly expect that all users spend the same amount of time or have the same amount of trust toward each other. In these scenarios, it's best to assign a weight to the links that encapsulates our knowledge about how strongly these users may want to communicate with each other. We strongly encourage you to use weights to capture strengths of relationships whenever possible; just as we have seen that there is a large variance between users in terms of overall activity, we can surely expect that users engage with some of their friends more than with others. From this point of view, if we don't use link strengths as weights in our calculations, we may think that some weak social links are of importance, whereas in reality, users may never interact through these links.

Imagine a scenario in which we would like to predict which friend of a user to target with a message if we want to reach the user in a "viral" manner. If we don't consider communication strengths, the best we can do is a random draw; however, if past communication frequencies are assigned to the links as strengths, we may want to pick the friend with the most frequent interactions with the user. Certainly, treating links where no communication happens the same way as the users' strongest communication partners would lead to less accurate results than trying to model the actual importance of the links. Many times, however, for the sake of simplicity or because of a lack of further data, we don't have a choice but to proceed with an unweighted description. Doing so may be all right though if the neighborhood is small (thus the diversity among link weights may be smaller), or we explicitly don't mind the fact that these links are unweighted.

Basically, we can generally think of every graph we previously mentioned as a *complete weighted graph*. By *completeness* we mean that every edge is present among all the nodes, or in other words we have a total of

$$L = \binom{N}{2} = \frac{N(N-1)}{2} \tag{2.1}$$

undirected edges in the graph if N is the number of nodes. Of these L edges in actual graphs, only, of course, a fraction is usually present. However, we can assign a weight to links that are not there in the original graph that equals 0 or infinity, depending on the interpretation of weights by the algorithm that processes the graph. If, for instance, we interpret the weights as the number of times two users communicated in a specific time frame, then 0 is a good choice for non-existing links. However, we could also think of a different scenario: The weights will describe in this case the expected time it takes for a user to deliver a message to another user. In this case we should rather choose an infinite weight for an edge through which the messages cannot be delivered; due, for instance, to the two users not being connected through a relationship, which would preclude that the sender could contact the potential receiver. This interpretation is shown in Figure 2.1. Then if we would like to know what the shortest time is to deliver a message from user S (source) in the graph to another user D (destination), we could run a shortest path finding algorithm (for instance, Dijkstra's) to find the shortest path among all possible paths between S and D. Obviously, a shortest path (if it exists) will not go through edges with infinite weights, so assigning infinite weights to edges that are not present was the right choice.

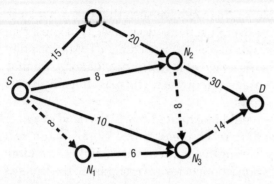

Figure 2.1: A small graph where the source *S* wants to send a message to destination node *D*. The time it takes for one node to relay the message to another one is shown on the links, and these are the weights of the links. To indicate that a node cannot contact another one, we can use infinite (∞) weights, such as between *S* and N_1 and between N_2 and N_3.

In practice, it is almost never a good idea to store edges with 0 or infinite weights, however, as this would increase the amount of space needed to store edges from $O(N)$ (if as in most cases, the number of edges grows linearly with the number of nodes) to $O(N^2)$, which is normally unaffordable. However, it may help to still think in terms of complete weighted graphs when a connection between any two nodes is possible, which is the case in online social networks.

Creating Graphs from Activities: Implicit Networks

Social networks are well described in terms of a graph, especially when we think of the connections among the users that they created to follow others' activities or to express a relationship. However, it can be equally important for us to discover relationships between users that they have not explicitly created, but would be useful for us to work with. Following are a few examples for relationships that do not exist per se but may be inferred from user behavior:

- When two users may know each other but have not yet explicitly indicated their relationship. This is also known as the link prediction or network completion problem, where we would like to predict with a high probability which two nodes in the network should be connected.

- When a user should be interested in consuming a specific piece of content or in buying a specific product. This connects two different kinds of entities, in this case users and other items (content or products). We would like to know which items users prefer over others, and in most cases, we are looking for the items that the user would rank highest among all possible choices. One method to discover such latent connections is called *collaborative filtering* because the ranking of the items is possible through observing the collective action of a lot of users.

■ In a more general sense, *personalization* refers to recommending content to users in a way that takes into account their personal preferences and differences. Personalization may happen on a more substantial level than just changing the order of recommended items. For instance, we can consider changing UI layouts based on who users are or targeting them according to their perceived preferences or demographic characteristics.

Let's proceed by looking at a few examples of graphs and their statistical properties. As an example of an implicit network, we can continue working with the relationships between Wikipedia editors. Although Wikipedia doesn't provide an explicit way to make connections between users, as is commonly used on other social networks (friendship or follow links), we can consider their conversations as they take place on the "user talk" pages as a signal for their connections. User talk pages also look like regular wiki pages; however, they belong to a specific user, and other users can edit these to leave a message for the owner or to discuss a topic. The user talk activities are also among the data we downloaded and parsed earlier; they are recorded only in a specific Wikipedia namespace. A namespace on Wikipedia is a specific prefix used for wiki pages that logically separates them from normal articles. (For example, there are namespaces for users, help pages, and multimedia files. For detailed information about Wikipedia namespaces, go to `http://en.wikipedia.org/wiki/Wikipedia:Namespace`). Within each of the namespaces there are also talk pages to facilitate discussions around an entry. We are interested in the user talk pages. The interaction network we will look at is created in the following way: If a user leaves a message on another user's talk page, there will be a directed link created from this user to the owner of the talk page. For this we obviously need to again specify a period over which we will collect interactions among the users: We used a month's worth of data. Listing 2.1 is a part of the Python script that creates a file for the weighted, directed connections, recording the author of the message, the target user, and how many times in the time window we have seen a message from the author.

Listing 2.1: Reading the Wikipedia activity file, we can decide which edit was made to a user talk page (in namespace "3"), and who the target user was, by parsing the user name out from the page title. We also removed robots whose name likely contains the "bot" word. We sorted the input activity file by timestamp beforehand, so we can simplify the matching of date range boundaries. (`create_network.py`)

```python
import gzip, re
from collections import defaultdict

INPUT_FILE = 'data/wikipedia/revisions_time_sorted.tsv.gz'
OUTPUT_FILE = 'data/wikipedia/talk_network.tsv.gz'

DATE_RANGE = ['2013-01-01T00:00:00', '2013-02-01T00:00:00']
```

```
# `edges` is a doubly-keyed dictionary to keep the number of times when
# an edit happened.
edges = defaultdict(lambda: defaultdict(int))
# The mapping between the user name and the arbitrary user integer
# index.
user_name_to_index = dict()


def map_string_to_index(mapping, string):
    '''Return the 0-based index for the user name, or a new user ID if
       we have not seen the user before.'''
    if string in mapping:
        index = mapping[string]
    else:
        index = len(mapping)
        mapping[string] = index
    return index


# The regexp pattern to parse out the user name from the page title.
pattern_user_name = re.compile('^User talk:([^/]*)/*.*')
# The pattern to identify a bot (any user name that contains a word that
# ends on 'bot').
pattern_bot = re.compile('.*[Bb][Oo][Tt]\\b')
input_file = gzip.open(INPUT_FILE, 'r')
for line in input_file:
    title, namespace, page_id, rev_id, timestamp, user_id, user_name,\
    ip = line[:-1].split('\t')
    if timestamp >= DATE_RANGE[1]:
        # The input file is sorted by time so we can finish the loop
        # in this case.
        break
    if namespace == '3' and user_id != '' and user_id != '0' and \
    timestamp >= DATE_RANGE[0] and timestamp < DATE_RANGE[1]:
        m = pattern_user_name.match(title)
        if m:
            commenter, target_user = (user_name, m.group(1))
            if pattern_bot.match(commenter) or \
            pattern_bot.match(target_user) or commenter == target_user:
                # A bot is making or creating the edit, or a self-edit.
                continue
            commenter = map_string_to_index(user_name_to_index,
                                            commenter)
            target_user = map_string_to_index(user_name_to_index,
                                              target_user)
            edges[commenter][target_user] += 1
input_file.close()
```

Similar to user activities, a lot of user talk edits were made by maintenance agents (robots). We also got rid of such edits by removing all users whose name contains the word "bot." This is obviously not an infallible way of identifying robots, though it's a practice on Wikipedia to name agents like this. Also, we can see that we mapped usernames to 0-based integer indices; this is not a technical necessity, but it's good practice to make it easier to work with data later that has been anonymized. In this way, we have built a network that contains approximately 100k users and 136k directed edges between them.

Visualizing Networks

Before we look at any further statistical properties of the graph, let's plot the connections between a subset of the nodes so that we can imagine how the network looks. We obviously cannot visualize the complete graph; although it would be computationally feasible to lay out 100,000 nodes on a big sheet of paper, we would not necessarily immediately gain more understanding from this than by taking a smaller number of nodes that can be laid out on a standard-sized page. But what is a good way to select a smaller part of the graph to plot?

In choosing this subgraph, we would like to show all links that exist between any of the selected nodes. Imagine, for a second, that we selected our target nodes *uniformly randomly* from among all the nodes; this is obviously not a great choice for seeing the local structure of the graph because

- it's not likely that there will be too many edges between random nodes;
- even if there were, there is no reason to believe that we will understand better how many connections nodes generally have, how they are clustered together, and what kind of behavior we can expect from algorithms that operate on local graph neighborhoods.

A better choice would be to perform a *snowball sampling* on the graph: Starting from a given center node, we would first include all the neighbors of the center, then all their neighbors, then the neighbors of the neighbors, and so on, up to a maximum distance from the center. The advantage of this (at least for visualization) is that we will see a part of a graph the same way its participants see it. We can implement snowball sampling using one of the well-known graph traversal algorithms: *breadth-first search*. This algorithm will walk through all the nodes, first visiting all the neighbors of a node before descending one level deeper and visiting the neighbors of the neighbors. (In contrast, a related algorithm, *depth-first search*, will always try to go deeper before exploring nodes on the same level.)

In snowball sampling, we still need to decide where to start. Which node should be the initial center? In fact, we will follow a simple strategy: We will choose the center randomly, walk the graph up to depth 3, and inspect the resulting subgraph. If it's dense enough but not *too* dense, we will likely have a layout that is not too busy, yet contains enough edges at the same time. We will also require that the node with the maximum degree has no more than 200 neighbors; these conditions are arbitrary, but because visualization is more art than science, we do not have to look for exact rules.

We will use the `networkx` module for Python (available at `http://networkx.github.io/`) to store and lay out the graph as shown in Listing 2.2. The layout was generated by the so-called embedded spring layout mechanism. This procedure essentially treats the nodes as electric charges that repel each other, whereas the edges are springs that pull them back together. By initially placing the nodes randomly on a plane, we let the nodes find their equilibrium position by simulating the forces that are exerted on them by other nodes and springs. When they stop moving, we can plot the graph using their positions.

Listing 2.2: We randomly select a center for snowball sampling and check whether the resulting small network sample would have the properties for amenable layout. (`plot_network.py`)

```python
import gzip, random
import networkx as nx
import networkx.algorithms.traversal.breadth_first_search as \
breadth_first_search
import matplotlib.pyplot as plt

MAX_DIST = 3
INPUT_FILE = 'data/wikipedia/talk_network.tsv.gz'

graph = nx.Graph()
with gzip.open(INPUT_FILE, 'r') as input_file:
    for line in input_file:
        commenter, target_user, times = line.rstrip().split('\t')
        if commenter != target_user:
            # Do not store self-edits.
            commenter, target_user = map(int, [commenter, target_user])
            graph.add_edge(commenter, target_user)

N = graph.number_of_nodes()
E = graph.number_of_edges()
print N, E

while True:
    # Choose a random node for a center.
    center = random.randint(0, N - 1)
    # The distances of the nodes from the center we have seen so far.
    distances = { center: 0 }
    # Walk the graph with a BFS, starting from 'center'. The edges are
    # returned in an order corresponding to BFS.
    for source, target in breadth_first_search.bfs_edges(graph, center):
```

```
        if target not in distances:
            if distances[source] == MAX_DIST:
                # The very first time we touch a node that is beyond our
                # maximum depth, we stop walking.
                break
            else:
                distances[target] = distances[source] + 1

# We create a 'small_graph' that contains only the nodes that we
# walked and the edges between them.
small_graph = nx.Graph()
for node_found in distances.iterkeys():
    for neighbor in graph.neighbors(node_found):
        if neighbor in distances:
            small_graph.add_edge(node_found, neighbor)

# We decide whether the local graph we found would look "good"
# (a medium density of edges, not too many nodes, and the node
# with the most connections has at most 200 neighbors).
edge_fraction = float(small_graph.number_of_edges()) / \
    small_graph.number_of_nodes()
max_degree = None
for node in small_graph.nodes():
    if max_degree is None or small_graph.degree(node) > max_degree:
        max_degree = small_graph.degree(node)
if small_graph.number_of_edges() < 3000 and \
edge_fraction > 2 and edge_fraction < 4 and max_degree < 200:
    # If this seems to be a good neighborhood, lay it out with the
    # force-directed spring layout algorithm.
    print 'Center:', center
    pos = nx.spring_layout(small_graph, iterations=200)
    colors = [(3 * [max([0, (distances[n] - 1.0) /
                MAX_DIST - 1)])]) for n in small_graph.nodes()]
    nx.draw(small_graph, pos, node_size=40, node_color=colors,
        with_labels=False)
    nx.draw_networkx_nodes(small_graph, pos,
        nodelist=[center], node_size=200, node_color=[1, 0, 0])
    plt.show()
    break
```

Figure 2.2 shows a part of the Wikipedia talk network obtained in the way we just described. Here, though, for laying out the graph, we made the talk network undirected: Whenever there was a directed edge between any two nodes in the graph, we replaced it with an undirected edge. We have also not considered the weights of the edges; as a simplification we made the network unweighted by keeping an edge if its weight (in this case the number of messages left) is at least 1.

center node

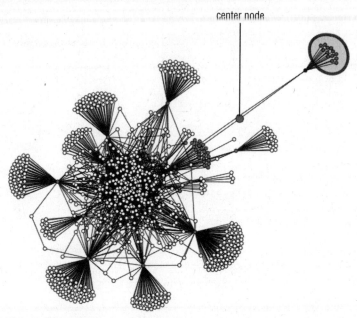

Figure 2.2: A small subset of the Wikipedia user talk connection network. We started from a randomly chosen center node (see callout), and performed a breadth-first search on the network to include all nodes with a distance of at most 3 to our center node. Only the connections among the included nodes are kept. Also, we shaded nodes according to how many hops they are from the center: Black nodes are at distance 1 (there're few of these), gray ones at distance 2, and white nodes are at distance 3.

The center from which we performed the walk is plotted with a larger size. We traversed the graph up to distance (depth) 3 from the center node and colored the nodes according to their distances. (Immediate neighbors are black, second neighbors are gray, and third neighbors are white.) We can see that aside from the dense region in the middle, where we find a lot of interconnections among users, there seem to be users who are connected to a relatively large number of other users, on the peripheries of the figure. We also notice that there are some "gray" (distance 2) users who are probably not connected to anyone else but only one other node. (Of the white nodes, at distance 3, we cannot say this with certainty, as that is the depth at which we stopped, so they may have other, unseen neighbors.) This all tells us that we should expect to find a lot of users who have few connections, but also there'll be some who have a lot, and they may be connected to each other. The next sections examine these questions in more detail.

Degrees: The Winner Takes All

Looking at Figure 2.2, we may intuit that similar to the large degree of diversity that we have seen for user activities previously, we will also find large variations among the connectedness of users to other users. This is easy to measure: For each user, we can determine how many other users they have contacted during the one month of our measurement. This is what we call the *out-degree* of a user: the number of outgoing edges in the graph starting from this user to any other. Similarly, the *in-degree* of a node is the number of incoming links to that node. In an undirected network, the *degree* measures the number of neighbors, and the out-degree, in-degree, and degree are obviously equal. Note that in this interpretation of the degrees the graph is considered unweighted as well.

The probability distribution function of the out-degrees and in-degrees of users in the Wikipedia talk network are shown in Figure 2.3. We can see from this that we indeed find users with vastly different numbers of connections in the network. Again, the straight lines on the log-log plot indicate that both distributions are approximate power laws. As we have already seen, this means that there are a few users who have many connections (these kinds of nodes in the network are sometimes called *hubs*), whereas there is a huge number of users who are connected to one other user only. One neighborhood of such users having *one* outgoing edge is shown by the shaded circle in Figure 2.2, for example.

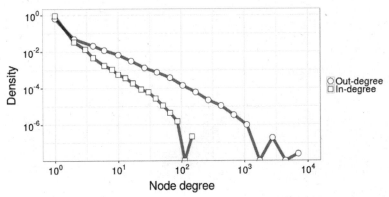

Figure 2.3: The in- and out-degree distributions of the Wikipedia talk network. We counted how many other users a given user contacted, or was contacted by, through talk; this is what we call out- and in-degree, respectively.

We can again see that the connectivity structure of the Wikipedia talk network is ostensibly governed by laws that result in peculiarly similar statistics to what we have seen for the highly skewed user activities in Chapter 1. Can this kind of behavior be universal, that is, be seen in other social media systems, and if so, is there a plausible explanation for such a characteristic we can observe in social networks?

Let's look at how users in the Twitter dataset we used in the previous chapter connect to each other. For Figure 2.4, we retrieved the number of followers and followees for many Twitter users. Remember, Twitter provides an asymmetrical social network, where users may follow each other, meaning that user *A* following another user *B* will get all status updates of *B*. However, when *A* decides to follow *B*, *B* doesn't need to reciprocate or even authorize this contact. Interestingly, according to Figure 2.4, the fraction of users who have a given number of followers or followees is approximately the same for any follower/ followee count, as these two density plots overlap to a high degree. This was not the case in the Wikipedia talk network. We can see, however, that these two systems have power-law network degree distributions, and the same is usually found in other social media systems as well. There has been extensive research in this area, and it has become clear that networks based on human interactions closely resemble the two preceding examples in terms of their degree distributions. (The exponents of the power laws generally differ, though, in their exact values from one system to another.)

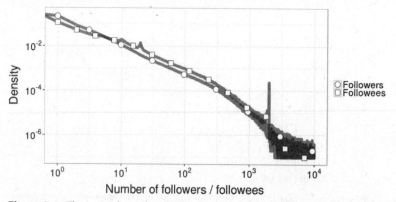

Figure 2.4: The in- and out-degree distributions of the Twitter follower network. Here the number of followers and followees were taken at a specific time for a sample of representative users. We can see an idiosyncratic spike for the number of followees at 2,000, which is because the Twitter service used to limit the number of other users a user may follow under normal circumstances at this count.

Counting the Number of Connections

As it can be instructive, we'll detail how we calculated the in- and out-degree histograms from the raw data. First, we retrieved the number of followers and followees for each user ID for our Twitter users using Twitter's API, resulting in a file with two columns for these counts and one row for each user. Now, we could have loaded all this detailed data in R and have created histograms and plots subsequently from the data frame; however, if we have a lot of edges, R may not be able to hold all that in memory. (This shouldn't necessarily be the case here, but to illustrate the workflow, we'll still proceed with this assumption.) However, it should be relatively easy to stream through this file and keep a tally of how many users we encountered with a given number of followers or followees. This way, we never need to keep the whole dataset in memory. In Python, we just need to keep a running count of the degrees as we read through the file, as shown in Listing 2.3. Because social media usually generates a lot of data, frequently we need to resort to solutions like streaming when we want to calculate aggregate metrics. Moreover, to highlight a useful data exchange mechanism between Python and R, we wrote this Python script in such a way that its results can be directly consumed from R, without having to use temporary files for the data exchange.

Listing 2.3: This Python function parses a file that contains integers for which we create frequency tables (histograms). This function will be called from R. (`twitter_followers_and_followees.py`)

```python
from collections import defaultdict
import gzip

FILE = 'data/twitter/followers_followees.tsv.gz'

def followers_followees_stat():
    followers_stat = defaultdict(int)
    followees_stat = defaultdict(int)
    with gzip.open(FILE) as f:
        for line in f:
            followers, followees = map(int, line.split('\t'))
            followers_stat[followers] += 1
            followees_stat[followees] += 1
    # We can only return vectors to R, no data frames.
    return [followers_stat.keys(), followers_stat.values(),
            followees_stat.keys(), followees_stat.values()]
```

What we obviously did in Listing 2.3 was to count the number of users with a certain number of followers and followees, respectively. Now in our R session we need to call this Python function and ingest the resulting vectors. With the help of the `rPython` R library (`https://cran.r-project.org/web/packages/rPython/index.html`), we can call out from R to Python. As Listing 2.4 shows, calculating the fractions of users with a given number of followers/followees requires only loading the script and executing a call to the function, after which we can create a data frame from the results.

Listing 2.4: A short example of how we can delegate some calculations to Python from R. It makes sense to run this simple task in Python, which is faster and more flexible at processing text files than R. (`twitter_graph.R`)

```
library(rPython)

python.load('src/chapter2/twitter_followers_and_followees.py')
ff = python.call('followers_followees_stat')
followers = data.frame(bucket=ff[[1]], count=ff[[2]] / sum(ff[[2]]),
 type='Followers')
followees = data.frame(bucket=ff[[3]], count=ff[[4]] / sum(ff[[4]]),
 type='Followees')
```

The Long Tail in User Connections

Let's now see if we can find a plausible explanation for why the long-tail behavior emerges in the connection graph, similarly to how we tried to explain the skewed activity distributions in the section "The Origin of the User Activity Distribution" in Chapter 1. There we found that the probability distribution functions of activities over different observation periods were unchanged, and the only analytic function that could satisfy this condition was the power law. To explain the observed distributions in graphs as in Figures 2.3 and 2.4, we'd like to find a generative model that could plausibly give rise to the measurements.

Consider now that social networks as we observe them are in general the result of users creating (and possibly severing) connections among each other, and what we can measure in terms of degrees is a snapshot of the evolution of the social network at the time we make the observations. By way of example, Twitter didn't always have as many users as it has today; it started with only a handful. On one hand, these users started following each other, and on the other, new users began to join the network through invitations and word-of-mouth effects.

A natural thought is that we are looking for a model that approximates the growth both in terms of the user base and their connections. We, of course, would just like to capture the most essential ingredients of the network evolution because there must be certain idiosyncrasies to each social network that only more detailed models could possibly describe: Obviously, the distributions in Figures 2.3 and 2.4 are different enough so that no one model could possibly characterize both systems equally well. However, they both display heavy-tailed power-law-like distributions for the in- and out-degrees. Our goal is to explain why a power law emerges for the degrees.

Imagine that a user decides to create a link to another user to befriend or follow her; essentially, we can model this as a random process in which the target user is chosen randomly (but with some strategy) from among all the users. We could assume that this choice is completely arbitrary, and any other user is chosen with the same probability uniformly randomly. Probably this is not a good model though; our intuition tells us that real connections are not created this way. Let's consider that there is usually a preference given to better known, more "popular" accounts. (This thinking is also motivated by the expectation that social media services usually also highlight popular items or users in the form of recommendations, or these users are just more visible due to their higher activity on the site.) Therefore, to capture this fact, let's assume that the more connections an account has, the more connections it will also attract: The probability that someone will connect to a given user will be greater for users with more connections. This, in essence, will enable users with more connections to accrue further connections at a higher rate.

Let's focus on the incoming degree distribution and how users gain followers. We can formulate the model in the following way: Assume that we have discrete time, and in every time step an incoming link may be added to one of the users. Obviously, links are added *by* someone in the social network, but we don't concern ourselves with *who* is making the connection now, as we would like to explain only the in-degree, and not the out-degree distributions. Following this reasoning, we need to pick one user randomly to whom the incoming link is going to be added. Because we think more popular accounts are more likely to attract further links, let's make the probability that a given user is picked *proportional* to the current in-degree of that user. If user A has 20 connections and user B has 10 incoming connections, we should pick A with twice the probability that we would pick B. This principle is called *preferential attachment*: The linking probability is linearly proportional to the actual degree of the target node (see A. L. Barabási and R. Albert, "Emergence of scaling in random networks," `https://arxiv.org/abs/cond-mat/9910332`).

Beyond having preferential attachment, we would also like to introduce new users into the network: Sometimes, instead of creating a link, we can create a new user. We can facilitate this by introducing a parameter, p, into the model. In every time step, with probability p, we are going to create a new user with one incoming link (so that the new user immediately becomes part of the network); with probability $1 - p$, we will proceed with the link addition as just described. With these two mechanisms, we have attempted to capture what we believe are the two main features of a growing social graph: the creation of links between the users, and the joining of new users to the network. Obviously, we didn't consider other dynamic processes in these networks: most importantly the removal of connections and the deletion of users themselves. Again, incorporating these could be refinements of the model above, but we're not considering these mechanisms now for simplicity.

A model based on similar analogies has been known and analyzed since the 1970s in probability theory. It's called *Pólya's urn model*, and specifically the *generalized Pólya's urn model*. This model, with a change of terminology, corresponds to the same process as we have described for the users. In Pólya's model, we are given a finite number of bins, and balls arrive one at a time. With probability p, we create a *new bin* for the ball to be dropped into, or with probability $1 - p$ instead, we drop the ball into one of the existing bins. In this latter case, we prescribe that the probability of a bin to be chosen must be proportional to the number of balls that bin already has. We can see that we could replace the word "users" with "bins" and "incoming degrees" with "balls" in our discussion of a social network, and we have a one-to-one correspondence between our simplified social network evolution model and the Pólya model. The benefit of doing this is that Pólya's model has been studied rather extensively, and we can immediately use those results.

One of the pertinent results for the urn model is that if the probability that a ball is dropped into a bin is indeed proportional to the number of balls in that bin, then the ball distribution across the bins will approximate a power-law distribution by the time we have dropped many balls. In fact, we don't just have to believe this analytical result, we can easily write a short simulation using a pseudorandom number generator to see if we can indeed recover the power-law distribution for the number of balls in bins.

Listing 2.5 shows the Python code for this simulation. It's relatively straightforward to understand: We are going through ROUNDS number of ball/bin additions, placing each ball into a bin according to preferential attachment, or creating a new bin.

Listing 2.5: Simulation of Pólya's urns. (`polya_preferential_attachment.py`)

```
0 # The number of total draws (time steps).
1 ROUNDS = 10000

2 # The parameter p of the model.
3 P = 0.2

4 import random
5 from collections import defaultdict
6 import matplotlib.pyplot as plt

7 # The number of balls in each of the bins; bins are indexed by
  # integers.
8 bin_balls = defaultdict(int)
```

```
 9 # Start with one bin having one ball only.
10 bin_balls[0] = 1

11 for round in xrange(0, ROUNDS):
12     if random.random() < P:
13         # Create a new bin with probability P.
14         bin_balls[len(bin_balls)] = 1
15     else:
16         # Else add a ball to a bin based on preferential attachment.
17         threshold = random.randint(1, round + 1)
18         s = 0
19         for b, balls in bin_balls.iteritems():
20             s += balls
21             if s >= threshold:
22                 # Choose this bin for the ball.
23                 bin_balls[b] += 1
24                 break

25 # Calculate the ball distribution across the bins.
26 ball_dist = defaultdict(int)
27 for k in bin_balls.itervalues():
28     ball_dist[k] += 1

29 plt.xscale('log'); plt.yscale('log')
30 plt.xlabel('Ball count'); plt.ylabel('Bin count')
31 plt.scatter(ball_dist.keys(), ball_dist.values())
32 plt.show()
```

With probability P in the code, we add a new bin, and otherwise we select a bin with a probability linear to the number of balls it contains for the ball to be added to. This selection is shown in lines 12–24, and the procedure is illustrated by Figure 2.5.

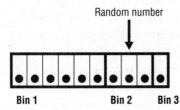

Figure 2.5: Suppose we have three bins, with six, three, and one ball in each, respectively. We would like to pick a bin (1 to 3) for a new ball to be put into, and this should happen with a probability proportional to the balls already in them.

For this example only the part where we are choosing the bin with a probability proportional to the number of balls in it needs explanation. The reason we highlighted how to simulate this process is so we can experiment with different choices of p and see how the power law changes as a result. Lines 17–24 implement the selection of a bin chosen with a probability proportional to the number of balls it holds: Following Figure 2.5, we line up the bins next to each other with as many balls as they contain and draw a random number between 1 and 10 (the total number of balls). In essence, we add the new ball "next" to the ball corresponding to the random index we draw. This means that we'll increase the number of balls in the bin where the selected ball belongs by one, and because we can do this as many ways as there are balls in this bin, we will indeed choose this bin with a likelihood proportional to the number of balls it holds. In this particular example, the random ball index drawn is 8; therefore, we will place the new ball in Bin 2.

Actually, if we run this simulation multiple times, we would see that it will be only the exponent of the power law that changes, but we will always have a power law. In particular, it has also been shown analytically for the generalized Pólya model that the exponent of the power law is exactly $1 + \dfrac{1}{1-p}$.

Beyond the Idealized Network Model

We now see why it was useful to spend some time looking at this simple model. We saw that both the model and the measurements result in qualitatively similar results for the degree distributions of the networks, and therefore we can say that the preferential attachment in growing social networks should be a major part of the explanation for the skewed degree distributions in the networks. Although we focused on the incoming links in the preceding section, similar arguments could be given why the outgoing links follow similar distributions—the more links someone already created, the more they will create later.

To recap, note that both *growth* (as expressed by the parameter p for the addition of new nodes) and *preferential attachment* (as expressed by the linking probability being proportional to the current degree) were necessary for the model to exhibit a similar power-law degree distribution as we found in practice. This means that we can expect for the same to hold in real-world social networks: For us to observe this, we need a constant (although minimal) influx of new users, and that popular users become more connected proportionally with their number of connections in time. Note that at this point we tried to find an idealized model that has a growth component for both the users and links with a plausible connection mechanism, and the preceding model was a simple one that had these and explained the observed statistic qualitatively. There could be intricacies, of course, in practice, that give rise to different degree distributions.

A further consequence of these growth rules is what we usually call the *winner takes all* phenomenon in terms of network connections. The winners in our case are the hubs, users with a lot of connections, and they indeed have a disproportionately large fraction of the connections. This is fitting as apparently only a few of the participants will possess most of the connections.

There are several omissions in this modeling framework that we didn't consider on purpose for simplicity, but that would be potentially needed if we wanted to more closely approximate reality. We didn't account for several other (more or less) important features the networks may exhibit:

- Edges may be removed from the network through users unfollowing each other or otherwise cutting their connections.

- Users may drop out of or cancel their subscription to the service altogether, reversing the effect of user growth.

- Users may discover each other through more "local" mechanisms than the global popularity-based preferential attachment, as previously described. We can expect, for instance, that "friends of friends become friends." This natural tendency of networks to form triangles may be important and form the basis for different recommendation schemes we could design. However, this local attachment mechanism may also show the signs of preferential attachment, except that we don't consider all nodes in the network, but only the local ones.

- The connection kernel (the function that specified the connection probability for a new link as a function of the target node's degree) may not be linear in reality but a different function of the degree or of other variables. Note that a power-law degree distribution in this model emerges only when the connection kernel is linear, but because we sometimes see deviations from a perfect power law, there might be one possible explanation for this. One commonly used feature of social media services, highlighting "most popular" or "most interesting" accounts prominently on the service, may especially be a good candidate for introducing deviations from this model. To address this issue, several more complicated models have been developed to describe the assumed difference between users' ability to "attract" more links—this varying ability of the network nodes has been called _fitness_, to refer to the fact that some nodes gain links faster than others.

- When user growth is irregular during some periods, we may see an enrichment in some parts of the degree distributions. If user growth slows, but link creation doesn't, we may see a shift toward higher degrees; if there is a time when there are a lot of new users joining the service, we could observe that the head of the distribution gets more pronounced.

Overall, insofar as online social networks approximate real-life social networks, we can be comfortable knowing that most or all social networks that researchers have looked at show the long-tailed degree distributions we have seen previously for Wikipedia and Twitter. Because these natural networks have displayed similar characteristics, a great deal of effort has been concentrated on their research. They have also been called *scale-free networks* for the reason that their degree distribution is similar to what we can observe in other physical systems where long-range interactions emerge, together with other measurable properties becoming power laws. The long-range interaction analogy holds here as well: The hub users with a lot of links form bridges between various communities in the network in one way or another.

Capturing Correlations: Triangles, Clustering, and Assortativity

In the previous sections, we worked with a high-level model for explaining the observed degree distributions in social networks. However, that model was simplistic, and didn't account for other plausible mechanisms that must play a role in network formation, such as the creation of communities. In this section, you'll take a look at some of these mechanisms that lead to local correlations in the networks' structures, and ways to measure and model them.

Local Triangles and Clustering

We mentioned at the end of the previous section that it's likely that real social networks will display a high degree of triangle formation, which we called "friends of friends become friends." This assumption, of course, was based on intuition only—we haven't seen yet why the scale-free social networks we are interested in should have more triangles than we would expect. First, let's quantify the triangles in the graph. For this, we will use the definition of the *local clustering coefficient*. The local clustering coefficient is a number between 0 and 1 for every node, and it's the ratio of the number of links among the node's *neighbors* to the maximum number of such possible connections. In the case of directed graphs, for neighbors we consider nodes at the other ends of both the incoming and outgoing edges of the node. If we have k_i such neighboring nodes for node i, the maximum number of links between them in a directed, unweighted graph is $2\binom{k_i}{2} = k_i(k_i - 1)$. Therefore, assuming we counted n_i directed edges between the neighbors, the local clustering coefficient C_i for node i is

$$C_i = \frac{n_i}{k_i(k_i - 1)}. \tag{2.2}$$

This calculation is illustrated by Figure 2.6 for the directed case. (If we have undirected graphs, the definition is the same, but we need to count each edge among the neighbors twice because they correspond to two directed edges going both ways—or equivalently, we can count the edges among neighbors only once, but divide by $k_i(k_i-1)/2$, the number of maximum possible *undirected* edges among the neighbors.)

Figure 2.6: An illustration of how to calculate the local clustering coefficient in a directed network. The central node *i* has $k_i = 5$ neighbors (considering both incoming and outgoing links). Among the neighbors, we find $n_i = 4$ links, but if all the connections were there, we could have $5 \times 4 = 20$ links. Therefore, the node's local clustering coefficient is $4/20 = 0.2$.

When a node has many triangles around it, we expect the node's clustering coefficient to be large (close to 1). To measure this, we can use a simple counting loop, as shown in Listing 2.6. We wrote this in Python, as R is not efficient with loops or hash table lookups; however, we can do the evaluation of the results in R.

Listing 2.6: Counting the number of edges a node's neighbors have among them. (`triangle_counts.py`)

```python
# The graph is a directed graph.
outgoing = defaultdict(set)     # The nodes at the ends of outgoing
                                # links.
incoming = defaultdict(set)     # The nodes at the other ends of
                                # incoming links.
users = set()                   # All the users.
with gzip.open(INPUT) as f:
    for line in f:
        # Convert node IDs to integers to save space.
        source, destination = map(int, line.rstrip().split('\t'))
        outgoing[source].add(destination)
        incoming[destination].add(source)
        users.add(source)
        users.add(destination)

with gzip.open(OUTPUT, 'w') as out:
    for u in users:                 # Need to iterate through all the users.
        triangle_links = 0          # The number of links among neighbors.
        neighbors = incoming[u].copy()
        neighbors.update(outgoing[u])           # Holds all the
                                                # neighbors.
```

```
for v in neighbors:
    if v in outgoing:
        # For all outgoing edges of v if it has any.
        for e in outgoing[v]:
            if e != u and e in neighbors:
                triangle_links += 1
# Just so we have all the data we store the out- and in-degree,
# the number of distinct neighbors, and the number of directed
# edges between the neighbors.
out.write('\t'.join(map(str, [len(outgoing[u]),
                        len(incoming[u]),
                        len(neighbors), triangle_links]))
        + '\n')
```

What does the clustering coefficient look like in actual social networks? First, we can look at the Wikipedia talk network that we used previously, where the talk network is composed of editors who can leave comments on the personal Wiki spaces of other users. The nodes of this graph are the Wikipedia editors, and we create a directed link starting from an editor who left a comment on another editor's page. We should be aware that this network could also be treated as a weighted network: In any time window, different editors may contact others a different number of times. The weight could be the number of times they left a comment on others' pages. However, as a simplification, we will consider this graph as an unweighted graph because our goal, again, is to expose the existence of triangles and not necessarily the exact details around them.

Figure 2.7 shows the actual mean of the local clustering coefficients measured as a function of the nodes' numbers of neighbors (this was calculated using the Python script in `wikipedia_triangles.py`). We chose to calculate the clustering coefficients by degree because this gives us more information about the structure of the graph than a single global average. As you can see in Figure 2.7, it tells us something interesting about triangle formation: It appears that nodes with a larger number of neighbors have relatively fewer triangles around them. (Mind the vertical axis. It's logarithmically rescaled, so the differences between the two ends of the degree scale are quite large, approximately 100–1000-fold.) We can see that editors with only a few editor "friends" have a relatively large fraction, approximately one-tenth, of the possible triangles completed around them. However, if an editor is prolific or popular in leaving/receiving comments, her connections are much less likely to be connected to each other; only fewer than 1 in 100 possible triangles are completed for editors with 100 or more neighbors. This suggests that users with many connections don't necessarily have neighbors who know each other. In a way, editors with few neighbors are part of communities that know each other well, whereas prolific editors with a lot of connections act more as bridges between communities of users rather than belonging to any particular one.

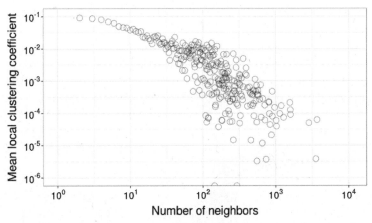

Figure 2.7: The average local clustering coefficients in the Wikipedia talk network as a function of the node's degree

To generalize beyond the Wikipedia talk network, you can also look at a different kind of social network, the LiveJournal friend network (`http://www.livejournal.com/`). LiveJournal is an online journal keeping and blogging service, whose users can make other users "friends" of theirs, therefore allowing them to see what they blog about. A snapshot taken of the directed LiveJournal friend network from approximately December 11, 2006, is available at `http://socialnetworks.mpi-sws.org/data-imc2007.html`. It counts 5.3 M users and 77.4 M directed links. This is a sufficiently large network for our purposes. It also differs from the Wikipedia talk network in the sense that whereas the Wikipedia network was a public communication network, LiveJournal links do express a certain level of trust, or, plausibly, actual friendly relationships between the users. How does the clustering coefficient look in this network?

Figure 2.8 shows the coefficient for the LiveJournal friendship network. For now, just consider the curve on top with circles. It shows a lot of similarity with the Wikipedia graph. However, you can also see that LiveJournal users with degrees between 200 and 1000 have increased clustering coefficients compared to what you would expect if the apparent power-law relationship held there as well, as evidenced by the "bump" in the function. This kind of behavior is not unexpected in actual social media systems; specific design choices of the service may have a profound influence on network formation. This is especially true if you consider that the fraction of users with relatively large degrees like this is small: Whereas it seems that the neighbors of these users are connected to each other more than you may have expected, it is also true only for a relatively small number of users in the entire social network. There can be several reasons for this. Features can exist on the site that encourage triangle formation for the active users; these users may be the early and closely connected adopters; user recommendation algorithms may work better for high-degree users; or such users may be spammers (we don't claim they are). Any or all these reasons may be just speculation, and we leave it to the interested reader to investigate this further. In short, though, we always see the idiosyncrasies of the specific service reflected in most statistical measures, but in general we strive to understand the generics of human behavior online, which emerge even considering the differences between the different social media services.

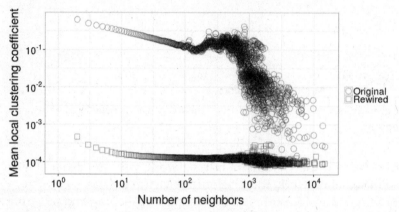

Figure 2.8: The average local clustering coefficients in the LiveJournal social network as a function of the node's degree. We show both the actual measurements (circles) and the reference rewired version (squares), as described in the text.

The question remains whether we should consider the degree of triangle formation that we observed strong or weak. We definitely find triangles in social networks online; for LiveJournal, we have an average clustering coefficient in the approximate range of 0.1 to 0.6 for neighbor counts smaller than 100. This appears to be rather large, considering that this is the fraction of all edges that could maximally be present among the neighbors of a node.

To prove that this is indeed a relatively large fraction, we need to have a "null hypothesis" or a reference that we can compare these results to. One such reference graph can be a social network where all the same users are present as in our original one, but let's assume that they don't have a specific preference to forming triangles. We can create such a reference network by randomly rewiring the edges in the graph: By rewiring we mean that we'd like to keep both the in- and out-degrees of the users but would like to simulate what would have happened if the users chose who they follow completely randomly. If after this rewiring we still find the same number of triangles, we can say that even a random linking process on the part of the users could have created them.

The rewiring follows a procedure as shown in Figure 2.9: We randomly select a pair of edges in the graph, and we simply swap where they point to in between them. How many times should we repeat this rewiring? A good lower bound for the number of iterations is one-half the number of edges, such that each edge is expected to be selected at least once. The result will be a graph where both the outgoing and incoming degrees of the nodes are preserved, but the links no longer point to where they used to, and are randomized. In other words, we can consider this graph a model of a network formation process where users have the same innate ability to create and attract as many edges as we have in the original network (this means that the degrees are preserved) but otherwise randomly select who they connect with. The Python script in Listing 2.7 performs this randomization.

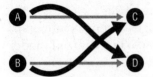

Figure 2.9: The repeated procedure through which we rewire the graph to get a reference graph for comparison for the clustering coefficient. Originally, nodes *A* and *C*, and *B* and *D* were connected, respectively, as shown by the thinner arrows. After we rewire the pair, *A* and *D*, and *B* and *C* will be linked.

Listing 2.7: We read in the directed links, and go over the edges, randomly selecting a pair and swapping the targets for the two edges between themselves. We repeat this 10 times the number of edges so that we have a good number of randomizations. (`rewire.py`)

```
edges = list()                    # The list of all edges with (from, to)
                                  # tuples.
with gzip.open(INPUT) as f:
    for line in f:
        # Convert node IDs to integers to save space.
        source, destination = map(int, line.rstrip().split('\t'))
        edges.append([source, destination])

print 'The number of edges:', len(edges)

rewire_rounds = 10 * len(edges)            # The number of
                                           # randomization steps.
for rewire_round in xrange(0, rewire_rounds):
    e1 = random.randint(0, len(edges) - 1) # Choose the first edge
                                           # randomly.
    e2 = random.randint(0, len(edges) - 1) # Choose the second edge
                                           # randomly.
    e2_dest = edges[e2][1]                 # Swap the edges (we don't
                                           # need to
    edges[e2][1] = edges[e1][1]            # watch out for the case
                                           # when
    edges[e1][1] = e2_dest                 # e1 == e2, it just won't do
                                           # anything).
```

The reason we created the randomized network was to see if we would get as many triangles in this one as we would have in our original LiveJournal network. The answer is no; we see markedly fewer triangles in this reference graph. Now look at Figure 2.8 again considering both curves. As before, the measured correlation coefficients in the original network are shown with circles, whereas the clustering coefficients in the new, rewired graph are shown with the square symbols. The difference is obvious: The rewiring resulted in clustering coefficients that are approximately a *thousand times smaller* than what we measured in the actual network. The interpretation of this finding is that the network couldn't have been the result of a process in which users pick other users to be friends completely randomly. There exists a very strong clustering effect in the network formation, one that gives rise to a lot more edges among neighbors of any node than we could expect in comparison to a simple randomized model. As in real life, online users do form smaller cliques, at least on the level of triangles. Sometimes, this process is called *triadic closure*, which means that open triangles around nodes tend to close up when the neighbors fill in those links.

NOTE   You may also be interested in higher-order *network motifs* beyond triangles; these are small subgraphs in the social network that have a structure. Triangles are examples of motifs, as are four nodes forming a fully connected "square," or a square with one diagonal. In essence, they are structures created by a small number of nodes that occur significantly more frequently than in some random (or similarly to the preceding, randomized) graph. If you find these in social networks, they are often a reflection of an underlying social hierarchy or users' tendency to form the motif that has some benefit for them for a specific reason.

Triangles are common in social networks. Knowing this, you can actively explore different mechanisms to encourage the creation of triangles, such as when you design a service to recommend users to each other. Even without knowing the exact details of *why* triangles are formed by the users, you can see that it may be more likely that users know each other when they have a common neighbor.

Assortativity

A further way to look at correlations in local neighborhoods of a social network is to consider the degrees of connected nodes. The question we ask is the following: Given a node with degree k, what is the average degree of its neighboring nodes? In other words, if a node has a small or, conversely, a large number of links, will its neighbors also have a small or a large number of links, respectively? Again, you can consider both incoming and outgoing degrees for your inquiry, and different social media systems will likely yield different results.

To answer this question quantitatively, we can take nodes that have the same degrees and measure what degrees their neighbors have. Because we have a directed social network, we also need to agree on whether we take the incoming or outgoing links to decide who the "neighbors" are, and when we create the statistics for the neighbors, if we take their in-degrees or out-degrees. This gives us four possible combinations to consider among in- and out-degrees, and we'll proceed like this with the following example. We see that to calculate this, we would need to iterate through all the nodes in the graph, determine their degrees, and iterate through all their respective neighbors to add their in- or out-degrees to a running average.

To implement this in Python, we could use one of the graph libraries (for instance, `networkx` or `igraph`) to store the whole graph, nodes, and edges, and simply follow the previous recipe. However, these graphs are large, and it may be that we cannot store all the edges in memory, a common situation with actual social networks nowadays. Let's say that there's enough RAM to store only *some* data associated with nodes. It's normally expected that we can do at least this much. A modern computer should be able to store hundreds of millions of nodes with a few numeric attributes.

In this case, iterating through the nodes, and then in turn iterating through their neighbors, will use information from every directed link twice: Once for each end node in the loop when we consider the other node as a neighbor to calculate averages over. However, our idea is that we can turn the node iteration around and do iterations over the edges instead. The order of the averaging will be changed, of course, but that's no problem as we can perform additions in any order. The benefit of this is that we don't have to keep all the edges in memory, as we can just stream through the file containing the directed edges. Let's look in detail what we need to do:

1. Because you need to have the in- and out-degrees for every node for the edge iterations and averaging, you need to have them calculated by the time you do the iterations for the assortativity calculations. This requires a first pass through the edge file when you count how many incoming and outgoing edges any node has.

2. There's a second pass through the file when you consider every edge again: For both end nodes, update the averages for the appropriate incoming (or outgoing) direction by taking the out- (or in-) degree of the node at the opposite end of the edge, respectively.

In this way, you have to read the edges file twice instead of the one time you would have had to do if you stored the graph in memory, but you can at least carry out the calculations with more limited RAM as well. (It's also not obvious that computation time should be longer, as reading and maintaining a dynamically growing graph also takes time.)

The code snippet to perform this operation is shown in Listing 2.8. Note that we have used another trick to calculate the averages (and the variances, in case we need them): The class `OnlineMeanVariance`, instead of simply keeping a running sum of the sample items to calculate the means in the end, employs a simple online algorithm that, at any time, keeps track of the mean explicitly (in the `self.mean` variable). There's another benefit of this, which is that this algorithm is numerically more stable. In the common case, when we keep track of the sum of the items as $\sum_{i=1}^{N} a_i$, and add a new item, a_{N+1}, to it, a_{N+1} can be much smaller than the sum of all the previous items before it. This can lead to the loss of significant digits if we use floating point variables. In the online algorithm, however, we try to minimize these losses by matching the order of the numbers in the additions. (You can double-check why this algorithm works in Listing 2.8 by simply considering what happens to the running average when you add a new item to the sample by writing down the formulas.) The update rules for the variance are similarly easy to derive and carry the same numerical benefits as the procedure for the mean does.

Listing 2.8: To calculate the degree–degree correlations, we make two passes over the tab-separated values (TSV) file containing the directed links of a graph in `"source destination"` format. We calculate the averages and variances of the neighbor degree distributions using an online algorithm. This algorithm also mitigates floating point rounding errors because it adds together real numbers that are of the same magnitude, instead of what happens in a simpler "running" sum for the averages, for instance. (`degree_correlations.py`)

```
class OnlineMeanVariance():
    '''Online mean and variance calculations.

    For the details see for instance
    https://en.wikipedia.org/wiki
    /Algorithms_for_calculating_variance#Online_algorithm
    '''
    def __init__(self):
        self.mean = 0.0               # The running mean, make this a
                                      # float.
        self.count = 0                # Number of items added so far.
        self._M2 = 0.0                # The sum of squares of differences
                                      # from the running mean, float.
    def add(self, x):
        '''Register a new item.'''
        if x > 0:
            self.count += 1                    # Increment the count.
            delta = x - self.mean              # Follow the
                                               # calculations for the
            self.mean += delta / self.count    # online algorithm.
            self._M2 += delta * (x - self.mean)
```

```python
    def variance(self):
        '''Calculate the unbiased sample variance.'''
        if self.count <= 1:
            return None
        else:
            return self._M2 / (self.count - 1)


# First pass: count the in- and out-degrees of every node.
outdegrees = defaultdict(int)        # The out-degree for every node.
indegrees = defaultdict(int)         # The in-degree for every node.
with gzip.open(INPUT) as f:
    for line in f:
        source, destination = map(int, line.rstrip().split('\t'))
        outdegrees[source] += 1
        indegrees[destination] += 1

# Second pass: calculate the means and variances of the neighbor degree
# distributions.
# stats is a dict of dicts, the first level is for the
# in- & out-degrees, the second level is for the degree of the node
# under consideration.
stats = defaultdict(lambda: defaultdict(OnlineMeanVariance))
with gzip.open(INPUT) as f:
    for line in f:
        source, destination = map(int, line.rstrip().split('\t'))

        # Update the statistics for the four in- and out-degree
        # combinations, and two end points.
        stats[('in', 'in')][indegrees[source]]. \
            add(indegrees[destination])
        stats[('in', 'out')][indegrees[source]]. \
            add(outdegrees[destination])
        stats[('out', 'in')][outdegrees[source]]. \
            add(indegrees[destination])
        stats[('out', 'out')][outdegrees[source]]. \
            add(outdegrees[destination])

        stats[('in', 'in')][indegrees[destination]]. \
            add(indegrees[source])
        stats[('in', 'out')][indegrees[destination]]. \
            add(outdegrees[source])
        stats[('out', 'in')][outdegrees[destination]]. \
            add(indegrees[source])
        stats[('out', 'out')][outdegrees[destination]]. \
            add(outdegrees[source])

# Write the results to a file.
with gzip.open(OUTPUT, 'w') as out:
```

```
for direction, dir_stats in stats.iteritems():
    for deg, stat in dir_stats.iteritems():
        out.write('\t'.join(map(str, [direction[0],
        deg, direction[1], stat.mean, stat.variance()])) + '\n')
```

Having seen how we can in practice calculate the degree-degree correlations, what are the results? Figure 2.10 shows the average degree of the neighbors of the LiveJournal network as a function of the node's degree (which we call a reference node in the figure). Again, we have four possible combinations: We can look at only neighbors of the reference node that it either connects to (on the outgoing edges) or is connected to by (on the incoming edges), and we can then calculate either the in-degree or the out-degree of these neighbors. These four cases are shown by four separate functions in the figure.

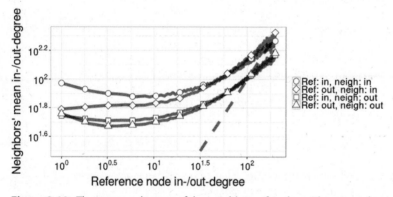

Figure 2.10: The average degrees of the neighbors of nodes with a given degree. We call the latter *reference nodes*. We consider both in- and out-degrees for the neighbors, and neighbors were also taken as nodes on the other ends of both the incoming and outgoing edges of the reference node. We only show reference node degrees up to 200, beyond which the data becomes noisy. The dashed line shows the $y = x$ identity relationship.

We can observe that except for small degrees of the reference node (up to degrees $10^{0.75} \approx 5$ or so), the larger the degree of the reference node, the more connected its neighbors are going to be as well. The average degree of the neighbors is increasing with the increasing reference degree. Such a property of the social network is called *assortative mixing*, which expresses a kind of homophily (connected nodes are similar to each other) in the graph. In other words, well-connected people tend to be connected to other well-connected people. The result of this is that there will be a core of the network in which users with high degrees are clumped together. This makes these networks fast to traverse from one node to another because the high-degree nodes provide shortcuts between distant parts of the graph. Social networks usually exhibit assortative mixing, whereas technological networks (such as the WWW and Internet routers) and biological networks (protein interaction networks, food webs, and neural networks) are often *disassortative*: The functions shown for these systems, as in Figure 2.10, would be monotonically decreasing.

There is another interesting fact to note about the mean degrees of the neighbors: For most nodes in the network, the neighbors' degrees are *greater* than the degree of the reference node. We can see this in Figure 2.10 because the means are almost always above the identity, shown with a dashed line in the plot. The easy interpretation is that an individual's friends are usually more popular than the individual is. However, we should be aware that, as we observed for degree distributions, the neighbor degrees are also distributed in a highly skewed way. This means that when we calculated averages over them, a few *highly* connected neighbors could bias the means toward higher values. It's not too surprising, though: A lot of the less connected users must connect to these popular ones because this is what made them have a high degree in the first place. Therefore, for many users in the lower degree ranges, these highly connected neighbors dominate the means; it is thus possible to observe counterintuitive findings like this.

Summary

This chapter focused on the connections between the users that create a social network. These networks have a profound role in keeping users informed of others' activities and enable them to express trust in each other in different ways.

- You can take explicit links that users have created to each other and build a graph of social connections from these.

- You can also create graphs inferred from related activities in the service and use the same methods to analyze them as you would for explicit networks.

- An important measurable on social networks is the distribution of degrees that their users have. Degrees are the number of neighbors in the social graph, giving the number of connections that each user has. You saw that the degree distribution, in many respects, is reminiscent of the activity distributions in the previous chapter. They are long-tailed, power law-like distributions, suggesting that, indeed, huge variations can exist among the "popularities" of the users. The implications of these kinds of distributions are similar to what we have seen: Outliers have great influence on averages, most connections are concentrated on a small fraction of the users, and most users still have a small number of connections.

- For social networks, you can equate this phenomenon with the presence of hubs in the network, which play the role of social centers, connecting different parts of the network.

- The preferential attachment mechanism can give a good account of how these networks grow. The networks are called scale-free because their structures (manifested through the power-law distributions) don't define any "typical" size for communities or clusters. Preferential attachment creates "winners" in the network who will possess a large fraction of the total number of connections.

- There is a strong tendency in social networks for forming triangles of users. Triangles are formed because people who know each other are likely to share common friends as well. The degree of triangle formation can be described by the clustering coefficient.

- In social networks, highly connected users usually are connected to other users who are themselves highly connected. This is captured by the assortativity metric of the network. A high assortative mixing in social networks finds that users connect to others who are likely to be similar to themselves (homophily).

The next chapter switches gears, turning to another important aspect of understanding the behavior of users in social media: The role of time and the temporal characteristics of users' actions.

## CHAPTER 3

Temporal Processes: The *When* of Social Media

This chapter explores the role time has to play in social systems and tools to help you understand that role. You start by looking at models of how you intuitively think of and form assumptions about the timing of social media events. Then you revise these assumptions by observing that the temporal characteristics of actions differ considerably from what you expected on data sets of Tweets and Wikipedia posts. As in the previous chapters, these observations may seem counterintuitive at first but hint at the presence of large variances along the temporal dimension.

The way we live our lives is strongly determined by the cyclical flow of time on many different levels. The repetition of days, weeks, seasons, and years suggests that there have to be similar patterns observable among the events in social media as well. We identify these trends in our data as well and present a framework on how you can use these to your advantage and forecast future metrics in time.

What Traditional Models Tell You About Events in Time

In any dynamic system time plays a role. A social system has many events in time: Users join the network, add edges, click links, make searches, and send messages. All these events have a time associated with them. This chapter shows how to analyze streams of events in time quantitatively.

The most complete way to represent a series of events is as a sequence of timestamp–event data pairs, where the event data represents some interesting data, and the timestamp characterizes the precise instant that the event occurred. For example, event data may be that User 12 tweeted "I love goldfish!" and the timestamp for this event might be represented as 1,374,622,532 seconds since Jan 1, 1970. When all the event data objects are the same, for example, when they're all "`http://wikipedia.org` was clicked," you can simply think of the event stream as a series of timestamps, without always explicitly mentioning the event.

The time between two consecutive events, the *inter-arrival* time, is an important statistic for understanding any event stream. An event stream with timestamps (0, 2, 4, 6, 8) has completely regular inter-arrival times: (2, 2, 2, 2). This kind of stream is called *periodic* because the time between events repeats as a pattern, which in this case is 2. The ticking of a clock's second hand has a periodic inter-arrival time, which is 1 second. Periodic event streams do not need to have the same time between each event but rather between each repetition of the pattern. Consider the inter-arrival times (2, 3, 4, 2, 3, 4, 2, 3, 4,…). Every 9 seconds in this stream, the pattern repeats itself. This is also a periodic stream.

During a soccer match, the time between Tweets after a goal is scored may decrease dramatically. Imagine the spectators who watch the match on television; at the moment a goal is scored, they may post to support their team, visit their team's page, or search for messages about the team. During the normal operation of a social system, you can expect some apparently random values for inter-arrival times: Users may randomly have a moment in the elevator to check their messages, or perhaps they are waiting for an appointment and spend the time reading news. These events are influenced by chaotic events in the real world, such as traffic, weather, encounters with other people, and so on. Observing changes in the statistics of inter-arrival times can identify periods of interest around corresponding events and can help you distinguish unusual times from the usual fluctuations you expect in day-to-day activities.

Although the inter-arrival times are an almost complete description of an event stream, a coarser view is often useful. By tracking event counts in windows of time, you can observe much of the same behavior that you see by tracking inter-arrival times. In the previous example of events at time (0, 2, 4, 6, 8 . . .), you see the window between [0, 7) has a count of 4 and the window from [7, 14) has a count of 1. By counting over wider time windows, you can expect to see many events in each window and therefore apply standard statistics to the values you observe for the counts. Considering the soccer example, if you count total events every minute, the minutes nearest a goal will have higher than average numbers of events. The next section looks at these two representations of events for uniform event arrivals.

When Events Happen Uniformly in Time

When events happen uniformly in time, they don't have any dependence on prior history. What can you expect from such a uniform system that has events with *no memory* of the past? It may seem that a periodic pattern is expected because the time between events for a simple period is uniformly a constant. This is not what is meant by uniform in this case. A clock clearly has memory: It knows not to move the second hand again until another second has elapsed. So, uniform, in this definition, doesn't mean periodic. Here *uniform* means that the probability that the next event arrives after a time $T + \tau$, given that you have already waited for time T, depends only on τ, but not T. To reiterate: When the system has no memory, the time you have to wait for the next event does not depend on how long you have already waited. This can be expressed as a formula with conditional probabilities:

$$P(wait > T + \tau \mid wait > T) = P(wait > \tau) = f(\tau), \tag{3.1}$$

where for simplicity the right-hand side is called $f(\tau)$. Using the definition of conditional probability and that all waiting times are greater than zero:

$$P(wait > T + \tau \mid wait > T) = \frac{P(wait > T + \tau)}{P(wait > T)} = P(wait > \tau). \tag{3.2}$$

This tells you that $f(T + \tau) = f(T) f(\tau)$. What kind of function f satisfies this? Although you can prove this more rigorously, it's only true if f is the exponential function:

$$f(\tau) = e^{-\lambda \tau}. \tag{3.3}$$

We also had to introduce the so-called rate λ because the equality $f(T + \tau) = f(T) f(\tau)$ holds true for any arbitrary choice of a constant λ as well.

You now have the answer: When events occur uniformly, without memory, the probability that you wait for more than τ is $e^{-\lambda \tau}$ for some constant rate λ. Random processes that have no such memory for waiting times as assumed are called *Poisson processes*. The mean and standard deviation of the exponential distribution are both $1 / \lambda$. Therefore, a quick check to see if an event stream is memoryless is to compare the standard deviation to the mean of the inter-arrival times: A large difference implies some memory or periodicity in the events.

Now consider an event stream as a *counting process* (which determines the number of events in a given time window), for example, where you wonder how many new followers you can acquire after a given window of time, or how many clicks your profile page can get in the next 24 hours. These processes are the sum of random events that have some time between successive occurrences. Knowing how many events to expect can help identify unusual or interesting times.

You can't predict exactly the number of events in advance, but can you derive the probability distribution of the number of events observed in equal time windows, assuming a memoryless Poisson process? Let's introduce $P_k(T, T+d)$, which is the probability that you count k events in the window of time $[T, T+d)$. When $k = 0$, you ask the same preceding question: What is the probability you will wait more than an interval d to see the next event after time T? You already know that answer: $e^{-\lambda d}$. But how can you compute the distribution for other values of k?

This probability is given by the famous Poisson distribution, as follows:

$$P_k(d) = \frac{(\lambda d)^k e^{-\lambda d}}{k!}. \tag{3.4}$$

In other words, in a memoryless Poisson process, your event counts should follow the previous statistic for any time interval d.

An interesting feature of the Poisson distribution as given in the preceding formula is that its mean is equal to its variance (not the standard deviation, as with the exponential distribution):

$$mean(k) = var(k) = \lambda d. \tag{3.5}$$

Now you see again why λ is called the *rate*: Because after a time d, you expect on average to see λd events (which is the expectation value of the Poisson distribution). λ is therefore the average speed of an event arrival, or the average number of events in one unit of time. Because the standard deviation is the square root of the variance, after a time d you expect to see $\lambda d \pm \sqrt{\lambda d} = \lambda d \left(1 \pm \dfrac{1}{\sqrt{\lambda d}} \right)$ events. This means that the number of events in each time bucket of length d may differ from each other by a relative difference of $1/\sqrt{\lambda d}$. So when you make buckets with $d = 10,000 / \lambda$, which is to say you expect approximately 10,000 events in each bucket, then the number of events you'll find in each bucket should agree within approximately $1/\sqrt{10,000}$ or 1%.

Is this model appropriate to describe the timing of events in social media? Figure 3.1 depicts the distribution of time between Tweets referencing the word "lunch" on a semi-log scale collected over two timescales. A perfectly memoryless process would be a straight line on this plot. Notice that when we include only data over 1 hour, we get a closer agreement to the memoryless process. However, when we collect data for a day, we see a deviation from the exponential process due to the daily periodicity observed on Twitter. In both cases, we see the effect of cutoffs after about 10 seconds.

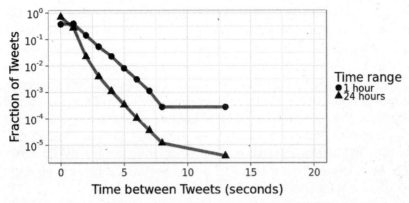

Figure 3.1: The distribution of times between Tweets mentioning "lunch" over a 1-hour, and a 24-hour period, respectively. Tweet arrival times could only be measured in seconds. The vertical axis has been rescaled logarithmically to show correspondences with the exponential function.

Only for short periods of time are the uniform models as good for many social systems as we would expect. If the uniform model, then, is not good, what is a good model? What kind of process could have generated the patterns that we see that is still simple enough to handle in code or mathematically? Remember that we certainly expect that some periods of time are more "interesting" than others, and therefore elicit higher activity rates than others, so the simple Poisson process would not apply. One simple change to still apply the Poisson model to social temporal data is to imagine that you have not one fixed rate λ, but many different rates: $\lambda_1, \lambda_2, \lambda_3, \ldots$, and the actual time series is generated by a mixture of these Poisson distributions with different rate parameters. You could imagine that your social system has a hidden state $S = 1, 2, 3, \ldots$, each state with a corresponding rate. As interest and activity levels change, you can model that by changing the state from one with a lower rate to one with a higher rate. For instance, at a soccer match, when a goal is scored, the system might shift to a higher rate of activity, but over a short enough time scale, the rate might stay constant and appear uniform.

Inter-Event Times

Despite our lapses, humans do have memory. We send a Tweet saying "Good Morning" when the sun comes up, and "Good Evening" when the sun goes down. Such patterns cannot be captured with a Poisson process. The fundamental property of memorylessness is foreign to human experience. When I wait for a friend to arrive, how long I have waited changes the probability that I have to wait longer. If I have been waiting far longer than expected, there is a good chance one of us is confused and the meeting is not about to take place. If we followed a memoryless process, which is to say a Poisson process, the expected wait time is independent of how long one has already waited. This is what we see in Las Vegas at the roulette wheel. How long do we have to wait for the next occurrence of the number 5 to appear? We are easily confused and might have some intuition that if we haven't seen the 5 in a while, we are due for a 5 to appear, but if the roulette wheel is fair, we have a constant probability on each turn of seeing 5, and the history does not matter in the slightest.

Perhaps our incorrect intuition for certain random systems is due to how seldom humans encounter truly memoryless processes. The human notion of time focuses on cycles: The earth around the sun, the moon around the earth, the hands of a watch around a circle. Certain things predictably happen periodically, such as morning commutes, weekend celebrations, yearly holidays, and special events. Human affairs naturally have states that follow such periods. But much is not predictable with a periodic pattern. The exact configuration of cars in the morning traffic, the outcome of sporting events, or disclosure of political information are all difficult to predict. Each can change the baseline of behavior in the time afterward.

As an example what you might guess to be a non-memoryless process, look at the time between people mentioning "lunch" on Twitter, as we did in the previous section. Of the hundreds of millions of Tweets in a day, lunch appears only in few of them, but because most people eat lunch every day, you can expect that there will be some periodicity, and thus memory, in the pattern you observe. We collected the data and recorded the timestamp in seconds since the epoch and stored them in one column. When we look at our data set, we see that our first Tweet about lunch was just after 7 a.m. UTC. Now that we have our events as a sorted list of integer timestamps, let's plot them! A first question we ask is how many mentions per second do we observe. To count this, we write a small function to put each event into exactly one bucket of time and then count how many events fall into each bucket in Listing 3.1.

Listing 3.1: Counting the number of Tweets in time buckets. (`tweet_interevents.py`)

```
import itertools

def bucket(timestamps, bucket_size):
    '''A function to count items in intervals of size bucket_size.'''
```

```
    sortedTs = sorted(timestamps)

    def bucket_of(ts):
        return int(ts / bucket_size)

    bucket_count = dict((b, len(list(vs))) \
                    for (b, vs) in itertools.groupby(sortedTs, bucket_of))
    max_bucket = max(itertools.imap(bucket_of, timestamps))
    min_bucket = min(itertools.imap(bucket_of, timestamps))
    return map(lambda bucket: bucket_count.get(bucket, 0),
               range(min_bucket, max_bucket))

  mentions_per_minute = bucket(lunch_timestamps, 60)
```

Our algorithm uses Python's built-in module, `itertools`, which offers tools for dealing with objects that support iteration. The approach is to sort the timestamps and then use `groupby`, which groups adjacent items together according to some key. If the key is the bucket, the size of the group is the count of that bucket. Finally, we output a list that is ordered from lowest to highest bucket and suitable for plotting; Figure 3.2 shows the generated chart.

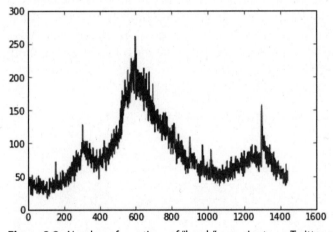

Figure 3.2: Number of mentions of "lunch" per minute on Twitter on a given day

You can see a big peak between 500 and 800 minutes after midnight GMT, which corresponds to 8:20 to 13:20 Pacific time, or in other words, the lunch hours of the United States. An alternative view of this same data, as shown in Figure 3.3, focuses on the time between adjacent Tweets.

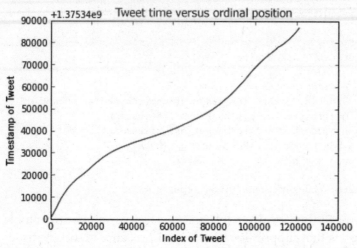

Figure 3.3: Time of the ith mention of "lunch" on Twitter

This figure shows the times that each Tweet containing "lunch" came in. It's much harder to immediately see a signal in this representation. There seems to be something going on, but it is hard to be sure. Certainly, there seems to be a higher rate, evidenced by the slope, from approximately 10,000 to 30,000, as compared to what follows after this. But let's be more direct. For each Tweet about lunch, let's plot how long it has been since the most recent Tweet about lunch; for this, use Listing 3.2 to calculate the time differences between consecutive Tweets (Figure 3.1 was created this way).

Listing 3.2: Calculating the inter-event times between the arrivals of Tweets. (tweet_interevents.py)

```
def make_diffs(items):
    '''A helper to make a stream of the differences in times of an
    iterator.'''

    prev = None
    for x in items:
        if prev:
            yield x - prev
        prev = x


diffs = list(make_diffs(lunch_timestamps))
```

When we view the time between this Tweet and the previous, we can certainly see something going on, as shown in Figure 3.4. It's quite noisy, but there are periods of time in which the intervals are consistently smaller. To smooth this data, we applied a commonly used smoothing technique, the *exponential moving average*, to the data. In Listing 3.3, you can see the algorithm to compute the exponential moving average as a linear difference equation. The exponential moving average is a simple technique to smooth out a time series by mixing together the previously smoothed value with the current time series value to arrive at the average (in effect, deweighting the previous values in an exponentially growing fashion to contribute to the result).

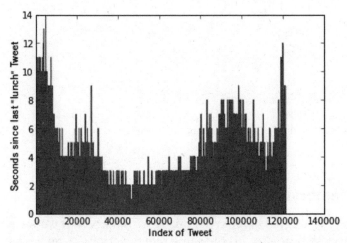

Figure 3.4: Time between successive mentions of "lunch" on Twitter on a particular day. Note that the solid-looking black plot is the result of high variances between the inter-event times of the adjacent Tweets.

Listing 3.3: Calculating the exponential moving average of a series of inter-arrival times. (`tweet_interevents.py`)

```
def exp_ma(items, decay=0.95, init=0.0):
    '''Exponential moving average calculation.'''

    for x in items:
        init = decay * init + (1.0 - decay) * x
        yield init

moving_ave = list(exp_ma(diffs, 0.999))
```

Applying the moving average in Figure 3.5, you see some prominent features easily. What are the times of the extrema? It seems to roughly meet our expectations. We see the time between lunch Tweets decreasing until approximately 9:41 Pacific time (16:41 UTC) and then rise until 13:25 Pacific (00:25 UTC).

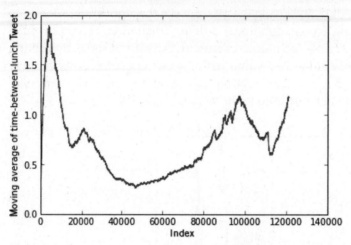

Figure 3.5: Exponentially smoothed time-between-mentions of lunch

Comparing to a Memoryless Process

How do you know there is a signal here? What might we have seen if we were dealing with a memoryless process with the same rate of activity? Can we be sure this is not just a fluke of a memoryless process? Let's determine the mean of the inter-arrival times of the Tweets and generate data with a Poisson process with the exact mean that we measured, in Listing 3.4. The inter-arrival times for all the events generated this way are shown in Figure 3.6.

Listing 3.4: Generate a Poisson time series with the same mean as what we measured, to check whether our actual data is similar to this. (`generate_poisson.py`)

```
import numpy as np


mean0 = mean(diffs)
# A constant to correct for the truncation, but keep the means the same.
correction_due_to_quatization = 1.22


memoryless = np.random.exponential(
    1.0 / (correction_due_to_quatization * mean0), len(diffs)).astype(int)
print mean0, mean(memoryless)
```

If we compare the standard deviations of the Poisson process with that of the measured time series (which, recall, is the square root of its mean), we can see that there is not a huge difference between these, which could be a support for our actual data being close to a Poisson process at first glance.

There does not appear to be much signal in this synthetically generated data set, and indeed there is not as this is identically exponentially distributed random data. The rate appears fairly constant as we expect with a memoryless process. Originally, we looked at the number of events per minute by bucketing the data, which we can also do with our memoryless process, as shown in Figure 3.7.

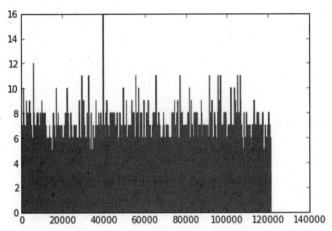

Figure 3.6: Inter-arrival times for the memoryless (Poisson) process as a function of the event index

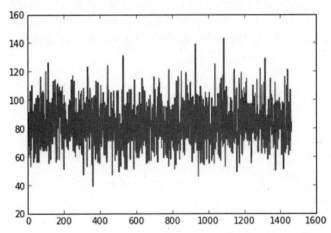

Figure 3.7: Counts in windows of 60 seconds for the memoryless, Poisson data

In the bucketed view, notice two things compared to the actual data. First, the variance between adjacent buckets is much higher in the random case. Second, the average number in each bucket appears fairly constant. This later fact can also be seen in the moving average of the time between these random events, as shown in Figure 3.8.

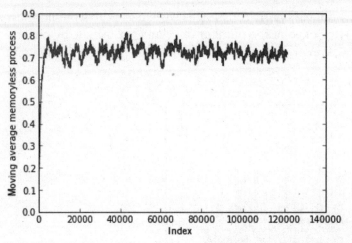

Figure 3.8: The exponential moving average of the memoryless, generated data

As expected, when we average, the rate converges quickly to a constant near the mean. We can have a better way to check if the arrival times between the Tweets do or do not follow an exponential distribution, as would be the case with the memoryless process. One technique for comparing two distributions is to plot each quantile of one distribution versus the other. When comparing against a known theoretical distribution (the exponential), you can exactly derive the theoretical quantile value. Now look at this plot, called the *quantile-quantile*, or Q-Q plot, of the inter-arrival times of the Twitter data, compared against the exponential distribution (Figure 3.9). The Python code that created this plot is shown in Listing 3.5.

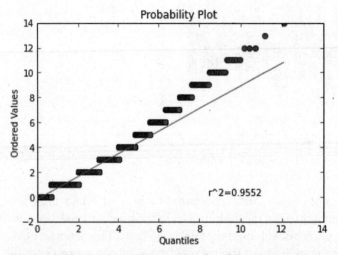

Figure 3.9: The Q-Q (quantile-quantile) plot of the measured inter-arrival time distribution of the Tweets versus the theoretical exponential distribution. You want to test if the measured distribution follows an exponential. You can see that at the higher quantile ranges, the distributions differ.

Listing 3.5: Code to generate a Q-Q plot of the measured and the theoretical exponential distribution. We show the plot in Figure 3.9. (`tweet_q-q_plot.py`)

```
import scipy.stats as stats

stats.probplot(diffs, dist='expon', plot=pylab)
pylab.show()
```

The Q-Q plot shows a significant deviation from the exponential, as when we looked at the moving average. One explanation for this is that the process of users sending Tweets is indeed not memoryless. For this reason, take a look at a final approach: autocorrelation.

Autocorrelations

Autocorrelation is the correlation of a signal with itself, lagged by a certain amount of time. One way to explain correlation is that it is the covariance of two signals, divided by the standard deviation of those signals. Another way to say this is that correlation is the inner product of the signals, after centering to the mean and normalizing. If x_i and y_i denote two ordered samples, then the *Pearson correlation coefficient* between the two samples is expressed as follows:

$$C(x,y) = \frac{\sum_i (x_i - \bar{x})(y_i - \bar{y})}{\sqrt{\sum_i (x_i - \bar{x})^2 \sum_i (y_i - \bar{y})^2}}. \tag{3.6}$$

This is the same formula as the cosine distance between two vectors with components x_i and y_i if their respective means are all 0. If you recall your trigonometry, this equivalence implies that correlation must range between -1 and 1, exactly like cosines do. In simple terms, correlation expresses the degree of linear coupling between x and y: if it's strong (close to 1), changes in either x or y are reflected in proportional changes in the other variable, in the same direction. For strong negative correlations, the same holds, except increases in x from the mean result in decreases in y, and vice versa.

The autocorrelation of a signal is the correlation between the signal and itself when we shift it in time by a certain number of time steps or lags. If j denotes the lag in terms of time steps, then the autocorrelation for the time signal x is given by

$$A(x,j) = \frac{\sum_i (x_i - \bar{x})(x_{i+j} - \bar{x})}{\sum_i (x_i - \bar{x})^2}. \tag{3.7}$$

Naturally, the autocorrelation at $j = 0$ is perfect ($A(x, 0) = 1$) by construction. But as we increase the lag, j, the correlation of the signal with itself might change. If we created x by drawing random numbers independently, there should be no autocorrelation. This calculation is shown in Listing 3.6.

Listing 3.6: Calculating the autocorrelation for different laqs for the Tweets time series. (`tweet_interevents.py`)

```
import numpy as np

def autocor(data):
    centered = np.array(data) - (np.ones(len(data)) * mean(data))
    normed = np.divide(centered, np.std(centered))
    pos_and_neg = np.correlate(normed, normed, mode='full')
    # Normalize the window size.
    ones = np.ones(len(data))
    denom = np.correlate(ones, ones, mode='full')
    win_normed = np.divide(pos_and_neg, denom)
    # The autocorrelation is symmetric, return the right half, and only
    # the first half of overlaps (0.5 to 0.75) to make the plot more
    # compact.
    return win_normed[win_normed.size / 2 : int(0.75 * win_normed.size)]

plot(autocor(mentions_per_minute))
```

Now look at the autocorrelation as a function of the lag for our Twitter mentions-per-minute time series data. This plot is shown in Figure 3.10 and is compelling. We see values as extreme as 0.95 and −0.8. We see that for short times, there is almost perfect autocorrelation. By the time 180–240 minutes have passed, there is almost no correlation. Put differently, if we see a lot of Tweets about lunch now, that does not mean we will see a lot in 200 minutes. However, seeing a lot now means we can expect fewer than average after 500 minutes, or approximately 9 hours later. Conversely, few Tweets now suggest an increase may be coming after approximately 9 hours.

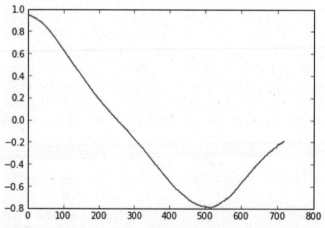

Figure 3.10: Autocorrelation of the time between mentions of lunch, as a function of the number of time step lags, which is measured in minutes

One last test you can perform to make sure you are not fooling yourself is to shuffle the data. This technique is useful when you want to test whether correlations are among your data points in time because a random shuffling would destroy such correlations if they exist. Clearly, after a shuffle, no real correlation exists, but what does your function and plot have to say? Figure 3.11 shows that shuffling the order of the time between Tweets, as it did, make all correlations disappear.

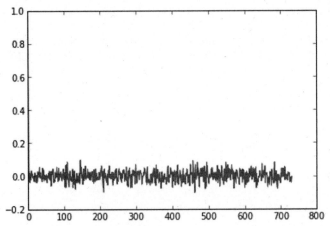

Figure 3.11: Autocorrelation of the shuffled data: not much to see

Deviations from Memorylessness

You have seen in detail how a process that has no memory of the past must be a Poisson process, which is to say having an exponential waiting time between events. However, it's obvious that actual human activities are not memoryless. But how are these deviations from memorylessness created? Let's illustrate that with a toy model and consider a process in which a totally memoryless process is fed to an agent with just a little bit of memory. That agent can choose to delete the event but never introduces an event of its own; otherwise it just passes the event on. To be concrete, we say it remembers the last time an event came. If that time is greater than t_0, the agent lets it pass; otherwise, it is discarded. You can actually derive the time between events in this new case:

$$P(t > \tau) = \begin{cases} 1, \text{ if } \tau \le t_0 \\ \dfrac{P(t > \tau \cap t > t_0)}{P(t > t_0)} = \dfrac{P(t > \tau)}{P(t > t_0)} = e^{-\lambda(\tau - t_0)}, \text{ if } \tau > t_0 \end{cases} \qquad (3.8)$$

In this formula, we also used the definition for conditional probabilities that $P(A \mid B) = P(A \cap B) / P(B)$. The point is that the waiting time distribution of this agent with memory deviates from the exponential in that it cuts out the smallest times, but it does not actually change the shape.

What if after each time an event comes that is too soon ($< t_0$), the agent decreases t_0 by a factor? This is like lowering our standards: We haven't seen something good enough for a while, so we are willing to accept a lesser value. After we finally find an event, we reset our memory back to the initial standard. Let's call this process the *impatient filtering agent*. Deriving the waiting time probability analytically is harder in this case, so instead we can simulate it and plot it directly, as shown in Listing 3.7.

Listing 3.7: Simulating an impatient filtering agent that doesn't let any event go through that comes earlier than a given parameter `minDiff`. However, if we haven't seen an event for this amount of time, we'll lower the filtering time parameter. (`agent.py`)

```
def agent(start, minDiff):
    '''Return a function that transforms an input iterator according to
    the impatient filtering.'''

    def __inner__(interTimes):
      now = start
      thisDiff = minDiff
      lastTime = now
      for interval in interTimes:
        now = now + interval
        if interval > thisDiff:
            yield now - lastTime
            thisDiff = minDiff
            lastTime = now
        else:
          # We get impatient and lower the barrier.
          thisDiff = thisDiff * 0.25

    return __inner__
```

To make it more interesting, imagine that someone down the line from our first agent could do the same trick. Such coupled networks of agents sending and filtering events can be useful modes of network dynamics. Figure 3.12 shows the inter-event time distributions for the original memoryless process and the effect when we introduce one or two filtering agents. So, even a little bit of memory results in a clear difference from a memoryless process. If filterings like this occur in social systems of interacting agents, our final timings will be different from what we'd expect for a memoryless process.

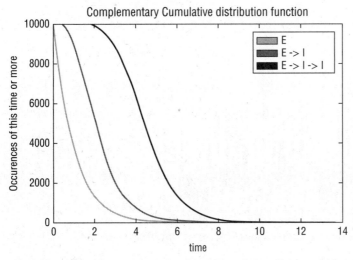

Figure 3.12: Time between events after 0 (E) and after chaining 1 (E→I) and 2 (E→I→I) impatient filtering agents

Periodicities in Time in User Activities

So far, we looked in detail at one particular day and identified a few features. The data is noisy; there appears that from one moment to the next we cannot make an exact prediction. However, there was a strong signal that you can make out immediately, referred to in Figure 3.2. In this section, we look in closer detail at the time correlations that exist. Lunch time comes at the same time every day, but what we choose to send a Tweet about is difficult to predict, and only a small fraction of Tweets contain the string "lunch." By looking at the pattern over a month, you might see more clearly the predictable and periodic signal, and what remains will be the part you have yet to predict.

Figure 3.13 shows the Tweets per minute containing the word "lunch," again, but this time for 30 days. If you look carefully, you can already see a lot of structure. Every 10,000 or so minutes, you see a gap. Between 10,000 and 20,000 you see five peaks. Surely those must be peaks on each weekday. Indeed, the week has 7 × 24 × 60 = 10,080 minutes. The distribution of the number of Tweets per minute for the same dataset is shown by Figure 3.14.

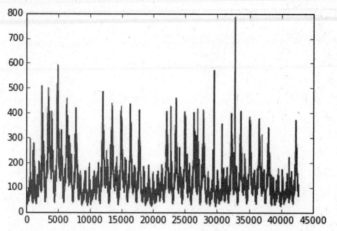

Figure 3.13: Tweets per minute containing the string "lunch" for 30 days

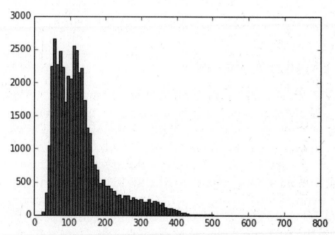

Figure 3.14: Distribution of the number of Tweets containing the word "lunch" per minute for 30 days

Figure 3.15 shows the total number of Tweets for 30 days plotted by minute of the day. Here, you can see what appears as several peaks that look nearly Guassian: the biggest two approximately 600 minutes (10 a.m. GMT, 6 a.m. Eastern, and 3 a.m. Pacific) and 1300 minutes (9:40 p.m. GMT, 4:40 p.m. Eastern, and 1:40 p.m. Pacific). Now we have broken the problem into two: What causes this clean daily pattern? What causes the deviations from the daily pattern? We won't spend much time on the first one, but we can suggest an approach.

Some Tweets about lunch are because you are about to eat, or just ate, and some are not about a particular recent event and decoupled from the time the sender ate. The reasons for randomness in this process are many: Due to geographic distribution, not all users send a Tweet at the same time; not all users in all locations use English words; and not all users in all locations use Twitter at the same rate. By developing a model on those four variables, you could perhaps explain this curve as arising mostly from geographic and language differences. The key point to make is that when you have an idea how to partition the data, that is, there is a daily cycle and a difference from that, you can look at those two signals separately.

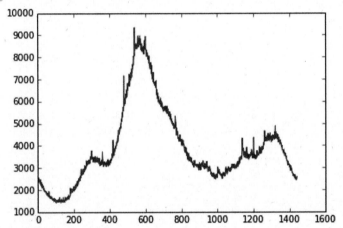

Figure 3.15: The total number of Tweets that fell on each minute of the day for each day of a 30-day period

Figure 3.16 shows the difference from the daily average. Note that although there are still spikes, the size is much smaller: Almost all of them are less than 200 Tweets/minute, meaning that there is almost never more than 200 extra Tweets in a minute relative to the daily expected amount at a given time. Before we removed the daily average (refer to Figure 3.13), we were seeing regular spikes above 400 Tweets/minute and several above 500 Tweets/minute. So the daily cycle certainly accounts for much of the variance, but the weekdays and weekends are still quite visible in Figure 3.16.

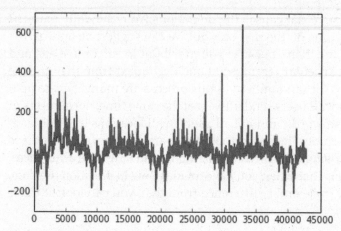

Figure 3.16: Difference of the actual number of Tweets per minute from the average daily cycle

Figure 3.17 looks at the distribution of differences from the daily cycle. It is much closer to a normal distribution. There is the hint of two smaller normals hidden inside: one at approximately –150 and one at approximately –25. These mixtures may be the result of the weekends and that you have yet to account for the slight down trend as the week goes on. You can test this by subtracting not the average rate for each minute in the day, but the average rate for each minute in the *week*.

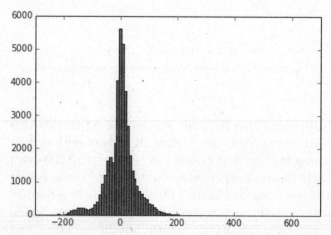

Figure 3.17: Distribution of the difference from the number of Tweets per minute and what we expect from the daily average cycle. Note how much closer to Gaussian this is.

How do we determine what the expected Tweet rate would be for a given minute and day in any given week? We do it by averaging over several weeks within bins that correspond to a minute within the week. For each of the 10,080 minutes in the week, we have a bin, and we compute the average number of Tweets for that bin. In this example, we are looking only at data for one month, so each bin holds four values. See the result in Figure 3.18. You can notice several features. First, as the week goes on, you see that the peak is lowering: On average, people were sending more Tweets about lunch earlier in the week. Second, the gap between the first peak and the second peak appears to disappear on the weekend. It's not clear why. Third, it is not nearly as smooth as Figure 3.15, which had 30 days averaged in each minute compared to only 4 here. As a result of fewer samples, Figure 3.18 is considerably spikier.

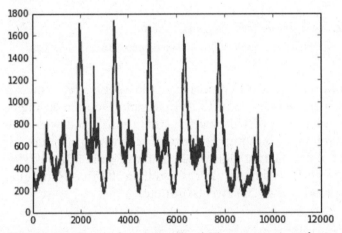

Figure 3.18: Minute-of-week total "lunch" Tweets per minute for 4 weeks

Taking the average over the 4 weeks and subtracting it, you get Figure 3.19. With the weekly pattern removed, you see something much closer to the independent random noise referred to in Figure 3.8. At this stage, what are we doing? We are saying that the overall signal can be modeled as a weekly background that is due to features such as time-of-day, geography, language, and geo-specific adoption rate. Several features still remain visible. Early in the month, there seems to be a deficit and then surplus of Tweets. Then there are many large spikes still: The largest is nearly 500 extra Tweets per minute approximately 33,000 minutes into the month. Almost anything could be the cause of such a blip: log collection issues at runtime, a funny line on a TV show, a news headline, a restaurant running a special, and so on. If we actually need to explain that peak, we might start by looking at the text of the Tweet and the accounts of the senders, as we will do in Chapter 4.

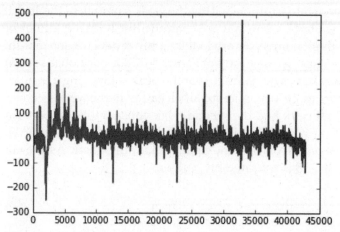

Figure 3.19: Difference of the actual data and the 4-week average referred to in Figure 3.18

Looking at the distribution of the differences from the weekly cycle, you can see a nice, normal-like distribution in Figure 3.20. In this plot, you can no longer see multiple peaks as in Figure 3.17. This suggests that those peaks were due to the weekly cycle; therefore, accounting for them causes them to be removed. Also look at how much more narrow Figure 3.20 is than Figure 3.17. The difference from the weekly period is almost always less than 100 Tweets/minute, but the daily cycle is spread within 200 Tweets/minute.

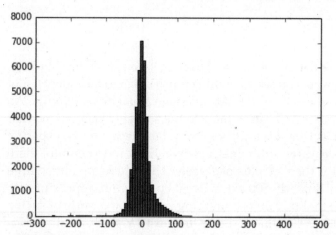

Figure 3.20: Distribution of difference in "lunch" Tweets per minute from the weekly cycle average

So the weekly cycle has reduced the variance, but at the expense of having 10,080 bins to average over. By contrast, the daily model has only 1,440 bins to explain. A compromise approach is to create a model with 1,440 + 6 values:

one for each minute of Monday and 6 more to scale days relative to Monday. Of course, we can also reduce the number of bins we track each day. More than 1,000 may be overkill. Perhaps that curve could fit reasonably well with as few as 12 variables: 4 normal distributions each with a mean, variance, and a maximum. The name of the game is to use as few parameters as possible to give the smallest error in the residual model.

The reason we looked at the daily and weekly Tweet-rate patterns was to highlight some of the periodic behavior that is necessarily part of social media systems; we'll take a more in-depth look at how we can actually use these discovered periodicities in the "Forecasting Metrics in Time" section later in this chapter.

Bursty Activities of Individuals

Up to this point, you have looked at the aggregate, system-level timing of events, such as when you can observe any Tweet with the word "lunch" in it. This was obviously the result of the activities of a lot of users considered together. In this section, you consider *individual* users instead, the smallest "unit" of a social system. For this you take the revisions made by Wikipedia editors on any page and focus your attention on these activities. The data we have are the times when a user made an edit anywhere. To better understand the trends for individual users, you can choose a short time window (such as 1 hour) and count how many actions a user took within a given time window, as you did before. The most straightforward way to do this is to take time windows that do not overlap and that cover the entire date range you selected for the data collection. For example, in Figure 3.21 we took the first week of 2013, when Wikipedia had fewer users, and counted the hourly number of edits four randomly chosen users had during this time. (We chose users who had a comparatively large total number of edits during the one week; see `wikipedia_edit_interevent_times.R`).

You can see from these graphs that users' activities tend to cluster into sessions when the user is active for a relatively short period of time, then goes inactive for a longer period of time, then makes some edits again. These short periods of high activity are the *bursts* that characterize temporal human activity patterns and are markedly different from the more "uniformly spaced" events that a Poisson process would result in, as we could see in the previous sections.

In Figure 3.22 we take one randomly chosen Wikipedia editor and show her windowed edit rates over time. For comparison, we also show how the edit rates would look if the user made edits according to a Poisson process, as a baseline (in essence modeling the user as if she decided completely randomly whether to make an edit at any given moment). It is apparent that the actual bursty user activity patterns look different from the simple Poisson model qualitatively. How can we describe these differences?

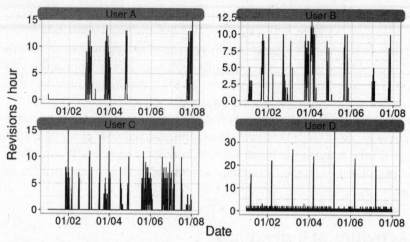

Figure 3.21: The number of revisions per hour for four randomly selected Wikipedia editors, during the first week of 2013. We partitioned the 1-week date range by non-overlapping hours and counted the times that a particular user made edits in any hour. User *A* was active at irregular times but made quite a few edits on 4 days; User *B*'s pattern is similar to this. User *C*, however, made edits more often and was active for longer times in a "session." In User *D*'s time series, you can see low levels of activities most of the time and active hours 7 times on each day at approximately the same hour during the week.

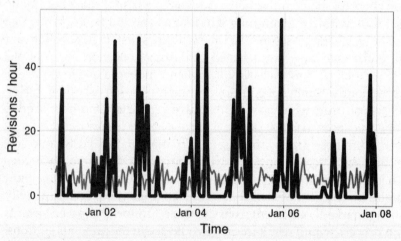

Figure 3.22: The bold line shows the revisions per hour for a randomly chosen (but high-activity) Wikipedia editor. The lighter line is a simulation of a Poisson process that results in approximately the same number of total events during the whole week as the chosen editor had (approximately 1,200). We achieve this by choosing the rate parameter of the Poisson process such that the expected number of events per time unit is the same as the number of events we observed for the given user, $\lambda = $ *(# of events)* / (1 *week*).

The first thing we should be looking at is again the inter-event time distribution of the user edits. The way to measure inter-event times is first to sort the activity records by the timestamp, and then we can take the differences between successive timestamps for every user. In Python/R, we would do this by reading in the edit records into a data frame, followed by sorting on the timestamp, and finally grouping on user ID and taking a `diff` in every group on the timestamps. Although this would work, for large amounts of data we could possibly run out of memory. Instead, it's a better solution to sort the timestamps first with external sort (such as with the sort Unix command that uses the disk when necessary for temporary storage, Listing 3.8), and then stream through the file in Python. We can keep a dictionary that stores the last seen timestamp for every user ID as we go, and calculate the time differences as soon as we see a new timestamp coming for the user. This solution would be both fast and use only the available working memory. An even better approach would be to filter the input dataset first to contain only the desired date ranges, and sort only after; our intent was to highlight an easy way to perform sorting even on large datasets.

Listing 3.8: Sorting the Wikipedia revisions pre-processed dataset by revision timestamp, using multicore processing. (`wikipedia_sort_by_time.sh`)

```
# Sort the Wikipedia revision file with parallelized external sort and
# compression, using half of the RAM.

pigz --decompress --stdout < data/wikipedia/revisions.tsv.gz | \
sort --key=5 --field-separator=$'\t' --buffer-size=50% --parallel=
$(nproc) | \
pigz --stdout > data/wikipedia/revisions_time_sorted.tsv.gz
```

Next we'll take a time range (the first 3 months of 2013), and all the users' edits in this time interval, and calculate inter-event times by taking the differences between the successive edits of the individual users. Because we already have the revisions sorted by increasing timestamps, we can just go through the records sequentially and take the differences between successive timestamps of a user; Listing 3.9 illustrates this.

Listing 3.9: After the revisions file is sorted by timestamps, it's easy to compute the inter-edit time histograms. We do this here with logarithmic binning. This script streams through the revisions and records the inter-event times between the edits of *users* and between the edits on *pages*, separately. (`wikipedia_edit_interevent_times.py`)

```
'''
Calculate the inter-edit times for both Wikipedia editors and pages.
'''

import sys, gzip, math
from collections import defaultdict
from datetime import datetime
```

```python
INPUT_FILE = 'data/wikipedia/revisions_time_sorted.tsv.gz'
OUTPUT_FILE_PATTERN = 'data/wikipedia/interedit_times_%s.tsv.gz'

class IntereventTimes():
    '''A class to keep track of inter-event times between arrivals of
       certain events, such as for user edits and page changes.'''

    # Create 50 logarithmic buckets for 10000 seconds (chosen
    # arbitrarily).
    LOG_BUCKET = math.log10(1e4) / 50

    def __init__(self):
        self.last_seen = dict()
        self.interevent_times = defaultdict(int)

    def discretize(self, value):
        '''Determine the index of the logarithmic bucket for this
        value.'''
        if value == 0:
            return -1
        return int(math.log10(int(value)) / IntereventTimes.LOG_BUCKET)

    def add(self, key, time):
        try:
            last_time = self.last_seen[key]
            dt = self.discretize((time - last_time).total_seconds())
            self.interevent_times[dt] += 1
        except KeyError:
            pass
        self.last_seen[key] = time

interevent_times = dict()
for entity in ['users', 'pages']:
    interevent_times[entity] = IntereventTimes()

input_file = gzip.open(INPUT_FILE, 'r')
for line in input_file:
    title, namespace, page_id, rev_id, timestamp, user_id, user_name, \
    ip = line[:-1].split('\t')
    if user_id != '' and user_id != '0':
        user_id = int(user_id)
        page_id = int(page_id)
        timestamp = datetime.strptime(timestamp, '%Y-%m-%dT%H:%M:%SZ')
        interevent_times['users'].add(user_id, timestamp)
        interevent_times['pages'].add(page_id, timestamp)
input_file.close()

for entity in ['users', 'pages']:
    output_file = gzip.open(OUTPUT_FILE_PATTERN % entity, 'w')
```

```
for dt, count in interevent_times[entity].interevent_times. \
iteritems():
    output_file.write('\t'.join(map(str, [dt, count])) + '\n')
output_file.close()
```

We can then take the union of all the inter-edit times for all the users as our sample and see how these times are distributed, as shown in Figure 3.23. (In this way what we're looking at is how the inter-edit times would be distributed for an "average" user measured over a long time.)

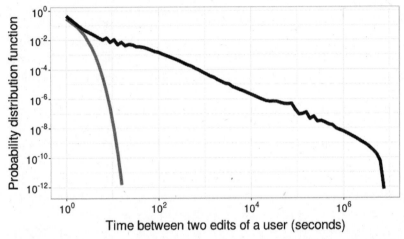

Figure 3.23: The empirical probability density function of times between two edits of any given user, with a bold line. The measured inter-edit time distribution has a power-law exponent of approximately −1.3. With the lighter line, we show the probability density function for a Poisson process with a rate parameter λ that would result in the same number of total edit events as what we have in the measurement. We used logarithmic binning to compute the empirical PDF for the Wikipedia inter-edit times.

The first thing you can observe is that the inter-event times for users' edit activities follow a power law, in contrast to the exponential distribution that you would see for a Poisson process. To make this comparison to the Poisson process more apparent, you can also plot the probability density function for a Poisson process that would result in the same expected number of edits as what you have observed. You know that the PDF of the inter-event times t of a Poisson process is $\lambda e^{-\lambda t}$, with a mean inter-event time of $1 / \lambda$. Given that in this actual case we can count approximately 13.6 million edits for 90 days, the mean average inter-event time will be

$$\frac{1}{\lambda} = \frac{90 \ days}{13.6 \cdot 10^6}.$$ (3.9)

From this it's easy to determine that $\lambda = 1.75$ / second. (We chose seconds as our time unit.) Figure 3.23 also shows the PDF of the exponential distribution with this exact λ parameter. The difference between the Wikipedia inter-edit times and the Poisson process is apparent: Although both result in the same number of total events, you can observe longer inter-event times on Wikipedia than the uniform Poisson model would suggest. Considering the previous figures with the example time series of some selected users, this is the reason you saw long periods of inactivity interspersed with activity bursts: These periods when users are inactive are relatively frequent given the long-tailed distribution of inter-event times.

In a similar way, we can also turn our attention to pages and look at the distribution of the time that elapses between two edits on a given page. Similarly to how we did it for the users, we then take the inter-edit times of all the pages together, and plot the PDF for the entire data set. Listing 3.9 was used to calculate the empirical PDF with logarithmic binning. We plotted the resulting density function in Figure 3.24, from which it is apparent that again we have a power-law tail for the inter-edit times. However, in this case we can also see that the distribution has a peak at approximately 1 minute, but then for longer times it becomes the familiar power-law distribution again. In Figures 3.23 and 3.24, for the inter-event times you can see that at the 90-day mark (90 days $\approx 7.8 \cdot 10^6$ seconds) the distributions are cut off, for the natural reason that you cannot measure larger differences between two events than these 90 days.

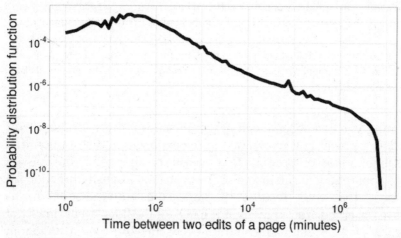

Figure 3.24: The PDF of the times between two edits on any Wikipedia page for the first 90 days of 2013. We consider all pages together here, similar to how we aggregated all users for Figure 3.23.

What have you learned, overall? You have seen that if you consider either individual users' actions or actions related to individual content (Wikipedia page edits), events *do not happen uniformly* in time, as would be suggested by a Poisson model. Single users act in bursts in which longer periods of inactivity are interrupted by sessions where they show a lot heavier activity.

Correlations and Bursts

We considered the autocorrelation function of the number of binned Tweets in the "Autocorrelations" section earlier in this chapter as a measure of the deviations from memorylessness over time in the aggregate user activities. In this section you'll focus on the presence of correlations in the activity patterns of *individual* users, as opposed to what happens when you consider all activities at once, as we did previously.

In Figure 3.22, you saw that when users make edits, they are usually active for a short time and then go inactive again. This suggests that for inter-event times, short periods should be followed by similarly short periods between two successive events. How can you check this hypothesis with measurements?

You need to recognize that what you want to measure here is a *conditional probability density function*: Given the length of an inter-event time, what will be the length of the following inter-event time for a user? If the first one is short, will the next one also be short? In the language of probability theory, the conditional probability of an event A, given another event B, is denoted as $P(A \mid B)$. This means nothing more than that we require that B must have happened before we consider by what probability A will also take place. In other words, in our concrete Wikipedia example, we would like to measure the conditional probability density function $f(t_2 \mid t_1)$, where t_1 is the first inter-event time, and t_2 is the inter-event time immediately following this one. (Note that we need to have three consecutive events for this.) We also know that after we fix t_1 to a concrete value, the distribution of t_2's has to be a probability measure, or in other words just a regular probability density function. Therefore, its area has to be 1: $\int f(t_2 \mid t_1)dt_2 = 1$. We will use this property shortly.

Following are steps to measure the conditional PDF in practice:

1. By going through the file containing the edit events, you can keep track of events that a particular user made. Because you're looking for successive inter-edit times, you need to keep track of only the last inter-edit time that you have seen for this user.

2. Any time a new event occurs, we calculate how much time has elapsed between this and the user's last event, and at the same time we can output in two columns the previous inter-event time (which we have kept in a variable for the user so that we can use it now) and the current inter-event time.

3. Naturally, we then replace the last inter-event time with the current one, and the last time an event was seen with the current time of the incoming event.

This task is again better implemented as a streaming algorithm, and we just note that the script is similar to Listing 3.9 and can be found in `wikipedia_edit_times_for_conditional_probs.py`. Also, we would like to calculate the conditional probability density function of t_2 following t_1, which we can approximate by calculating a histogram over binned values of both t_2 and t_1. This procedure is extremely similar to how we would calculate histograms over just one random variable, except here we're given two random variables instead of one, but conceptually we're performing the same operations. Also, because we know that the inter-event times have a long-tailed distribution, we'd better use logarithmic binning as a discretization method of the inter-event times.

Then it's straightforward what we need to do: As we calculate the (t_1, t_2) pairs using the revision data, we could immediately bin these values and keep a frequency count of how often these pairs are encountered, using a dictionary in Python. However, for the sake of illustrating a useful practical method, we'll forgo this simple solution in favor of a slightly more complicated one that enables us to introduce *reservoir sampling*.

Reservoir Sampling

Now assume that we want to create the histogram in R, instead of Python, so the Python script should output only the raw (t_1, t_2) pairs of successive inter-event times, whose number of occurrences we would count later in R. However, because we have a lot of inter-event times, we could quickly generate more rows than R can process. We perhaps don't even need a lot of records; all we want is to create a decent histogram, but we don't need extreme statistical resolution beyond a certain point. One solution to this is to start reading the revision data, and we could just stop when we reach the wanted number of output rows. (Ten million seems to be a good number.) However, if we have a lot of dense data, we may have covered a short overall time range only. (In our actual case, if we start reading revisions starting on Jan 1, 2013, we'll reach 10 million records by March 13, so this is not a problem. If we have more users, the time range covered may shorten significantly.) Then we could be worried that this time period may have some biases because it's too short. For instance, if it were only one night, we wouldn't capture the daily patterns fully.

To work around this, we can downsample the data uniformly by streaming through the items and keeping each one in our output with a probability p, choosing p so that we'll approximately get the wanted number of rows in the end. Again, this works if we know the number of records we'll read through in advance; however, if it's an "infinite" stream of items, we probably don't know this. All we want is to read through the stream, and by the end of the run have a given number of records (say, 10 million) at our disposal that should be selected from the stream *uniformly* and *randomly*. This procedure is accomplished by performing the reservoir sampling. The way it works is this: If the desired number of items we want to select from the stream is k, we first allocate room for k items in a reservoir. Then, we take items from the stream one by one, first completely filling up the reservoir. After we fill up the reservoir, we need to periodically replace items in the reservoir from the stream to maintain the requirement that every item should have the same probability of being chosen. Say that we're at the ith element in the stream. We then generate a random integer r between 1 and i, and if r is smaller than k, we replace the rth element in the reservoir by the current i^{th} element from the stream. (In essence, we replace a random item in the reservoir with probability k / i.) This procedure is illustrated by Listing 3.10. It can be easily proven that in this case every element from the stream will be represented with equal probability in the reservoir by the time we reach the end of the stream.

Listing 3.10: Class that implements the reservoir sampling algorithm. The add_item method is used to let the class know that we have a new item in the stream. By the time we reach the end of the stream, the self.items list will contain items chosen from the stream with equal probability. (reservoir_sampling.py)

```
import random

class ReservoirSample():
    '''Perform reservoir sampling to get a uniform sample from any
    number of elements.'''

    def __init__(self, sample_count):
        '''sample_count is the desired number of sample points.
           self.items contains the sample after we're finished.'''
        self.items = []
        self.sample_count = sample_count
        self.index = 0

    def add_item(self, item):
        '''Add an item to the reservoir.'''
        if self.index < self.sample_count:
            self.items.append(item)
        else:
            r = random.randint(0, self.index - 1)
            if r < self.sample_count:
                self.items[r] = item
        self.index += 1
```

Then if we perform a reservoir sampling on our successive inter-event pairs, we can produce an input file of a given length that now can be easily consumed from R. What is left is only the discretization (binning) of the inter-event times and the normalization of the histogram to 1 for every single binned t_1 value. Figure 3.25 shows the results for the Wikipedia inter-event time correlations.

This is a heatmap of the conditional probability density function of t_2, given that the previous inter-event time was t_1. The gray scale represents the values of the PDF in every (t_1, t_2) bin. The probability values add up to 1 for each column of t_1.

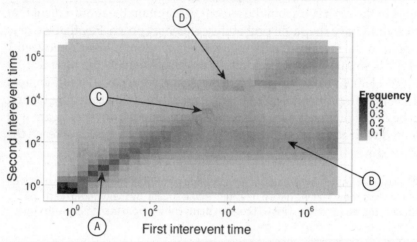

Figure 3.25: The heatmap of the conditional probability density function of an inter-edit time, given that it follows another inter-edit time of a certain length. (Both axes are in seconds, and the times are logarithmically binned.) The way to look at this plot is to imagine that we have three successive edits made by a Wikipedia user, which gives us two inter-edit times. The first inter-event time is represented by the x axis in this figure, and assuming we fix that, the distribution of the second inter-edit time is given by the corresponding column. Therefore, the columns of the heatmap sum to 1, and the shade of the cells is a representation of the value of the PDF at that point.

How do we read this figure? We know that if any t_2 was completely independent of the choice of t_1, then for every t_1 we should get the exact same distribution over t_2, and therefore the columns of Figure 3.25 should be equal, or on the heatmap as shown, equally shaded. However, in this specific case, this holds only in the neighborhood of approximately $t_1 = 10^6$ seconds, where each column corresponding to slightly different t_1s is approximately the same. (These conditional PDFs have two peaks, at approximately $t_2 = 10^2$ seconds and $t_2 = 10^6$ seconds, respectively.)

However, when we look at other t_1 values, especially in the 10^0 to 10^2 range (1 sec–2 min, marker *A*), we can see that the conditional PDFs are different for each t_1: They are different because their peaks occur at different values of t_2 (the vertical axis). This is obvious because there's a diagonal dark line in the figure, which means that the peaks of the conditional distributions happen at approximately $t_2 \approx t_1$. The peaks are also rather sharp because the diagonal is well defined in the plot. What this means is that if the user has just made two edits that are less than approximately 2 minutes apart, then he will make an edit again after the same amount of time with a high probability. He's probably making the edits that are all either quick or take a few minutes of time.

This qualitative picture changes however for t_1 values that are larger than approximately 2 minutes (10^2 seconds). In this region, indicated by B in the figure, we can see that the darker area, with approximately $t_2 = 100$ seconds, becomes more likely. It can also be seen that in this regime the peak at approximately 100 seconds becomes *independent* of t_1, which means that if the user makes an edit now, and the previous edit was more than 2 minutes ago, then he will have the next edit between 10 and 1,000 seconds from the current one (this is roughly the extent of the darker area), no matter when the previous edit happened. In a way, in this case the user doesn't "remember" any more when the previous edit took place and acts as if he would be starting over again, which is slightly reminiscent of the memoryless Poisson process.

As for specific patterns related to daily cycles, consider the parts of the distribution with the markers C and D. C points to a bin that is slightly more likely to appear than its surrounding bins—this corresponds approximately to the hourly cycles. (The location of the bin on the logarithmic axes for hourly differences is $\log_{10}(60 \cdot 60) \approx 3.56$, because we use base-10 logarithm on the axes for time differences in seconds.) Similarly, the more pronounced area pointed to by D is for $t_2 = 1$ day ($\log_{10}(24 \cdot 60 \cdot 60) \approx 4.94$, which is the position of the darker area on the vertical axis). Again, this means that it's relatively likely that the time difference between two edits of a user is about 1 day, perhaps because these users (or maybe automatic agents) have a daily schedule to make edits to Wikipedia pages.

In summary, you have seen that when users are active, there are strong correlations among their activities. When they have activities in a quick succession after one another, it's likely that there will be quicker activities happening shortly after that. However, when users have not had activities for a little while (in our Wikipedia case, for approximately 2 minutes), they act more or less independently of how long they hadn't done anything. Just as you have seen for the autocorrelations of Tweet counts around a topic previously, individual user actions display similar correlated behavior over time. The two alternative ways of looking at autocorrelations should convince you that significant short-term memory effects exist in social media, either because of the external events that happen at particular times or because the users attend to their online activities in bursts.

Forecasting Metrics in Time

You looked at the basic characteristics of the timing of social media events and how they differ from a simple baseline model. However, you did this on short-time horizons, a few days or weeks, in which you saw that the metrics suggest correlations in time. This section considers the long-term evolution of user metrics and how you can model this to make predictions.

You might want to track several metrics in social media platforms. Examples are the daily/weekly/monthly number of active users representing the total count of users logging in, the number of requests to servers representing the load on a particular server, or the number of posts to the platform in the form of text or media. It is often crucial to forecast future values of these metrics. For instance, if you are a reliability engineer, it's critical for you to know a peak time in server loads before any incidence and get ready for the load. If you are in the finance department, it's critical to know future revenue to plan for company investments. Tracking user statistics such as the number of daily active users (the number of unique users using the platform on a daily basis) is important for social media platforms. It is crucial for understanding growth and for planning for the load on the servers supporting the service ahead of time. This section uses Wikipedia data as an example data set, and the number of daily active users who contribute content to Wikipedia as the time series.

Each of these problems consists of some numerical values on successive days, weeks, months, or years. In other words, there is a time unit in which the metric is tracked, and there is a value for the metric in that time frame. A series of such (time, value) pairs forms a *time series*, and given values of such pairs, predicting any future value in time is called *time series forecasting*. The commonality between all the preceding examples is that all of them can be considered as a time series forecasting problem. This section explores some of the basic techniques for time series forecasting and related problems.

We denote the pair (time, value) of the metric we track as X_τ representing the value at time τ of the metric X. Suppose our full-time series is denoted via $X_{1:t}$, and we want to estimate X_{t+1}. To get an accurate forecast, we need to understand our data and the underlying dynamics. We focus on two different aspects of time series in this section: *Trends* and *seasonality*.

Before we go any deeper, a visual inspection of the time series is useful. Often at different time segments varying dynamics dominate the evolution of the time series. For example, as shown in Figure 3.26, we have two qualitatively different stages of the evolution of the daily number of editors on Wikipedia: a fast growth in the early period (until around mid-2007, the "first stage"), and a down-trending state (after that until we decided to window data for clarity in 2013, the "second stage").

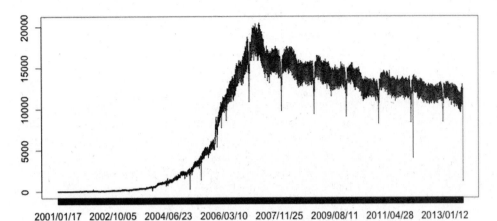

Figure 3.26: The daily number of unique editors on Wikipedia who contribute some content (make an edit) at least once a day. The first stage shows accelerating growth, whereas the second stage shows declining daily user counts and has a strong apparent periodic component.

Often a simple transformation of the data helps with both extracting insights and forecasting future values. For example, we want to understand the different dynamics of the first stage and the second stage of the Wikipedia time series. Because it appears that in the first stage growth is accelerating, we can perform a logarithmic transformation of this stage, which is shown in Figure 3.27. The log-transform of the user numbers is linear; therefore, the growth in this stage was exponential. It's a good practice to check the log-transform of a time series when there is such a quick growth in a metric because an apparently fast growth can occur due to a polynomial increase as well. However, with the log-transform we can understand whether it is exponential or polynomial. If the growth is exponential, the log-transform results in a linear function, whereas a polynomial growth shows up as sublinear after the transformation.

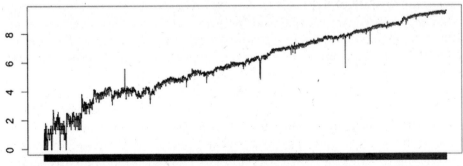

Figure 3.27: The first stage of the time series describing the number of daily active users on Wikipedia, this time on a logarithmic vertical axis

A typical and common relation type between time and the metric we're measuring is linearity, meaning that the best function to be fit on the longer trend is linear. In actuality, this is not always the case; for example, the first stage of Wikipedia's user base shows exponential growth. We found that a log-transformation helped recover a simpler, linear relationship, and at this point both the first stage and the second stage could possibly be modeled through less complex models, as we explain in the following sections. The only difference for the first stage is that after making the forecast on a log-scale, we need to transform it back to complete the prediction.

Following are important observations we can make at this point:

- A time series might get into different stages in which the dynamics are qualitatively different from each other.

- Within each stage, a separate model might be more useful, which is selected and fine-tuned for that stage.

- Each stage requires careful analysis on its own. For instance, the first stage of the Wikipedia user growth can be modeled using an exponential function. In this case the question is the rate of this exponential growth. For the second stage, it may be more important to describe the apparent cyclic patterns.

We explore all these questions in the remaining sections of this chapter. We want to remove the trend and seasonality from the time series and explain and model them, and after the removal we will be left with random, otherwise unexplainable noise only. Then we can look for outliers.

Finding Trends

One reason we want to perform time series analysis is to find the direction of certain metrics, for instance, to understand how some specific metrics in a social media platform are evolving. As mentioned, you may want to track trends in the number of daily active users or content production.

In general, we can try to understand a time series by decomposing it into three different components: a trend, a seasonality, and a noisy or irregular component. We assume that the time series is given as the sum of these components, $X_\tau = T_\tau + S_\tau + N_\tau$. (In other scenarios it's also worthwhile to try to decompose a time series into *multiplicative* components, in contrast to the *additive* relationship we just assumed for this model.) When we can describe these three simpler components, we can make predictions, assuming the statistics of these are the same in the future as they were in the past. If we can capture the trends and seasonalities, we can use forecasting to detect anomalies and take early actions if the time series start deviating from what we'd expect based on what we've seen as "normal" in the past. Anomalies in social media platforms can happen in both the infrastructure of the platform, or they can happen in certain locations or groups of the users due to special events or changes in the regular dynamics.

For example, we could alert the relevant engineering team if we detect a service anomaly, or when we see anything unexpected in user behavior, it might give us important insights for marketing or business strategies.

In what follows, we focus on *trends* in time series. The underlying trend in the time series in its simplest form is found through moving averaging techniques (a small example of this we already saw in the "Inter-Event Times" section, where we uncovered the underlying trends in Tweet counts with exponential moving averaging). When doing this, we go through the time series with a sliding window that is significantly shorter than the entire time series, but long enough so that it spans a considerable time range, and calculate some kind of an expected value for the time series using the data the window is covering. The rationale for this is that by taking the summary statistics (for example, average) of the points within the window, we can get rid of the noise component N_τ overlaid on the other two regular components, where we assume the noise has zero expectation value, thereby the summing in the averaging canceling N_τs out.

We expect that our moving average should be robust against the underlying noise, which is true if the noise is bounded, and is coming, as usually assumed, from a normal distribution with zero mean and a finite variance, and no correlation between successive noise values. However, if what we've seen until now is any indication, we could expect that social media systems can be subject to rare events whose occurrence may be better modeled by long-tailed distributions rather than the exponential-like decays in the tail that Gaussian distributions exhibit. In other words, these "rare events" may not be that rare after all in systems influenced by human dynamics, and we could expect to see spikes in our metrics. As we know, averages over long-tailed distributions are problematic and may be sensitive to the outliers in the noise that we are bound to encounter. Therefore, we may want to look for a stronger technique in which we are robust not only to Gaussian noise, but also to the fat-tailed noise distributions.

For this reason, in this section we consider another technique called *median filtering*, which is a powerful technique for noise reduction in signal processing. In time series analysis this can also be used to find trends in a way that is more robust to the presence of bursts in the noise component. Similarly to the moving average technique, the main idea is to go over the data with a time window, and now we replace each item with the median of the values in the window. The important difference is to take the median instead of the average in the window because the median is robust also to potentially long-tailed noise distributions. We use the `robfilter` R package to demonstrate this method in Listing 3.11.

Listing 3.11: Running median filtering on our time series data. (`median_filtering.R`)

```
library(robfilter)

# See "?adore.filter" for the meaning of the parameters.
filtered = adore.filter(data$count, min.width=300, max.width=350,
    p.test=80, extrapolate=TRUE)
```

Here the median filter is applied via the `adore.filter` function where the window length is selected between the minimum and maximum length parameters via a goodness-of-fit test by the function. The trends found using this technique are shown in Figures 3.28 and 3.29. These show that in the first stage there is an increasing trend, whereas the second stage is decreasing, as expected, naturally.

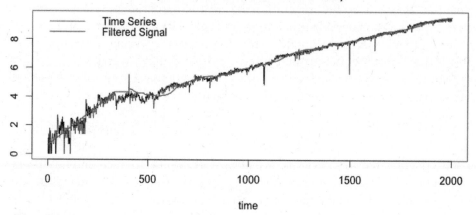

Figure 3.28: Trend found using median filtering on the log-transformed first stage of editor growth in Wikipedia

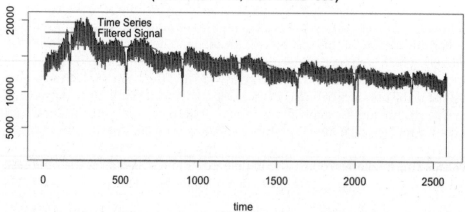

Figure 3.29: Trend found using median filtering, second stage

After we find the trends, next we want to remove these from the signal to be left with the seasonal and noise components only. We can do this by simply subtracting the calculated median trend from the signal (note that we choose to work with the additive time series model). The time series after trend removal are given in Figures 3.30 and 3.31, respectively. After this, we see that there is some periodicity left in the time series, especially in the second stage. To efficiently identify unexpected outliers or anomalies and to forecast future time series values, we still need to understand and remove this component as well from the detrended time series.

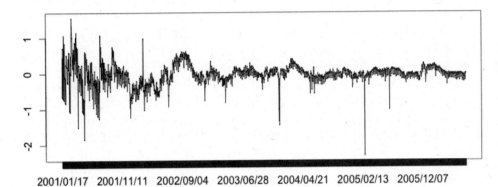

Figure 3.30: The trend removed from the log-transformed signal, first stage

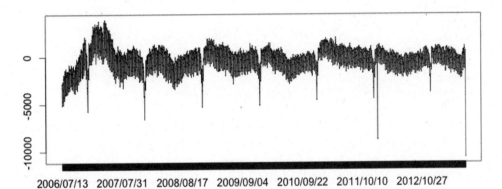

Figure 3.31: The trend removed from the original signal, second stage

Finding Seasonality

Seasonality can be defined as the periodic pattern in time series data, and a *periodic signal* is one that repeats its values at regular intervals. To accurately predict future values in a continuous signal, we should first extract these patterns. In the next section, we see that we need to determine the parameters of the periodic behavior (such as the length of the period) to perform a more fine-grained modeling. The purpose of this section is to extract these parameters about the periodic part of a time series.

Though visual inspection helps us figure out whether a time series has apparent seasonalities, we must quantify the periodic part in a way that we can use for forecasting. Suppose we have a hypothesis that the signal has a pattern repeating itself with a 1-day periodicity. If this is true, then if we shift the signal by a day, we should be seeing a high correlation with itself. Let's say that we repeat the same procedure for all possible such hypotheses—lag the signal more and more, and take the correlation with itself, as we have seen in the "Autocorrelations" section earlier in this chapter. Then we have a function mapping lag values (for example, 0, 1, 2, 3, ...) to correlations (for example, 1, 0.3, 0.5, –0.9, ...). We already know that at lag 0 we have a perfect (auto)correlation of the signal with itself, the correlation coefficient being 1.

We can use autocorrelation to discover the seasonality for both stages of the time series. First, we apply the R autocorrelation function `acf` to the detrended data. For compactness, we consider only the second stage for seasonality analysis. However, we encourage you to follow the same procedure for the log-transformed first stage. The code snippet for detecting seasonalities is as follows in Listing 3.12.

Listing 3.12: First, we apply the `acf` R function to see the lagged autocorrelation coefficients, up to lags 370. Then, when we see that the correlations are strong at lags 1 and 7, we can subtract the signal twice from itself lagged with those lags, and check if the autocorrelations indeed disappear. (`acf_apply.R`)

```
# `detrended` contains the detrended time series, one point for each
# time index.
acf(detrended, lag.max=370)

# diff takes the differences between the elements of the vector at the
# given lag distances:
# diff(x, lag=L)[i] == x[i + L] - x[i]
acf(as.vector(diff(diff(detrended, lag=1), lag=7)), lag.max=370)
```

As you can see in Figure 3.32, the detrended time series has strong correlations with itself at lags 0 (the correlation coefficient is 1 because this is the signal's correlation with itself), 1, and 7. The correlation coefficients at these lags are larger than 0.5, which is a good practical threshold for significant correlations. These correlations mirror the daily and weekly periodicities in user behavior.

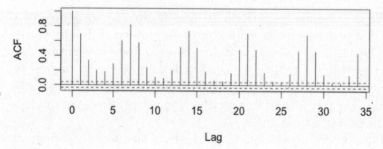

Figure 3.32: Autocorrelation of the detrended signal

If the periods we just found are indeed present in the data, then if we subtract the time series from its lagged self at a lag in which the correlation coefficient is strong, the autocorrelations should be mostly destroyed. This is because if the signal is indeed periodic with that period length, we essentially cancel it out with itself. However, if we were to subtract it from itself at a lag *other than* its own period length, and looked at the autocorrelation function of the result, we should still see strong autocorrelations at the period length because the difference function stayed periodic with the original period. Figure 3.33 shows that taking the difference of the time series from itself at lags 1 and 7 (as the preceding code snippet demonstrates) indeed gets rid of all the autocorrelations in the difference function. This way we ascertained that our original time series had daily and weekly periodicities.

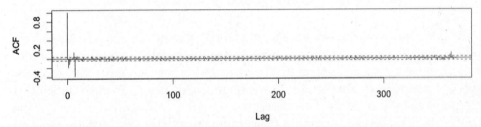

Figure 3.33: Autocorrelation of the signal with the daily and weekly seasonalities removed

When you know the longest period of the time series, you can perform the same procedure as we did in the "Autocorrelations" section, namely splitting up the time series data by this period length averaging the splits out to cancel out the noise terms, and to recover the periodic component, S_τ.

Forecasting Time Series with ARIMA

Now you've learned how to transform and detrend time series and how to determine the periodicity of its seasonal component. This section shows how to forecast future values. Because it's flexible in capturing a lot of structure in time series data, we use the *Autoregressive Integrated Moving Average* (ARIMA) model to discover historical patterns in the data. ARIMA can describe both the underlying trend and seasonality in the time series, so why did we just go through the exercise of finding these ourselves? First, these two steps were necessary to have a thorough understanding of what components the actual time series data contains, and second, these steps can help us build and parametrize an ARIMA model appropriately so that we can use it to predict future values.

The family of ARIMA models consists of three separate parts: an autoregressive part, parameterized by a parameter p ("AR"); a differencing part, parameterized by d ("I"); and a moving average part, parameterized by q ("MA"). The notation

ARIMA(p, d, q) is used when we want to express that we fitted the ARIMA model to the data with given p, d, and q parameters, respectively.

We now discuss the three components of the model separately: The autoregressive part, the differencing part, and the moving average part.

The Autoregressive Part ("AR")

An autoregressive model states that future values of a random process should be in linear association with past data and that future values of the time series are correlated with values in the recent past. It has a parameter p specifying the length or steps of historical dependence, or in other words, how far back we expect to go to see linear correlations with our current value. The autoregressive model is defined as

$$X_t = \sum_{i=1}^{p} \Theta_i X_{t-i} + \varepsilon_t,$$

(3.10)

where X_t represents the value we want to forecast at time t, and p is our parameter telling how many values we consider to be correlated with X_t in the recent past. ε_t represents a noise term that by assumption has zero mean and constant variance. Finally, Θ_i are the unknown weights to be determined, and they correspond to how strongly X_t is determined by the ith historical value. On the right side of the model, everything but Θ_i and the variance of the noise term are given: p is something we choose, and X_{t-i} are the historical data we're performing the training on. Therefore, it's Θ_i and the variance of the noise term are the parameters we should be learning from the time series. Finding Θ_is is part of a fitting procedure that we have a function in R available for (together with the "I" and "MA" parts, naturally).

When the best model parameters are learned, we can find an estimate for X_t by computing $\sum_{i=1}^{p} \Theta_i X_{t-i}$ using the by now known values of Θ_i. This yields the expectation for this time series value, given what information about the past correlations the autoregressive model could encode. X_t also naturally has an estimation error, which is determined by the variance of the noise term ε_t. If we want to bring this forward and estimate any X_{t+T} at a future time T, we can compute it recursively in a similar manner: We'll just use the generated predictions as best-guess historical values when we forecast the next time series value.

Every such prediction can be considered as a random variable coming from a given distribution, and if we take a significant number of steps into the future, this variance of the distribution keeps widening as our certainty about values into the future drops further and further.

The Moving Average Part ("MA")

The moving average model uses the forecasting error from the recent past to predict the forecasting error for future values of the time series, or in other words assumes that there are correlations between the noise terms in time. The predicted value is a linear combination of the past q prediction errors, shifted by a constant expectation for the signal (Equation 3.11). The moving average forecasting model should not be confused with the moving average smoothing technique.

$$X_t = \mu + \varepsilon_t + \sum_{j=1}^{q} \varphi_j \varepsilon_{t-j}. \tag{3.11}$$

Similarly to Equation 3.10, ε_t represents the noise term with zero mean and constant variance. μ is the parameter for the expected value of X_t. Note that there is a distinction between ε_t and ε_{t-j} here: ε_t is a random variable describing our uncertainty about the prediction, whereas ε_{t-j} are actual, calculable error differences between our past predictions and the realized values. φ_j are the parameters to be estimated through model fitting, for which specialized techniques exist.

A practical point for deciding between the AR and MA models is that AR models sometimes can be sensitive to outliers. This is a reason why when using AR models to predict long-term time series into the future we should make sure that we have no large outliers among the latest p data points just preceding the time when we start making the forecasts. For example, if there're eventful days when we see spikes in our user activity metrics (such as when there's a sports or political event of great importance), we have to avoid starting to make the predictions close to these days. If the time series on which we would like to train the model is short and contains obvious outliers, we have to take the results with a grain of salt. One should be careful and cross-check the trained model with historical data by validating the predictions on hold-out parts of the time series.

The Full ARIMA(p, d, q) Model

One last additional item we consider here is the differencing term. The main assumption of both the AR and the MA model is the *stationarity* of the random process governing the time series. This practically means that our model dynamics do not change in time. For instance, when we assume that the error term has zero mean and constant variance, this should be the case throughout all the time steps. However, in practice this isn't usually true. The error not only might change in time, but we also often have periodicities in the signal. In the "Finding Seasonality" section earlier in this chapter, we used a differencing operation to remove seasonalities from a time series. In this section, instead of separately removing the seasonalities, we use the *integrated* part of ARIMA to model nonstationarities, such as seasonal effects. This is parameterized with the d variable. When the AR (Autoregressive), I (Integrated), and MA (Moving Average) terms are all part of the model together, they form the full ARIMA(p, d, q).

One question here is how to specify the model parameters p, d, and q. Generally, we want to find the minimum length of dependence to the historical values. This not only reduces the potential complexity due to unnecessary computations, but it also reduces the chance of overfitting. Our goal should be to find the model with minimum complexity explaining the observed data best. The trend finding, autocorrelation analysis, and seasonalities we observe in the data are all techniques we can use to learn more about our time series, and we can use this knowledge to fine-tune the model. Often a cross-validation on historical data might be required to choose the best parameter set from a pool of candidate values.

According to the observations we made so far about the number of daily active users in Wikipedia, Listing 3.13 shows the demonstration of the application. We use the `arima` function from the `stats` package in R.

Listing 3.13: Fitting the ARIMA model to a downsampled version of the Wikipedia user count data. We chose every 7th day from the dataset to speed up the fitting procedure. (`arima.R`)

```
library(forecast)

len = length(data$count)
# For simplicity, we sample the data uniformly.
sampled_data = data$count[seq(1, len, 7)]

fitted_tps = arima(sampled_data,
        order=c(0, 1, 7),
        seasonal=list(order=c(0, 1, 2), period=52))

prediction = forecast(fitted_tps, 90)
plot(prediction)
```

As shown in Figure 3.34, our model seems to be able to create reasonably good predictions. Without loss of generality, we sampled the data to make the run faster for this demonstration. You can instead use weekly active users as well to simplify the computation. In this example, we used a differencing term with $d = 1$. The motivation for this choice is as follows: In the seasonality analysis, we found that there is a weekly seasonality. Due to the downsampling by a factor of 7, this weekly seasonality can be eliminated via the integrated part of 1. In addition, we know that there is a yearly seasonality. Again due to sampling with a ratio of 1 / 7, this yearly seasonality corresponds to 52 weekly values in the sampled data. (There are 52 weeks in a year.) This was the reason we picked a period parameter of 52. See `?arima` for a more detailed explanation of the seasonal parameter of the function call. The choice of 7 as the MA parameter is empirical. It could easily be 6 or 8. Again, in the seasonal part, we prefer lower values because we try to minimize model complexity. We observe that this is enough for our problem. We also chose two levels of history in seasonality with one differencing, but these parameters are also best determined through some trial and error. In Figure 3.34, we also plot the confidence intervals for the prediction. One thing we observe is that as the length of the prediction increases, the variance of the prediction increases. This is due to the accumulated variance in time. In other words, the Day 2 estimation variance incorporates the Day 1 estimation variability, and Day 3 incorporates both Day 1 and Day 2.

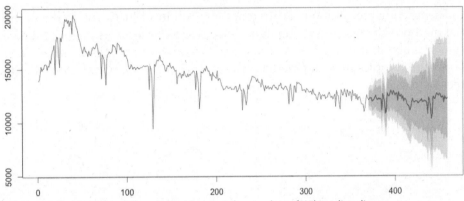

Figure 3.34: ARIMA model applied to forecast the number of Wikipedia editors

Summary

This chapter covered the basics of the temporal analysis of social media events. Starting from the most obvious assumptions encapsulated by the Poisson model, we worked our way through to describing events by considering their periodic and correlation structures. Following are the main topics we covered in this chapter:

- Although the Poisson process is a good model to use many times when describing random temporal processes, it's not the best one for periodic events in social media, especially because these events also show autocorrelations over time.

- Autocorrelations were the way to describe the presence of memory in our systems. There is obviously memory in social media events because these usually revolve around news in the real world, which last a shorter or longer amount of time.

- Another consequence of memory over time is that events have a bursty nature as seen though social media data, either about users' activities or times when content changed. The times between events were interestingly described by long-tailed distributions again, drawing a parallel between temporal phenomena and prevailing characteristics of users' actions (in Chapter 1), and their networks (in Chapter 2).

- Because many times we'd like to forecast the numbers of certain events in the future, we can employ various models to capture the cyclical and trend structures in the metrics. One of the models, the ARIMA model, is flexible enough to describe these patterns so that we can fit a model and project out time series.

The next chapter is about a different topic and introduces you to the essential methods of trying to understand in aggregate _what_ users of social media converse about. It focuses on selected topics from text analysis to understand how to find topics in social media posts and what the statistical properties of these topics are.

Content: The *What* of Social Media

This chapter focuses on textual content in social media and answers the question of how you can classify the subjects that users talk about. Because you obviously would like to see emerging, large-scale trends among the individual textual content you can find in online databases, you need to find a way to capture the meaning of the documents in a computational way. Becoming familiar with these methods will comprise a large part of this chapter.

You'll also see that after encoding text, you can find topics among the posts or documents. How popular are these topics, and how do they relate to each other? This is another important question we'll pay attention to in this chapter. You'll also see how to use these models to make predictions about users and how to further improve your understanding of text using the network connections among your users.

Defining Content: Focus on Text and Unstructured Data

In the following sections you work with datasets that highlight how individuals create and consume content, focusing on text analysis and the essential notions that you can use to understand what people are writing about. At first sight, it may not be straightforward how to make sense of text even when it's written in the same language by all users, and how to map it to concepts to structures that you can gain insights from.

To make our investigation more concrete, we'll work with a publicly available dataset of user-generated content from a leading topical question-answering service, Stack Exchange. The Stack Exchange network has made data dumps from its sites available at the Internet Archive (`https://archive.org/details/stackexchange`). Of interest to us, these dumps contain all the questions and answers, and the related metadata pertaining to the posts: author IDs, times and dates of creation, the number of times the post has been favorited, tags that users assigned to a question, and even the number of times a question has been viewed. An example of a post as it appears on the Stack Exchange site is shown in Figure 4.1.

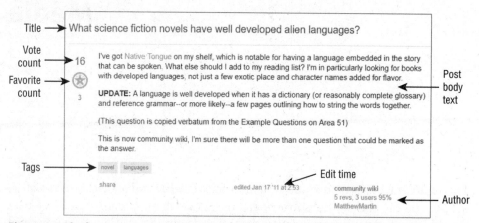

Figure 4.1: The first question posted on Stack Exchange in the "Science Fiction & Fantasy" category (`http://scifi.stackexchange.com/questions/1/`). We labeled the parts of the post that are also stored as part of the downloadable data from the site. Although the body of the post is obviously easy to parse for a human reader, we need to transform it into a format that is amenable for automatic analysis by a computer.

Because data is available for download for every network site, we have chosen one particular sub-site, with the subject title "Science Fiction & Fantasy." This Stack Exchange site had approximately 46,000 questions and 88,000 answers in early 2018 after about 7 years in existence, and we settled on this site because it will provide us with a moderately sized dataset that we can process even on personal computers. Another reason was that we believed this sub-site contains somewhat less jargon than more frequented sub-sites, such as Stack Overflow or Mathematics, where both the questions and the answers may be about jargon-heavy topics. Given that our intent is to highlight how to discover topics and how to analyze them based on textual features, a broader natural language use and topical coverage may be beneficial. (This is an assumption on our part, so you may well find that parsing program code or formulas also leads to interesting insights.)

Similar to several of the Wikipedia data dumps, the Stack Exchange data is also in XML format, which we can reshape into a tabular format as we did with the Wikipedia data sets in Chapter 1. We'll soon proceed by preprocessing the data stored in the XML file in Python and then use R to look at the statistical properties of both the text and the related user activities. However, before we get to that, let's review how to make sense of free-flowing text to determine what people are talking about.

Creating Features from Text: The Basics of Natural Language Processing

We are interested in how topics of interest are distributed on the site and how users attend to these topics. For this, we need to define what a topic is for a post, or in other words assign a post to a bucket that describes a topic for human observers with a good degree of accuracy. Motivated by this goal, we'll highlight one of the most common methods in natural language processing for canonizing text for machine processing. This is called the *bag-of-words approach* in which we treat a piece of text as a collection of words together with the number of times they appeared in the text, but we disregard the order and the context that these words appeared in. Although we lose grammatical cohesion this way, we are in a much better position to represent and work with the text as only a set of words, where we keep track of only the frequency of any word appearing in a post. However, where we talk about posts, the text mining literature usually refers to them more generally as *documents*; so when we see expressions such as "document-term matrix," we'll know that in this case we're referring to the matrix where the rows refer to documents of texts (posts), the columns refer to words (terms), and the matrix entries are the counts of any word in each document.

To represent posts as a set of words, therefore, means that we need to split up the post at word boundaries: whitespaces, and punctuation marks. We can then also define a "vocabulary" or "dictionary," which will be formed by all the words that appear in any of our posts. At this point, though, we should consider that for our purposes a lot of words seem similar: "Universe," "universes," and "universal," for instance, convey similar meanings, especially given that we'll treat the posts as a bag of words. The process of reducing each word to a token that still retains its meaning but removes inflections is called *stemming*. After the word is stemmed, it may (usually) or may not (less frequently, but it happens) resemble the original word. We'll use the so-called *Snowball stemmer* here, which, while providing a reasonably good approximation to the root of the word, still retains understandability after stemming. Some other stemmers in use differ in the degree they chop the words down to their roots and therefore sometimes it's hard to understand what the original word may have been. For the three particular words just mentioned, for instance, the Snowball stemmer result is "univers." Stemming words is an important part of text processing, as we'll reduce the dimensionality of our vocabulary significantly without losing much of the meaning of the words, and therefore we can also expect to have better cross-comparisons among the documents in our corpora. As languages and their grammatical rules are different, we have slightly different stemmers for every language (at least for the most common ones for which stemmers have been developed).

Furthermore, some words do not convey much meaning besides making the grammar of sentences proper or enhancing style: "And," "which," "just," and "because" are such words, for example. We need them in spoken and written language, but to detect what subject a text covers, for instance, they have little to add. In other words, we can consider that they are so common that the occurrence in any text is not surprising and does not add new information. For this reason, they are usually also deleted from the bag of words, through a process called *stop word removal*. The list of stop words can be fixed and formed by most common English words or can be determined after creating the vocabulary for a set of documents and selecting the most common terms from it to be treated as stop words. We use a fixed list here, but conceptually both approaches are valid and can be used at your discretion.

Fortunately, a lot of natural language processing routines have been developed as part of the high-quality `nltk` package in Python: We can use its tokenization and stemming facilities, and also use its stop word list. Listing 4.1 showcases the snippet that processes the text body for the questions and answers of the Science Fiction & Fantasy XML file of the Stack Exchange data. In addition to using the `nltk` library, we also used one function from the `BeautifulSoup` Python library that helps with parsing HTML data. As posters of questions and answers on Stack Exchange may use HTML markup to indicate different font and paragraph styles, we would also like to get rid of this formatting, for which we can use `BeautifulSoup`'s `get_text`.

Listing 4.1: Reading the Stack Exchange XML data files to preprocess the text. (`process_stackexchange_xml.py`)

```python
import xml.sax, gzip, reimport bs4
import nltk.tokenize
import nltk.corpus
import nltk.stem.snowball


class StackExchangeXMLReader(xml.sax.handler.ContentHandler):

    def __init__(self, record_processor):
        # Precompile the regex pattern for keeping alphanumeric
        # characters only.
```

```
        self._alphanumeric_pattern = re.compile('[\W_]+')
        # Use NLTK's built-in stop word list for the English language.
        # The stopwords corpora may need to be downloaded for NLTK, the
        # command for this would be:
        # python -c "import nltk; nltk.download('stopwords')"
        # For the details see http://www.nltk.org/data.html
        self._stopwords = set(nltk.corpus.stopwords.words('english'))
        self._stemmer = nltk.stem.snowball.SnowballStemmer('english')


# ...
# further code omitted in print for readability
# ...


    def tokenize_text(self, text):
        # Clean up the text from HTML tags first.
        html_cleaned = bs4.BeautifulSoup(text).get_text()
        # Break words at whitespaces and punctuation marks next.
        tokens = nltk.tokenize.wordpunct_tokenize(html_cleaned)
        result = []
        for token in tokens:
            # Keep only the alphanumeric letters in the words.
            token = self._alphanumeric_pattern.sub('', token)
            token = self._stemmer.stem(token)
            if token:
                result.append(token.lower())
        return result


# ...
# further code omitted in print for readability
# ...
```

We show only the code pertaining to tokenizing the text body: In the `tokenize_text` method, we first use `BeautifulSoup`'s functions to clean up the HTML markup and to remove the HTML tags that are present in the data. (With other datasets when we have plain text, this may not be necessary.) We then call `nltk`'s `wordpunct_tokenize` to break up the text at whitespaces and punctuation marks into "tokens" (words), and finally for each token we remove the non-alphanumeric characters and stem the word using the Snowball stemmer.

The first few words of Figure 4.1's post after tokenization and stemming, for instance, look like this: `novel languages ve got nativ tongu shelf notabl languag embed stori spoken els add read`…. Although it'd be hard to reconstruct what the author meant from tokens like this, this kind of representation is useful to find posts similar to each other, for example.

The benefit of representing text as a bag of words is that you can use any traditional data mining method that operates on numerical vectors without having to modify the algorithms to this unstructured, textual data format first the other way around.

The Basic Statistics of Term Occurrences in Text

After extracting the stemmed forms of words for all the posts, we can ask how frequently any term appears across the posts. Although doing so may just look like a theoretical curiosity at first, remember that our goal is to find topics in the text, so learning about the distribution of terms may motivate us later to design re-weighting schemes around the terms: Frequently occurring words may have less "specific" meanings, after all. As we mentioned previously when discussing stop words, we might want to de-emphasize frequent terms, yet make infrequent ones more important so that when they appear we know the author mentioned a niche topic. On the stemmed terms, therefore, we measured how frequently they appear and plotted this in Figure 4.2. Apparently, the term frequency distribution follows a power law with a high degree of accuracy.

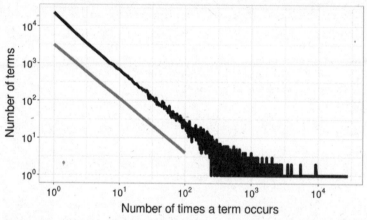

Figure 4.2: The distribution of the number of times a given term appears in any post in the Science Fiction & Fantasy section of Stack Exchange. Apparently, the stemmed term frequency distribution follows a power law, which has an exponent of −1.45. (We performed the linear fit on the double logarithmic axes in the range indicated by the lighter straight line, but naturally shifted this line down by approximately one-half a decade so that the curves do not overlap each other.)

A close variant of this observation is called *Zipf's law*, which says that if we rank words occurring in a natural language text according to their frequencies so that the most frequent word has rank 1, the second most frequent has rank 2, and so on, then their counts will be inversely proportional to their ranks (until some rank 1000). Although here we have already removed some of the most frequent words using `nltk`'s stop word list and we have also changed the appearance of words through Snowball stemming, we can still see that we are left with a word frequency distribution that is similar in nature to those observed in larger corpora by Zipf and others. In fact, our ten most frequent stemmed roots are `would one time like use could know onli book also,` where we can see that `time` and `book` probably made it into the top-10 list because of the topical idiosyncrasies that the forums in the science fiction section cover.

What is the significance of the frequency of the terms following a power-law distribution? We'll see it in the next section where we explore how we can find the sets of similar posts.

Using Content Features to Identify Topics

A major goal of why we performed the transformations on the text of the posts is that we can use the resulting features for identifying topics in the posts, in other words find the posts that are similar to each other based on the words that they contain. Ultimately, we would like to find *groups* of posts that can be considered similar to each other, not only pairs of such posts. However, we'll need to define both what *similarity* means and what a *grouping* of similar posts means.

First, let's focus on how we would find groups of posts that are similar, or *close* to each other, in the term space; then we can look at good ways for us to define the similarities. Because it's easier to imagine how a technique works when we can visualize it, consider Figure 4.3, where we placed 12 dots on the plane, and our task is to find those dots that form groups. We circled a few of the dots to show what we would naturally recognize as groups of nearby dots. Intuitively, what we are looking for are dots that among themselves are close to each other, while at the same time the distances between dots belonging to different clusters are comparatively large.

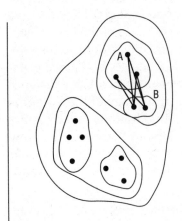

Figure 4.3: Assume that the items we would like to find groups of can be situated in a two-dimensional Euclidean space, and their "similarities" are exactly the distances between them: The further away they are, the less similar they are to each other. This is a natural way of looking at clustering, where for instance the items are fishing boats on the sea, and we're looking for groups of fishermen who are fishing together.

Then we surrounded the *groups* of dots with larger circles to show that after finding the smaller groups, we can repeat the procedure and form larger clusters composed of smaller groups. Conceptually, this higher-level clustering is similar to what we did with the dots. Now we just need to define distances between existing *clusters* of dots that we are trying to pull together into bigger clusters.

Although most problems we encounter are not amenable for embedding in 2-D space and visualization such as shown in Figure 4.3, the concept of defining distances between the items and then creating clusters based on their distances is a general characteristic of unsupervised clustering methods. (Clustering is *unsupervised* because we don't need "labeled examples" or ground truth to find clusters of nearby items; the distances should specify the clustering.)

Let's now also formalize the clustering method that we'll use to find posts that are topically similar to each other. This clustering is called *hierarchical agglomerative clustering* because it places the items in their own standalone clusters initially, and then proceeds by merging clusters one by one until only one cluster is left. All through this we of course keep track of the order we performed the merges. Stepwise, it works as follows:

1. **Initialize**—We first calculate the distances between all pairs of items that we'd like to cluster. The "distances" don't have to have geometrical interpretation as is the case for Euclidean distances. Initially, every item forms its own cluster.

2. **Merging items**—Find the two closest clusters to each other, and join them together to form a new cluster. Consider the new cluster as a new one on its own, and replace the two clusters just merged with this new cluster.

3. **Redefining distances**—We, therefore, have decreased the number of clusters by 1, as we replaced two clusters by one in Step 2. However, we see that by doing so, we need to redefine the distance of the new cluster to any of the remaining ones. We'll do this by creating a derived distance between clusters as a function of the pairwise distances between the distances of the original items they contain. For our purposes, the distance between two clusters will be calculated as the average of the distances between all pairs of their respective items. This choice is called *average linkage* for calculating derived cluster distances. In Figure 4.3 we drew lines among the original items of clusters *A* and *B* over which we would take an average of their original distances when calculating the distance between clusters *A* and *B*.

4. **Stopping criterion**—Repeat beginning with Step 2 until there is only one cluster left. (This will contain all the items; there're no more clusters to merge it with.)

You can see why this procedure is called hierarchical: There is a certain order to follow in merging the clusters, and the distances at which mergings occurred between clusters kept increasing monotonically. In other words, with every iteration, we discovered more and more loosely connected clusters, on a higher level of the hierarchy.

As a remark for Step 3, we could have chosen a different linkage criterion for calculating the distances between clusters of several items each. Two other linkages are called *single* (take the minimum of the distances between the items), and *complete linkage* (take the maximum of the distances between pairs of items from the two clusters each). The average linkage provided good results, but we encourage you to repeat the clustering also with different linkage choices (see Listing 4.3 later in this chapter).

Until now we have avoided the question of how we would define the "distance" between posts. We know that we represented the posts as bags of words, meaning that we map every post to a vector where the components of the vector are the number of times that a given stemmed word appears in the post. Now let's see how we would calculate the distances between posts. A straightforward definition of similarity or distance between posts is to what degree the terms in them overlap: If two posts contain the words "trek" and "star" several times, we are reasonably safe to say that they are about the show "Star Trek." If at the same time, they both contain the less frequent word "warp," then we can guess that the two posts are both about the fictional warp drive propulsion system of the space ships appearing in the episodes. Is there a way we can capture this similarity with a single number, similar to how Euclidean distances describe the relative positions of items with respect to each other in Figure 4.3?

A frequently used natural metric for measuring similarity in the term space is the *cosine similarity* between the term vectors of posts. If u_t is the number of occurrences of term t for a post u, and v_t is t's number of occurrences for a post v, then their cosine similarity is the dot product of their respective normalized term vectors:

$$S(\mathbf{u}, \mathbf{v}) = \frac{\sum_t u_t v_t}{\sqrt{\sum_t u_t^2}\sqrt{\sum_t v_t^2}} = \frac{\mathbf{u} \cdot \mathbf{v}}{\|\mathbf{u}\|\|\mathbf{v}\|} = \frac{\mathbf{u}}{\|\mathbf{u}\|} \cdot \frac{\mathbf{v}}{\|\mathbf{v}\|}. \tag{4.1}$$

The cosine similarity is a well-known distance metric between vectors, and in common terms it means that we take the sum of the products of the pairwise corresponding vector components, normalized by the product of their Euclidean lengths. (It's called "cosine" because $S(\mathbf{u}, \mathbf{v})$ is exactly the cosine of the angle between the vectors.) This is what the sum in the numerator stands for, which is also the same as taking the dot product $\mathbf{u} \cdot \mathbf{v}$ of the vectors. The value of the cosine similarity will be between -1 and 1 for any two vectors in general. In our case, because our vector components (the counts of the terms) are all positive, the cosine similarity will be between 0 and 1. If the posts don't share any terms, their similarity will be 0, whereas if they share all the same terms the same exact numbers of times, their similarity will be 1.

Returning to how we would use cosine similarity for agglomerative clustering, we saw that the clustering algorithm operates with distances and takes them in increasing order, so it is only the ordering, and not the absolute value of the distances, that matters. Therefore, if we want to use cosine similarity as a distance metric, we'll just make highly similar items (with a cosine similarity close to 1) have a short distance, and highly dissimilar items (with a cosine similarity near 0) have a large distance. A usual way to define the distance of two post vectors $\mathbf{u}$ and $\mathbf{v}$ is therefore $d(\mathbf{u}, \mathbf{v}) = 1 - S(\mathbf{u}, \mathbf{v})$. However, because it's only the ordering of the distances that matters, we'll define the distances as $d(\mathbf{u}, \mathbf{v}) = -S(\mathbf{u}, \mathbf{v})$. (We explain the reasons a little later in this section.)

After we remove the stop words from a post and properly tokenize and stem its words, we can assign a feature vector to this post so that we can calculate the cosine similarity between these vectors. As mentioned earlier in this chapter, the components of the vector are going to be related to the counts of how many times each term appears in the post. Naturally, when considering the full vocabulary of words appearing in all the posts, this will be a long vector, but at the same time, it's also very sparse with only a small fraction of all the components present. In the post shown in Figure 4.1, for example, there are only 54 different terms, and in the science fiction sub-category, we could count approximately 116,000 different terms. This means that these feature vectors should be represented for instance as dictionaries in Python, storing only the terms as keys that do appear in a text, together with their counts as values in the dictionary.

An issue with creating similarities between posts is that we've seen that some words occur much more frequently than others, as we can see in Figure 4.2. Obviously, we would like to de-emphasize the importance of words that are common and appear in many of our posts, such as those at the top of the word frequency list: would, one, and time. (If we hadn't removed the stop words, they would certainly be on the top of our list as well.)

A solution to this is to give different weights to terms in the document vectors based on their frequencies in the given document and also other documents. For instance, because the term time appears so frequently, it doesn't have much discriminating power among topics, so we want to give it less weight when it appears in any given post. A usual weighting scheme for term frequencies is the so-called *term frequency–inverse document frequency* weighting scheme, commonly abbreviated as *tf–idf*. This statistic is defined as the product of the term frequency in each document and the inverse document frequency. The inverse document frequency is large if the term occurs only in a few documents and a small value if it appears in many documents, so in other words it captures how *specific* the term is to the given document only. The tf–idf score for a given term

t in document d is shown in the following equation (if the set of all documents is denoted by D):

$$\text{tf} - \text{idf}(t, d, D) = \text{tf}(t, d) \cdot \text{idf}(t, D) = \text{tf}(t, d) \cdot \log \frac{|D|}{|\{d \in D : t \in d\}|}. \qquad (4.2)$$

For the tf(t, d) "term frequency" term we'll take the number of times that term t appears in document d. (There could be other options, such as also dividing the counts by the number of all terms in d.) The idf part, as we can see, divides the total number of documents by the number of documents d that actually contain the term t. This ratio is never less than 1, so the log is always positive.

The reason we want to use tf–idf to re-weight the term frequencies in the term vectors is because we would like to highlight the necessity of using a weighting scheme, and tf–idf is one of the most commonly used schemes. However, you can experiment with different kinds of weights, and it's likely that the results will be qualitatively similar, as long as the scheme logarithmically downweights frequent terms. We can also see why it makes sense to use logarithmic rescaling for the relative frequencies, given that this way power-law term distributions similar to Figure 4.2 will be transformed into a bounded range, mitigating the exponential differences among the counts of terms.

Let's see how we can calculate the cosine similarities across our posts in practice. For this consider Equation 4.1 again, and especially the form where we first normalize the term feature vectors; then take their dot products, as this is the order that we'll follow. The R code for this is shown in Listing 4.2.

Listing 4.2: Creating a distance (dissimilarity) matrix for posts using only the stemmed terms that appear in their text bodies, as produced by Listing 4.1. (`stackexchange_text.R`)

```
 0 library(tm)              # Package for text mining.
 1 library(Matrix)          # Package for sparse matrix operations.

 2 # Read in the stemmed post terms and metadata created by
 3 # process_stackexchange_xml.py .
 4 posts = read.table(gzfile('data/stack_exchange/posts.tsv.gz'),
 5         sep='\t', stringsAsFactors=F,
 6         col.names=c('id', 'post.type.id', 'parent.id',
 7                 'owner.user.id', 'creation.date', 'view.count',
 8                 'favorite.count', 'tags', 'terms'))

 9 # Consider only questions, no answers for simplicity.
10 posts = subset(posts, post.type.id == 1)

11 # Create a Corpus object from the terms for the tm package.
12 corpus = Corpus(VectorSource(posts$terms))

13 # Build a sparse term-document matrix, and weight the terms in the
```

```
14 # documents using tf-idf.
15 term.doc.matrix = TermDocumentMatrix(corpus,
              control=list(weighting=weightTfIdf))

16 # Transform the TermDocumentMatrix into a traditional sparse matrix
17 # for the subsequent operations.
18 tdsm = sparseMatrix(i=term.doc.matrix$i, j=term.doc.matrix$j,
            x=term.doc.matrix$v, dims=c(term.doc.matrix$nrow,
              term.doc.matrix$ncol))

20 # Normalize the column vectors of tdsm by their lengths
21 # for the cosine similarity.
22 normalized.term.vectors =
              tdsm %*% Diagonal(x=1 / sqrt(colSums(tdsm ^ 2)))

23 # Calculate the cosine similarities of posts using the term vectors,
24 # and create distances (dissimilarities) by flipping their values.
25 # To keep the matrix sparse we only take the negative of the
26 # similarities to just reverse their order.
27 post.dissimilarities = -crossprod(normalized.term.vectors)
```

First, in lines 4–15 we read in the posts texts and create a term–document matrix from it with tf–idf weighting, using the appropriate functions from the `tm` package. The `term.doc.matrix` variable is already stored as a sparse matrix, but we explicitly convert it to a sparse `Matrix` object in line 18. Second, in line 22 we essentially divide each column vector by the norm (the length) of the vector. Finally, line 27 calculates the cosine similarities between all pairs of the column vectors by calculating $\mathbf{N}^T\mathbf{N}$ (where $\mathbf{N}$ refers to the `normalized.term.vectors` matrix) with a call to `crossprod`. We then also take the negative of the result to reverse the order of the similarities and to have the proper order for the distance interpretation. Normally, you would take $1 - \mathbf{S}$ to convert a cosine *similarity* matrix $\mathbf{S}$ into a *distance* matrix, knowing that the cosine similarities are between 0 and 1. However, this would immediately destroy the nice sparse property of the matrix, filling up the distance matrix with mostly 1s, as relatively speaking there are only few pairs of posts that have a cosine similarity that is not zero. For the sake of keeping the sparse property, we'll omit the 1 in this step but will add it back in the next one.

The next step to find topics in the posts is to perform the hierarchical agglomerative clustering introduced earlier in this section. For this consider the short R source shown in Listing 4.3. We simply convert the dissimilarity matrix to a distance matrix object expected by `hclust` and then do an average linkage clustering on this distance matrix. At the end, we add the 1 back to the *merging heights* that we omitted from the distance matrix.

Listing 4.3: Run the hierarchical agglomerative clustering method `hclust` on the post dissimilarities. (`stackexchange_text.R`)

```
# Perform a hierarchical agglomerative clustering with average linkage.
h = hclust(as.dist(post.dissimilarities), method='average')

# Convert the merging heights back to a dissimilarity scale of [0; 1].
h$height = 1 + h$height
```

But what are the merging heights? They are the distances at which the merging of any two clusters happened during the run of the algorithm, as calculated by the linkage method (average linkage in our case). There are $N - 1$ mergings if we have N posts to start with, so we'll also have $N - 1$ merging heights. The reason they are called "heights" is because of the usual way that the clustering is visualized: On a dendrogram, as shown by Figure 4.4, the distances between two clusters that were merged into a larger one are shown as heights in the binary tree.

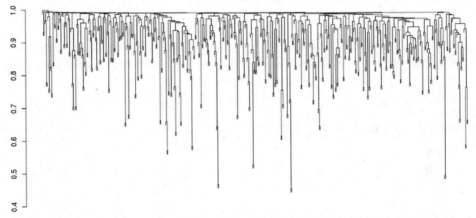

Figure 4.4: A small illustrative dendrogram for a clustering on posts. The leaves of the tree (the small, hanging stubs) correspond to the original items in the clustering, and the horizontal lines represent the distance at which the merging occurred for the two sub-clusters into a new cluster.

Notice that every branch of the tree has two children that represent the two clusters that were merged at that point. If we were to place a ruler horizontally on the bottom of the tree, and slowly moved it upward, we could retrace how the clustering algorithm merged the clusters: Any time we would cross a horizontal line on the dendrogram, there would be a merging. The height of this crossing would indicate the distance at which the merge happened. This way we can also immediately see where similar or dissimilar clusters are located, because if there's a cluster that lies deep compared to when its next merge happened up in the tree, then that means that cluster was relatively far, even from its closest neighbor at the time, when it got merged with it. Therefore, it is probably about a distinct set of posts topically separated far from the rest of the posts.

While Figure 4.4 was just an illustrative example, we introduced dendrograms so that we can easily select some representative topic branches from the full set of posts we have at our disposal. In this case, however, we cannot hope to plot the full dendrogram, as we have too many posts as leaves and the tree would get visually dense. Not that we even would like to, as at this point we're not interested in the low-lying parts of the tree that would correspond to the small clusters; we'd like to see bigger topics appearing among the questions that the Stack Exchange users asked.

For this, Listing 4.4 shows the R code to cut the dendrogram at a height of 0.9. (Recall that distances/dissimilarities between posts are in the range 0 to 1.) At the same time, we would also like to know what kind of posts selected subtrees contain. To visually summarize several documents, *word clouds* are a frequently used technique, and we're also creating those in Listing 4.4.

Listing 4.4: R code to plot the upper part of the dendrogram of cluster merges, at distances of 0.9 and higher. We also show how to interactively select subtrees of the dendrogram and create word clouds for them. (`stackexchange_text.R`)

```
# Convert the result of clustering into a dendrogram that 'cut' can
# handle.
h.dendr = as.dendrogram(h)


# Cut the dendrogram, and keep only the merges that were done at a
# distance of 0.9 or higher.
h.dendr.upper = cut(h.dendr, h=0.9)$upper


# Plot only this upper part.
plot(h.dendr.upper, leaflab='none', ylim=c(0.9, 1))


# Select the branches with a left click, exit with a right click.
identified.branches = identify(h, N=10, MAXCLUSTER=length(h$height) + 1)


# Create tag clouds for the branches that we selected.
library(wordcloud)
invisible(lapply(seq_along(identified.branches),
    function(i) {
        leaves = identified.branches[[i]]
        # The number of times a term appears in the leaf posts
        words = rowSums(as.matrix(term.doc.matrix[, leaves]))
        words = words[words > 0]
        words = words / max(words)      # Normalize the counts.
        wordcloud(names(words), words, max.words=50,
                scale=c(4, 0.5))        # Plot the word cloud.
        # Create a word cloud also for the tags associated with
        # the posts.
```

```
tags = unlist(strsplit(posts$tags[chosen.posts[leaves]], ' '))
tag.counts = table(tags)
tag.counts = tag.counts / max(tag.counts)
wordcloud(names(tag.counts), tag.counts, max.words=10,
          scale=c(4, 0.5))
}))
```

Figure 4.5 shows with shaded boxes the truncated dendrogram and the subtrees that we selected. The word clouds show that indeed the subtrees comprise of posts that are about similar topics: Subtree **A** contains terms relating to the "Lord of the Rings," and **B** has posts on the "Star Trek" series. Subtree **C** is harder to identify as anything related to a story or show, as we see general words such as "remember," "book," and "alien." If we look at some of the specific posts that are in this subtree, we would notice that many of them are in fact about users looking for a book or story that they had read or heard about in the past. A common theme among these posts is not the subject of the post, but the intent of the users, and apparently the lack of words in the texts that would identify a more specific topic strongly.

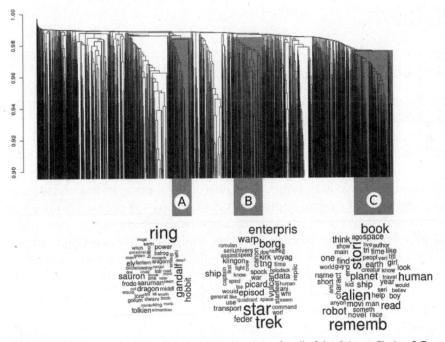

Figure 4.5: The hierarchy of post cluster merges shown for all of the Science Fiction & Fantasy questions on Stack Exchange, for the merges that took place at a distance of 0.9 or higher. This way we highlight the last stages of the agglomerative clustering algorithm, only already operating on larger clusters that are below the area shown. Using Listing 4.4, we selected three subtrees of the dendrogram, shaded and labeled as A, B, and C. Underneath each subtree we also show the word clouds of the most frequently appearing terms in their leaf posts. The size of the terms is proportional to the number of times they appear in the union set of all the subtree posts.

On Stack Exchange, users can also use _tags_ to attach to their questions, as Figure 4.1 shows in the bottom-left corner of the post. Figure 4.6 shows the tag clouds for the three respective subtrees: They seem to agree well with the topics that we identified. In particular, the tags given to subtree **C** underpin our assumption that the questions in this section of the cluster tree are about finding stories that the users want to recollect.

Figure 4.6: Word clouds for the _tags_ that users attached to their questions, in the same subtrees A, B, and C as in Figure 4.5.

The Popularity of Topics

You have just seen that it's possible to find topics in user-contributed content by using clustering defined on the texts of the questions that the users ask. You want to know, though, what subjects are the most interesting to the users, or in other words, if there are some topics that attract more questions than others. We'll look at this from the point of view of how many questions have been _asked_, instead of looked at or commented on. (But, of course, this would also be possible, especially if we had impressions data on posts.) For this, the simplest way to proceed would be to consider the tags that users attached to their questions: These are good approximations of the topics that the question is about. On many occasions a question has also more than one tag attached to it. At this point we're interested in knowing the diversity of subjects (as captured by the tags): We'll measure how frequently a tag appears on any post. Are subjects equally popular, or are there some that elicit disproportionately more questions than others?

The answer to this question can be given after seeing how the tags are distributed, as shown in Figure 4.7.

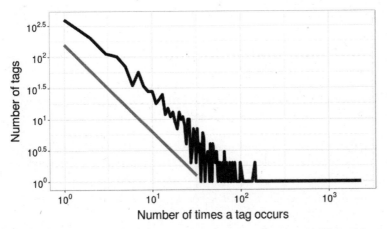

Figure 4.7: The number of times that any given tag appears together with any of the questions. We can see a power-law distribution again, with an exponent of −1.4.

The straight line on a double logarithmic scale suggests the presence of a power-law distribution, similar to what we observed for user activities. We can draw an analogy with the user activity distributions in the following way: If we make the tags analogous to users, the number of times a tag is "active" follows the same type of statistical distribution as the number of times that a user was active in a time period (see Chapter 1). Curiously, we could discover this similarity between two seemingly unrelated domains of social media activities. The commonality though is that they both originate from human behavior and interest.

This means that as we have seen before in Chapter 1 in the "Diversity of User Activities" section, we'll have a few tags that are popular across all questions: In fact, the most frequently used tags in the Science Fiction & Fantasy category of Stack Exchange are `story-identification`, `harry-potter`, `star-trek`, `star-wars`, `movie`, and `lord-of-the-rings`. Not surprisingly, these topics happened to be among the clearest clusters that we identified in Figure 4.5.

In addition to looking at the tags attached to questions, there's another way we could quantify the "popularity" of certain subjects. Because we have already run the clustering (which could be visualized as the dendrogram of cluster merges), we could just as well decide to stop the clustering at an arbitrary point and look at what kinds of clusters we have at that point. In particular, given that we'd like to see how large topics get in terms of questions asked in that topic, we could count the number of posts that were merged into any given cluster when we stopped the clustering. Stopping the clustering is equivalent to cutting the dendrogram at a certain level as well, in which case the clusters will be the separate branches under the cutting height.

Because, as we said, the point at which we stop the clustering/the height at which we cut the dendrogram is arbitrary, we'll choose three different heights under which we'd like to determine the cluster size distributions: These will be 0.5, 0.7, and 0.9, in terms of bag-of-words distances, as we used before. Listing 4.5 is the piece of R code that performs this cutting and calculates the size distribution of the branches left behind by the cut. These branches now will contain posts that are similar to each other, such as the examples in Figure 4.5.

Listing 4.5: This is how we work with the dendrogram of cluster merges to determine what kinds of clusters we had at some point while running the hierarchical agglomerative algorithm. (`stackexchange_text.R`)

```
# Cut the full dendrogram at different heights, and determine the size
# distribution of the topic clusters under the cuts.
h.dendr = as.dendrogram(h)
cut.heights = c(0.5, 0.7, 0.9)
branch.size.distrib = data.frame()
for (cut.height in cut.heights) {
    # Cut the final dendrogram to see what clusters we had at that
    # point during the run of the hierarchical clustering.
    dendr.cut = cut(h.dendr, h=cut.height)
    # The 'members' attribute of a branch is the number of leaves on
    # the branch.
    branch.sizes = sapply(dendr.cut$lower, function(b) attr(b,
            'members'))
    # Calculate the size distribution on this branch.
    size.distrib = ddply(data.frame(size=branch.sizes), .(size),
            summarize, count=nrow(piece))
    # Store the distribution together with a column storing the height
    # of cut.
    branch.size.distrib = rbind(branch.size.distrib,
            data.frame(size.distrib, cut.height=cut.height))
}

# branch.size.distrib now has three columns: size, count, cut.height
# for the number of post counts in branches of size 'size', at a given
# height.
```

If, moreover, we now look at how *big* these branches are in terms of posts, we get distributions as shown in Figure 4.8. What we can see in this figure is that although we still have power-law distributions for the topics sizes (roughly speaking only; for distance 0.9 small topics start to disappear), the distributions are qualitatively different. As we go higher in the dendrogram (let the clustering proceed further), we start to see the distributions shift toward larger cluster sizes, away from small clusters. However, the distributions still appear to retain their power-law nature. These two facts together mean that the exponent of the distribution must change toward "shallower" values so that we'll have a shift toward the larger clusters.

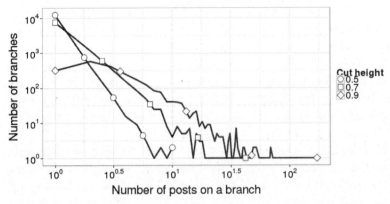

Figure 4.8: The distributions of the numbers of posts (questions) we find in the clusters if we were to stop the clustering at distances of 0.5, 0.7, and 0.9, respectively. We didn't actually stop the algorithm at any point but instead calculated these sizes using the history of cluster merges with Listing 4.5.

To recap, this all means that no matter at what granularity we are looking at the topics created by users, we seem to observe long tails in the "interest distribution" as measured by the number of posts in any topic cluster.

How Diverse Are Individual Users' Interests?

To this point in this chapter, we have looked at the extent to which topics attract attention based on questions posted. Equally interesting questions may be coming from the users' perspective: How many topics are users interested in? Are they posting questions into a lot of different categories, or are most people interested in a restricted set of topics only?

One thing is clear: Users' interests are not the same. If, taking the above dataset, one user is a "Lord of the Rings" fan, it doesn't necessarily make him a fan of "Star Wars," for example. However, if two different users have only one question in either of these categories, we can say that they are both only interested in their respective categories, and nothing else (as far as we can tell from the data, at least). However, if there is a user who has four posts in the topic "Comics," and one post in the topic "Matrix," we can assume that she is four times more interested in "Comics" than in the "Matrix." What would be the best way to measure this bias in user interests?

If we don't care about what topics users like, only about the relative strengths of their interests in any of the topics they posted into, then we can *rank* the labels designating their interests and work with a list of their ranked interests that we take in decreasing order: The interest where they posted the most will have rank 1, the second most frequent one will have rank 2, and so on. Also, we'll approximate users' interests by the tags that they associated with their questions. (In a similar vein, we could have used the clusters we obtained from clustering on text in the section "Using Content Features to Identify Topics," but for simplicity's sake we'll take the tags.)

After ranking users' tag frequencies in a decreasing order, we also need to normalize them so that the interests' weight sum to 1 for a user: This is necessary so that we can have the same metric for the relative importance for the topics for every user, irrespective of how active the users are individually. (We have seen that this activity has large variances across users, so we don't want any long-tail behavior to dominate our statistics.) Finally, to have a system-level view, we can just take an average over the relative interest strengths over all the users as a function of the topics' ranks. This procedure is shown in Listing 4.6.

Listing 4.6: Ranking users' tags by decreasing normalized frequencies and then taking an average over all users as a function of the tags' ranks. We finally normalize the distribution to have an area of 1. (`stackexchange_text.R`)

```
0  # Create a list of tag vectors for all post tags.
1  all.tags = strsplit(posts$tags, ' ')

2  # Create a data frame where the user.id column is the poster's ID,
3  # and the tag column is all the tags they used on any of their posts.
4  users.tags = do.call(rbind, lapply(seq_along(all.tags), function(i)
5                       data.frame(
6                                  user.id=posts$owner.user.id[i],
7                                  tag=all.tags[[i]]))))

8  # Convert factors to strings.
9  users.tags$tag = as.character(users.tags$tag)

10 # For each user, count and normalize their tag frequencies, and sort
11 # in decreasing order of normalized frequency so we get ranks.
12 users.ranked.tags = ddply(users.tags, .(user.id), function(df) {
13             # Count the tags.
14             tag.freqs = as.vector(table(df$tag))
15             # Normalize the frequencies.
16             tag.freqs = tag.freqs / nrow(df)
17             # Rank them.
18             tag.freqs = tag.freqs[order(tag.freqs, decreasing=TRUE)]
19             data.frame(rank=1 : length(tag.freqs), freqs=tag.freqs)
20         })

21 # Average the relative frequencies as a function of the tags' ranks.
22 mean.ranked.tags = ddply(users.ranked.tags, .(rank), summarize,
23          mean.freq=sum(freqs))
24 mean.ranked.tags = within(mean.ranked.tags, {
25             mean.freq = mean.freq / sum(mean.freq)
26         })
```

When we perform the re-ranking of users' topics and take an average over all users, what we'll get is that in an aggregate sense, how much users are interested in their most important topic versus the second, versus the third, and so forth. For the actual values we're getting for the average ranked tag frequency distribution per user, see Table 4.1.

Table 4.1: The expectation for the relative frequency of the top five most used tags by any individual user. On average, the most frequently used tag appears in 52.1% of a user's posts, the second most frequent tag appears 25.8% of the time, and so on.

RANK OF THE TAG	RELATIVE FREQUENCY PER USER
1	52.1%
2	25.8%
3	11.0%
4	4.2%
5	2.1%

Note that, naturally, different users have different total numbers of tags they have used; in the preceding calculations, we implicitly assumed that if a user has less than 5 tags altogether, any possible tag beyond rank 5 counts as 0—this is what the normalizations in lines 22–26 of Listing 4.6 are about. To expand on Table 4.1, we can also see in more detail how the ranked tag frequency distribution scales with the rank in Figure 4.9.

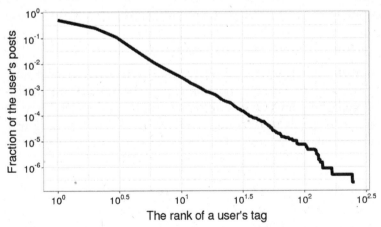

Figure 4.9: The expected relative frequency of how often a user uses a tag, versus the rank of a tag. Again, we had to rescale both axes logarithmically to see the function in full detail.

What can we conclude from Figure 4.9? It looks like that the per-user interests also follow a power law (although with a different exponent than what we saw for the overall topics distribution, as shown in Figure 4.7). We can be sure, though, that not everyone is interested in the same topic, and that's why we have re-ranked the per-user tag frequencies. When we consider user interests, though, it's appropriate to say that it appears that individual interests are governed by similar laws that are in effect for global user activities and content popularity.

Extracting Low-Dimensional Information from High-Dimensional Text

We explained how to represent text so that we can use it in our algorithms in the "Creating Features from Text: The Basics of Natural Language Processing" section earlier in this chapter. This section discusses the problem of high dimensionality of this type of data.

Social media text in the form of Tweets, blog posts, or status updates are often short in length but high in dimensionality. For the English language, when we consider the top 1 million words and with the bag-of-words representation, a simple Tweet like "Good morning!" will be denoted by a 1 M dimensional sparse vector, where only two items, "good" and "morning," are non-zeros, and all the unused terms are just zero. The human brain can easily extract meaning or a theme taking into consideration the time and sender of the message, and more; however, this is not that trivial for computers due to the high dimensionality of the data. So, computational tasks such text summarization, classification, and computing similarity based on content are challenging.

High dimensionality is a problem for two main reasons:

- Extracting meaning/a theme is algorithmically challenging. Often the underlying information within text documents is low dimensional, which means that often there are just a couple meaningful notions encoded in the text that we can come up with after reading. For instance, a paragraph from a news article is probably about one topic, such as sports, politics, or architecture. Though we read hundreds or thousands of words, we can easily come up with one of the few meanings. Our brain simply maps these words to meaningful themes. Here, instead of us reading, we perform that mapping task algorithmically. However, transforming the information from millions of terms/words to those few themes is a many-to-one mapping, and there is more than one way of doing that. Computer algorithms should solve this problem so that a few words from a certain user should be interpreted the right way, and information should not be buried under the high dimensionality of the data. We need advanced algorithms handling these issues.

- High dimensionality produces computational challenges. Even if we have advanced algorithms that can automatically extract meanings from the text, often those algorithms do not scale to large datasets with millions of dimensions and millions of users, which is often the case in social media. For those reasons, we need to reduce dimensionality.

We can explain the algorithmic challenge as follows. Suppose there are two Tweets:

1. "Today's soccer match was amazing!"
2. "The right winger could have scored that goal."

Let's assume you want to compute the similarity of these two Tweets. If you use only a term-based approach, as we did previously, and compare these two strings using string match, the similarity will be 0 because there are no overlapping words. However, we can easily realize that both Tweets are about a soccer match, where the second Tweet talks about a specific position in the game. If we want to find the similarity, we should find the latent theme representing the overlapping meaning in both Tweets. The algorithm we propose should associate the word "soccer" and "match" in the first Tweet with "right winger," "scored," and "goal" word so that it can give some non-zero similarity between these two Tweets.

Topic Modeling

The area of machine learning that performs dimensionality reduction on unstructured text is called *topic modeling*. The family of algorithms in this area takes raw unstructured text and any other metadata such as a social graph, time of sending, or labels as input, and learns a group of low-dimensional thematic representations of the text within the data, called *topics*. For instance, in Figures 4.10 and 4.11 we observe that two Tweets from one of the book's authors have significantly different themes and meanings. The first one is about a music instrument/event and mentions another user who is likely to be interested in/ related to the same topic. By just capturing words such as "music," or "instrument," we could easily identify that this Tweet is about music. Similarly, another example is shown in Figure 4.11, where the theme is a TV broadcast about the Olympiads.

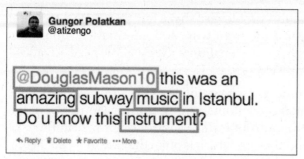

Figure 4.10: A Tweet about music. Keywords in tags represent clues for the message. The users are interested in music, and we explicitly see words such as "music" and "instrument" that might help us decide that this Tweet is about music indeed.

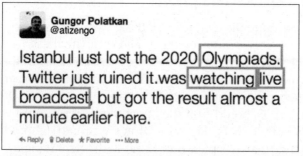

Figure 4.11: A Tweet about TV broadcast news. Keywords in boxes tell us that this Tweet is about a piece of news as it appeared on television.

While we are performing these actions, our brain simply looks at the words and associates those words with an underlying possible thematic space, as illustrated in Figure 4.12. The goal of topic modeling is to algorithmically perform or approximate this operation using computers, as shown in Figure 4.13.

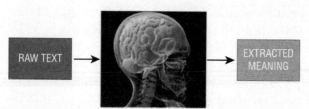

Figure 4.12: The human brain processes raw text and associates it with latent semantic themes.

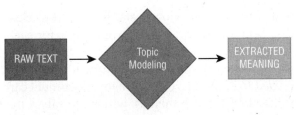

Figure 4.13: Topic modeling analyzes raw text and finds what topics it is most likely about.

Extracting information from text is critical in many computational problems within social media. In any user classification problem, you can use raw text/ status updates/posts of the users to model user interests based on both content produced and content the user engaged with. Another example is social media search tools. Often a search engine associated with the social media platform returns the most relevant users or posts based on a query. Link recommendation (such as friendship recommendation in a mutually linked graph, or "who to follow" problems in directed social graphs) is another big problem in social media platforms, where content produced and consumed by the users plays an important role for high-quality recommendations. In all these problems, using raw words only is often not the best idea for both algorithmic accuracy and computational complexity. You need to compactly represent this giant dataset and summarize the meanings in latent low-dimensional semantic structures, which we called topics here.

As mentioned, the mapping performed from high-dimensional word space to low-dimensional topic space is many-to-one. This means that often there are multiple topic representations that can explain the existing dataset. Though the human brain is smart enough to pick the right ones using other covariates such as the temporal relevancy and the user who sent the message, computer algorithms should be specifically instructed to do so. The following three sections present topic modeling algorithms based on the type of assistance performed in the social media platform:

- Unsupervised topic modeling
- Supervised topic modeling
- Relational topic modeling

Each approach will be explained in more detail as we go along.

Unsupervised Topic Modeling

This set of algorithms uses only the raw text to learn topics/themes inside the documents. It is called *unsupervised* because there is no class label or any other metadata other than the text that has been used. The most famous approach in this group of algorithms is the Latent Dirichlet Allocation (LDA) algorithm.

LDA takes a set of text documents (for example, blog posts, Tweets, messages, or emails) as input and outputs a set of topics and topic proportions for each document, and it operates only on the raw text to learn those.

The fundamental idea of LDA is that every single text document consists of one or more themes that can be used to summarize it, and a text document can also be represented as a mixed member of those themes, which are called the topics. We can see examples of this in Figures 4.10, 4.11, and 4.14. For instance, Figure 4.14 shows that when there are two topics such as "blogging" and "technology," this Tweet can be represented as a mixed member of those topics.

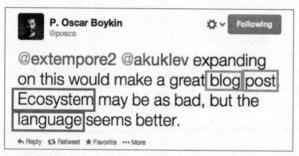

Figure 4.14: A Tweet about a proposal to write a blog post about a programming language. We can claim that this Tweet consists of two topics: (1) social/blog: "blog post" is a clue; and (2) tech/computer science: "ecosystem" and "language" are keywords.

The way LDA models data is the same as this principle. Every single text document is generated as a mixed member of a set of topics, where topics are probability distributions over the entire dictionary used anywhere in our corpus. The way words in the dictionary are weighted in those distributions tells us the characteristic of that topic. For instance, a topic on sports will probably have high weights on words such as "football," "basketball," and "defense," whereas a topic on politics will have high weights on words such as "democrat," "republican," and "government."

For each document, first a topic is generated. Topic proportion for a document represents the amount each topic will be used in it. For instance, a news article might be approximately 80% "Sports" and 20% "North America." These proportions are generally far from uniform because we know that a short text document may only contain a few topics. For instance, a news article about the topic "Sports" mostly talks about sports, whereas an article about "Economics" talks about money, markets, stocks, and more. But it is almost impossible to find an article that talks about everything at the same time, for example, politics, sports, economy, and science.

After topic proportions are generated, then for each word we pick a topic according to the proportions—if the "Sports" topic is weighted at 80%, approximately 80% of the words will belong to the "Sports" topic. This process defines the way data is modeled. The next question is how we can infer topics and topic proportions, given concrete textual data.

Inference

To give a flavor of how the LDA topics are determined, the next few paragraphs describe the basic principles based on which it's done. If you are more interested in the practical applications, you can to skip to the next section.

A way to visualize dependence relations between the entities of the approach and the generative process is to use probabilistic graphical models. The graphical model for LDA is shown in Figure 4.15.

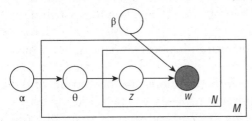

Figure 4.15: A graphical model for Latent Dirichlet Allocation (LDA). Shaded node *w* represents the observed words in the text and unshaded nodes represent the latent variables such as topics β, topic proportions θ, and per-word topic assignments *z*. α is a fixed parameter to the model. The plates represent replications; for instance, there are *M* documents in the corpus and *N* words within each document.

Each node represents a random variable. Shaded nodes represent the observed variables, and unshaded nodes represent the latent variables. The directed edges denote a "parent-of" ("conditionally-dependent-on") relationship between the corresponding variables. For instance, Θ is a parent of **z**, and **z** is a parent of *w*. While explaining the inference, instead of working on each random variable separately, we will group them into three buckets:

- The observed words (*w*).
- Latent variables (topics β, topic proportions Θ, and per-word topic assignments **z**).
- Parameters of the LDA model (α).

Without loss of generality, let $\mathbf{X} = \mathbf{x}_{1:N}$'s denote the observations (in our specific model LDA words in the text, *w* in Figure 4.15), $\mathbf{Z} = \mathbf{z}_{1:M}$ the latent variables (topics β, topic proportions Θ, and per-word topic assignments **z**), and a set of $\mathbf{Q} = \mathbf{q}_{1:T}$ parameters of the model that are fixed. A probabilistic model can be defined as the set of relations between all of the random variables and the set of conditional distributions that when combined define the joint distribution $P(\mathbf{X}, \mathbf{Z}|\mathbf{Q})$. A given probabilistic model means that the joint distribution $P(\mathbf{X}, \mathbf{Z}|\mathbf{Q})$

is defined, and the dependence among all of the random variables is specified. For instance, the graphical model for LDA given in Figure 4.15 defines the joint relations of the observed text, topic assignments, and topic proportions.

The next stage is the inference. Our overall goal here is to learn the *posterior distribution* of the latent variables, given the parameters and observed variables. That is to say, we are interested in computing the posterior distribution,

$$P(\mathbf{Z}|\mathbf{X},\mathbf{Q}) = \frac{P(\mathbf{X}|\mathbf{Z},\mathbf{Q})P(\mathbf{Z}|\mathbf{Q})}{\int_{Z}P(\mathbf{X}|\mathbf{Z},\mathbf{Q})P(\mathbf{Z}|\mathbf{Q})}, \tag{4.3}$$

where we've rewritten the conditional probability using Bayes' theorem. The first term on the right side, $P(\mathbf{X}|\mathbf{Z}, \mathbf{Q})$, is called the *likelihood*, and the second term, $P(\mathbf{Z}|\mathbf{Q})$, is called the *prior*, which expresses our initial belief on the distribution of the latent variables.

Computing the posterior distribution using the likelihood and the prior—which links the data and the model—is called the *inference*. This is the algorithm that learns topics from the data. The posterior distributions are the outputs of the algorithms that we can find several different purposes for, such as summarization of the text, features in a classification system, and so on. Computing the numerator of Equation 4.3 is easy: Just the values of some configuration of the hidden variables should be embedded into the probability distributions provided by the model. However, the denominator is problematic, because as the data size and dimensionality grows, the computation of the integral becomes harder, and the problem becomes intractable.

To solve this issue, approximate posterior inference algorithms were proposed. These methods are used when the exact computation of the posterior is infeasible. Generally, we solve this issue using either Markov Chain Monte Carlo (MCMC) sampling or variational inference.

Experimental Demonstration

This section focuses on practical applications of LDA and real data in R. In this section, we use the lda R package, available on CRAN (Comprehensive R Archive Network). The lda package contains example document and corpus data as well, which we use in the next code examples.

Next, we show how we process our own text documents and get term counts from them. As explained earlier in this chapter in the section "Creating Features from Text: The Basics of Natural Language Processing," we need to first convert the text to vectors so that we can run numerical algorithms on them. For this purpose, we use the lexicalize function of the lda package shown in Listing 4.7. For instance, in the example we process a set of raw text documents stored as an array of strings, consisting of three documents. lexicalize returns a list of two items: the document-term matrix in sparse form, and a list of words, the vocabulary of the corpus (enumerating all the terms that appeared in any of the documents).

Listing 4.7: Creating terms and a vocabulary from documents in R. (`create_tdm_small_example.R`)

```
library(lda)
library(tm)

documents = c(
        'I love football and Messi is my favorite player',
        'The demonstration on the football field was spectacular',
        'This is just a demonstration for the LDA package'
)

corpus = lexicalize(documents)

# Use the stop words list from the `tm` package.
stop.words = stopwords('en')

# Get the list of words. This is a function in LDA package.
words = word.counts(corpus$documents)

# Specify which words in the vocabulary are stop words.
words.to.be.removed = as.numeric(names(words)[corpus$vocab %in%
 stop.words])

# Filter out those words from the corpus.
docs.filtered = filter.words(corpus$documents, words.to.be.removed)

corpus$vocab
 [1] "i"            "love"        "football"       "and"
 [5] "messi"        "is"          "my"             "favorite"
 [9] "player"       "the"         "demonstration"  "on"
[13] "field"        "was"         "spectacular"    "this"
[17] "just"         "a"           "for"            "lda"
[21] "package"

docs.filtered
[[1]]
     [,1] [,2] [,3] [,4] [,5]
[1,]    1    2    4    7    8
[2,]    1    1    1    1    1

[[2]]
     [,1] [,2] [,3] [,4]
[1,]   10    2   12   14
[2,]    1    1    1    1

[[3]]
     [,1] [,2] [,3] [,4]
[1,]   16   10   19   20
[2,]    1    1    1    1
```

In the `corpus$documents` list element, the first row represents the word indices (starting at 0), and the second row tells us how many times that index appeared in the document. The other constituent of the corpus is the vocabulary, the total set of unique words appearing in any of the documents, with the same index used as in the first rows of the documents. In this code we also removed the stop words, as we did earlier in this chapter.

One main issue in the case of social media text is the noise in the data. Often people are not careful while sending an email or Tweet, or posting a message. Text is often full of typos. This causes an inflation in the number of words, and many of those additional words are meaningless. Earlier in this chapter, we discussed how stop word removal and stemming may alleviate this; while fitting a topic model to a text corpus, we definitely do not want the stop words to dominate our topics.

The remainder of this section uses a different example: the Cora data set from within the `lda` package. It consists of 2,410 scientific articles, with links and titles from the Cora search engine. Cora was a prototype portal for computer science research papers (see `?cora` in R for more details). In Listing 4.8, `cora.documents` and `cora.vocab` have the same data structure as `corpus$documents` and `corpus$vocab` in Listing 4.7.

Listing 4.8: Getting a feel for what the example corpus contains. (`lda_analysis.R`)

```
library(lda)

# Load the Cora data set.
data(cora.documents)
data(cora.vocab)
data(cora.titles)

# Inspect data, seeing explanation, top rows and length.
?cora.documents
head(cora.documents)
length(cora.documents)
head(cora.vocab)
length(cora.vocab)
```

Fitting the LDA topics model is demonstrated by Listing 4.9. In this case, we wanted to fit 10 topics to our corpus. We can observe that each topic has its own characteristic. For instance, topic 1 is about genetic programming, whereas topic 3 is about Bayesian modeling. Topic 10 is about research and universities in general, whereas topic 5 is about reinforcement learning (which is a big branch of machine learning).

Listing 4.9: Fitting the LDA model to the Cora corpus and inspecting the most important terms. (`lda_analysis.R`)

```
# The number of topics.
K = 10
```

```
# Setting the random seed for reproducibility.
set.seed(867101)

# Model fitting with the Gibbs sampler. It only takes the document-term
# matrix (with vocabulary).
result = lda.collapsed.gibbs.sampler(cora.documents,
        K,                          # The number of topics.
        cora.vocab,
        50,                         # The number of iterations.
        0.1,                        # Parameters.
        0.1,
        compute.log.likelihood=TRUE)

# Get the top words in the cluster. Top words are the characteristics of
# the relevant topic.
top.words = top.topic.words(result$topics, 5, by.score=TRUE)

top.words
        [,1]            [,2]          [,3]        [,4]          [,5]
[1,] "genetic"       "functions"   "bayesian"  "learning"    "reinforcement"
[2,] "programming"   "parallel"    "models"    "decision"    "learning"
[3,] "robot"         "function"    "data"      "inductive"   "algorithm"
[4,] "system"        "neural"      "markov"    "induction"   "methods"
[5,] "crossover"     "control"     "model"     "concept"     "state"
        [,6]            [,7]          [,8]        [,9]          [,10]
[1,] "algorithm"     "reasoning"   "network"   "genetic"     "research"
[2,] "learning"      "knowledge"   "neural"    "search"      "grant"
[3,] "error"         "design"      "networks"  "fitness"     "university"
[4,] "bounds"        "case"        "input"     "optimization" "report"
[5,] "classification" "system"     "training"  "selection"   "technical"
```

While learning topics, we also learn topic proportions per document as well. Those proportions are the low-dimensional representations in the topic space of the corpus. So LDA can be considered as a dimensionality reduction technique as well. Using those proportions and top-topic words, we can summarize the articles and perform a sanity check on whether the learned topics make sense: Next, we randomly pick 10 documents and compare the text in those articles with their topic proportions with Listing 4.10.

Listing 4.10: Spot-checking the model results for 10 randomly chosen documents from Cora. (`lda_analysis.R`)

```
# Number of documents to display.
N = 10

# This is a normalization for assignments in the Gibbs sampling.
topic.proportions = t(result$document_sums) /
    colSums(result$document_sums)

# Take 10 random samples.
```

```
index = sample(1 : dim(topic.proportions)[1], N)
topic.proportions =  topic.proportions[index,]

# There might be empty documents.
topic.proportions[is.na(topic.proportions)] =  1 / K

colnames(topic.proportions) = apply(top.words, 2, paste, collapse=" ")

# Prepare the data for ggplot.
topic.proportions.df =
      melt(cbind(data.frame(topic.proportions), document=factor(1 : N)),
      variable.name="topic",
      id.vars="document")

ggplot(data=topic.proportions.df, aes(x=topic, y=value)) +
      geom_bar(stat='identity') +
      coord_flip() + facet_wrap(~ document, ncol=5) +
      theme(axis.text.x=element_text(angle=90, hjust=1))

cora.titles[index]
  [1] "Using dirichlet mixture priors to derive hidden Markov models for
      protein families."
  [2] "Incremental self-improvement for lifetime multi-agent
      reinforcement learning."
  [3] "Stochastic pro-positionalization of non-determinate background
      knowledge."
  [4] "Linden (1998). Model selection using measure functions."
  [5] "On the informativeness of the DNA promoter sequences domain
      theory."
  [6] "(in preparation) \"Between MDPs and semi-MDPs: learning, planning,
      and representing knowledge at multiple temporal scales.\""
  [7] "\"Gambling in a rigged casino: the adversarial multi-armed bandit
      problem,\""
  [8] "The Pandemonium system of reflective agents."
  [9] "\"The weighted majority algorithm\","
  [10] "\"The Complexity of Real-time Search.\""
```

In Figure 4.16, we show the topic proportions of the same documents. Matching indices, we can see that the titles make great sense compared with the highest weighted topics in the figure. For instance, the first document is about Dirichlet mixtures and Markov models; in the plot the same document has the highest weight in the Bayesian modeling topic, which is indeed the broader area to which these two subject areas belong. Similarly, the second document is about reinforcement learning, and in the plot we can see that the corresponding topic label has indeed been identified.

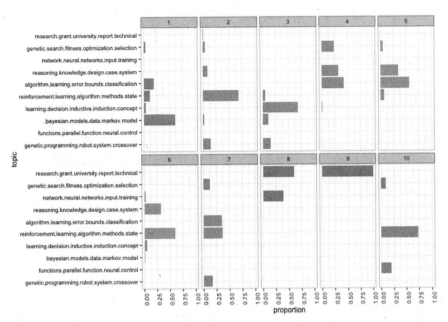

Figure 4.16: Topic proportions of 10 samples from the corpus. To characterize the topics, we pick the top 5 words from them and concatenate them with periods. The bar height of a topic within each subplot represents the weight of that topic in the corresponding document. The sum of topic proportions within each subplot is 1.

Another interpretation for topic modeling is clustering, just as we demonstrated earlier in this chapter, when we analyzed the topics appearing in the questions on Stack Exchange. Topics can be considered cluster centers in an unsupervised clustering algorithm that runs on textual data. In the case of LDA, the assignment of documents to those clusters is soft, though, as we have the topic proportions as well, which are real valued. By thresholding, you can perform a hard assignment as well, picking the topic with the maximum weight for instance as the cluster assignment of the corresponding document.

Supervised Topic Modeling

In vanilla LDA, we used only the raw text and learned topics and topic proportions in an unsupervised way. In social media data mining problems, there is often metadata or a covariate related to the text or message of the user. This type of additional information can be used to assist the topic modeling process. However, we can also use content produced by a user to predict such additional response variables, for example, to identify whether the user is a spammer or a regular user. Indeed, we can perform any type of user classification/modeling based on the text data produced by the user. In these types of problems, in addition to raw unstructured text, we can use the response (label) data (for example, whether the user producing the content is a spammer, the age or gender of the user, and more) as supervision to our topic modeling algorithm. The algorithms considering this type of additional data are called supervised topic models because we provide ground-truth input to the algorithm. We will specifically look at the supervised Latent Dirichlet Allocation model as a more advanced version of the LDA model we studied in the previous section.

Response variables on a user or post basis are common in social media platforms. Some examples include covariates about users, such as gender, age, or income, as mentioned. These types of information can be useful while trying to identify the underlying meaning in a text document. As mentioned in the previous section, mapping from words/text to topics is a many-to-one operation, meaning that there might be multiple different sets of topics, each with different quality and interpretability, but which all fit the observed data in some way. It may be challenging for the topic modeling algorithm to find a high-quality set of topics, and supervision in the form of these additional covariates may make the resulting topics more accurate. The main idea of sLDA (supervised LDA), and a fundamental difference from unsupervised LDA, is exactly this point. sLDA uses the additional response variables to assist the topic learning process. This helps to learn not only higher quality topics, but also provides more interpretability and insights regarding the response variable.

Insight is one key component here. It is common to ask questions in social media problems about what content is correlated with certain user actions. What type of things do certain types of people talk about? How does the content change based on the demographics of the user? While answering these kinds of questions, it is critical to consider both the content (text produced by the users) and the response variable (gender, age, political bias, and so on). sLDA is an algorithm proposing a solution to these kinds of questions.

In Figure 4.17, we present the probabilistic graphical model for sLDA. Differing from LDA in Figure 4.15, we also have response variables Y representing the additional information (age, gender, spam/regular user). We have latent variables η, for supervision, explaining how the learned topics affect the supervision.

In classical regression problems, a model is fitted to get the regression weights to explain the relation between the covariates (also called *attributes* or *features*) and the response variables. sLDA follows a similar route to learn the relation between topic proportions and the response variables. In addition to LDA, there is a regression part embedded within the model such that topic proportions play the role of covariates, and response variables are what we want to predict using the covariates. The specific equation modeling the response variable is given as

$$P\left(Y \mid z_{1:n}, \eta, \sigma^2\right) \propto \exp\frac{\eta^T \bar{z}}{\sigma^2}, \tag{4.4}$$

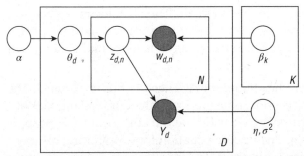

Figure 4.17: A graphical model for supervised Latent Dicirichlet Allocation (sLDA). The shaded node W represents the observed words in the text as in LDA, and Y represents the response variables (for example, age and gender of a user). Unshaded nodes represent the latent variables: for topics β, topic proportions Θ, per-word topic assignments Z, as in LDA. Moreover, we added supervision parameters η and σ^2. Similarly to LDA, α is a fixed parameter passed to the model. (For the meaning of the parameters, see `https://arxiv.org/abs/1003.0783`. The figure appeared in this paper originally also.) The plates represent replications. In particular, there are D documents in the corpus, N words within each document, and K topics to learn.

where $\bar{z} = \frac{1}{T}\sum_{t=1}^{T} z_t$ is the empirical topic proportion computed over T samples of topic assignments in the Gibbs sampler. A model fit on the observed data (when Y and W are given) will learn the latent variable η. η is a vector of length K, denoting the regression coefficients over the topic proportions. Because topic proportions are variables with positive values between 0 and 1, the higher the weight, the more important role the topic k plays with the response variable.

This parameter is important for two reasons:

■ You can use η on a new document without a response variable and predict the response variable using topic proportions. For example, by just looking at the content produced, you can predict whether a user is male or female.

■ η is a good way to summarize the content's relation to the response variable. For example, you can summarize what content groups of a certain age or gender produce. We'll see a practical demonstration of both next.

Inference

Inference for sLDA is a simple modification of the inference for LDA. There are two main parts which are different, though:

■ Topic assignments are not done in an unsupervised manner any more. Assignments are weighted according to how well the assignment fits the response variable of the document. Let's say we are trying to decide if we should assign word to either the topic "Sports" or to the topic "Home/gardening," and our response variable is whether the user that generated this content is male or female. Suppose that the current state of η states that "Sports" is highly correlated with the gender male; and "Home/

gardening" is highly correlated with female. Then if a document belongs to a male user, it's more likely that it will be assigned to the "Sports" topic; and if it belongs to a female user, then it is more likely that it will be assigned to the "Home/gardening" topic.

▪ Given an assignment, on the other hand, we need to find η. As usual, the inference stage for η starts with some random valued initialization. With the current topic assignments, we estimate the empirical topic proportions, and then update η. The update equation for η is nothing different than a classical regression in this case. The inference procedure continues iteratively, sampling topic assignments where η is fixed and later updating the η by solving a simple linear regression problem with given topic assignments.

Experimental Demonstration

This section continues using the `lda` R package. However, to make things a bit different, we'll use a collection of 773 political blogs' data this time as our corpus. The response variable will be whether the authors of the blogs are politically conservative or liberal.

So, in addition to the documents and vocabulary files, we also load the ratings file denoting the response variable in Listing 4.11. The data set consists of 309 conservative users and 464 liberal users.

Listing 4.11: The political blog dataset we'll use to demonstrate the sLDA topic detection. (`slda_analysis.R`)

```
library(lda)

# Load the data.
data(poliblog.documents)
data(poliblog.vocab)
data(poliblog.ratings)      # It is important--we also have ratings per
                            # document.

?poliblog.documents

table(poliblog.ratings)
poliblog.ratings
-100   100
 464   309
```

Next, in Listing 4.12, we initialize the parameters and start fitting the model.

Listing 4.12: Training the sLDA model on the political blog dataset. (`slda_analysis.R`)

```
num.topics = 10

# Initialize the parameters.
params = sample(c(-1, 1), num.topics, replace=TRUE)
```

```
result = slda.em(documents=poliblog.documents,
        K=num.topics,
        vocab=poliblog.vocab,
        num.e.iterations=10,
        num.m.iterations=4,
        alpha=1.0,
        eta=0.1,
        poliblog.ratings / 100,
        params,
        variance=0.25,
        lambda=1.0,
        logistic=FALSE,
        method='sLDA')

# Pick the top words for each topic.
topics = apply(top.topic.words(result$topics, 5, by.score=TRUE), 2,
        paste, collapse=' ')

topics
 [1] "wright hes people said just"
 [2] "tax money oil new make"
 [3] "mccain said president john mccains"
 [4] "clinton obama voters vote percent"
 [5] "obama barack hillary obamas clinton"
 [6] "democratic race election party primary"
 [7] "senator like media dont debate"
 [8] "war house iraq bush law"
 [9] "government just people political federal"
[10] "senate district republican candidates house"
```

Here we feed the algorithm with documents and a vocabulary that comes with the content produced by the bloggers, and additionally we include ratings as well. The `num.e.iterations` is a parameter for how many samples we are going to collect before updating η, and `num.m.iterations` is a parameter for how many times we are going to update η. For `num.e.iterations = 10` and `num.m.iterations = 4`, η will be updated 4 times and for each time we will collect 10 samples of topic assignments.

sLDA outputs three main variables:

- Topics, denoted as β in the model.
- Topic proportions and assignments (Θ and $\mathbf{Z}$).
- Supervision weights (η).

In Listing 4.12 we also present the top five highest-weighted words within each topic. We observe that topics include different debate verticals, such as justice, money, and economy, as well as political polarizations around democrats and republicans.

As we mentioned earlier, one important aspect of topic modeling is the exploratory power it provides. In particular, sLDA is even richer in its interpretation of textual data than LDA is. We can answer questions like "What is the difference in topics that followers of @justinbieber and @ladygaga discuss? "; "What kind of content do people supporting Obama produce, and what kind of different content do people supporting McCain produce?"; "What did people talk about on New Year's Eve, given their gender?" These questions can all be summarized as one single question: "What type of things do people in group *A* talk about, compared to people in group *B*?" sLDA can answer questions like these. To be specific, in Listing 4.13 we analyze the regression coefficients η of the model previously fitted, which will tell us what topic usage is more representative of conservatives and democrats, respectively. We first extract the coefficients and order them by magnitude, and then plot the weights versus the topics, as shown in Figure 4.18.

Listing 4.13: Here we extract the η coefficients, linking topics to the response variable. (slda_analysis.R)

```
# Get the coefficients for the regresssion.
coefs = data.frame(coef(summary(result$model)))
coefs = cbind(coefs, Topics=factor(topics,
        topics[order(coefs$Estimate)]))
coefs = coefs[order(coefs$Estimate),]

qplot(Topics, Estimate, colour=Estimate, size=abs(t.value),
      data=coefs) +
      geom_errorbar(width=0.5,
            aes(ymin=Estimate - Std..Error, ymax=Estimate+Std..Error)) +
      coord_flip()
```

High positive weight is correlated with the blog being conservative, and high negative weight is correlated with it being liberal. According to this analysis, as shown in Figure 4.18, conservatives talk about "tax, money, and oil," as well as opponents "Barack Obama" and "Hillary Clinton." However, liberal bloggers talk about "republican candidates," "McCain," and "the Iraq war." This figure is important for insights because with just one plot, we can summarize both topics and their relations to the grouping of users generating the content. It would be almost impossible to look at thousands (or millions, in a real-world social media scenario) of posts to extract such insights.

We can also check if the topics used by the bloggers are any indication for their political leaning. For this, we use the `predict` function to see how well our predictions of the response variable compare with the ground truth in Listing 4.14. This function first finds topic proportions given the topics within the fitted model, and then it estimates the response variables, as was shown in Equation 4.4 earlier in this chapter. We then compute the density of predictions segmented via the ground truth. For instance, we could use a decision threshold to assign each blogger to either ends of the political spectrum. In this case, the overlapping area of the ratings in Figure 4.19 represents potentials for prediction error, as in this case both conservatives and liberals appear in the dataset for the same rating.

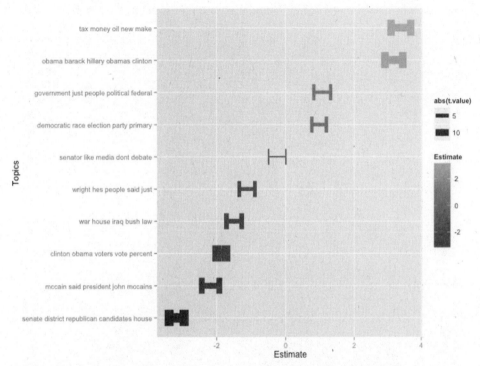

Figure 4.18: Coefficients η for each topic connecting topics with political ideology. The higher the coefficient of a topic on the *x* axis, the higher the probability that the conservative bloggers talk about it, and the lower the coefficient, the higher the probability that liberal users talk about the topic.

Listing 4.14: We perform a prediction using the previously fitted model, for the political view of the blog, and then check how it compares to its actual label. (slda_analysis.R)

```
predictions = slda.predict(poliblog.documents,
        result$topics,
        result$model,
        alpha=1.0,
        eta=0.1)

qplot(predictions,
                fill=factor(poliblog.ratings),
                xlab='predicted rating',
```

```
                ylab='density',
                alpha=I(0.5),
                geom='density') +
        geom_vline(aes(xintercept=0)) +
        theme(legend.position='none')
```

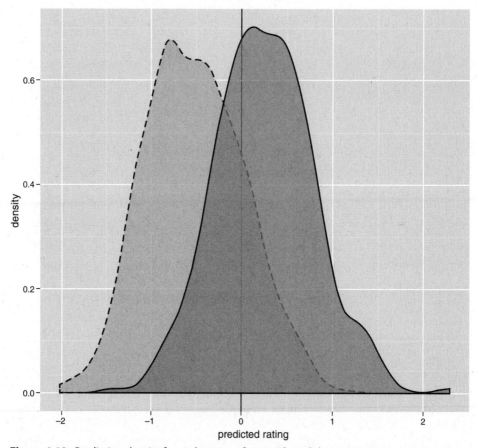

Figure 4.19: Prediction density for each group of users. The solid curve represents conservative, and the dashed curve represents liberal. Overlapping areas represent potential errors either as false positives or false negatives, depending on a decision threshold.

Relational Topic Modeling

In the preceding section, "Supervised Topic Modeling," we studied how to incorporate a response variable into topic modeling and use it to improve topic quality, as well as to learn a predictive model for the response variables. The key motivation was that the transformation of words/raw text to a low-dimensional meaning/topic space is many-to-one—there are multiple topic candidates that can fit the observed data—and any further supervision into learning can let our algorithms pick more meaningful and higher quality topics. In this section, we will follow a similar path, but in this case we are going to incorporate relational information into topic modeling.

Relational information is widespread in modern data sets, but in social media it is often the heartbeat of the data. Any social graph (whether directed or undirected), hyperlinks among web pages, connections among emails, or a citation network among research articles can be considered as relational information. In this section, we study how to incorporate such relational information into topic modeling. For instance, while we learn topics from Tweets, how can we incorporate the follow graph? Or while we learn topics from research articles, how can we incorporate the citation network? These are the questions we will try to answer.

Similar to what we studied with supervised topic modeling, in this section, we work on a modification of LDA. The model is called *relational topic modeling* (RTM). Different from LDA, RTM gets the relational information (such as a social graph) as input to the model, and in addition to vanilla outputs of LDA, it also produces a model for link prediction. There are two main motivations for RTM:

- The mapping from words to topics is not unique. To assist topic modeling, we want to use the social graph: Graphs generally include rich information. For instance, for social media, people follow or befriend each other carefully and this tells a lot about the relation of the users. The content they produce is likely to be related as well. For one-way public graphs, for instance, relationships in the network are mostly interest-based. So, if you follow another user, this is a strong signal that you are interested in what content this user produces and the content you produce is also likely correlated with it. Another example is citation networks of scientific publications. For such graphs people do share another paper they used, while generating the content in the existing paper. Hence, knowing this information is critical to understand the underlying thematic structure in the text.

- Link prediction is an important problem in graph data mining. RTM proposes a solution to predict links in graphs using content generated by nodes in the graph. This has the underlying assumption that link generation has its dynamics within the content produced by both sides. By using this tool, we can predict the non-existent (but potential) links in any relational graph, for example, a social graph.

Similarly to sLDA, extracting insights is one important component of RTM. Our goal while mining the content on social media is not only to learn topics and the model for link prediction, but also we want to understand and summarize the data. One important problem is to find out what content plays an important role in link generation. For instance, do people talking about politics follow each other? Does a mutual interest in sports, or in politics play a more important role forming the social graph, respectively? We can use RTM to answer these types of questions.

In Figure 4.20 we present the probabilistic graphical model for RTM. Different from LDA in Figure 4.15, we have relational variables $y_{d,d'}$ representing the additional information such as links in a social graph or citation networks, and we have latent variables η for modeling the correlation between relational information and the topical match between two nodes.

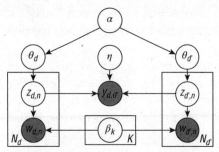

Figure 4.20: A graphical model for relational topic modeling (RTM). *d* and *d'* represent two nodes in the graph, respectively. Shaded nodes w_d and $w_{d'}$ represent the observed words in the content generated by user *d* and *d'*, and $y_{d,d'}$ represents the link variable (e.g., friends in a social graph, citations between documents). Unshaded nodes represent the latent variables such as topics β, topic proportions Θ_d and $\Theta_{d'}$, per-word topic assignments z_d and $z_{d'}$ as in LDA, and relational parameters such as η. Similarly to LDA, α is a fixed parameter to the model. The plates represent replications; for instance, there are $N_{d'}$ words within each document and *K* topics to learn. The figure and more explanations can be found in http://proceedings.mlr .press/v5/chang09a/chang09a.pdf.

The relational information is modeled similarly to the approach in sLDA; an exponential function connects the match in the topic proportions to the link. The match in topic proportions is formulated as the dot product in empirical topic proportions $\bar{z}_d \cdot \bar{z}_{d'}$, where $\bar{z} = \dfrac{1}{T}\sum_{t=1}^{T} z_t$ is the empirical topic proportion over *T* samples of topic assignments in the Gibbs sampler and "·" corresponds to the dot product of two *K*-length vectors. The *k*th item of $\bar{z}_d \cdot \bar{z}_{d'}$ is high only when both documents have a high proportion on the *k*th topic, which means a match in interest on topic *k*. For the link variable

$$P\left(y_{d,d'} \mid z_d, z_{d'}, \eta\right) = \exp(\eta^T (\bar{z}_d \cdot \bar{z}_{d'})). \tag{4.5}$$

A model fitted on observed data (with $y_{d,d'}$ and *w* given) will learn the latent variable η. Similarly to sLDA, η is a vector of length *K*, denoting the regression coefficients over the topic proportions. Because topic proportions are variables with positive values between 0 and 1, the higher the weight, the higher the topic k plays a positive role.

This parameter is important and differentiates RTM from LDA for two reasons:

- You can use η on two new documents without a link, and predict the possibility of two users in the social graph or two papers in the citation network getting connected using topic proportions. For example, by just looking at the content produced, you can predict whether user A might be interested in connecting to user B in the social graph.

- η is a good way to summarize the correlation between the existence of a link and the match in the content produced by two nodes. For example, you can summarize what role the content match plays in predicting the existence of a link between two nodes.

Inference

Inference for RTM is a simple modification to the inference for LDA as was also the case for sLDA. We will not give the full derivation, but we will explain the main ideas behind the algorithm. There are two main parts that are different from LDA:

- Topic assignments are not done in an unsupervised manner any more. Assignments are weighted according to how well the assignment fits the graph structure or the relational information. Let's say we want to decide assigning word w_i in document d either to the topic "Sports" or to the topic "Home/gardening." Suppose the current state of η states that mutual interest with your network in "Home/gardening" is highly correlated with link generation. Then if w_i belongs to a user with many friends with high interest in "Home/gardening," then it is very likely that it will be assigned to the "Home/gardening" topic because the supervision coming from the relational information tells the algorithm to do so.

- Given the topic assignments, we want to find η. As usual, the inference stage for η starts with some random valued initialization. With the current topic assignments, RTM estimates the empirical topic proportions. In sLDA, if the response is binary (for example, spam, not spam), then updating η is like a classical logistic regression problem because there are both positive and negative samples. In RTM, often the relational information is in the form of a graph, and in this case either there is an edge in the graph or not. This means that we do not have negative samples—there is nothing like a non-edge in the graph. To solve this issue, RTM uses regularization with some parameter assuming the existence of some non-edges in the graph. This is intuitive because we know that a user in the social graph is not interested in becoming a friend with everybody. So, excluding some people and assuming that these people have uniform interest in all topics is reasonable. Taking this into account, the update equation for η is also a regularized regression in this case. The inference continues iteratively sampling topic assignments where η is fixed, and later with given topic assignments updating the η by solving a regularized regression problem.

Experimental Demonstration

This section continues using the `lda` package from the CRAN. We use the pre-processed Cora data set shipped with the `lda` package again, which we also used in the section "Unsupervised Topic Modeling" with the LDA model. Here, we additionally use the links between the documents representing which papers cited others.

In Listing 4.15, we fitted LDA and RTM to this data set. In contrast to LDA, RTM also used the citation links between the research articles as additional data. The topics both LDA and RTM generated look similar. The indices are different, though. This is due to the identifiability problem (that is, the topic about neural networks is indexed at topic 1 in LDA, but at topic 7 in RTM). Though looking at the top words give us some idea about the quality of topics, it is hard to quantify the difference between the two models.

Listing 4.15: Fitting an RTM model to the Cora data set, considering the citation network as the relationships given among the publications. (`rtm_analysis.R`)

```
library(lda)

# Load the data.
data(cora.documents)
data(cora.vocab)
data(cora.titles)
data(cora.cites)                 # Now we also have citations.

# Inspect the data and seeing the explanations.
?cora.documents
head(cora.documents)
length(cora.documents)
head(cora.vocab)
length(cora.vocab)

# The number of topics.
K = 10

# Fit an RTM model.
rtm.model = rtm.collapsed.gibbs.sampler(cora.documents,
        cora.cites,              # Links are input to the model.
        K,
        cora.vocab,
        35,
        0.1, 0.1, 6)
```

```
# Fit an LDA model to the topics.
lda.model = lda.collapsed.gibbs.sampler(cora.documents,
        K,                      # The Number of topics.
        cora.vocab,
        50,                     # The number of iterations.
        0.1,
        0.1,
        compute.log.likelihood=TRUE)

top.words.rtm = top.topic.words(rtm.model$topics, 5, by.score=TRUE)
top.words.lda = top.topic.words(lda.model$topics, 5, by.score=TRUE)

top.words.rtm
        [,1]            [,2]            [,3]            [,4]            [,5]
[,6]
[1,] "learning"  "genetic"       "bayesian"      "decision"   "research"
"markov"
[2,] "networks"  "optimization"  "data"          "tree"       "grant"
"chain"
[3,] "training"  "control"       "belief"        "trees"      "university"
"sampling"
[4,] "network"   "neural"        "model"         "crossover"  "science"
"distribution"
[5,] "features"  "design"        "regression"    "examples"   "supported"
"error"
        [,7]            [,8]            [,9]            [,10]
[1,] "network"   "reinforcement"  "algorithm"  "knowledge"
[2,] "neural"    "genetic"        "queries"    "design"
[3,] "networks"  "algorithm"      "time"       "reasoning"
[4,] "visual"    "fitness"        "learner"    "system"
[5,] "recurrent" "population"     "query"      "planning"


top.words.lda
        [,1]        [,2]        [,3]            [,4]            [,5]
[,6]
[1,] "neural"    "visual"    "logic"         "theory"         "knowledge"
"bayesian"
[2,] "networks"  "network"   "instruction"   "error"          "learning"
"models"
[3,] "network"   "model"     "clauses"       "generalization" "system"
"model"
[4,] "learning"  "neural"    "processor"     "belief"         "reasoning"
"data"
[5,] "recurrent" "system"    "programming"   "learning"       "planning"
"networks"
        [,7]        [,8]            [,9]            [,10]
[1,] "search"    "genetic"        "algorithm"  "research"
[2,] "algorithm" "evolutionary"   "algorithms" "grant"
```

```
[3,]  "decision"   "programming"   "bayesian"   "university"
[4,]  "trees"      "fitness"       "decision"   "science"
[5,]  "genetic"    "population"     "data"       "report"
```

For a better comparison we perform the following experiment: We sample 100 existing edges sampled from the graph. We then predict the probability of the existence of edges using topics and topics proportions generated by both LDA and RTM. Listing 4.16 performs this operation.

Listing 4.16: Predicting the existence of sampled edges in the citation graph using both RTM and LDA. (rtm_analysis.R)

```
# Randomly sample 100 edges.
edges = links.as.edgelist(cora.cites)

# Sample the edges and find the probabilities.
sampled.edges = edges[sample(dim(edges)[1], 100),]
rtm.similarity = predictive.link.probability(sampled.edges,
        rtm.model$document_sums, 0.1, 6)
lda.similarity = predictive.link.probability(sampled.edges,
        lda.model$document_sums, 0.1, 6)

# Compute how many times each document was cited.
cite.counts = table(factor(edges[, 1],
                levels=1 : dim(rtm.model$document_sums)[2]))

# Which topic is most expressed by the cited document.
max.topic = apply(rtm.model$document_sums, 2, which.max)

qplot(lda.similarity, rtm.similarity,
                size=log(cite.counts[sampled.edges[, 1]]),
                colour=factor(max.topic[sampled.edges[, 2]]),
                xlab='LDA predicted link probability',
                ylab='RTM predicted link probability',
                xlim=c(0, 0.5), ylim=c(0, 0.5)) +
        scale_size(name='log(Number of citations)') +
        scale_colour_hue(name='Max RTM topic of citing document')
```

In Figure 4.21 we plot the probabilities generated by LDA and RTM for the 100 edges sampled, respectively. If both models had generated exactly the same probabilities, the 100 sampled edges would have aligned on the diagonal line with a 45-degree angle with both axes. However, the two models generate different scores for almost all edges, and the scores are higher in the case of RTM, showing that topic proportions allow for RTM to make better predictions (note that we trained and predicted on the same data set for the sake of example, but this should otherwise be avoided). This shows that using relational information in topic modeling helped us learn topics that can be more useful for making predictions about links in turn.

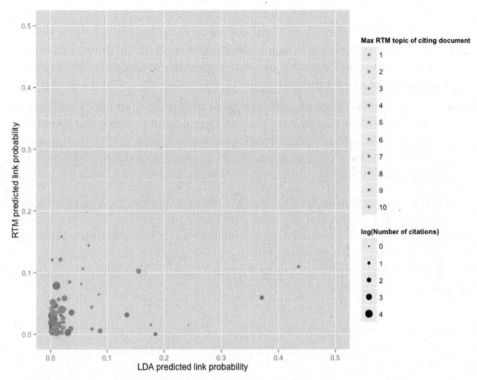

Figure 4.21: Link probabilities by RTM versus LDA for a sample of 100 existing edges.

Summary

Although content is arguably richer than the textual contributions of users (think of images, video, and music, as additional types of content), we turned our attention to text to model and simplify so that we can still discover something about what people are interested in in social media. You saw how to map a sequence of words to topics, and how these topics are represented in a series of posts.

- One of the most basic realizations made is that you can treat text as a collection of words and use the frequencies and co-occurrences of words to find related documents.

- In terms of how popular topics are, you saw that some topics evoke vastly more interest than others, in a long-tailed fashion. This can be expected because they are also the result of human activities, which showed similar characteristics. There are also a large number of differing topics that only a few users show interest in.

- We found a way to cluster individual documents together and to describe the hierarchical structure of the topics. Moreover, you also saw how to use different methods to have soft assignments of documents to topics, because it's likely that actual texts (especially long ones) cover several topics at the same time.

- What people talk about can be used to predict further characteristics of these users, and you saw this in the later part of the chapter. Moreover, using the social links and further covariates can also help in refining our predictions about the content of their conversations and textual contributions to social media.

So far we have considered the characteristics of users, their networks, the role of time, and the properties of the textual content that users produce in social media. Next we turn our attention to how we can practically process the large amounts of data that is normally associated with social media usage, and what kinds of algorithms are at our disposal to make these large-scale tasks computationally feasible.

Processing Large Datasets

The most popular social websites have hundreds of millions to more than a billion users. Logging the actions that users take, such as messaging, adding and removing network relationships, and clicking, rapidly amounts to terabytes (one thousand gigabytes) to petabytes (one million gigabytes) of data. To make a ballpark estimate, with 10 million users spending 10 minutes a day on your site, viewing 10 items per minute, you can expect to record to the logs approximately one billion items a day. If every item costs approximately 1000 bytes to record, you can expect approximately 1 terabyte (TB) of data per day. This rough estimate may even underestimate by an order of magnitude or more if you consider server systems logs. Clearly, keeping any analysis going that can keep up with such a rate of data requires considerable computation.

A single processor cannot keep up with the flow of Internet-scale social data. Analysis must rely on sampling, approximate, or parallel algorithms. This chapter focuses on MapReduce, a model of parallel computation that enables you to structure your problems so that you may harness hundreds or even thousands of computers to process your data faster than it accumulates. The chapter also introduces algorithms to carry out computations with fewer resources than one would see from traditional approaches, while delivering approximations to the expected results within guaranteed bounds.

MapReduce: Structuring Parallel and Sequential Operations

MapReduce is named for two functions from the functional programming literature: *map* and *reduce*. These functions represent the purely parallel (map) and sequential (reduce) parts of a computation. Classically, these are higher-order functions or functions that take functions as arguments. Versions of these two functions are standard in Python as well, and are illustrated in Listing 5.1.

Listing 5.1: An illustration of the MapReduce paradigm with a simple Python example. (`mapreduce_def.py`)

```
def map2(fun, items):
    '''The Map operation in MapReduce.

    Slightly different from Python's standard "map".
    '''
    result = []
    for x in items:
        result.extend(fun(x))
    return result


def reduce(fun, items):
    '''The Reduce operation in MapReduce.'''
    result = None
    for x in items:
        if result is not None:
            result = fun(result, x)
        else:
            result = x
    return result


def times2(x):
    yield 2 * x


def add(x, y):
    return x + y


if __name__ == '__main__':
    print map2(times2, [1, 2, 3])
    # Prints [2, 4, 6]

    print reduce(add, [1, 2, 3])
    # Prints 6
```

Google developed a system based on these two functions called MapReduce. A similar implementation in Java was created at Yahoo called Hadoop, which became hugely popular as an open-source implementation of the approach. An additional twist that MapReduce and Hadoop put in the toy example presented in the preceding code is that the output of the map function is a pair that is considered as a key and a value. Then, rather than a single reduce function seeing all the map output, for each key, the reduce function is applied to the groups of records having the same key.

These systems harness hundreds or thousands of computers, each with some subset of a global filesystem on the local disk. Thus, the first phase, or map phase of the operation, can be performed on computers that are already storing the input data. After the map tasks run, the output is a key-value pair, and all pairs with the same key are sent to the same reducer task.

A toy implementation of something similar to the MapReduce or Hadoop model is presented in Listing 5.2.

Listing 5.2: An illustration of the MapReduce paradigm with a simple Python example. (`keyed_mapreduce.py`)

```python
from mapreduce_def import map2


def keyed_mapreduce(items, mapfn, redfn):
    # Do the Map phase.
    mapped = map2(mapfn, items)
    # Partition values by key.
    keyed_values = {}
    for (key, value) in mapped:
        values = keyed_values.get(key, [])
        values.append(value)
        keyed_values[key] = values
    # Do the reduce phase.
    for (key, values) in keyed_values.iteritems():
        for out in redfn(key, values):
            yield out


def map1(x):
    '''A sample map function.

    Notice that we return something iterable. We can use this to filter,
    or expand the input by returning 0 or more than 1 items, respectively.
    '''
    key = x % 3
    value = x
    yield (key, value)
```

```
def red1(key, values):
    '''A sample reduce function.

    Again, we return something iterable for flexibility.
    '''
    yield (key, sum(values))


if __name__ == '__main__':
    print dict(keyed_mapreduce(range(0, 100), map1, red1))
    # Prints {0: 1683, 1: 1617, 2: 1650}

    print {
        0: sum([x for x in range(0, 100) if x % 3 == 0]),
        1: sum([x for x in range(0, 100) if x % 3 == 1]),
        2: sum([x for x in range(0, 100) if x % 3 == 2])
    }
    # Prints the same as above
```

In this code, there are three phases: the *map phase*, the *partition phase* that is also called the *shuffle phase*, and finally the *reduce phase*. In this example, we use the MapReduce approach to bucket all integers from 0 up to and less than 100 into one of three buckets: Those with no remainder when divided by 3, those with remainder 1, and those with remainder 2. Finally, in each keyed bucket we add up all the values. This is not an exciting or directly applicable calculation, but it is something that should be simple enough to understand. When this example and code make sense, you can ask what other things you might compute in this model.

Counting Words

The canonical example computation is word count. In this problem, you are presented with many lines of text, each has some number of words. The output you want is the number of times each word appears. This simple problem is demonstrated in Listing 5.3.

Listing 5.3: The canonical word count example for MapReduce. (`word_count.py`)

```
import sys

from keyed_mapreduce import keyed_mapreduce


def mapfn(line):
    '''Split up a line into words.'''
    return [(word, 1) for word in line.split()]
```

```
def plus(key, values):
    '''Add up the values for the given key.'''
    yield (key, sum(values))


for wordcount in keyed_mapreduce(sys.stdin, mapfn, plus):
    print wordcount
```

Because the map phase is purely parallel, it could have harnessed any number of processors. Imagine if the list of items had billions of elements and was distributed to hundreds of machines. This example would have worked fine as long as all of them had work to do! This is quite powerful. Although structuring computation this way is not always the most natural, especially at first, after you do so, you can easily express parallel algorithms in a way that allows a system such as Hadoop to exploit the parallelism.

When describing a calculation like this, we often say we "group by" the word, and look at the size of each group, which we implement by making a value of 1, and summing those values in the reducer. The map phase is often preparing a key, which is what we group by, and a value, which is what we aggregate in the reducer.

Though it may seem that counting words is not exciting, we need to use only our imagination to see the relevance of this simple algorithm: Consider each appearance of the word as a vote and see that word counting as vote counting is a form of ranking. If instead of word count, you might want to count links to web pages. Links are written as strings without spaces called uniform resource locators (URLs), which usually begin with "http." Listing 5.4 is a URL counting job.

Listing 5.4: A variation of the word count example, this time counting distinct URLs in HTML files within a given directory. (`url_count.py`)

```
'''
Count the distinct URLs in all the HTML files in a directory.

Run as
python src/chapter5/url_count.py data/mapreduce/url_counting
'''

import sys
from os import listdir
from os.path import isfile, join
from HTMLParser import HTMLParser

from keyed_mapreduce import keyed_mapreduce


# Create a subclass and override the handler methods.
class UrlParser(HTMLParser):
    def __init__(self):
```

```
        HTMLParser.__init__(self)
        self.__urls__ = []

    def urls(self):
        '''Get the URLS from the last feed, and empty the list.'''
        for url in self.__urls__:
            yield url
        self.__urls__[:] = []

    def handle_starttag(self, tag, attrs):
        '''Get the links, which are in anchor <a href=""> tags.'''
        if tag == 'a':
            self.__urls__.extend(
                [url for (href, url) in attrs if href == 'href'])


def urls(fileline):
    '''Return 1 as the value for every URL appearing in the line.'''
    (filename, line) = fileline
    parser.feed(line)
    return [(url, 1) for url in parser.urls()]


def plus(key, values):
    yield (key, sum(values))


def filesource(files):
    '''Creates an iterator of (filename, line) pairs.

    Allows us to operate on many files.
    '''
    for fname in files:
        with open(fname, 'r') as f:
            for line in f:
                yield (fname, line)


if __name__ == '__main__':
    # Each mapper will need an html parser to read the anchor tags.
    parser = UrlParser()

    path = sys.argv[1]
    htmlfiles = [join(path, f) for f in listdir(path)
                    if isfile(join(path, f)) and f.endswith('html')]
    for urlcount in keyed_mapreduce(filesource(htmlfiles), urls, plus):
        print urlcount
```

Notice several things about this URL counting job. First, note that most of the code is spent on issues of preparing the data and identifying URLs, and the MapReduce formalism fades into the background. Indeed, the reduce operation here is the same as the one used in the word count example. The mapper function, which is called `urls`, appears hardly more complex, but that is because the work is delegated to the parser, which in addition to using custom logic in this code also relies on its base functionality coming from the Python standard `HTMLParser`. To describe this algorithm succinctly: Group by URL, and then count the size of each group.

In addition to the map function and the reduce function, a new concept appears in the preceding example, which is an *input function*. This concept is called an InputFormat, Loader, Tap or Source in Hadoop, Pig, Cascading, and Scalding, respectively. Whatever the name, the concept is the same: It provides a way to partition and read the input data so that many independent tasks might simultaneously read the entire dataset. Note in this case, the `filesource` lists all the `.html` files in the directory passed as an argument by the user, and then, for each file and for each line, emits a pair that is the current file name and the current line. You may need to know which file you are reading to determine the output of the computation. For instance, if your URL counter is to be more than a toy, it needs to understand relative links. To do that, you must know the file from which an `href` attribute inside an `a` tag comes. Consider "`blog/2014/01/01.html`"; this does not appear to be a URL, but if that were loaded in the file fetched from the URL `http://example.com`, you see that the full URL is `http://example.com/blog/2014/01/01.html`.

Remember, although word count sounds like a boring computation, many interesting big data computations are just variations of word counts over large data sets.

Skew: The Curse of the Last Reducer

As shown in the MapReduce model, parallelism in the reduce phase is determined by partitioning on the key space. The reduce operation, unless it is an associative operation, is not generally parallelizable. Of course, the complete MapReduce job is not finished until the last reducer is finished. What if one or a few keys have far more values associated with them than the rest? Then, the job can take a long time to complete as just a few reduce tasks process a large number of values and we wait.

Why does this happen? As we have seen, power-law distributions common to networked systems produce a few values that are far larger than the rest. Consider the number that follow Barack Obama on Twitter (the 3rd most popular account with more than 100 million followers as of this writing). You or I might have less than 100 or 1,000 connections. If we run a job that for each user returns the follower who has the most followers, what would that look like?

Assume you have data for three columns: user, follower, and followers' follower count (FFC). The MapReduce job is easy. The map phase does nothing but puts the user into the key and the pair (follower, FFC) into the value. The reduce phase for each key goes through all the values and returns the first follower such that FFC is greater than or equal to all the rest. For @BarackObama, you need to inspect a list of more than 100 million followers. The reducer handling that node takes considerably longer than handling a user with 100 followers. You can call @BarackObama a "hot key" in this context. There are two common approaches to deal with hot keys. Now look at each.

If your reduce operation is *associative*, that is:

$$\text{reduce}(\text{reduce}(a, b), c) = \text{reduce}(a, \text{reduce}(b, c))$$

and *commutative*:

$$\text{reduce}(a, b) = \text{reduce}(b, a)$$

then on the mappers, before you send to the reducers, you can apply the reduce operation partially on records residing on that mapper. This ensures that for each key on each mapper, you send only one value to each reducer, instead of one for every record. There are two common ways to apply the reduce operation on the mapper. The first is to replicate the behavior of the reduce and do a partitioning of the data by key, and then for each key group apply the reduce operation. This approach does not take advantage of the fact that you could reduce values one at a time due the associative and commutative property.

A second approach is to maintain an in-memory hashtable of each key. As a new value comes, directly combine it with the existing value for the key. This creates a memory overhead in proportion to the cardinality of the keyspace on each mapper. If you can't keep all the keys in memory, that is okay, too. Notice that you don't have to reduce *all* the values for a given key because the reducers are still going to combine data from multiple mappers. Thus, it is sufficient to keep a cache that is as big as possible without exhausting memory and simply evict the least often used keys. After you pass over all the data in the mapper, you can flush the entire cache out to the reducers.

Which approach is faster depends somewhat on the data, but many implementations (such as Pig, Cascading, and Scalding) prefer the in-memory cache-based approach. When designing data pipelines, which are scheduled and run regularly, ensuring that commutative reduce operations are run on mappers can be a significant performance enhancement. When using higher level systems (Scalding, Spark, Pig, Impala, and Hive) you generally won't need to worry about it.

Multi-Stage MapReduce Flows

Although many cases can be handled with one map stage and one reduce stage, commonly you need more than one MapReduce stage to do your job. For libraries on top of MapReduce-like systems, you do not need to make this multistage plan by hand. However, it is helpful in writing efficient code and for debugging problems to have some understanding of how higher-level operations in multistage flows are executed.

The nice thing about MapReduce is that there are only three primitives: *mapping* (one item at a time), *partitioning* (reorganizing the data by a key), and *reducing* (for a given partition, processing all the values to produce a new collection of values). These primitives are highly amenable to implementation in a distributed setting, thus the popularity of such systems. This simplest example is the single-stage computation graph of MapReduce using our Python library from before:

```
from keyed_mapreduce import keyed_mapreduce

# Logically: Map -> Partition -> Reduce
result = keyed_mapreduce(load(), mapFn, redFn)
```

To build more complex flows, think about more complex graphs. Of course, some operations don't require reducing. Consider transforming data from one format to another. This is just mapping records of type A into type B:

```
# Here is an identity reduce operation.
# Logically: Map
def identity_reduce(key, values):
    for value in values:
        yield (key, value)

result = keyed_mapreduce(load(), mapFn, identity_reduce)

# We could have skipped the shuffle entirely such as this:
result = (mapFn(x) for x in load())
```

Hadoop supports such map-only jobs without needing to do the key-based shuffle partitioning to a set of reducers. Another extension to our computation graphs is to write data out in one job and read it in the next. This creates effectively the following:

```
# Map -> Partition -> Reduce -> Map -> Partition -> Reduce
result1 = keyed_mapreduce(load(), mapFn1, redFn1)
result2 = keyed_mapreduce(result1, mapFn2, redFn2)
```

This is more powerful but still a linear sequence of operations. A good example of this kind of computation is creating a histogram of frequencies. Rather than counting words, suppose you want to know how many words appear N times for all values of N. Does this curve look like an exponential or a power law, for instance? The snippet in Listing 5.5 shows how this looks in MapReduce.

Listing 5.5: Frequency histogram in MapReduce. (`word_freq_hist.py`)

```python
import sys

from keyed_mapreduce import keyed_mapreduce


def mapfn(line):
    return [(word, 1) for word in line.split()]


def plus(key, values):
    yield (key, sum(values))


def get_count(word_count):
    yield (word_count[1], 1)


# Read the words from stdin.
word_counts = keyed_mapreduce(sys.stdin, mapfn, plus)
# Calculate the histogram of word counts.
histogram = keyed_mapreduce(word_counts, get_count, plus)

# Print the histogram in decreasing order of the frequencies.
for (freq, count) in sorted(histogram, key=lambda x: x[1],
reverse=True):
    print "%i\t%i" % (freq, count)
```

This calculation is the word count computation applied on itself: Group by word, and then count to get the frequencies, and then group by frequency and count. It answers the question: If you randomly select a word uniformly over all the words in the sample, how frequently did that word occur in the corpus? Analyses such as these can be useful in language processing.

Next, consider the two most common (and related) methods to create non-linear flows of computation.

Fan-Out

The first, almost trivial, construct is to read the previous output of a single MapReduce job by not one but two subsequent jobs. Call this a *fork* or a *fan-out*:

```
# We have to save this result (in a list here, but on Hadoop we write to
# disk) to read it twice.
result1 = list(keyed_mapreduce(load1(), mapFn1, redFn1))

# Now that we have saved the output of the first job, read it in two
# different ones.
result2 = keyed_mapreduce(result1, mapFn2, redFn2)
result3 = keyed_mapreduce(result1, mapFn3, redFn3)
```

Examples of this are easy to imagine. As shown in the "Counting Words" section earlier in this chapter, many interesting calculations are identical to word count. Suppose your first job computes clicks on each page in each hour. This is just word count where the words are page-hours on your site. For instance, one word might be "home-20180201T1200" meaning a click on the home page of your site, at the noon UTC on February 1, 2018. Given enough visitor log data, this becomes a big data problem. After you count the visitors for each page-hour, you might want other reductions of this data. Suppose you want to know the top 10 hours for each page. You might also want to report the top pages in each hour. Both later computations are derived from the first and can happen in parallel.

Merging Data Streams

Merging is the reverse of fan-out. This is when two jobs run independently, and then you want to consume both of their outputs in a single job, which is a *merge*.

```
def merge(first, second):
    for item in first:
        yield item
    for item in second:
        yield item

result1 = keyed_mapreduce(load1(), mapFn1, redFn1)
result2 = keyed_mapreduce(load2(), mapFn2, redFn2)
merge(result1, result2)
```

Merge is not difficult to implement when building a system, as in the preceding snippet. On Hadoop it is accomplished with the MultipleInputs class. In most higher-level systems, it is usually a single function.

A common case would be running daily jobs to count the number of clicks on each page each hour. You might run this job once a day after all the logs are in place. You get an output for each page-hour. Now, once a month, you might want to look at the total number of clicks in each of the 24 hours. You don't want to run through all the log data again. Instead, merge the aggregated page-hour counts into one input, remove the date portion, and sum up the counts, as Listing 5.6 illustrates.

Listing 5.6: The total number of clicks per hour of the day over a given month. (`aggregate_month.py`)

```python
import sys

from keyed_mapreduce import keyed_mapreduce


# Assumes the input is a pair (page-datetime, count).
def mapfn(pagedatehour_count):
    (pagedh, count) = pagedatehour_count
    (page, dh) = pagedh.split('-')
    (date, hour) = dh.split('T')
    yield ('%s-%s' % (page, hour), count)


def plus(key, values):
    yield (key, sum(values))


def merge(inputs):
    for inp in inputs:
        for item in inp:
            yield item


input_data0 = [('home-20180201T01', 100)]
input_data1 = [('home-20180203T01', 10)]
input_data2 = [('home-20180214T13', 127)]
input_data3 = [('home-20180222T13', 1)]
input_data4 = [('home-20180228T23', 42)]

# Get the page-hour counts.
mergedin = merge(
    [input_data0, input_data1, input_data2, input_data3, input_data4])
pagehourcounts = keyed_mapreduce(mergedin, mapfn, plus)

for phc in sorted(pagehourcounts, key=lambda x: x[1], reverse=True):
    print '%s\t%i' % phc

# Outputs:
# home-13 128
# home-01 110
# home-23 42
```

So, you've seen MapReduce, fan-outs of MapReduce jobs, and merges of MapReduce jobs. Next, you'll see an interesting application of merges with a special kind of reduce to perform lookups or joins.

Joining Two Data Sources

Joins are a common operation in the database world. Consider two lists of key-value pairs. An inner join, for each key, creates the cross product of values associated with that key. For instance, an inner join of [(0, 1), (0, 2)] and [(0, 3), (0, 4)] would be

$$[(0, (1, 3)), (0, (2, 3)), (0, (1, 4)), (0, (2, 4))].$$

Listing 5.7 shows how this operation is implemented in Python.

Listing 5.7: The definition of an inner join in terms of MapReduce operations. (join_definiton.py)

```python
from itertools import groupby


def get_0(item):
    return item[0]


def get_1(item):
    return item[1]


def to_dict(key_values):
    '''Build a dict of key, and the list of all values for that key.'''
    return dict([(k, list(v)) for (k, v) in
                groupby(sorted(key_values, key=get_0), get_0)])


def concat_map(f, xs):
    '''Map each element x to f(x), which is itself a list, then
    concatenate.'''
    return [y for x in xs for y in f(x)]


def cross_product(list1, list2):
    return [(x, y) for x in list1 for y in list2]


def innerjoin(list1, list2):
    '''Return a list of (k, (v, w)) for all k, v, w such that
    k, v is in list1, and k, w is in list2.'''
    table1 = to_dict(list1)
    table2 = to_dict(list2)

    # Here's is the cross product for each key.
    def key_cross(k):
```

```
        return map(lambda v: (k, v), cross_product(map(get_1, table1[k]),
                                                   map(get_1, table2[k])))

    both_keys = set(table1.keys()) & set(table2.keys())
    return concat_map(key_cross, both_keys)


if __name__ == '__main__':
    print innerjoin(map(lambda x: (x / 2, 2 * x), range(0, 5)),
                    map(lambda x: (x / 2, 3 * x), range(0, 3)))
# Prints:
# [(0, (0, 0)), (0, (0, 3)), (0, (2, 0)), (0, (2, 3)), (1, (4, 6)),
# (1, (6, 6))]
# because 0 / 2 == 1 / 2 == 0, etc.
# so the first list is  [(0, 0), (0, 2), (1, 4), (1, 6), (2, 8)]
#    the second list is [(0, 0), (0, 3), (1, 6)]
# cross product for key 0 = [0, 2] x [0, 3] = [(0, 0), (0, 3), (2, 0),
# (2, 3)]
# cross product for key 1 = [4, 6] x [6] = [(4, 6), (6, 6)]
# cross product for key 2 = [8] x [] = []
```

If there is only one value associated with each key, the join is equivalent to a lookup for that key. For each key, two values from different lists, or tables, are brought together. For instance, one list might be a list of user ids with their click count for this week, and the second list might be the same data from the previous week. If you join on user ID, you can see which users clicked more or less this week than last.

Another example comes from analytics. Suppose you have logs of what your users click. At the time of the logging, you might only know the user ID. Previously, users might have given you some information, such as their interests or from whom they want to see updates. Suppose you want to know, for each interest, how many clicks you receive on a given page. If you know this, you can start to look for correlations and mutual information between some of your variables. An inner join gives exactly this functionality: Join on the user ID, and then group by the interest, page pair, and sum. Incidentally, this pattern of joining, then ignoring the key, and followed by group by sum is exactly matrix multiplication between the *userxpage* matrix and the *userxinterest* matrices, which is a nice exercise work out to confirm your understanding.

Now you have seen what a join is, how it can be implemented in Python, and how to use it in an analytics setting, but how can it be implemented in MapReduce? Although you probably would never need to implement join in MapReduce, as all commonly used frameworks have join built in, it is helpful to understand how it is implemented when debugging performance problems.

A commonly used algorithm is the *sort-merge join*. This algorithm does the cross product in the reducers for each key, by sorting the two value sets. This may seem round-about, but keep in mind, our only primitive operations are map, shuffling, and reduce. We decorate the values so that we can see if they came from the right or left. Then in the reducers, we sort. Although we see items from the left, we save them in memory or on disk. For each item on the right we see, we emit the cross product of that item with all the items from the left. The snippet in Listing 5.8 shows an implementation.

Listing 5.8: The sort-merge join with MapReduce operations. (`mapred_join.py`)

```
from keyed_mapreduce import keyed_mapreduce


def innerjoin_mr(list1, list2):
    # First do the map-only operation to add the decorator to tell
    # right from left.
    def decorate(index):
        '''Return a function that we can use to map and add a
        decorator.'''
        def __dec__(kv):
            (key, value) = kv
            yield (key, (index, value))
        return __dec__

    def identity_reduce(key, values):
        for value in values:
            yield (key, value)

    decleft = keyed_mapreduce(list1, decorate(0), identity_reduce)
    decright = keyed_mapreduce(list2, decorate(1), identity_reduce)

    # Now do the reduce-only operation to cross product on each key.
    def identity_map(x):
        yield x

    def merge(left, right):
        for l in left:
            yield l
        for r in right:
            yield r

    # Here is the cross product algorithm as a reduce function.
    def sort_merge(key, leftandright):
        left_first = sorted(leftandright, key=lambda v: v[0])
        lefts = []
        # We only go through this once:
        for item in left_first:
            value = item[1]
            if item[0] == 0:
                lefts.append(value)
            else:
```

```
        # We have all the lefts, start emitting on the right
        for left in lefts:
            yield (key, (left, value))

    return keyed_mapreduce(merge(decleft, decright), identity_map,
        sort_merge)


if __name__ == '__main__':
    print list(innerjoin_mr(
        map(lambda x: (x / 2, 2 * x), range(0, 5)),
        map(lambda x: (x / 2, 3 * x), range(0, 3))))
# Prints:
# [(0, (0, 0)), (0, (0, 3)), (0, (2, 0)), (0, (2, 3)), (1, (4, 6)),
# (1, (6, 6))]
```

If you look carefully, you can see a potential problem with this algorithm. Note that the parallelism in the reduce phase comes from the fact that each key is processed in parallel. The job is only done when all the reducers are done. So, if some key has many values, it becomes a bottleneck for the entire job. However, in the case of joins, it is even worse: We have a quadratic algorithm going on in the cross product! Consider the problem of finding all pairs of users such that both follow a common user, which is to say they are second neighbors on some social graph. We can do this by joining the list of edges, (A, B) where A is followed by B, by itself. This produces a list like $[(A, (B, C)), (A, (B, D)), ...]$. If A is followed by N users, the cross-product in the join requires emitting N^2 pairs! For a system like Twitter, and a user like @BarackObama who is followed by more than 100 million, this results in more than 10 quadrillion (10,000 trillion) pairs. However, a user followed by only 10 users will emit 100 pairs. This has the potential to create enormous skews in the time required to process the join. The thing to note is that when you see a single or a few reducers taking far longer than the rest in a join, often the problem cannot be solved by simply throwing more reducers in. In such highly skewed cases, the join algorithm needs to change.

Joining Against Small Datasets

The previous section includes a join algorithm that is the default implementation for most MapReduce systems, that uses the key-based shuffle along with a sort-merge to implement joins. This algorithm works great when there are many keys, and each of the keys has roughly the same number of values. Let's look at the communication cost of the sort-merge join. If there are L records on the left and R records on the right, we need to partition and shuffle all $L + R$ records in the reduce phase. But what if one of the data sets is *much* smaller than the other? Let's think about it.

A join follows a specific algebraic formula. If we consider a single key, a join is a cross product on the list:

```
def cross_product(list1, list2):
    return [(x, y) for x in list1 for y in list2]
```

If we define addition on lists as concatenation, which is what Python does when we write `[1, 2] + [3, 4]`, then these two operators obey the distributive law:

$$\text{cross\_product}(a + b, c) = \text{cross\_product}(a, c) + \text{cross\_product}(b, c)$$
$$\text{cross\_product}(a, b + c) = \text{cross\_product}(a, b) + \text{cross\_product}(a, c)$$

If we say that L_i is the partition of the left data that is accessible by mapper i, we see that to get a cross_product:

$$\text{cross\_product}(L, R) = \text{cross\_product}\left(\sum_i L_i, R\right) = \sum_i \text{cross\_product}(L_i, R)$$

This equation means that we could get the same logical result, though distributed across machines differently, if we replicate *all of R* to each of the mappers and locally do a join. How much would this cost?

The sort-merge join costs $L + R$ in the shuffle. Assuming we have M_L mappers holding the L records, the map-side join costs us $M_L \times R$ communication cost. So, that means we should prefer the map-side join when $M_L R < L + R$, or equivalently when $R < \dfrac{L}{M_L - 1}$. Because the number of mappers is often in the range of 100 to 1000 on even larger clusters, as a rule of thumb, if one side of the data is more than 100–1000 times larger than the other side, a map-side join should be considered.

Models of Large-Scale MapReduce

So far you have seen MapReduce jobs, map-only jobs, merges (reading many inputs in one job), fan-outs (reading a single output multiple times), and joins (which are an application of MapReduce with a merge). Describing and organizing many MapReduce jobs can be tedious. If one step in the flow fails, you should consider all the flow to have failed. Because of this, unless jobs are simple, rarely do people directly program MapReduce jobs using the Hadoop APIs these days. Despite that, it is difficult to understand how to design and debug large flows without some understanding of the underlying implementation.

There are two models of MapReduce programming emerging. One style is to make an SQL-like language that is presented to the user and then plan the query into a series of MapReduce jobs that run on the cluster. This style is used by Pig, Hive, Impala, Spark SQL, Cascading-Lingual, and some others. The second style might be called the distributed collections model. Here we consider the cluster to hold distributed collections of items, like lists whose members are stored across many machines. The reduce operations are like building distributed maps that for each key hold a list of values. The libraries supply many of the familiar operations of collections. This is the model of Scalding, Spark, Scoobi, Crunch, Scrunch, and others.

Patterns in MapReduce Programming

The previous section discussed the basic building blocks of MapReduce flows; this section combines them to see how we can implement interesting and useful calculations. First, we discuss static computations. By static, we mean the input is given and the computation produces a single output. For example, given a graph, how many edges does it have? How many nodes have more than 1000 edges? What are the 1000 nodes with the most edges?

Second, in addition to such static calculations, we commonly deal with time. In these cases, we do some computation, and then more input comes in, and we want to make an incremental update to our previous result. A lot of common analytics tasks fall in this category. A common example here is counting the number of clicks into large time buckets, such as weeks. Given our count for this week from yesterday, we produce the new count by adding today's clicks to the count we have so far. More complex examples might be doing an incremental update to a PageRank computation by using yesterday's result as an approximation of today's result to save the effort of starting from scratch. At the far extreme of this category is real-time computation where the computation is updated every time a new event arrives. To get real-time results, we need to use a platform other than Hadoop, such as Storm or Spark, but the MapReduce style of thinking will be valuable still.

This section moves from our toy implementation of raw MapReduce and instead use Scalding and the Scala language, which is a distributed collections model library for programming Hadoop. All these examples are executable.

Static MapReduce Jobs

Many interesting machine learning or ranking algorithms can be expressed as operations on matrices. The columns and rows of these matrices are usually things like user IDs, page IDs, topic IDs, action IDs, and so on. The values of the matrices are sometimes boolean 0/1 values, or for instance floating point numbers that represent probabilities. The first algorithms we consider are matrix math algorithms.

How do we store large matrices? A simple way to store matrices is to write each row as a line in a text file, with a separator, such as comma, space, or tab character, between column values for that row. Because we want to process the file line by line, this approach works well as long as we can keep all the columns in memory at once. As a rule, with more than a few thousand columns, it is generally better to use an alternative approach. One alternative is to write three values in each line: Row number, column number, matrix value. We call this a sparse representation. This potentially increases the storage costs by almost 3x because now instead of writing one value we write three. However, no matter how large the matrix, each line of the file is a constant size. This constant size irrespective of data size is a valuable property when our algorithm needs to grow to web scale. On the other hand, many matrices are in practice mostly filled with zero values. In the sparse representation, we omit lines that have the value of zero. Thus, for many common matrices we get a huge savings by using the sparse representation. Consider a Twitter graph. Let's put the user IDs on the rows and columns. Let's set the matrix value at row R, column C to 1 if R follows C; otherwise to 0. This matrix has hundreds of millions of rows and columns, but for each row and each column, almost all the values are 0 because most people follow only a smaller number of other users. Let's say the average user follows 100 users hypothetically: This means we must store only 100 values in each row. The same savings appears if we consider matrices of web page link structure, product–buyer matrices, or Wikipedia page–editor matrices.

Let's consider how we do math with such a representation. Matrix addition is simple to express: For each row and column, we add the values in that row and column to produce the new value. The snippet in Listing 5.9 shows the code for this.

Listing 5.9: Matrix addition for sparse matrices in Scalding. (`MatrixSum.scala`)

```
0 def job: Execution[Unit] = Execution.getConfig.flatMap { config =>
1   def input(name: String) =
2     TypedPipe.from
         (TypedTsv[(Long, Long, Double)] (config.get(name).get))

3   val leftInput = input("smdma.left")
4   val rightInput = input("smdma.right")
5   val output =
         TypedTsv[(Long, Long, Double)] (config.get("smdma.output").get)

6   (leftInput ++ rightInput)
7     .map { case (row, col, value) => ((row, col), value) }
8     .sumByKey
9     .map { case ((row, col), value) => (row, col, value) }
10    .writeExecution(output)
11 }
```

The Scalding code to implement matrix sum from tab-separated input files is given in this snippet. Let's look at each part of the code. An `Execution` is a box around a set of operations that runs as a series of MapReduce jobs and has a final result. The first line of this code declares a method `job` that returns an `Execution` that, when executed, reads two matrices from disk, performs the algorithm, and writes the result to disk. To know which files to read, we take input arguments from the user. Those are passed in the `Config` when the `Execution` is eventually run.

The code on line 0 means that we are creating a new `Execution` after reading the `Config` into a value called `config`. Lines 1–2 define a short function we reuse. This function defines how to create input `TypedPipes` from a tab-separated value file. `TypedPipe` is the name for what Scalding calls the imaginary collection of values that you can imagine flows through your computation. It is like an unordered list, but parts of that list live on many different computers. Line 2 gets the name from the config and creates a `TypedTsv`, which is a tab-separated value file with three columns, two `Long`s (signed integers less than 64 bits in size) and a `Double` (a floating point number that is stored with 64 bits). We call this input function twice to create the left and right matrices on lines 3 and 4. The user must pass arguments that we selected to be called `smdma.left` and `smdma.right`, but they could have been anything. On line 5 we create an output file to store the results.

The logic begins on line 6. The goal is to get the values from the right and left side for a row and column together and then add them. To accomplish this, we merge the two pipes, group by the row and columns and sum the values. Note, if there is no entry for a given row or column on the right, when we group we get a single value. If there is no entry on either side, we won't find a group with the corresponding row and column preserving the sparse format. To look at the code directly, line 6 handles the merge using `++` between two `TypedPipes`. Line 7 puts the row and column into the key position of a pair and moves the value into the value position. Line 8 calls `sumByKey`, which as the name implies groups by the key, in this case the pair row and column, and then for each group sums the values. On line 9 we unpack the pair format back into the tuple of size three for output. We create the resulting execution by writing the three-tuple into the output file on line 10.

In the `scalding_examples` directory, we can run this example code on our local machine:

```
cd src/chapter5/scalding_examples
./sbt "run --local " \
    "-Dsmdma.left=data/small_matrix1.tsv " \
    "-Dsmdma.right=data/small_matrix2.tsv " \
    "-Dsmdma.output=test"
# Select the "MatrixSum" class to run.
```

Now if you inspect the lines of the newly written file called `test`, it should be the element-wise sum of the values in two input files. Running jobs locally on small data sets is a great way to check the correctness of the algorithm and spot check performance before you scale it up to gigabytes and terabytes of data on tens or hundreds of machines.

At this point, even if all the Scala code is not 100 percent clear to you yet, you should see how the structure of the algorithm matches what we developed in our toy MapReduce implementation. We made use of merges, a group by, and the most common reduce operation that is numeric sum. Next, we use a concept not used in the previous algorithm: join.

After matrix addition, you might want to do matrix multiplication. The basic approach of multiplication is related to the interesting graph applications that follow, such as finding second neighbors, finding triangles, and computing PageRank. Let's see what the matrix multiplication algorithm looks like in Scalding. To understand matrix multiplication, you need to understand dot products first. A dot product of two vectors is the sum of the point-wise products. For instance, dot([1, 2, 3], [4, 1, 2]) = 1 × 4 + 2 × 1 + 3 × 2 = 12. The matrix product of two matrices **A**, **B** returns a matrix whose value at row i, column j is exactly the dot product of row i from **A** and column j from **B**. This formula can be written as $M_{i,j} = \sum_{k} A_{i,k} B_{k,j}$. To translate that into MapReduce, we can see that for each k we do a multiplication, then to a sum for each i and j. We already saw sums. To do the multiplication we use a join. We set up the input and output like we did in the previous example. Let's focus on the rest of the job in Listing 5.10.

Listing 5.10: Multiplying matrices in Scalding with a join. (`MatrixProduct.scala`)

```
0 val leftByCol = leftInput.map { case (r1, c1, v1) => (c1, (r1, v1)) }
1 val rightByRow = rightInput.map { case (r2, c2, v2) =>
    (r2, (c2, v2)) }

2 leftByCol.join(rightByRow)
3   .map { case (joiningKey, ((r1, v1), (c2, v2))) =>
    ((r1, c2), v1 * v2) }
4   .sumByKey
5   .map { case ((row, col), value) => (row, col, value) }
6   .writeExecution(output)
```

The first step is to take the three tuples from the previous example and prepare them as key-values. The key we want first is the join key between the left and the right. As our formula indicates, we want to connect the kth column of the left with k^{th} row of the right. We do this by assigning the join key to the column on the left and the row on the right. We move the rest of the data into the value position of the key-value pair. This is shown in lines 0 and 1. We execute the join on line 2. The default Scalding join is an inner join. This is what we want because if one value or the other is absent, that means the same as zero, and zero times anything is zero. Line 3 shows where we do the multiplication. Each element of the `TypedPipe` at that point carries the join key, which is *k* as we called above, the values from the left and the values from the right. We want to just keep the row `r1` and column `c2` numbers from the left and right, respectively, along with the product of the two values. Recall that join is a kind of a cross product that can greatly expand the size of the data. In this example, values in the `r1, c2` pair may be repeated many times. We need to sum them together. Lines 4 to 6 are identical to Lines 8 to 10 in the previous example in Listing 5.9.

We can run this example locally with the following command:

```
cd src/chapter5/scalding_examples
./sbt "run --local " \
        "-Dsmdma.left=data/small_matrix1.tsv " \
        "-Dsmdma.right=data/small_matrix2.tsv " \
        "-Dsmdma.output=test"
# Select the "MatrixProduct" class to run.
```

When we run this, if we look carefully, we can see that there are two MapReduce jobs in the product code: The first does the join and the second does the sum.

Now let's turn our attention to networks or graphs. Like the canonical MapReduce example of word count, suppose we want to do follower count. How do we count how many followers each user has? Why would we want to know this? One common reason is for rankings and recommendations. A simple approach to recommendation is to recommend the most popular items. A second reason to know follower count is to report to users how many they can reach, which is an important metric for people using social systems for publishing.

Let's assume that our input data uses a sparse format like we did with the matrices. For a graph, that means we have a file with two values in it: The source of the edge and the destination of the edge. Put another way, the follower is in the first column and the followee is in the second column. This is classic MapReduce with which by now we are quite familiar (Listing 5.11).

Listing 5.11: Determining the degrees (number of followers) of users in a social follow graph. (`DegreeCount.scala`)

```
0 edges.map { case (from, to) => (to, 1L) }
1   .sumByKey
2   .writeExecution(output)
```

The first thing we do is discard the follower ID. When counting followers, you need to know only how many; you don't need to identify the nodes. Line 0 discards the follower and puts the followee in the key position. In the value position, we put the number `1L` that instructs Scala to use a 64-bit number here. (Hint: For big data, it is best to always use `Longs` to count things because normal integers in many languages can count only to a few billion). Line

1 triggers the reduce that sums all the 1s to create a total count. Finally, we write it to an output expecting two columns of Longs. You can run this example with

```
cd src/chapter5/scalding_examples
./sbt "run --local -Dsmdma.edges=data/small_graph.tsv " \
"-Dsmdma.output=test"
# Select the "DegreeCount" class to run.
```

As we know, word count is hugely important. Again, it rears its head: Degree count is word count by another name. If you squint you might see how our matrix sum example is close to this degree count. We put a 1 everywhere there is a follower-followee row-column pair, and then we sum the columns of that matrix to produce a vector. Not everyone prefers that matrix representation of such problems, but it's often valuable to look at a problem from different perspectives.

Just as degree count is similar to matrix sum, the problem of finding second neighbors on a graph is similar to matrix multiplication. The algorithm is presented in the book's example source code as SecondNeighbors.scala, and in Listing 5.12.

Listing 5.12: Determining the degrees (number of followers) of users in a social follow graph. (SecondNeighbors.scala)

```
0  edges
1    .map { case (from, to) => (to, from) }
2    .join(edges)
3    .map { case (middleNode, (from, to)) => (from, to) }
4    .distinct
5    .writeExecution(output)
```

As before, we omit discussion of the common code to read the input and set up the output as it is virtually identical in all these examples. In line 1 and line 2, we reverse the order of an edge. The idea here is we want $A \to B \to C$ triples. We group by B in the previous equation or "to" in line 1 and perform an inner join to find all pairs of nodes that connect via that node. After the join, we can disregard the middle node we pass through: It is irrelevant when considering the second neighbors. Because there may be more than one path between a pair of nodes, we must distinct the pairs on line 4. Finally, as always, we write out the result.

Second neighbors can be great candidates for recommendations as well. If A and B are linked, and B and C are linked, often A and C will be related, as you saw in the "Capturing Correlations: Triangles, Clustering, and Assortativity" section in Chapter 2. Can you think how to change the previous algorithm if we want to know how many paths there are between the pairs of nodes? On line 4, rather than distincting the nodes, we could again use our old friend word count: Group by the pairs, count the number of paths. With this, we could build a recommendation so that we recommend to each user the second neighbors as long as there are enough paths between them. This is sometimes called "triangle closing," because if the user makes an edge to a second neighbor, a triangle in the graph will be created.

In the preceding example, we have seen an important fact: If we want to walk edges in a graph, the way to do it is with a join. We must be careful with highly skewed graphs. Some nodes may be hubs through which many or even most of the paths pass. If we run this algorithm on such a graph, we find a few of the reducers executing the join run for much longer than the rest. The common signature of this problem is when one looks at the reducer time, there is a high variance across the nodes. When you see this, if the run time is not acceptable, a skew-join technique must be used. Many high-level MapReduce libraries support such a primitive. However, unless you deal with extremely large and highly skewed graphs, it might be better to keep solutions simple as long as possible.

As mentioned, second neighbors are useful because we could recommend a connection. That connection creates triangles in the graph. How can we find triangles? We have seen some hints. Joins are walks in the graph. A triangle exists when your second neighbor is also a first neighbor. One approach is to generate all the pairs, as we did previously, and then take one more step on the graph to see if we can get back to the start. Let's look at the algorithm here in Listing 5.13.

Listing 5.13: Finding triangles in a follow graph. (`Triangles.scala`)

```
0  edges.map { case (from, to) => (to, from) }
1    .join(edges)
2    .map { case (middle, (start, end)) => (end, (start, middle)) }
3    .filter { case (end, (start, middle)) =>
4      (end > middle) && (end > start)
5    }
6    .join(edges)
7    .filter { case (end, ((start, middle), start1)) =>
8      (start1 == start)
9    }
10   .map { case (end, ((start, middle), start1)) => (start, middle,
         end) }
11   .writeExecution(output)
```

You can run this example with

```
cd src/chapter5/scalding_examples
./sbt "run --local -Dsmdma.output=triangles " \
       "-Dsmdma.edges=data/small_graph_with_triangles.tsv"
# Select the "Triangles" class to run.
```

The first two lines are identical to the second neighbor algorithm. After we create a path of length two, we need to take the next step. On line 2, we put the end of the length 2 path into the key. If we are not careful, we could count a triangle three times: Starting at each of the nodes. To prevent this, we choose the representation where the end node has the biggest value. On line 4 we filter so that we keep only 2-paths where the end is bigger than the middle and the start. It is important to do that before the last join so that we don't have to shuffle data that we will filter later. This is worth reiterating: Always filter data as soon as you logically can. Some optimizers can help you, but currently it is hard for optimizers to beat a human's understanding of the algorithm to maximize performance.

By line 5 we have prepared candidate triples, and on line 6 we take one more step. What we are left with is a bit complicated. See it on line 7: The key is the third node (called `end`), and the value is an element of the cross product of all the length-2 paths to the `end` with all the nodes `end` can reach in one hop (which we call `start1` on line 7). Each row represents a triangle if and only if `start` == `start1`, which is exactly the filter we apply on line 8. After we have the data we want, on line 10, we prepare it into a tuple of size 3 for writing on line 11.

By now we have covered quite a few common graph computations in a MapReduce setting, but all of them share the feature that the steps do not depend on the input data. Put another way, no matter what the input, the algorithm is the same. Some algorithms, especially some approximate or randomized algorithms, do not have this property. In the next section, you see two examples of iterative MapReduce algorithms that run until some termination criterion is met.

Iterative MapReduce Jobs

Often the algorithm we would like to execute on our large datasets is expressed in terms of iterations—in other words, consecutive steps in a loop that take as input some or all of our data, and also, the results of the algorithm's run from the previous step. We normally stop the run of the process when some accuracy or running time criterion is met. We're going to focus on some of these algorithms in the following sections.

PageRank for Ranking in Graphs

One of the earliest "big data" algorithms was PageRank, which Google used as a feature to rank searches. The fundamental problem with web search is that there are so many hits for almost every query that ranking is immensely important for the search to have utility. The idea of PageRank is to model the web surfer as someone that randomly clicks one link on a page, or with a small probability randomly jumps to a page on the web. If this random surfer keeps following this process for long enough (in practice, not that long, as such random processes are known to converge quickly), then we can associate a probability of walking to each node no matter where the walker starts. A simple search engine could search for pages matching a query string and then rank them by the probability that such a random walker would reach them. Because authoritative sites are likely to have a lot of incoming links, a random walker has a higher chance of walking to them.

Because we can't walk infinitely long to compute PageRank, we instead update the rank of each node at each step of the algorithm. After each step, we look to see how much the squared error has changed with respect to the previous step. After it drops below a threshold, we terminate the algorithm. One minor difference from the probability description of the algorithm is that we generally prefer to normalize so that the sum of all the PageRanks is N, the number of nodes, rather than 1. This is so that as the network changes in size, the rank of individual nodes, on average, does not change. Also, we avoid having to compute the total normalization although that is a trivial cost compared to the rest of the algorithm.

At this point, it is important to understand something about what Scalding calls an `Execution`. An `Execution` is a set of MapReduce jobs that can be run and produce some kind of result. The useful thing about `Execution`s is that they have a method that for historical reasons is called `flatMap` but might be called `readAndThen` because what it does is this: Given one `Execution`, you can read the value it would produce and then create a new `Execution`, and that whole process can be considered yet a larger set of MapReduce operations, which is to say can be an `Execution`. We use this `flatMap` (`readAndThen`) to create `Execution`s that can loop.

The main rank propagation step is written in Listing 5.14.

Listing 5.14: The rank propagation step of the PageRank algorithm. (`PageRank.scala`)

```
def doPageRankStep(alpha: Double, graph: TypedPipe[(Long, (Long, Int))],
    oldPR: TypedPipe[(Long, Double)]):
  Execution[TypedPipe[(Long, Double)]] =
    graph.outerJoin(oldPR)
      .map {
        case (from, (Some((to, fromDegree)), Some(weight))) =>
          (to, weight / fromDegree)
        case (from, (Some((to, fromDegree)), None)) => (to, 0.0)
        case (from, (None, _)) => (from, 0.0)
      }
      .sumByKey
      .map { case (node, newWeight) => (node, (1.0 - alpha) *
        newWeight + alpha) }
      .forceToDiskExecution
```

This function takes three inputs: `alpha`, `graph`, and `oldPR`. `alpha` is the probability the walker randomly jumps. `graph` represents the graph in the shape `(from, (to, degreeOfFrom))`. Note, we need to know the out-degree of each "from" node to split the rank to each of its neighbors. `oldPR` is the page rank at the previous step: For each node that we store as a `Long` integer, we have a `Double` holding the rank. The first thing we do is an `outerJoin` of the graph and the previous PageRank. An outer join is a join that gives some value for every key. If one side is missing, it is like instead a special value called `None` was present. Otherwise, all values are wrapped so that *x* becomes *Some(x)* meaning that it was present. Why might nodes be absent? Some nodes might have no out-degrees. There are pages that don't point anywhere. As for the `oldPR` we expect all nodes to have a score previously, so this code is a bit defensive in using a full outer join. A careful algorithm could instead use a right join.

After the join, we have one of three cases:

1. the `from` node points somewhere and had a prior rank (called `weight` in this code);

2. `from` points somewhere but previously had no rank value;

3. the node points nowhere.

In the first case, on average 1 / `fromDegree` of the from node's weight will be sent to each node it points to. So, we omit the pair `(to, weight / fromDegree)` in that case. In the second case, `from` has no weight that we interpret as 0.0; clearly each node it points to gets an additional 0.0 weight. Last is the case in which `from` points to no node. We want to make sure we don't drop nodes from the dataset, so in this case we omit `from` in case no one is pointing at `from`.

For each destination, we add up the weights with the `sumByKey` call. Let's not forget the random jump. With probability `alpha` a random jump is executed so with probability (1 − `alpha`) we keep our old rank and though the explanation is a bit more complex, and the probability theory beyond what is needed to understand the algorithm, it contributes `alpha` to each node. The last command, `forceToDiskExecution` is a way to tell Scalding this block should be executed before proceeding to the next phase.

Look back at the algorithm for the matrix product in Listing 5.10. Notice it is a join followed by a group and sum. That's the same algorithm we see in PageRank, and no wonder: This algorithm can be thought of as multiplying a vector of the previous PageRank by a transition matrix given by the graph. But so far, we have just seen one step. We can't run the algorithm forever; so instead we set a threshold on the mean-squared difference between the two most recent results. How do we compute the mean-squared difference? The equation is simple: $\sum_i (v_i - w_i)^2$ for two vectors *v* and *w*.

To compute mean-squared in MapReduce, we need a join to bring the components with the same index together. Because we use a sparse representation, where zero values may be omitted, we must deal with the case in which one or the other side is missing a value. An outerJoin is used here and gives us an Option value, which as we saw earlier with rightJoin may be None or Some. We do the outerJoin on line 2 in Listing 5.15. After the outerJoin we do the subtraction, taking care to replace empty values with 0.0 using .getOrElse or the Option values. On line 5, we return a tuple so that we can see the number of non-zero elements as well as the sum-of-squared-difference, which we sum. On line 8, we see a new Scalding privative, called toOptionExecution, which gives us the computation of a single value (in this case the total sum done on line 7) wrapped in an Execution. If we sum no items, we get None so that is why this must give you an Option value. On lines 10–11, we handle both the case of the missing (None) and present (Some) cases. The result of this function is an Execution that produces a double precision number, which is the mean squared difference between oldPR and newPR, the two most recent PageRank vectors for all the nodes.

Listing 5.15: Computing the mean-squared difference between the page rank vectors of the PageRank steps. (PageRank.scala)

```
0 def computeRMSError(oldPR: TypedPipe[(Long, Double)],
1   newPR: TypedPipe[(Long, Double)]): Execution[Double] =
2     oldPR.outerJoin(newPR)
3       .map { case (node, (oldv, newv)) =>
4         val err = (oldv.getOrElse(0.0) - newv.getOrElse(0.0))
5         (1L, err * err)
6       }
7       .sum
8       .toOptionExecution
9       .map {
10        case None => 0.0
11        case Some((n, err)) => err / n
12      }
```

We have the main pieces in place now. As in most of our examples, we will skip the code that reads the input graphs as it is similar to previous examples, but it is, of course, included in the code that accompanies this text. Instead the snippet in Listing 5.16 focuses on the newest aspect of this algorithm: the looping.

Listing 5.16: The main iterative loop of the PageRank algorithm. (PageRank.scala)

```
0 def run(graph: TypedPipe[(Long, (Long, Int))],
1         oldPR: TypedPipe[(Long, Double)]): Execution[Unit] = for {
2   newPR <- doPageRankStep(alpha, graph, oldPR)
3   err   <- computeRMSError(oldPR, newPR)
```

```
4   unit  <- if (err < threshold) newPR.writeExecution(output) else
        run(graph, newPR)
5 } yield unit
```

This shows the main looping code for PageRank. As is common in functional code, Scalding code generally uses no mutable variables. To execute a loop without a mutable variable, we write a recursive function. Secondly, the previous example uses a special syntax in Scala, the *for* syntax, to combine multiple Executions. We start the loop off on line 0 with the graph and an input PageRank vector. Initially, the vector can have the value of 1.0 for each node, or it could be the result from yesterday's run, with all the new nodes initialized to 1.0. On line 2 we take one step on the PageRank algorithm we discussed earlier. The newPR <- syntax means run the Execution and take the result and put it in the value newPR. On line 3 we take oldPR, which was passed in, and the newPR that we just computed and compute the mean-squared difference. Using the for-syntax err <- we take the result of the computeRMSError execution and put it in the value err. Lastly, we check, on line 4, if the error is below the threshold, and if it is, we write the newPR to the output; otherwise, we call the function again with the newPR as the argument. Both writeExecution and run return Executions holding a value of type Unit. Unit is a special type that has only one value so we don't care what it is. Unit in Scala is somewhat like void in C or Java, except that it has a value associated with it. Unit is like boolean, which has one of two values, true or false, but Unit has only one value which is written as () in Scala. Because all for-expressions must yield some value, on line 5 we return the unit we got on line 4. (But as we mentioned, there is only one possible value here.)

Now you have seen how to implement a looping algorithm on MapReduce. The idea is to do some fixed number of MapReduce jobs and then check some condition to see if you need to continue creating more MapReduce jobs. You can run the PageRank example using the following:

```
cd src/chapter5/scalding_examples
./sbt "run --hdfs -Dsmdma.pagerank.output=prout " \
      "-Dsmdma.pagerank.graph=data/small_graph.tsv"
# Select the "PageRank" class to run.
```

k-means Clustering

PageRank is a great algorithm to generate features useful for ranking in social systems. It can be of use for recommending top users in each topic or for filtering spammers that have a low reputation from the entire graph. Another useful algorithm that involves iteration is *k*-means clustering. In *k*-means clustering, we fix the number of clusters *k* we would like to find, and we cluster vectors around the centers of those clusters. At each step, we move each vector to the cluster whose centroid the vector is closest to. The algorithm stops when no vectors change clusters for an entire step. This algorithm is conceptually simple, but expressing it in a MapReduce style is a bit of work.

Like Python, Scala values have a type associated with them such as `Int`, `String`, `Double`, `List`, and so on. Unlike Python, Scala must infer the type of all values when you compile your code. This can be a bit of frustration sometimes, but for big data computations that will take hours or sometimes days to run, the type-safety can be a huge boon to productivity. In the following code snippet, we make some type aliases so that our type declarations are not so verbose in later snippets in this section. Let's look at each declaration and what they mean for our algorithm.

```
type Vect = Map[String, Double]
type LabeledVector = (Int, Vect)
type ClusterPipe = ValuePipe[List[LabeledVector]]
type PointPipe = TypedPipe[(String, LabeledVector)]
```

Because we are dealing with sparse vectors that often have most of their values as 0, we define our `Vect` type as a `Map[String, Double]`, which means it has a `String` key to represent the non-zero dimensions and the value space is over doubles. There are at least two other ways to do this. We could have defined `Vector` to be an `Array[Double]`, which is to use a dense vector. This can save space if we don't have many zero elements in our vectors. Alternatively, we could make the vectors themselves distributed and not store the whole vector in a single row of data; instead, we would store at most some upper-bound size that could fit in memory. Such a distributed representation significantly complicates the description of the algorithm, so we will not use it here. However, a careful student of the algorithms presented in this section should generalize this algorithm if the non-zero vector size does eventually reach the 10s of millions that would overwhelm this representation.

When we have our `Vect` type, we need to put a cluster label on each vector. For that we can use a tuple of `Integer` and `Vect` and call it `LabeledVector`. There are two parts to the data we are computing: Clusters and the set of vectors. For the clusters, we just have a `List` of `LabeledVectors` but because we must compute that `List` in MapReduce, Scalding puts such a value in a box called a `ValuePipe` (value because it is a single item; pipe because that is what Scalding calls data streams that will be computed in the cluster). Lastly, we have the set of all the vectors we want to cluster. We call this type the `PointPipe` in the preceding snippet, and it consists of a name for each vector we are clustering and the `LabeledVector` representing the vector. We keep a name with each vector because usually the numeric representation might not be the whole story.

Listing 5.17 is the function definition. We take the current set of clusters and the current labeled vectors and return an `Execution` that can tell us three things: The number of vectors that changed in this step, the new centroids, and the new labeled vectors. Let's look at each portion of the algorithm.

Listing 5.17: *k*-means clustering: Finding the closest cluster for a vector. (`KMeans.scala`)

```
def kmeansStep(clusters: ClusterPipe,
  points: PointPipe): Execution[(Long, ClusterPipe, PointPipe)] = {
  val next = points.leftCross(clusters)
    .map {
      case ((name, (oldId, vector)), Some(centroids)) =>
        val (id, newcentroid) = closest(vector, centroids)
        (name, id, vector, oldId)

      case (_, None) => sys.error("There were no centoids")
    }
    .forceToDiskExecution
```

The first portion of this algorithm computes the closest centroid for each vector and returns that with an old cluster ID, `oldId`, so we can see how many vectors move. We use the Scalding function `leftCross`, which is a cross product that attaches the `ValuePipe` argument to each value on the left side, in this case the vectors contained in `points`. After checking that the centroids do indeed exist, the code gets the name, `oldId`, and vector from the `PointsPipe`, and then uses the normal Euclidean norm to find the closest centroids in our `List`. Finally, we return the `name` of the vector, the new `id`, the `vector` itself, and the `oldId`. Note: This `leftCross` is a broadcast operation that replicates all the clusters to all the nodes holding vectors. Because the number of clusters should be much smaller than the number of vectors, this scales fine. With this we have done the main logical step, but we need to compute three things, as shown in the following snippet: The number of vectors that changed, the new centroids, and discard the `oldId`s from the vectors. Listing 5.18 shows the next step of the algorithm: counting how many vectors have changed clusters.

Listing 5.18: *k*-means clustering: Counting how many vectors have changed clusters. (`KMeans.scala`)

```
// How many vectors changed?
val changedVectors: Execution[Long] =
  for {
    pipe <- next
    changes <- (pipe.collect { case (_, newId, _, oldId) if (newId !=
      oldId) => 1L }
    // sum on a pipe adds everything in that pipe
    .sum
    .toOptionExecution)
  } yield (changes.getOrElse(0L))
```

This code uses the Scala `for` syntax to reach inside the `Execution` in the next value and get the pipe holding the results. From that pipe, we collect only the cases in which the IDs have changed, and for each one of those we emit a `1`. We sum these up to get the total count, and, because there might not be any, we get the computation as an `Option` (`toOptionExecution`). If the changes are empty, that means there were no changes at all, or 0 changes. This snippet is unwrapping to `Executions`. The first is `next`, which we discussed earlier. The second is counting the number of changed vectors. That is why there are two "unwrapping" left arrows (`<-`). Next we need to compute the new centroids by averaging all the vectors together. That is shown in Listing 5.19.

Listing 5.19: *k*-means clustering: Computing the new centroids. (`KMeans.scala`)

```scala
val nextCluster: Execution[ClusterPipe] =
  for {
    pipe <- next
    clusters = ComputedValue(pipe
      .map { case (_, newId, vector, oldId) => (newId, vector) }
      .group
      .mapValueStream { vectors => Iterator(centroidOf(vectors)) }
      // Now collect them all into one big
      .groupAll
      .toList
      // discard the "all" key used to group them together
      .values)
  } yield clusters
```

Again, we use the `for` syntax to unwrap the execution we defined in `next`. To compute the new centroids, we group by the cluster ID (`newId`) and then we take all the values and reduce them down to one. In Scalding, when you take an `Iterator` from the values to an `Iterator` of results, that is called `mapValueStream` in Scalding to indicate that you are mapping an entire stream of values onto another stream. Here the resulting stream has only one value, which is the centroid. We call a function, `centroidOf` that is just doing the element-wise average and is included in the source code for this book. All that is left is to reformat the vectors into the form needed to be input to the function, as shown in Listing 5.20.

Listing 5.20: *k*-means clustering: Preparing the results for the next iteration. (`KMeans.scala`)

```scala
val nextVectors: Execution[PointPipe] =
  for {
    pipe <- next
    nextVs = pipe.map { case (name, newId, vector, oldId) => (name,
      (newId, vector)) }
  } yield nextVs

Execution.zip(changedVectors, nextCluster, nextVectors)
```

Yet again, we use the `for`-syntax to unwrap the execution we defined in "next". After we have the pipe result from `next`, we have a tuple with four items: Vector `name`, the new cluster ID (`newId`), the `vector` itself, and the previous cluster ID (`oldId`). We can discard `oldId` and produce a tuple in the format expected by our `PointPipe` type, which is as a reminder: `(String, (Int, Vect))`. The last line of the `kmeans` function is to combine the three `Executions` we made into one, which is done by the `zip` function on `Execution`.

So, we have seen how to convert two non-trivial iterative algorithms into something that can be done in a MapReduce style by using the composable `Execution` type that Scalding offers. The main challenges in such algorithm design are bringing the right data together in the right way. As we saw in these examples, this is often done using a join. All the communication inherent in the algorithm must be done via the shuffle and reduce. As we saw earlier in the chapter, even joins are implemented this way. In the *k*-means example, you can imagine a processor working on each cluster to compute the new centroid. When we group by the cluster ID and shuffle, this is analogous to sending a message to a node with that cluster ID with the payload being the list of values. Hopefully, this section has given you some useful ideas on how to structure large computations using a MapReduce style.

Incremental MapReduce Jobs

If you plan to run an algorithm repeatedly, say, for instance, you want the latest PageRank all the time; an incremental algorithm can be a big savings. By incremental, we mean that with some incremental amount of new data, we do a somewhat proportionally incremental amount of work to incorporate that data. In the case of PageRank, as we saw in the previous section, the algorithm iterates using a constant graph to update a converging vector. Suppose you have run this algorithm to convergence yesterday. Today, you can take the newest graph, which is probably only slightly different than it was yesterday and start the algorithm converging from yesterday's solution. In the case of PageRank, we need to first do a join to initialize all new nodes with a rank of 1, because the total sum of all the ranks should be the number of nodes.

In *k*-means, we can do something similar. Using the cluster definitions from the previous output, we can assign all the new vectors to the cluster to which they are closest, and then start the iteration from there. This means we can generally converge much faster, especially if the clusters are robust over time. In such cases, it is likely that only one or two steps of the algorithm will suffice.

For such iterative and converging algorithms, the first run might be expensive, but as long as the updates are done frequently and with little incremental change of the input data, the cost can be manageable.

Temporal MapReduce Jobs

One of the most common applications of MapReduce is to count events that happen in some system over a period. For each hour, for each web page from each country, how many views, clicks, logins, and others were there? This kind of job builds dashboards to keep you aware of what happens in a system with many users and to summarize what happened in the past. If the counts change dramatically, something unusual is going on, for example, a failed upgrade or a news event that directed more than the normal number of users to your site. This is a straightforward word-count style of a job: One needs only to decide what the words are. We will go beyond the obvious generalization of word count to look at how we can make queries more efficient and aggregate values other than numbers.

Recall that the "Skew: The Curse of the Last Reducer" section earlier in this chapter presented the definition for associative: $fn(fn(a, b), c) = fn(a, fn(b, c))$ and commutative: $fn(a, b) = fn(b, a)$ functions. Addition, multiplication, and max and min are examples, but there are many more. When we aggregate a stream of events by hour, and if we later want to know the aggregation over a window of time, we can use the fact that addition is associative to look up the values for each hour and add them up quickly. Figure 5.1 shows how associativity alone is enough to aggregate a function over a range of time quickly. Therefore, keeping periodic associative aggregations is a useful trick in answering time range queries.

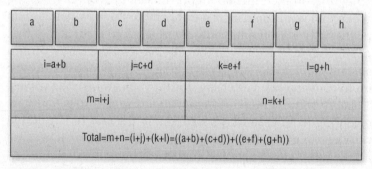

Figure 5.1: Associativity functions, here written as +, allow aggregation over a range of size T with time complexity $O(\log T)$ assuming maximal parallelism

Addition is certainly the associative operation most commonly used in aggregation. By aggregating over minutes, hours, days, weeks, years, and so on, we can quickly compute range. To see how this works, imagine we have aggregated some base unit of time T in exponentially increasing sized blocks. So, we have N aggregations for every bucket of size T, $2T$, $4T$, $8T$, $\ldots$, $2^{(N-1)}T$.

Now, we want the aggregation over a range $[x, y)$ by which we mean the range including x but less than and not including y. How do we compute this? The idea is to cover the range with the fewest buckets. For instance, if $N = 3$ and $T = 1$, then we have bucket sizes of 1, 2, 4. If we want to query the range $[3, 12)$ we could cover it with 9 buckets of size 1 starting at 3. But because we also have buckets of size 2, we could do 4 buckets: $[4, 6)$, $[6, 8)$, $[8, 10)$, $[10, 12)$, and then include one bucket of size 1: $[3, 4)$. That's 5 queries rather than 9. Of course, we also have buckets of size 4, so we could have instead used just 3 buckets: $[3, 4)$, $[4, 8)$, $[8, 12)$. This is the core idea behind "rollups" or data cubing. These two terms are used for similar ideas. A *rollup* refers to a prematerialization of queries that helps you answer a large set of queries faster. *Data cubing* often refers to a specific way of creating those prematerializations.

Rollups and Data Cubing

The simplest example might be aggregating the number of events for each hour. But as we just saw, if we later, after reading through our giant logs, want to know the number of events for 2 days, we would query 48 keys representing each hour that we had aggregated. In this example, there is only one key: Time. In a real system, you might have several items in a key tuple: For instance time and geographic area. If we make a data cube with these three key types, we would put each event in 4 buckets: (*time, geo*), (*time, None*), (*None, geo*), (*None, None*). If we want to query for a certain time in all geos, we read our aggregated value for (*time, None*). If we want all times in a certain geo, we read (*None, geo*). Here *None* used as a wildcard value that matches all keys. Each key "point" becomes a hypercube, and thus the name *data cube*. In this case, we started with a 2-dimensional key and resulted in a 2^2-dimensional key. If we had 3 dimensions, we would expand out into $8 = 2^3$ dimensions. For an n-tuple key we need to put each bucket in 2^n dimensions. Obviously, this approach is not scalable in the size of the tuple of the key. Because a data cube is only an optimization to reduce reads, we could always choose to not materialize some of the expansion if that wildcard is not needed. For instance, it makes little sense to expand gender this way because there might only be two keys to begin with. But country, however, might have more than 100 values already, so adding one more key will not consume much more space in your storage.

To show how this works, what follows is an example of a data cubing job. For this example, we use the Amazon reviews finefoods data set, which is a collection of the Amazon reviews for its category of products known as "Fine Foods." (The data can be obtained from the Stanford Network Analysis Platform library, `https://snap.stanford.edu/data/web-FineFoods.html`, and is also automatically prepared when running the `download_all.sh` script as described in this book's Introduction.) This data set has many keys: `product/productId`, review/userId, review/profileName, review/helpfulness, review/score, review/time, review/summary, and review/text. We can use the review/time field to build a rollup of distribution of score over time. How have reviews grown in time? Do people make reviews on some days more than others? The rollup lets us quickly answer these questions by prematerializing the results of a large set of queries. Let's look at some Scalding code that builds a simple rollup of the reviews from Amazon.

We first extract the relevant data from each row. We write a function to do this called getData. In this case, our parser converts rows on a single line into a Map with String keys and values. Because we don't have a true enforced schema on this data, any row might be incorrect. In Python you might return None for missing data. In Scala we do the same, but if the data is present, we return Some(data). An Option is either None or Some. When we get a key from a Map, it may be None. In Scala we can handle unwrapping and short-circuiting Options using a for statement, as Listing 5.21 shows.

Listing 5.21: The function to extract the fields from the pre-processed Amazon food reviews data set. (AmazonReviewRollups.scala)

```
def getData(record: Map[String, String]): Option[(RichDate, Double,
  String, String)] =
  for {
    dateSeconds <- record.get("review/time")
    // scalding RichDate keeps time in milliseconds since 1970
    date = RichDate(dateSeconds.toLong * 1000L)
    score <- record.get("review/score")
    dscore = score.toDouble // score is a string
    helpful <- record.get("review/helpfulness")
    uid <- record.get("review/userId")
  } yield (date, dscore, helpful, uid)
```

What the for statement does is this: Each Option is unwrapped when we use it with the "<-" characters. The values defined with "=" are just regular values. At the end, if any of the Options were None, then None is returned. Otherwise, Some(date, dscore, helpful, uid) is returned. Another way to think of an Option is that it is a List that can have either zero or one item.

We start by making a text source that returns each line of the text file as a single record. Next, we use a function, included in the source code for this text, to convert a line of text into a Map. This function is called AmazonReviewParsing.parse. To get the data from the map, apply getData, which we discussed previously.

We use flatMap in Listing 5.22 because, recall, an Option is like a List with zero or one item. If the option is None, flatMap removes it from our set. If it is Some, it unboxes the Some to get the contents. The flatMap function means map and then flatten, which is to say remove the inner data-structure that is in this case an Option.

Listing 5.22: Perform the parsing of the Amazon input data. (`AmazonReviewRollups .scala`)

```
val input = TextLine(conf.get("smdma.amazon.reviews").get,
  textEncoding = "ISO-8859-1")
// Use the parsing code we have already developed:
val parsed = TypedPipe.from(input)
  .map { line => AmazonReviewParsing.parse(line) }
  .flatMap { record => getData(record) }
```

Now that we have completely prepared the input data, it is time to determine the keys and values, and then to apply our data cubing to the keys. In this example, we put the date, score, and helpfulness as the key, and we want to know how often each key combination appears (Listing 5.23).

Listing 5.23: Select the keys that will be used in the data cubing. (`AmazonReviewRollups .scala`)

```
val prepared = parsed.map { case (date, score, helpful, uid) =>
  val key = (date, score, helpful)
  // We just count each occurrence of the key
  val value = 1L
  (key, value)
}
```

The last step of this code is to apply the data cubing expansion. In this example, we put each timestamp into three bucket types: year, year and month, and day of week. Human behavior is highly periodic. The most interesting periods are the daily, weekly, and yearly cycles. This example shows two reasons for rollups: The first is for query efficiency. We could just use the year-month buckets and sum 12 buckets up every time we want to query for a year. However, if there are enough values in your rollup and you query years a lot, it is better to prematerialize. Adding a bucket for the whole year just makes 13 buckets where there were previously 12, so the marginal cost is quite small. A second reason for rollups is to answer two orthogonal queries. With the monthly counts, I have no way to recover the counts for the Mondays. Likewise, if we know the total counts for each of the 7 days, there is clearly no way to compute the total count for a year.

The most interesting dimension we cube on here is time, but in this example, the key has two other parts: how helpful the review was rated and the score. For Amazon, the helpfulness is rated m/n to mean m out of n votes rated it helpful, so there could be any integer there. To allow seeing the total count, we put an example helpfulness 4/5 into two buckets: None, Some("4/5"); likewise, with the rating, which can be 1.0, 2.0, 3.0, 4.0, 5.0. Here we don't need to have an "all" bucket because we could just query 5 times and do the sum as we inspect the results, but again we increase the bucket count only marginally by adding an "all" bucket represented by None. In this example, every input item goes into $3 \times 2 \times 2 = 12$ buckets. After we have all the data in (*key, value*) form, we just `sumByKey` and we are done in Listing 5.24.

Listing 5.24: Perform the actual data cubing. (`AmazonReviewRollups.scala`)

```
val timezone = java.util.TimeZone.getTimeZone("UTC")
prepared.flatMap { case ((date, score, helpful), value) =>
  val timeBuckets =
    Iterator(date.toString("yyyy")(timezone), // year
      date.toString("yyyy.MM")(timezone), // year and month
      date.toString("EEE")(timezone)) // just day of week, e.g. Mon,
                                      // Tue, etc...
  for {
    dates <- timeBuckets
    scores <- Iterator(Some(score), None)
    helpfuls <- Iterator(Some(helpful), None)
  } yield ((dates, scores, helpfuls), value)
}
.sumByKey // Just add them up for each key
```

The Amazon Fine Foods dataset should have already been downloaded if you run the `download_all.sh` script as recommended to get all the datasets for the examples. With that we can run the rollup on the input:

```
cd src/chapter5/scalding_examples
./sbt "run --local " \
      "-Dsmdma.amazon.reviews= " \
      "../../../data/amazon_finefoods/finefoods.txt " \
      "-Dsmdma.output=rollup"
# Select the "AmazonReviewRollups" class to run.
```

When it completes, you can use the common search tool called `grep`, to inspect the results. For instance, to see reviews by day

```
grep "(...,None,None)" < rollup
```

You should see (in possibly a different order):

```
(Mon,None,None)  85363
(Tue,None,None)  85857
(Wed,None,None)  85994
(Thu,None,None)  87078
(Fri,None,None)  79682
(Sat,None,None)  71689
(Sun,None,None)  72791
```

Though this chapter is about how to aggregate data and write algorithms using a MapReduce style and not about data analysis, it is interesting to note that we see an almost constant number of reviews Monday through Thursday, and then a dip over the weekend. Similarly, we can see average distribution for a product review on Amazon:

```
grep "(2012,Some(..0),None)" < rollup

(2012,Some(1.0),None)    20368
(2012,Some(2.0),None)    11208
(2012,Some(3.0),None)    15603
(2012,Some(4.0),None)    28938
(2012,Some(5.0),None)    122542
```

Interestingly, in 2012 at least (the last year for which data was available from this source), the average distribution is bimodal: 1 is almost twice as common as 2. From this distribution, we can easily compute the average rating, which is 4.12. Consider how this rollup example would change if we are also interested in week-of-year (0–52) to see effects around holidays.

The main take away is understanding the pattern of data cubing, especially over time, and to see an example of constructing a compound key that is cubed in several dimensions.

What if instead of just asking for counts of ratings, we also want to know how many *users* gave ratings in each of our buckets? Is there just one user making all the ratings, or perhaps does each user write only one or two ratings? To see this, we don't add to the key, but to the value. In addition to aggregating the integer representing the count, we could also make a `Set` containing the user ID. It is natural to define sum on `Set`s as the union of those sets, and indeed the Algebird library that Scalding uses for sums does exactly this. After the sum, we can get the size of each set before we write it out.

The following Listing 5.25 shows the minor modifications needed to also track the number of uniques. See if you can identify the differences.

Listing 5.25: Instead counts, we keep track of sets of unique users. (`AmazonReviewRollupSet.scala`)

```
val prepared = parsed.map { case (date, score, helpful, uid) =>
  val key = (date, score, helpful)
  /*
   * We will count each review once, but also aggregate the set of
   * all users that make reviews so that we can see how many users
   * are active in each of our buckets.
   */
  val value = (1L, Set(uid))
  (key, value)
}
val timezone = java.util.TimeZone.getTimeZone("UTC")
prepared.flatMap { case ((date, score, helpful), value) =>
  val timeBuckets =
    Iterator(date.toString("yyyy")(timezone), // year
```

```
      date.toString("yyyy.MM")(timezone), // year and month
      date.toString("EEE")(timezone)) // just day of week, e.g. Mon,
                                       // Tue, etc...
  for {
    dates <- timeBuckets
    scores <- Iterator(Some(score), None)
    helpfuls <- Iterator(Some(helpful), None)
  } yield ((dates, scores, helpfuls), value)
}
.sumByKey // Just add them up for each key
.mapValues { case (count, uniques) =>
  // convert the Set object into a number:
  (count, uniques.size)
}
```

The only things we had to change were to expand the value to include a set of the user ID and then after the aggregation to get the size of those sets. This works because the sum of two sets is their union. Unfortunately, this approach is not scalable, as the sets take as much memory as their size. For large user bases, this results in memory problems. We see an approximate solution to this problem in the "Sampling and Approximations" section a little later in this chapter.

We can run this code the same way but by selecting the AmazonReviewRollupSet job.

Querying the result:

```
grep "(...,None,None)" < rollup

(Mon,None,None)  (85363,48097)
(Tue,None,None)  (85857,47551)
(Wed,None,None)  (85994,47425)
(Thu,None,None)  (87078,46225)
(Fri,None,None)  (79682,44229)
(Sat,None,None)  (71689,39824)
(Sun,None,None)  (72791,40755)
```

We can see that not only do the total reviews go down on the weekends, the number of users making reviews does as well. If we look at reviews per user, we see that it is between 1.8 to 1.9 regardless of day, so the drop in reviews on the weekend looks like it is due to a drop in unique users, not users making fewer reviews.

We have seen the core ideas of the rollup pattern of MapReduce jobs. When we have the output, we can do several things with it. Because the rollup data is a small fraction of the size of the original data, we might analyze it with traditional data analysis tools. We might load the output into a spreadsheet or an SQL database. We might further analyze it with R or Python. In this way, the rollup is a tool for making small or medium data from big data.

Expanding Rollup Jobs

We have seen the basic pattern of the rollup job in the previous section. The pattern is: Read and prepare the keys and values to roll up, expand the keys as desired to prematerialize interesting queries, and sum all the values for each key (word count!). Note that we didn't need to read raw data to roll up. We could have first performed some joins to get details for keys or values that might not be present in our log data. For instance, consider a log that has only user ID, as our Amazon data set does, but not how long the user has been active on the site. We might first do a join to get the number of months the user has been on the site and make that part of our key. In this way, our rollup can help us see if more ratings are coming from newer or older users. Another example would be the price of product reviewed, which we could not see in our dataset. If we joined the price into the key, and perhaps made buckets such as $0–$0.99, $1.00–$1.99, $2.00–$3.99, $4.00–$7.99, and more, we could see if ratings are more or less positive for expensive items.

Suppose we are doing a rollup for all time but our data arrives incrementally. This is a common case. Each hour we get a new batch of logs and we want to update our total counts for the day, month, and year. In this case, we could change our code a bit. We could load the total count so far, which is the output of a previous job, and merge that with the data after we expand the keys in the rollup but before we do our final sum. Because we have focused on the common case of associative operations in rollups (numeric sum, set union are good examples, but most common aggregations have the associative property), the computation gives the correct result. A sketch of the code follows:

```
val batchId = getCurrentBatchId()
val prepared = loadPrepared(batchId)
val previous = loadPrevious(batchId)
val newSum = (previous ++ (prepared.flatMap { r => bucketsFor(r) }))
  .sumByKey
newSum.write(outputSink(batchId)) // this will be read in
                                  // loadPrevious(batchId + 1)
```

Because the previous output has already been bucketed, we don't bucket it again. We just do a merge of the output after we bucket the prepared data from the current batch. After the merge, we sum each bucket as before. With this technique, we can build dashboards that are updated with the latest results. After each batch is aggregated, we can export that data into an SQL database and use standard JavaScript libraries (for instance D3) to view the data that a server collects from a database.

We have covered the basics of MapReduce jobs. Most jobs match one of the patterns we have discussed in this section. It can be a bit of an adjustment to move from a style of programming that assumes mutable state and shared global memory, but the style of functional programming matches the MapReduce model very well. If you are stuck writing a MapReduce algorithm, a good first step would be considering how to write the algorithm without any mutable variables, and hopefully at that point one of the solutions discussed in this chapter will be familiar.

Challenges with Processing Long-Tailed Social Media Data

So far, we have generally not worried about a critical question: How long will the jobs take to run? We don't ask this question too much because of the parallelism of the map phase and because reducing different keys happens in parallel, so in principle throwing more processors at the data works to a large degree. The mappers are always parallelizable, but the reducers can run only as many parallel tasks as there are keys, in general. What if one of the keys has a large fraction of the values? This is not uncommon. Consider social networks where a few users have millions of followers but most have only a handful. Consider a video site where a few videos are viewed millions of times but most videos are viewed only a few times. When data like this makes it into our pipelines, how do we avoid getting blocked on a few keys taking too long to finish? This problem is particularly acute for many-to-many joins that multiply the number of items for a key. Such joins could turn keys with millions of values into keys with trillions of values that become infeasible for a single reducer task to handle.

This section discusses a general solution and three patterns to apply it. The general solution is to leverage some algebra of the reduce function: The associative, commutative, and distributive laws. You saw in the previous section how associative operations can parallelize reduce functions. When you have a commutative and associative operation, reduction becomes even easier. Lastly, as discussed earlier, joins distribute over merges. By leveraging the distributive property of joins, you can parallelize heavy keys at the expense of increased communication costs between mappers and reducers. In practice, you might rarely need to implement any algorithms to do these optimizations because many MapReduce libraries provide them; however, you need to understand how they work and when you might need them when running into scaling problems with your MapReduce jobs.

Before discussing solutions, how can you diagnose skew in the keys? One simple check is to ask if one reducer or a few reducers take much longer than the others. It is not unusual for some reducers to take twice as long as the average, but 10 to 100 times longer should be a concern. Look at how many records were processed by each reducer. Most MapReduce systems, including Hadoop, give access to counters and logs that directly answer this question. If there is a skewed keyspace causing problems, one reducer should receive many more records than the average. If the logs don't indicate such record skew, look elsewhere to improve the performance. A way to reduce the skew is to reduce the variance between the number of records sent to each mapper. Consider a few ways to do this.

First consider the case of commutative and associative reductions. Many aggregations fall into this category including the following:

- Numeric addition and multiplication
- Maximum/minimum
- Harmonic mean: $hm(x, y) = 1 / (1 / x + 1 / y)$
- Set union and intersection
- Boolean and/or/xor
- Vector operations of any of the above

When the reduce function for each key is one of these operations, you can pre-reduce on each mapper. It works like this: Each mapper takes some input and output key-value pairs. For each key, because the reduce operation is commutative, the mapper can reduce all the values. Then the mapper transmits only one value for each key to the reducers. There are at least two ways to accomplish this. The mapper can keep a hash table of all the keys and the currently reduced values and update that for each record. The hash table does not need to fit all keys. Instead the hash table could use a caching approach and evict least used key-value pairs into a buffer that is transmitted to the mappers. An alternate implementation, which is similar to the implementation that Hadoop uses, is to sort the keys after the mapper runs; then values for the same key are adjacent to one another and can be reduced. The sort can be an external sort that uses disk instead of memory and, therefore, is scalable. In practice, the caching approach tends to be preferred because hot keys that have multiple values are exactly the items that tend to stay in the cache, and the cache avoids the cost of doing any key sorting. Some high-level MapReduce libraries perform this optimization automatically, including Scalding. Many of the earlier example code listings took advantage of this optimization.

Although most interesting associative reduce functions are also commutative, not all are. Some reduce functions are only associative and not commutative, for example:

- list/string concatenation
- first: $f(x, y) = x$
- last: $l(x, y) = y$

Concatenation is not much of a reduce function. It does not decrease the size of the data being considered, so it is not of much use in most cases. Similarly, taking the first or last item usually does not make sense unless the items are sorted in some way, but then you could have used the maximum or minimum functions as your reduce and not sort the data. So, generally, almost all common MapReduce applications use commutative reduce functions, and thus leverage map-side partial reducing.

Sampling and Approximations: Getting Results with Less Computation

On independent and randomly generated observations, the central limit theorem states that the arithmetic mean of the variables approaches a normal distribution as the number of samples taken increases, regardless of the underlying distribution, assuming the variance is finite. In social media analytics, however, normal distributions are not that interesting, and the variances can be extremely large. What we are excited about is events and patterns that stand out in some way and capture public interest.

In many cases, you don't need exact results, and even if you want them, they would be too costly to obtain. There is a definite trade-off in throughput and reliability of log collection. Most practical log collection systems might lose one in 10,000 or even one in 1,000 messages. In this environment, using a similar accuracy–throughput trade-off to reduce computation makes sense. When the wanted outcome of analytics is to identify events that are significant orders of magnitude stronger than the average events, the absolute precision of measuring those events becomes insignificant. Approximations of measurements become more important than the precise measurement of the event when, for example, you need to identify all messages that get reposted a thousand or tens of thousands times more often than the average message.

When counting unique elements, for example, how many users have viewed and accepted our updated terms and conditions, we usually try to place a hash of each element in a bag. If the hash does not already exist within the bag, then we increment the unique counter. If the hash already exists, that means that we have already counted the cardinality. An implementation using an in-memory hash set means that we require space proportional to the number of unique elements. When each element in the hash set requires 32 bytes (which is often the case on Java-based systems, for instance, 12 bytes header + 16 bytes data + 4 bytes padding) that means we need 32MB of memory for every one million unique elements. Considering that modern social networks are often 10 million to 1 billion users, the direct approach is costly.

Precise implementations are not memory-friendly and work in *linear space*. Storing n items in a collection requires O(n) space. On huge data streams that is unaffordable, or at least uneconomical. Even if we persist an entire collection, it takes significant resources to process and query that collection. Also for streaming data applications, we usually see the data just once and are expected to answer queries immediately on them without worrying about running out of memory.

So, there is a need for algorithms with a sublinear space nature. We can achieve that using techniques that are *lossy* and don't store all the data. As a result, they deliver results whose accuracy is guaranteed within specific bounds only.

A naïve lossy implementation would be random sampling: We can calculate statistics on partial data and build an estimator for the sampled data. However, building a new estimator for each parameter we might be interested in is difficult and requires specific expertise in statistics. An easier-to-apply technique is to use specialized data structures, some of which have been recently developed, to summarize the data. These data structures are highly parallelizable by design, work on sublinear space, and are based on associative and commutative operations. While the precise implementations use memory-hungry collections, probabilistic data structures enable us to trade precision of the estimation with memory consumption, with the additional benefit of distributing computations using MapReduce or other computational models.

To illustrate the substance of probabilistic data structures, let's assume we have a raw dataset that contains 1 billion random elements of 10 bytes representing user names that we know contains at most 10 million distinct elements (as many duplicates exist), and we are interested in querying this dataset for the following:

- The cardinality of the data set (the number of distinct elements).
- The most frequent elements, also known as heavy hitters or top-k elements.
- The frequencies of elements, especially for the most frequent elements.
- Testing whether a data set contains a specific user (membership queries).

If we were to keep in memory 10 million unique strings (with each element 10-bytes long), we would expect that the minimum memory requirements of that data structure would be 10 million × 10 Bytes = 100 MB. Furthermore, attaching a 24-bit counter to each element in the following structure to capture a frequency table requires 10 million × 13 Bytes = 130 MB of memory. The following code snippet illustrates this simple storage mechanism.

```
val unique_visitor = collection.mutable.Set[String]()
for (i <- 1 to 10000000) unique_visitor.add(util.Random.nextString(10) )
```

When looking for lossy implementations, we can instead hash each element into long integers of 3 bytes. Because of the hashing, we'll suffer from collisions resulting in approximate results, and we won't know precisely the error rate of the compressed collection, but we would save some space in memory.

With approximative algorithms, in contrast, we can specify the desired estimation error rate. If we decide that a relative accuracy (standard error) of 4 percent is tolerable, we can count cardinality using just 4 KB via the *HyperLogLog* (HLL) algorithm, create a frequency table of top hitters with 4 percent standard error using just 96 KB with the *Count-Min Sketch* (CMS) algorithm, and answer membership queries using an 8 MB *Bloom filter* (BF) data structure. We will expose these algorithms in the following sections. HLL, CMS, and BF achieve tremendous reduction in memory consumption by introducing lossy representations: We trade the precision of the estimation and CPU cycles for total memory consumption.

The algorithms are tunable, and, for example, if we decide that the expected error rate instead of 4 percent should be 0.25 percent, then the memory requirements for the previous dataset would be 9.1 MB for BF, 256 KB for HLL, and approximately 1.5 MB for preserving the frequency table of the top-100 frequent elements in a CMS.

At first this inaccuracy might sound strange, but if you think about it, this also happens to images, video, and sound recordings with modern lossy data compression techniques. Because users cannot detect a certain amount of information loss, performant compressions enable new types of applications. As it happens in the case of the JPEG image compression format, for instance, the creator can decide how much loss to introduce to make a trade-off between runtime and storage performance, and image quality.

There are many applications of approximate data structures. Table 5.1 lists the most common uses of the three algorithms discussed in this chapter, which are most frequently used to help perform calculations in social media systems.

Table 5.1: A Comparison of Traditional and the Corresponding Probabilistic Data Structures, and the Questions They Are Designed to Answer

QUESTION	APPROXIMATE DATA STRUCTURE	TRADITIONAL DATA STRUCTURE
Set cardinality	HyperLogLog	Set
Set membership	Bloom filter	Set
Frequencies count	Count-Min Sketch	Hash map or sorted IDs

Mathematically many, but not all, of the probabilistic data structures are *commutative monoids*. The monoid property means having an associative operation over the underlying set, with an identity element defined with respect to the operation. A commutative monoid is moreover commutative as well, as the name suggests. Having this property for an operation is valuable for fast execution in MadReduce or Spark because it enables a high degree of parallelism in the aggregation or reduce phase. (For a formal presentation, see "Monoidify! Monoids as a Design Principle for Efficient MapReduce Algorithms" by J. Lin at `https://arxiv.org/abs/1304.7544`.)

Putting the mathematical definitions aside, that means that we can think of combining complex data structures similarly to how we combine numbers using addition with the "+" operation (the identity element in the case of addition is the number zero). This analogy to, or generalization of, addition enables us to keep thinking of our computations as word counts, just with a different underlying structure to do the counting on. For example, if we count unique visitors to a web page using HLL and there are 100,000 unique visitors in 1 hour and 100,000 unique visitors in the following hour, summing the two HLL containers could result in 120,000 unique users if 80,000 users overlap in both datasets.

The main data types discussed in the rest of this chapter, HLL, BF, and CMS, are all commutative monoids. This makes their usage particularly efficient for distributed processing but also enables them in iterative processing, that is, storing the result of the processing on an initial set of data and then applying it to a newly arriving one.

The following sections present in detail these probabilistic algorithms and go over the practical rules and formulas that can help you determine the parameters and resulting memory requirements.

More specifically, we'll use the Algebird Scala library for probabilistic data structures (`https://github.com/twitter/algebird/`) and present the implementation using Scalding.

HyperLogLog

The HyperLogLog (HLL) is a probabilistic data structure for estimating the number of distinct elements in a set, known as the set's cardinality. The HyperLogLog algorithm was introduced by P. Flajolet, et al. in "HyperLogLog: The analysis of a near-optimal cardinality estimation algorithm" at the 2007 Conference on Analysis of Algorithms.

HLL uses a *small, fixed amount* of memory for approximating the number of unique elements in a *multiset*, a set in which members can appear more than once. How is this achieved?

HLL observes bit patterns, which is motivated by counting the longest run of heads when flipping a coin, starting the counting from the beginning of the flipping. If you flip coins, the probability that you have k heads in a row is $\left(\frac{1}{2}\right)^k$.

Therefore, if we repeat the coin flipping multiple times, and we observe that the most number of times we had heads come up in a row was k, it's likely that we had to restart our coin flipping 2^k number of times so that we could observe this one event.

Imagine taking random numbers uniformly distributed between 0 and 1. If you take N of these numbers, the expected value of the minimum is $1/(N+1) \approx 1/N$, if N is large, based on order statistics. So, if you just record the minimum random number from a series of such random numbers, you can estimate the number of unique numbers you have taken. Note that if a number appears twice or more, it cannot change the minimum, so this simple method would indeed count distinct appearances only.

Given the set of items whose cardinality we're interested in, we could use a strong hash function, apply it to the elements of the set, and interpret the hash result bit string as a binary number between 0 and 1. We could then take the minimum of these numbers and report the inverse of the minimum as the cardinality. (Instead of storing the actual minimum you could store its transformed value, $\log_2(1/\min)$, which is also approximately the number of leading 0s in the bit sequence of the minimum + 1. Then at the end of the run, report $2^{\log_2(1/\min)}$ as the estimate, similar to our deductions about the coin flipping above. This introduces a bit of noise but takes less data to store.)

Finally, to improve the accuracy, you could bucket the elements into 2^s substreams by taking the first s bits of the hash and consider that as the bucket number, and then apply this same algorithm for each bucket. This gives you 2^s estimates for the cardinality. At the end, let's take a mean of these 2^s cardinality estimation, but instead of the arithmetic mean, take the harmonic mean:

$$\frac{1}{C} = \sum_{i=1}^{2^s} \frac{1}{C_i}.$$ This improves the estimation of the cardinality C of the entire set.

The previous three techniques (hashing to generate numbers in [0, 1], bucketing the stream using the first few bits of the hash, and smoothing the resulting estimation using the harmonic mean) give you the HyperLogLog algorithm, which provides estimations on cardinality, using significantly less memory than storing all the distinct elements in the set. When a full set could require hundreds of megabytes to store, an HLL can count using just 256 bytes and give an estimate that is correct within about 10 percent error. The actual estimation error can be outside of ±10 percent because the error is approximately normally distributed, so ~5% of the time, it is more than 2 times this and 0.3% of the time it's more than 3 times this.

Table 5.2 illustrates the mean estimation error of HLL when specific memory is allocated to that data structure. By increasing the memory allocated to HLL to 256 KB, you can tolerate just 0.25 percent of inaccuracy. The standard error of HyperLogLog is 1.04 divided by the square root of m, where m is the number of *registers* used.

Table 5.2: The Estimation Error of the HLL as a Function of the Amount of Storage Allocated to It

MEMORY	256 Bytes	1 KB	4 KB	16 KB	64 KB	256 KB
ESTIMATION ERROR	10%	5%	2%	1%	0.5%	0.25%

Typically, the size of a register, which stores the $\log_2(1/\min)$, is 1 byte. For such implementations, you can expect to overflow the registers when you have more than 2^{256} elements in the stream. This is such an astronomical number (indeed, it could easily count distinct atoms in the universe) that you normally don't need to worry about this limitation.

Those are the trade-offs and benefits of using HLL in cardinality estimations. In social media analytics, counting is of paramount importance. Unique users, impressions, clicks, conversions, and many other statistics need to be calculated. The effectiveness of HLL makes this algorithm a first-class citizen in modern analytics.

The additional benefit is that HLL is a commutative monoid because it is based on taking a minimum, and clearly the minimum function is a commutative monoid. This means that you can calculate partial estimations and union intermediate results in a single estimation. For example, you can use HLL to count unique users per minute and then to count the unique users per hour, union all the minute-based data structures. Then you can also union all the hourly estimates to calculate the daily unique visitors. This capability to merge HLLs is an additional benefit beyond the memory savings. If you record the exact number of uniques on Tuesday and again on Wednesday, you have little idea how many uniques there were on Tuesday and Wednesday: It could be anywhere from the maximum of the 2 days to the sum. HLL gives you a great way to query your data in new ways without having to perform full recomputations of set cardinalities.

For further information about the HyperLogLog algorithm, refer to `http://research.neustar.biz/tag/hyperloglog/`.

HyperLogLog Example

To implement in Scalding an example that uses HLL, you need to first import the libraries `algebird` and `scalding` and define a case class that encapsulates your data, as follows.

```
import com.twitter.algebird._
import com.twitter.scalding._

case class Users(userID: Int)
```

Then define an HLL aggregator setting the estimation error to 2 percent. As HLL's error is approximately $1.04 / \sqrt{m}$, where m is the number of registers, by using $m = 2^{12}$ registers, you can expect a 1.6 percent average error.

```
val unique = HyperLogLogAggregator
  .sizeAggregator(12)
  // HLL needs a way to hash the record, converting to string is an
  // easy, if not terribly efficient way.
  .composePrepare[Users](_.userID.toString.getBytes("UTF-8"))
```

To simulate the exact experiment previously mentioned of a web page that has 100,000 unique visitors in hour 1 and 100,000 unique visitors in hour 2, you can generate synthetic data. Below we specifically instruct the data generator to have just 20,000 unique visitors across the two sets:

```
val hour1List = (1 to 100000).map(Users).toList
val hour1 = TypedPipe.from(hour1List)

val hour2List = (20001 to 120000).map(Users).toList
val hour2 = TypedPipe.from(hour2List)
```

Then aggregate and print each hour and then union both hours:

```
hour1
  .aggregate(unique)
  .map { x => println(s"Cardinality of HOUR 1 $x"); x }
  .write(TypedTsv("results/HLL-1stHour"))

hour2
  .aggregate(unique)
  .map { x => println(s"Cardinality of HOUR 2 $x"); x }
  .write(TypedTsv("results/HLL-2ndHour"))

val unionTwoHours = (hour1 ++ hour2)
  .aggregate(unique)
  .map { x => println(s"Cardinality of HOUR 1 & HOUR 2 $x"); x }
  .write(TypedTsv("results/HLL-BothHours"))
```

In the preceding code, we aggregate each dataset hour1 and hour2, and print out their cardinality estimation. We then union the two datasets and calculate the cardinality of their union.

In real-world use cases where you process massive amounts of data, you also need to take advantage of parallelism in the computations of HLL. Calculating the HLL of subsets and then aggregating the partial HLL together achieves that, and Scalding offers this out of the box: It calculates an HLL for every map task and then unions all intermediate HLL in a single reduce step.

The result of executing the previous code is

```
Cardinality of HOUR 1 97766.0
Cardinality of HOUR 2 97749.0
Cardinality of HOUR 1 && HOUR 2 118006.0
```

The actual estimation error on the first two sets is 2.25 percent, and when the two HLLs are unioned, the resulting error is 1.65 percent. That is correct because you expect a mean average error rate of 2 percent, and that is what occurs.

HyperLogLog on the Stack Exchange Dataset

To provide a more concrete example, now let's use an open data set from Stack Exchange. The data set contains 9 columns of data: `ID`, `PostTypeID`, `ParentID`, `OwnerUserID`, `CreationDate`, `ViewCount`, `FavoriteCount`, `Tags`, and `Keywords`. To work with this data set using the Scalding Typed API, first define a Scala case class and a companion object:

```
case class StackExchange(ID:Long, PostTypeID:Long, ParentID:Long,
  OwnerUserID:Long, CreationDate:String, ViewCount:Long,
  FavoriteCount:Long, Tags:String, Keywords:String)
object StackExchange {
  type StackExchangeType = (Long, Long, Long, Long, String, Long, Long,
  String, String)
  def fromTuple(t: StackExchangeType): StackExchange =
    StackExchange(t._1, t._2, t._3, t._4, t._5,t._6,t._7,t._8,t._9)
}
```

We can use Scala macros to generate this code, but overall the purpose of this block of code is to apply names and types on the dataset. To estimate using HLL the number of unique authors on Stack Exchange (with a mean accuracy of 2 percent), use the following code:

```
class HLLstackexchange(args: Args) extends Job(args) {

  val unique = HyperLogLogAggregator
    .sizeAggregator(12)
    // Convert OwnerUserID to UTF-8 encoded bytes as HyperLogLog expects
    // a byte array.
    .composePrepare[StackExchange] ( _.OwnerUserID.toString
      .getBytes ("UTF-8"))

  val stackExchangePosts =
    TypedPipe.from(
      TypedTsv[StackExchange.StackExchangeType](args("input")))
    .map { StackExchange.fromTuple }
    .aggregate(unique)
    .map { x =>
      println(s"Unique authors (cardinality estimation): $x"); x
    }
    .write(TypedTsv(args("output")))
}
```

This code can be executed against megabytes or gigabytes of data. In this case, we are testing with a small amount of data, but the exact same code on the exact same machine could count billions of uniques without exhausting the memory of the computer. Executing it against the sample Stack Exchange data, it returns the following:

```
Running HLL stack-exchange example took 1772 msec in --local mode
Unique authors (cardinality estimation): 9358 with 2.0 % error
```

Performance of HLL on Large Datasets

To clearly demonstrate the capabilities of HLL on large datasets, now evaluate the performance on a Hadoop cluster consisting of seven Amazon r3.8xlarge nodes (each offering 32 CPUs, 244 GB RAM and three 1TB magnetic EBS volumes). At the end of this chapter we briefly describe how to start such clusters.

For the performance evaluation, let's generate synthetic data consisting of 1, 10, 20, 40, 80, 100, and 500 million unique strings (one per line), and count the cardinality using precise and approximation algorithms. The results are demonstrated with Scalding (using HLL) and Hive (for the exact cardinality calculations). Hive is a popular data warehouse tool built on top of Hadoop, capable of executing SQL queries.

The on-disk sizes of the synthetic data sets are shown in Table 5.3 below.

Table 5.3: The Sizes of the Datasets We Generated for the HLL Performance Evaluation

UNIQUE ELEMENTS	1 million	10 million	20 million	100 million	500 million
SIZE ON DISK	30 MB	305 MB	610 MB	3.06 GB	15.3 GB

Executing accurate SQL queries on Hive or approximate HLL queries via Scalding results in similar execution plans. The results of many mappers are aggregated in a single reducer that calculates the cardinality.

Using HLL the execution time ranges from 35 seconds to 52 seconds, as shown in Figure 5.2, with most of the time spent on setting up the Hadoop containers and reading in parallel the dataset. When using Hive performing exact counts, the time and resources required are proportional to the dataset size.

Another interesting feature of HLL is that the expected estimation error is not affecting the execution time significantly. That means that counting cardinality with HLL with an expected estimation error of 0.1% adds 1 to 2 seconds of execution time only when we have the estimation error at 2 percent.

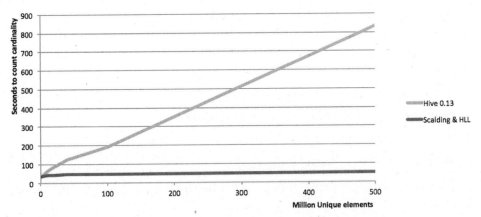

Figure 5.2: The runtime it takes to estimate the cardinalities of our toy data sets

Bloom Filters

A Bloom filter (BF) is a probabilistic data structure for membership queries first introduced by Burton Howard Bloom in 1970. A Bloom filter is nothing but a data structure for large sets that allows:

- Adding new elements to the set;
- Testing set membership.

Compared to an exact set implementation, it requires a smaller memory footprint and provides enhanced speed at the cost of a small percentage of false positives. When we query a BF for membership, we receive either a definitive "no," or a "maybe." "Maybe" means that there is a possibility for the item to belong to the set.

The definite "no" capability of the BF is usually utilized for filtering data in data mining, machine learning, bioinformatics, virus scanning, and other distributed applications. Typically, a BF is used as a filter before a matching phase. If the answer is no, the item is excluded, and if it is a maybe, usually there is another step carried out, which is an exact search. For example, the popular open source NoSQL database HBase uses BF to determine whether a key is contained within a block before reading it.

Similarly to HLL, you can tune the parameters of a BF at creation time to set what the expected trade-off is for the false positives you can tolerate. Another parameter you need to set is the relative size (the number of unique elements you expect to populate the set).

The mathematical definition of Bloom filters state that for any set with n number of items, a BF can be constructed to use k number of hash functions using m number of bits in the filter to yield false positives with a probability p. To summarize, the parameters of the filter are:

- n: The number of items in the filter.
- p: The probability of receiving false positives.
- m: The number of bits in the filter.
- k: The number of hash functions.

To shed some light on what these parameters mean, consider how the Bloom filter works.

Internally, a Bloom filter is a bit array of a specific size m, initially having each bit set to 0. When a new element is added to the filter, it is hashed by a number of k functions, each producing a value. These values are going to be used as indices into the bit array (thus taken modulo-m to arrive at an index between 0 and $m - 1$). The bits indexed at these positions are set to 1, as illustrated in Figure 5.3.

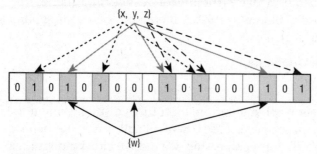

Figure 5.3: Bloom filter hashing to set specific bits of the bit array to 1

In this example, three elements { x, y, z } are added to a BF. Three independent random hash functions show the positions in the array of m bits that each set element is mapped to. Every element added into a BF changes the values of the bit filter to 1.

When we query the BF for a set membership, we similarly hash the element we are looking up through the k hash functions, and determine the bit locations in the bit array as we did during addition. However, if any of these bits are set to 0, we know that the queried element cannot be in the set. In the particular case shown in Figure 5.3, the BF responds with a definite "no" for a query on { w } because one of the bits it was indexed to is still 0. If all three locations where { w } was mapped to had the value of 1, then the answer would have been a "maybe."

Hashing new elements into a BF often results in indexes that have already been set to 1. Also, it's possible that { w } points to array locations already set to 1 by other items in the set. This is the reason that a BF responds with a "maybe", because it cannot be fully sure whether { w } belongs to the set, or there were collisions. This is what introduces the estimation error, a factor that is compensated for by having multiple hash functions for each element in the set.

There is a high correlation between the number of bits in the array and the probability of false positives. Usually, the BF is configured to use between 5 and 15 bits per element added, as shown in Figure 5.4, to arrive at a low-enough false positive rate.

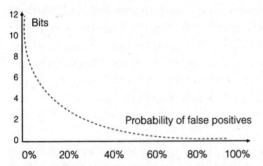

Figure 5.4: The number of bits per element in BF, and the resulting false positive rate

The second important factor when creating an efficient BF is the number of hash functions used. The optimal number of hash functions is roughly 0.7 times the number of array bits per element. Hash functions also play an important role as they heavily utilize CPU resources when adding or querying for elements, and hashing can be a potential bottleneck in query-intensive applications.

When using Algebird, all the BF optimization logic is encapsulated within the library. The library requires you to provide the number of unique items to be included in the BF and the estimation error. Algebird then automatically optimizes the number of bits per element and the number of hash functions to use, with the following calculation:

```
def optimalNumHashes(n: Int, width: Int): Int =
  math.ceil(width / n * math.log(2)).toInt
def optimalWidth(n: Int, p: Double): Int =
  math.ceil(-1 * n * math.log(p) / math.log(2) / math.log(2)).toInt
```

The memory requirements of a BF depend on the required false positive probability, and for every 100 K unique elements, Table 5.4 illustrates the size required.

Table 5.4: Bloom Filter Size Per 100 Thousand Elements

MEMORY	58 KB	76 KB	99 KB	114 KB	134 KB	152 KB
BITS PER ELEMENT	4.7	6.2	8.1	9.5	11	12.4
HASH FUNCTIONS	k=3	k=4	k=6	k=7	k=8	k=9
ESTIMATION ERROR	10%	5%	2%	1%	0.5%	0.25%

As a rule of thumb, note that for a 2% false positive rate, a BF requires 1 byte per element. Also, you can see that the number of hash functions is relatively low, usually in the range of 3 to 14.

The most important element when thinking about distributed computations and BF is the memory size. The BF overall is best-suited for moderate-size groups; calculating a BF for a few hundred thousand unique elements is fast. Using BF for anything more than a few million elements results in large records that Hadoop does not handle well and increases the cost of creating the BF in a suboptimal way. Recall, the "big" in big data is in terms of rows, not columns. So, we want each record to be reasonably small, and a multiple megabyte Bloom filter starts to violate that assumption.

The computational speed of adding new elements to the set and checking for set membership also depends on the underlying implementation of the hash functions and the number of hash functions used. One optimization on the computational speed comes by using only two hash functions to effectively implement a Bloom filter without any loss in false positive probability. For more information about this technique, see "Less Hashing, Same Performance: Building a Better Bloom Filter" by A. Kirsch and M. Mitzenmacher (http://www.eecs.harvard.edu/~michaelm/postscripts/rsa2008.pdf).

A Bloom Filter Example

We need to first import the algebird and scalding libraries and define a case class that can encapsulate our data to implement in Scalding an example that uses BF.

Algebird uses the efficient JavaEWAH library for a BF that provides a run-length encoding compression scheme and improves query processing time while introducing memory compression (https://github.com/lemire/javaewah/). The alternative java.util.BitSet class fails to scale without compression.

```
import com.twitter.algebird._import com.twitter.scalding._

case class SimpleUser(userID: String)
```

We then define a BF, setting the estimation error to 2 percent, and the size of the filter to 100,000. If we don't know the number of unique items in a priori, we can use HLL to get that approximately.

```
val bloomFilterMonoid = BloomFilter(numEntries=100000, fpProb=0.02)
```

We apply the BF monoid to an aggregator and specify that the filter capture just the `userID`.

```
val bfAggregator = BloomFilterAggregator(bloomFilterMonoid)
  .composePrepare[SimpleUser](_.userID)
```

We then generate the first 100,000 integers in-memory and place them into a Scalding typed pipe and aggregate the whole pipe into the BF. In the map phase, the values are hashed into a BF, and in a single reduce task, all the BF are unioned into a single Bloom filter.

```
// Generate and add 100K ids into the Bloom filter.
val usersList = (1 to 100000).toList.map{ x => SimpleUser(x.toString) }
val usersBF = TypedPipe.from[SimpleUser](usersList)
  .aggregate(usersBF)
```

The Scalding pipe now holds the BF, and we can easily perform set membership queries with the filter:

```
// Example for querying the BF.
usersBF.map { bf: BF =>
  println("BF contains 'ABCD' ? " +
    (if (bf.contains("ABCD").isTrue) "maybe" else "no"))
  println("BF contains 'EFGH' ? " +
    (if (bf.contains("EFGH").isTrue) "maybe" else "no"))
  println("BF contains '123' ? " +
    (if (bf.contains("123") .isTrue) "maybe" else "no"))
  bf }
```

Executing the preceding code results in

```
Running BF synthetic-data example took 4503 msec in --local mode

BF contains 'ABCD' ? no
BF contains 'EFGH' ? no
BF contains '123'  ? maybe
```

In addition, we can serialize the BF into a file (if we want to reuse it), by first converting the BF into a byte array and then storing it into a sequence file:

```
// Serialize the BF.
usersBF
  .map { bf: BF => io.scalding.approximations.Utils.serialize(bf) }
  .write( TypedSequenceFile("serializedBF")) )
```

The resulting serialized BF file is 103 KB and is in line with the original expectation of 99 KB, as we are also storing metadata about the BF in the form of some serialization headers.

Bloom Filter as Pre-Computed Membership Knowledge

An interesting property of all probabilistic data structures described in this chapter is that they can be serializable. This enables pre-computing information about a large dataset and storing the data structure for use later. Any convenient location such as HDFS, an SQL database, or a key-value store can be used to store a data structure, so subsequent applications can utilize it, as a quick approximate solution for membership queries, cardinalities, or frequency queries on datasets.

In this section, we read from disk and deserialize the BF we just generated and perform a set of membership queries. First, we read the sequence file and then map the byte array to a BF object:

```
val serializedBF = args("serialized")
val BF = TypedPipe.from(source.TypedSequenceFile(serializedBF))
  .map {
    serialized:Array[Byte] =>
    io.scalding.approximations.Utils.deserialize[BF](serialized)
  }
```

The method that deserializes looks like this:

```
def deserialize[T](byteArray: Array[Byte]): T = {
  val is = new ObjectInputStream(new ByteArrayInputStream(byteArray))
  is.readObject().asInstanceOf[T]
}
```

After we have loaded the pre-computed BF into a pipe, we can introduce the items to be queried against the BF from another location. For this demonstration, the items are loaded in-memory.

```
val itemsPipe = TypedPipe.from(List("ABCD", "EFGH", "123"))
```

We can then cross the items pipe with the BF and within a map function perform the membership queries. The contains method highlighted next returns an ApproximateBoolean object that either means that the answer is *false* with 100 percent confidence or *true* with a specific confidence level. In the following, we see that for the BF we construct, it reports a 97% confidence that the item is present.

```
itemsPipe.cross(BF)
  .map { case (item: String, bf: BF) =>
    val existsInBF = bf.contains(item)
    println(s"Item $item exists in BF : $existsInBF")
    (item, existsInBF.isTrue)
  }
  .write( TypedTsv("membershipResults") )
```

Executing this code prints on the screen:

```
Item ABCD exists in BF: ApproximateBoolean(false,1.0)
Item EFGH exists in BF: ApproximateBoolean(false,1.0)
Item 123 exists in BF: ApproximateBoolean(true,0.9707277171828571)
```

Bloom Filters on Large Social Datasets

Generating BFs in parallel is interesting both in MapReduce jobs that process large amounts of data and in real-time systems, where topologies distribute data in multiple streams that need to be periodically aggregated.

When we add an element to a BF, the operation that sets the indexed bits in the bit array to 1 can be thought of as one that takes the maximum of the value currently present at that location, and 1. In this way, BF bit arrays can be merged by taking bitwise maximums, and the BF itself is therefore a commutative monoid similar to the HLL.

Thus, we can execute in parallel many mappers, each adding via hashing many elements into a BF bit array. The resulting bit arrays from the mappers can be reduced in a single reduce phase with the bitwise OR operation, as shown in Figure 5.5.

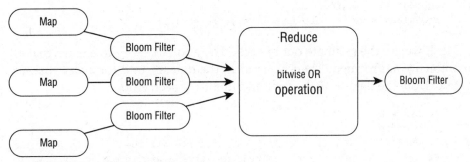

Figure 5.5: Aggregating Bloom filters on reducers

The following example parses a 20 GB dataset from Wikipedia containing article edits as we have seen before, and generates a BF for every month: Each BF contains all unique authors that edited an article during that month.

Initially, we define the case class and companion object for reading the data into a typed Scalding pipe.

```
object Wikipedia {
  type WikipediaType = (Long, String, Long, String)
  def fromTuple(t: WikipediaType): Wikipedia = Wikipedia(t._1, t._2,
    t._3, t._4)
}
case class Wikipedia(ContributorID: Long, ContributorUserName: String,
  RevisionID: Long, DateTime: String)
```

Because we do not know a priori how many unique authors edited an article, we use HLL to calculate cardinality estimation. To perform the calculation, we create an HLL aggregator using Algebird:

```
val hllAggregator = HyperLogLogAggregator
  .sizeAggregator(12)
  .composePrepare[Wikipedia](_.ContributorID.toString.getBytes("UTF-8"))
```

We then read the data and for every line in our dataset, extract the year-month from the date-time field:

```
val wikiHLL = TypedPipe.from(TypedTsv[Wikipedia.WikipediaType](input))
  .map { Wikipedia.fromTuple }
  .map {
    wiki => wiki.copy(DateTime = wiki.DateTime.substring(0, 7))
    // extract YYYY-MM
  }
```

Now we group all the wiki edits by year-month and aggregate using the HLL aggregator that has been set up to count unique contributor IDs, and take the estimation out of HLL.

```
wikiHLL
  .groupBy { wiki => wiki.DateTime }
  .aggregate(hllAggregator)
  .mapValues { hll => hll.approximateSize.estimate }
```

Next, we get the estimate out of each HLL and `sumByKey` to ensure that all months are aggregated. Then we read in the dataset, and for every line, we extract from the date-time the year and month of each edit:

```
  .sumByKey
  .toTypedPipe
  .groupAll                // Trick to force all results into a single
  .values                  // reducer--thus a single output file.
  // Also let's store the HLL results.
  .write(TypedTsv("results/wikipedia-per-month-HLL.tsv"))

// Example output is =>   Key = 2011-02 , Value = 149804
```

Another common scenario in which Bloom filters are used is in *needle in the haystack* joins. When joining massive amounts of data that we know that only a few entries from a much larger space will ever join, instead of replicating all data to hundreds of reducers, we can build a Bloom filter and perform a filter on the mappers. By filtering out most of the records that would not have matched anything on the other side of the join, significant performance gains can be achieved.

Count-Min Sketch

If we want to count how frequently items appear in a large data set, one option would be to perform a hash table-based counting or a distributed count as we have seen before in the word count example, for instance. However, if the data set is very large, as it usually happens in practice, we could run out of memory. A straightforward way to create a histogram of counts would be to sample the data first to solve this issue. But on large datasets, or infinite streams, sampling can still result in running out of memory. To effectively deal with histograms, we can use CMS, which is an approximative algorithm to estimate the frequencies of the incoming items.

A Count-Min Sketch (CMS) is a probabilistic data structure used to represent frequency tables. G. Cormode and S. Muthukrishnan introduced the definition of this sketch in 2003. As quoted in their original paper "An Improved Data Stream Summary: The Count-Min Sketch and its Applications" (`http://dimacs.rutgers.edu/~graham/pubs/papers/cm-full.pdf`):

> *Our sketch allows fundamental queries in data stream summarization such as point, range, and inner product queries to be approximately answered very quickly; in addition, it can be applied to solve several important problems in data streams such as finding quantiles, frequent items, etc.*

CMS is a data structure that is simple to implement and has an immense use in serving a certain class of frequency queries. It uses sublinear space to store histogram data: As far as storage is concerned, CMS counts frequencies using less space than the number of elements. However, we have to accept that the counts are not going to be exact, and the frequencies may be overestimated.

Similar to the other probabilistic data structures, we can tune the parameters to obtain the desired accuracy. CMS is similar to BF in many ways, as it also uses multiple hash functions on each element. The main distinction is that BF represents sets, whereas CMS represents multisets. In particular, CMS summarizes the frequency distribution, while BF represents which elements are present in a set.

CMS uses hashes to map items to frequencies in a memory-efficient way. For example, it can hold a frequency table of a multiset with billions of entries in just a few kilobytes. The trade-off is that due to hashing collisions, it overcounts some items. The estimation error can be tuned per sketch. The more memory is allocated for the sketch, the less the estimation error will be.

Internally, the CMS differs from a BF in another way. It allocates its working sketch data structure in memory in a 2-dimensional array with w columns and d rows. Every new incoming item is hashed by all of d independent hash functions to determine the column in the row of the matrix corresponding to the hash function. In that row and column now determined, we increment the value of the matrix entry by 1 (they all start out at 0). The procedure is shown in Figure 5.6.

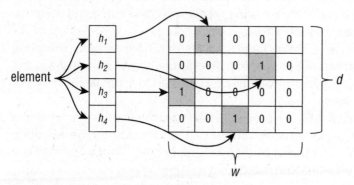

Figure 5.6: CMS increments the matrix values pointed to by the indices calculated from hashing the items with each of the d hash functions

During lookup, we similarly hash the queried element with all the hash functions, retrieve the values stored in the sketch matrix at the columns pointed to by the hashes, and return the *minimum* of all d values as the answer. This type of query the CMS supports is called a *point query*. This will return the estimated count of the queried element.

The CMS can also support *range queries*, where we can ask the data structure for the frequencies of items within a range. Using this, a CMS can also calculate *quantiles*, a feature often used in data science that can answer queries such as "find the top 5% of users who ...." We can find the total number of elements and then make multiple range queries to a CMS to discover the top 5 percent of the users with a binary search.

Another interesting query where CMS brings significant value in the context of data joins is called the *inner product query*. This allows us to query for the dot product of two sketched vectors. This can be useful to determine the approximate sizes of joined data sets, knowing that the CMS can keep track of the frequencies of items appearing in tables, on both sides of the join. A query optimizer needs to know the distribution of the keys of the data sets. Having a relative estimation of the join size enables a query planner to determine the best order in which to evaluate queries.

The error characteristics are stated in terms of two parameters: *Estimation error* and *delta*. CMS promises that the estimated count is at most $N \times$ (*estimation error*)

more than the true count, with probability 1 – *delta*. *N* here is the total number of items that we have added to the sketch. The data structure size is defined by the size of *d* (depth) and *w* (width), and high accuracy is achieved for CMS structures that range from a few kilobytes to a megabyte in size. Table 5.5 shows that at approximately 10 KB, we get error values of approximately 1 percent.

Table 5.5: The Count-Min Sketch Sizes as a Function of the Desired Error Bounds

MEMORY	2.5 KB	3.2 KB	9.8 KB	20 KB	37 KB	104 KB
WIDTH	28	55	272	544	1088	2719
DEPTH	3	3	5	6	6	7
ESTIMATION ERROR	10%	5%	1%	0.5%	0.25%	0.1%
DELTA	10%	5%	1%	0.5%	0.25%	0.1%

Another interesting point about CMS is that as long as it can fit in memory, the update rate is extremely high. A Xeon 2.8 GHz processor with 512 KB of cache and 4 GB of RAM can easily sustain 10 million updates per second.

As mentioned in the "Statistical Analysis of Sketch Estimators" by F. Rusu and A. Dobra (`http://www.cise.ufl.edu/~adobra/Publications/sigmod-2007-statistics.pdf`):

> *The performance of Count-Min sketches is strongly dependent on the skew of the data. For small skew, the error is orders of magnitude larger than the error of the other types of sketches. For large skew, CM sketches have the best performance— much better than AGMS and Fast-Count sketch (FC). The update performance is also very fast ranging between 50–400 ns.*

CM sketches have poor performance for distributions (close to) uniform. They have good accuracy as long as the data is skewed, and this is exactly what happens in social media analytics among other fields.

The next section uses this probabilistic data structure for identifying *heavy hitters*.

Count-Min Sketch—Heavy Hitters Example

As before, we need to first import the `scalding` and `algebird` libraries and the case class and companion object we build for the `Wikipedia` dataset:

```
package io.scalding.approximations.CountMinSketch

import com.twitter.algebird._
import com.twitter.scalding._
import io.scalding.approximations.model.Wikipedia
```

We can use an argument to define the size of the CMS at execution time. To use the CMS, we need to bring in the implicits. Then we can define our CMS monoid, passing in as parameters eps and delta that describe the desired confidence of our error estimates.

```
class WikipediaTopN(args: Args) extends Job(args) {
  val topN = args.getOrElse("topN", "100").toInt

  // Construct a Count-Min Sketch monoid and bring in implicit hashing
  // functions.
  import CMSHasherImplicits._
  val cmsMonoid = TopNCMS.monoid[Long](eps=0.01, delta=0.02,
    seed=(Math.random() * 100).toInt, heavyHittersN=topN)
```

The CMS uses the special TopNCMS monoid. The configuration in the preceding code builds a CMS that can count the histogram of the topN elements, with a 98 percent confidence that the results are within a 1 percent error rate.

To use it we need to define an aggregator that states that from within the Wikipedia objects we are interested only in counting the ContributorID:

```
val topNaggregator = TopNCMSAggregator(cmsMonoid)
  .composePrepare[Wikipedia](_.ContributorID)
```

After this set up, we can start reading the data from the filesystem and aggregate into the CMS:

```
val wikiData = TypedPipe.from(
  TypedTsv[Wikipedia.WikipediaType](args("input")))
  .map { Wikipedia.fromTuple }
  .aggregate(topNaggregator)
```

We can then use the CMS to display on the screen the heavy hitters, the top-*N* editors that made the most revisions. The CMS can also be serialized and stored on disk for future use:

```
wikiData
  .map { cms:CMS =>
    println(" + Total count in the CM sketch : " + cms.totalCount)
    println(" + Heavy Hitters : " + cms.heavyHitters.size)
    cms.heavyHitters.foreach( userid => {
      println("  - User ID : " + userid
        + " with estimated cardinality : " + cms.frequency(userid)
        .estimate)
    } )
    io.scalding.approximations.Utils.serialize(cms)
  }
  .write( SequenceFile(args("output")) )
```

Count-Min Sketch—Top Percentage Example

Instead of specifying the exact number of heavy hitters to track, we can also retrieve the heavy hitters that appear at least as many times (have made so many edits) as a fixed percentage of the total size of the data set (the total number of edits). To get the heavy hitters in this sense, we use the `TopPctCMS` monoid and the appropriate aggregator:

```
// Construct a Count-Min Sketch monoid and bring in helping implicit
// hash functions.
import CMSHasherImplicits._

val cmsMonoid =
  TopPctCMS.monoid[Long](eps=0.01, delta=0.02, seed=(Math.random() *
    100).toInt, heavyHittersPct = topPct )

val topPctaggregator = TopPctCMSAggregator(cmsMonoid)
  .composePrepare[Wikipedia](_.ContributorID)

// Algebird aggregators enable us to combine multiple monoid
// aggregations and perform a computation in a single pass:
val wikiData = TypedPipe.from(TypedTsv[Wikipedia.WikipediaType](input))
  .map { Wikipedia.fromTuple }
  .aggregate(GeneratedTupleAggregator.from2(topNaggregator,
    topPctaggregator))
  .write(TypedTsv(output))
```

Aggregating Approximate Data Structures

In the following example, we process the Wikipedia dataset and calculate multiple metrics:

- The 10 second time window in the full history where Wikipedia was receiving the highest number of writes per second.
- The 100 most active authors of all times.
- The histogram of edits per month.
- The histogram of edits per hour.

Here we create four aggregators, one to handle each aggregation mentioned. Algebird aggregators can be joined to make a single aggregator that can give all four results with a single pass over the data.

```
class WikipediaHistograms(args: Args) extends Job(args) {

  val input  = args.getOrElse("input",
    "data/wikipedia/wikipedia-revisions-sample.tsv")
```

```scala
val output = args.getOrElse("output",
  "data/wikipedia/wikipedia_multihistograms")
val seed    = (Math.random() * 100).toInt

import CMSHasherImplicits._

// Top-10 seconds with most writes/seconds.
val top10qpsMonoid= TopNCMS.monoid[BigInt](0.01, 0.02, seed,
  heavyHittersN = 10)
val top10qps = TopNCMSAggregator(top10qpsMonoid)
  .composePrepare[Wikipedia](x => BigInt( x.DateTime.getBytes ))

// Top-100 authors.
val top100authorsMonoid = TopNCMS.monoid[Long](0.01, 0.02, seed,
  heavyHittersN = 100)
val top100authors =
  TopNCMSAggregator(top100authorsMonoid)
    .composePrepare[Wikipedia](_.ContributorID)

// Top-12 months.
val topMonthsMonoid = TopNCMS.monoid[Long](0.01, 0.02, seed,
  heavyHittersN = 12)
val top12Months = TopNCMSAggregator(topMonthsMonoid)
  .composePrepare[Wikipedia](
    x => x.DateTime.substring(5, 7).toLong)

// Top-24 hours.
val top24HoursMonoid = TopNCMS.monoid[Long](0.01, 0.02, seed,
heavyHittersN = 24)
val top24Hours = TopNCMSAggregator(top24HoursMonoid)
  .composePrepare[Wikipedia](
    x => x.DateTime.substring(8, 10).toLong)

val wikiData = TypedPipe.from(
  TypedTsv[Wikipedia.WikipediaType](input))
  .map { Wikipedia.fromTuple }
  .aggregate(GeneratedTupleAggregator.from4(top10qps, top100authors,
  top12Months, top24Hours))
  .write(source.TypedSequenceFile(output))
}
```

Summary of Approximations

Rarely do we need exact answers to questions in the world of social media where what we are measuring is itself the result of a noisy process. Indeed, due to limits on our ability to perfectly collect input data, it is often wasteful to pay for an exact computation on imperfect inputs. We have seen three powerful algorithms—HyperLogLog, Bloom filters, and Count-Min Sketch—that give you approximate set size, approximate set membership, and approximate frequency counts, respectively. Each of these structures is a commutative monoid; they have associative and commutative merging operations, so we can leverage the parallelism of the MapReduce-style compute platforms to the fullest. Secondly, the monoid property enables us to merge the results of independent queries to get new answers. We can store summaries of aggregation buckets quickly, even for a dashboard, and then combine these buckets into larger units of aggregations to answer new questions.

Executing on a Hadoop Cluster (Amazon EC2)

Nowadays, multiple cloud platforms provide off-the-shelf distributed environments; however, it is useful to become familiar with the steps you would need to take to set up your own compute cluster "from scratch." This section presents the process of deploying a Hadoop cluster—specifically a Cloudera CDH distribution—on Amazon virtual machine instances. We set up VPC, Security Groups, Elastic IPs, and give you instructions on how to set up a working Hadoop cluster.

We also generate user credentials to share with collaborators working on the same cluster and then provide the means to gracefully shut down the cluster and spin it up on demand to minimize costs.

Installing a CDH Cluster on Amazon EC2

To set up a Cloudera Hadoop distribution on Amazon Web Services (AWS) EC2 instances on isolated Cloud resources, follow these steps below. (These steps should provide guidance for setting up a cluster on Amazon EC2, however, as technology evolves, these steps may not be up-to-date or fully accurate in the future.)

1. Log in to the AWS console (`http://console.aws.amazon.com`) and visit VPC. Select Start VPC Wizard ➪ VPC with a Single Public Subnet ➪ Select, set the name to `hadoop-vpc`, and press Create VPC with the default settings provided.

2. While in the VPC dashboard, create a new security group. Select Security Groups ➪ Create Security Group. Name the new group `hadoop-ports`, add a description, and select the VPC `hadoop-vpc`. As shown in Figure 5.7, add custom TCP rules to anywhere for the ports 22, 7180, 7182, 7183, 7432, 8088, 8888, 18088, 19888, 50070, and all ICMP traffic. Add all traffic on all ports to the VPC subnet (10.0.0.0/24).

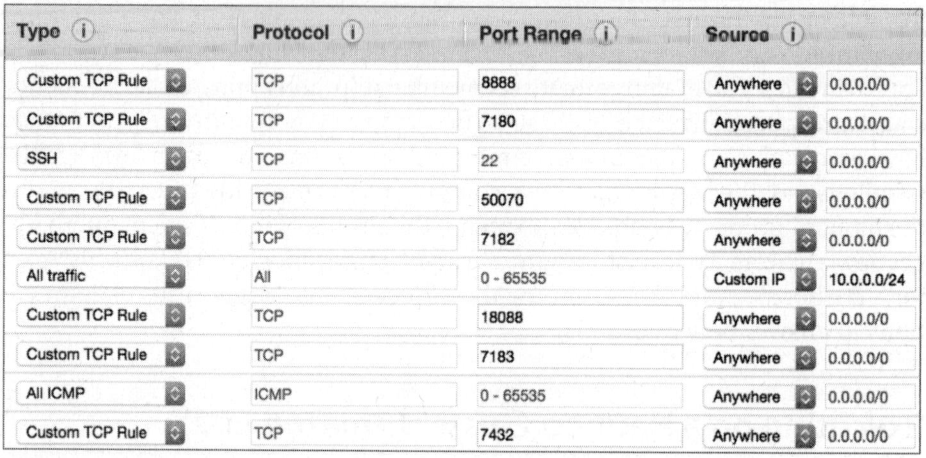

Type ⓘ	Protocol ⓘ	Port Range ⓘ	Source ⓘ	
Custom TCP Rule	TCP	8888	Anywhere	0.0.0.0/0
Custom TCP Rule	TCP	7180	Anywhere	0.0.0.0/0
SSH	TCP	22	Anywhere	0.0.0.0/0
Custom TCP Rule	TCP	50070	Anywhere	0.0.0.0/0
Custom TCP Rule	TCP	7182	Anywhere	0.0.0.0/0
All traffic	All	0 - 65535	Custom IP	10.0.0.0/24
Custom TCP Rule	TCP	18088	Anywhere	0.0.0.0/0
Custom TCP Rule	TCP	7183	Anywhere	0.0.0.0/0
All ICMP	ICMP	0 - 65535	Anywhere	0.0.0.0/0
Custom TCP Rule	TCP	7432	Anywhere	0.0.0.0/0

Figure 5.7: Setting up the Security Group to open the firewall for certain traffic

> **TIP**   You can add a rule for All Traffic with the source as your IP address.

3. Select Key Pairs ⇨ Create Key Pair, and name the new key pair `owner-key`. Download and store the file `owner-key.pem` under your home directory, that is, `~/.ssh/owner-key.pem`.

4. Launch four EC2 instances from the Dashboard. As shown in Figure 5.8, choose the `m3.large` (or similar) instance type that provides 4 CPUs, 15 GB of RAM, and SSD disks. For the Operating System (OS) choose Ubuntu 14.04 LTS or a newer version. Use the VPC as defined in Step 2: `hadoop-vpc` at the network settings and launch the instances with an appropriately sized SSD disk. On the step Configure Security Group, select `hadoop-ports` as the security group.

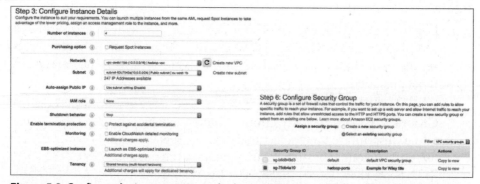

Figure 5.8: Configure the instance type, and select an appropriate VPC and security group

5. As the final step, as shown in Figure 5.9, select as a key pair the `owner-key` that we generated in Step 3 and then Launch the instances.

Figure 5.9: Selecting the user key

6. We assign Elastic IPs to the new instances. Select the Elastic IPs tab from the EC2 management console, and for each instance click Allocate New Address in VPC. Then select one address at a time and click Associate Address and assign it to one of your instances.

7. Add SSH to one of your instances.

> **TIP** If you install on CentOS or RHEL, you need to disable SELinux and reboot before proceeding with the installation. Download and run the Cloudera manager installer. (For information about disabling SELinux on CentOS, see `http://tinyurl.com/1rbhhkj` .) You need to replace your `<private-key-file>`, the `<username>`, and the hostname in the following command:
>
> ```
> $ ssh -i <private-key-file> <username>@ec2-xx-xx-xx-xx.compute-1.
> amazonaws.com
> ```
>
> **Then execute:**
>
> ```
> $ chmod 400 ~/.ssh/owner-key.pem
> $ ssh -i ~/.ssh/owner-key.pem ubuntu@ec2-xx-xx-xx-xx.eu-west-1.\
>   compute.amazonaws.com
> $ wget \
>   http://archive.cloudera.com/cm5/installer/latest/\
>   cloudera-manager-installer.bin
> $ chmod +x cloudera-manager-installer.bin
> $ sudo su
> $ ./cloudera-manager-installer.bin
> ```

8. Cloudera manager requires some time to fully start up but it will be soon accessible on `http://ec2-xx-xx-xx-xx.compute-1.amazonaws.com:7180`.

9. Log in with the default user name `admin` and password `admin`, and proceed with the installation of the Cloudera distribution. Review and follow the first two steps by choosing Cloudera Enterprise Data Hub Edition Trial.

10. As shown in Figure 5.10, specify hosts for your CDH cluster installation by searching the whole VPC network with the pattern 10.0.0.[0-255]. Select the hosts to be added and continue.

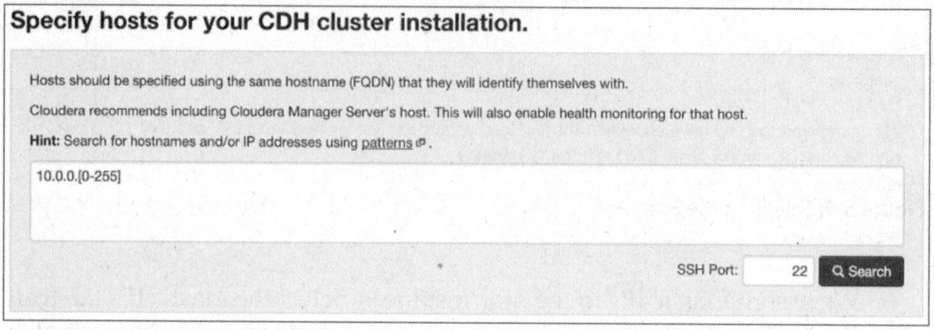

Specify hosts for your CDH cluster installation.

Hosts should be specified using the same hostname (FQDN) that they will identify themselves with.

Cloudera recommends including Cloudera Manager Server's host. This will also enable health monitoring for that host.

Hint: Search for hostnames and/or IP addresses using patterns ⌐ .

10.0.0.[0-255]

SSH Port: 22   Q Search

Figure 5.10: Discover hosts

11. Follow the wizard and choose the pre-selected defaults as shown in Figure 5.11; we need to provide SSH login credentials. Select ubuntu as the user and for authentication use the owner-key.pem private key file.

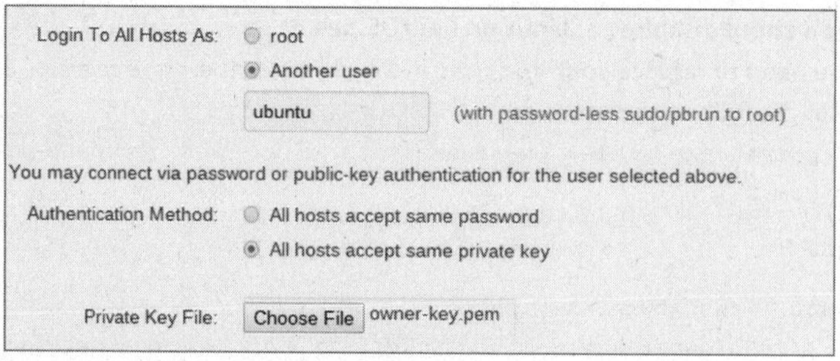

Login To All Hosts As: ○ root
                          ● Another user
                          ubuntu   (with password-less sudo/pbrun to root)

You may connect via password or public-key authentication for the user selected above.

Authentication Method: ○ All hosts accept same password
                          ● All hosts accept same private key

Private Key File: Choose File owner-key.pem

Figure 5.11: Set the user name and key

12. When the installation process completes successfully, we need to set up the new cluster from the Cluster Setup window:

   a. For the first step, select Core Hadoop or All Services depending on requirements.

   b. For the second step, select how Hadoop services will be distributed across the cluster nodes.

   c. For the third step, select Use Embedded Databases. You can write down the auto-generated passwords if you ever need to directly access the Hive metastore database. Click Test Connection and then Continue.

   d. For the fourth step, proceed with the default pre-selected settings.

Congratulations, you just set up your first CDH cluster. Notice that when a cluster starts, it takes some time for all services to start and report a healthy status.

Providing IAM Access to Collaborators

For generating account credentials to share them with collaborators, Amazon provides the Identity and Access Management (IAM) module. By providing access levels to our collaborators, they can access resources and even administer them. To generate such accounts, follow these steps:

1. Log in to the AWS console (`http://console.aws.amazon.com`) using the root credentials.

2. Select Identity & Access Management (`http://console.aws.amazon.com/iam`).

3. Select Users ⇨ Create New Users and add new user names for the collaborators.

4. Create and download the credential file as is shown in Figure 5.12. It contains the user name, the AWS Access Key ID, and the Secret Access Key.

Figure 5.12: Collaborator access key

5. Select Users from the AWS console and select the new collaborators. Then select User Actions ⇨ Manage Password and assign them a password, as shown in Figure 5.13. You can select one user at a time.

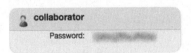

Figure 5.13: Collaborator password

6. Select Groups ⇨ Create New Group , and name the new group `hadoop-collaborators`. Then select Power User Access if you trust your collaborators; or Read Only Access if you want to provide limited access to the Amazon management components.

7. Select the new group and then Group Actions ⇨ Add Users to Group.

8. Visit the Dashboard and then share with your collaborators:

    a. The IAM users sign-in link (see Figure 5.14).

    b. And the user name/credentials and password.

> **Welcome to Identity and Access Management**
>
> IAM users sign-in link:
>
> **https://598575066668.signin.aws.amazon.com/console**   Customize | Copy Link

Figure 5.14: IAM access link

Adding On-Demand Cluster Capabilities

Familiarizing yourself with the capabilities of the cluster means that you can now start Hadoop clusters with the latest major distribution on a small number of nodes. This is the usual setup of lab clusters on the cloud, and we usually use a small number of 4 to 8 high-specification VMs that provide 32 CPU, 244 GB RAM, and multiple SSDs.

When building a cluster of any size, the cost of the infrastructure can easily become an issue. It's possible the cluster will be utilized only a few hours per day and stay idle most of the day. The wisest thing to do in that case is to take advantage of the scalability that the cloud provides and provide the means to release the CPU and memory resources when they are not needed. The long-term data, however, both on the operating system file system as well as the HDFS file system, need to be preserved.

As shown in Figure 5.15, you can shut down the cluster gracefully:

1. Stop the cluster in the Cloudera Manager status page.

2. Stop the Cloudera Management Service Actions.

3. Select and stop the Amazon instances on EC2, as shown in Figure 5.16.

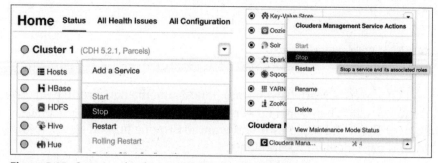

Figure 5.15: Stopping the cluster with Cloudera Manager

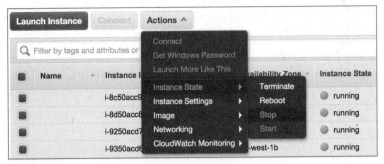

Figure 5.16: Stop Amazon EC2 instances

To bring the same cluster alive, just set the Instance State of the instances to Start. Within a few minutes the instances will run, and you can now access the Cloudera manager homepage to start up the cluster and the Cloudera Management Service Account.

Summary

This chapter discussed the essentials of processing the types of datasets that you are most likely to encounter while working with social media data. These datasets have properties that often make them challenging to work with, and which normally necessitate the use of distributed approaches. At the same time, we have seen that there are algorithms that allowed us to find computationally feasible solutions to answer the most common questions we're asking about the datasets that we can collect from these services.

- Given the nature of how frequently humans interact with social media services, you can expect that the logs collected on human activity will be very large, and thus we need to make use of distributed processing to analyze them. The MapReduce paradigm has emerged as one of the leading approaches for offline processing of large datasets, and you learned the essentials of how it works and what to consider when working with skewed datasets in the beginning of this chapter.

- You also saw a few different kinds of patterns for processing and preparing datasets that can speed up the most common types of calculations and queries on them.

- Human activity data itself is noisy, therefore we don't always require that our calculated statistics on them are exact. If we accept that our results are within guaranteed bounds of the expected answer, there are algorithms that can approximate several of these calculations with more efficient representations that can be better suited for a MapReduce-style processing as well.

- Finally, since cloud-side storage and processing has become commonplace, we briefly highlighted how to provision small clusters of servers on a cloud provider for distributed processing with Hadoop.

Learn, Map, and Recommend

User interaction is one of the most commonly collected type of data in social media platforms. People use online platforms to make decisions about what goods to purchase, what movies to watch, when to interact with friends, and so on. All these decisions constitute valuable information to help you understand users' behavioral patterns. Social media platforms also consist of several different components where people make choices and their choices can easily be logged for further processing. This chapter elaborates on how to model this type of data and extract meaningful, valuable information, and use this for decision making and recommendations.

Recommending items to users in social media has different problem stages depending on the age/state of the social media service we're working with. For example, suppose you have a new platform in which you jump start the product by providing new content to new users. This is a unique problem—the so-called *cold-start problem*. In another case, suppose there is some level of maturity in the product with some history of user engagement. This problem—the *mainstream problem*—is significantly different than the cold-start problem. This chapter starts by assuming some level of history and data liquidity. This can help you understand the fundamentals of making recommendations. The end of the chapter talks about edge cases such as the cold-start problem and incorporating covariates.

To discuss the mainstream problem, we divide the entire process into three pieces: Learn, map, and recommend. The first stage, *learning*, uses algorithms to extract information from the entire data set. The *mapping* stage maps users to the learned information space, in other words it finds how the learned models best fit for each. The final step, the *recommendation* stage, uses the mapped user data and the extracted patterns to make a prediction. The following sections elaborate on each of these pieces.

Social Media Services Online

Let us start with enumerating examples from different online consumer products that are already part of or can be directly embedded into today's social media platforms.

Search Engines

Search engines provide results based on a search query. Figure 6.1 shows an example: A list of websites with snippets summarizing the hyperlink found as a relevant result for the query. For social media platforms, these search results can be content posted on the platform (e.g., Tweets on Twitter), other users' profiles, or media such as photos or videos. Every search query is an explicit input from a user, and you can consider this data as users on one side of the relation, and the set of search queries on the other side. Any search action is an association of a user with that query where a user can search multiple queries and a query can be searched by multiple people. This can be viewed as consumption data where users *consume* from the pool of possible search queries.

This is not the complete story. After querying input, the engine shows relevant results based on a ranking algorithm. Users engage with the content based on not only the relevance of the item to their query, but also on their interest. This brings up the question of personalized results. How can you use such engagement data to rank items in a personalized way? This is a particularly big problem in social media platforms because there is a good chance that users from different regions of the world with different interests have different preferences of content as well.

Content Engagement

Videos watched on Netflix, items purchased on Amazon, Tweets favorited on Twitter are all examples of content/items presented to the users on those platforms. Within each consumer product there is a choice, and the user picks one to interact with following their personal interests. For Netflix, movies are considered to be on the items side and an association between users and movies could be made if a user watches a movie to the end. For Amazon, customers are the users, and they're linked with items to be purchased or if they view an item's page. On Twitter, users can be associated with Tweets based on whether they for instance favorite/retweet the particular Tweet.

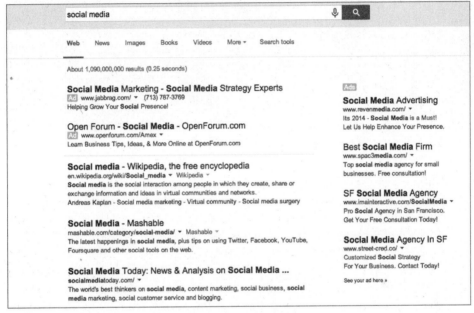

Figure 6.1: A typical Web interface for search engine results

Content is one of the most important aspects of social media platforms (Figure 6.2 shows a Netflix on-demand movie library). We have discussed how to process and make use of this information in Chapter 4. However, in this chapter the focus is to model the user's engagement with particular pieces of content. Engagement might be defined differently within each consumer product: At an online merchant, it might be defined as the product view, whereas on Netflix, it might be watching a movie. For social media platforms, it is often about the social interactions the platform provides to the user. It is sometimes a link click, a share, a comment, a retweet, or a favorite, depending on what kind of service we're talking about.

Figure 6.2: Netflix on-demand movie library

Content engagement is important for several reasons such as boosting interest and attracting more users to the platform. It is important to recommend the right item to the user at appropriate locations at the right time to boost the engagement. For instance, a new user's on-boarding process and the items recommended at this stage can be critical for user retention.

Content engagement is also important for monetization. One way to monetize social media platforms is to provide promoted/sponsored content. A common, organic way of content delivery is through the follow/friendship graph of the user. For example, if user A follows user B, then any content produced by user B will show up on the home page/timeline of user A. However, if user A does not follow user C but user C wants to show its content to user A, this is normally not possible through the usual ways as designed by the service. Many social media platforms invented can promote products wherein user C pays the platform, and in return the platform shows the promoted content to user A. Often, user C is charged only when user A interacts with the content. This means that given an impression, the engagement rate is important for the efficiency of the monetization strategy. The whole area of advertisement targeting uses engagement data to present the most relevant promoted content to users. The goal is often to keep the engagement rate as high as possible, while not decreasing user satisfaction.

Interactions with the Real World

One important direction in social media is *location-based activity*. This is an additional dimension different from the usual content-based activities a user can perform on social media. Using this, you can extract valuable information about users or directly recommend new items/locations depending on the product focus.

Social media *check-ins* are the most common way a user expresses her location as well as the detailed explanation of the place (i.e., is this a shop? A restaurant? If it is a restaurant, did you like it? Did you give a rating? How many times have you been there before?) The first task in generating this type of information is to recommend new locations (e.g., new restaurants, cafes, and shops) based on previous check-ins/ratings of the users. However, you can use this information to recommend other regular content. For instance, certain age/gender groups or users belonging to different economic classes such as middle income might regularly check in at certain restaurants. Knowing that a user is at that location can provide those additional pieces of demographic information about the user. You can then use this information in restaurant recommendations in turn. Figure 6.3 shows an example screenshot of Foursquare check-ins.

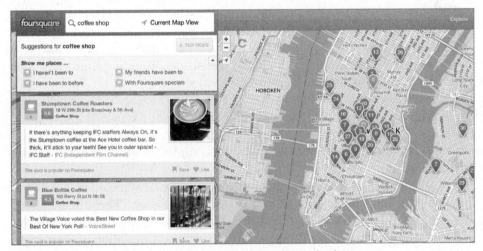

Figure 6.3: A location-based social media service: Foursquare check-ins

Interactions with People

Another important (and probably the most distinctive) aspect of social media platforms is the people forming their user bases. In these platforms, the main difference from other consumer products is the social aspect. People are connected to each other to form a social graph, either in a directed manner (with a one-way follow action from one user to the other) or in a friendship-like manner (users should mutually agree to be connected). It is vital to get connected to the right users as soon as possible to have the right experience of the product, because the content you see generally comes from the people you are connected to. So, it is also important to suggest the right users to follow/become friends with.

One way of representing either directed or undirected social graphs is to place users at one side of the associations we have been discussing, and the accounts they follow/friend with on the other side. With this interpretation, the format is not that different from the ones mentioned when we talked about content engagement or search engines earlier in this chapter. Potential users to follow are the items available for selection and performing the follow/friend action is equivalent to choosing/consuming the item.

We have just discussed some actual applications where the relationships between users and content, or among users, can be represented in a very similar problem formulation: that of associations among these entities. In mathematics and computer science, this format is also known as a *bipartite graph* where one set of nodes represents the users and the other set of nodes represents the items, and the association is denoted with the edges of the graph. A directed follow graph can be interpreted as an adjacency matrix also.

This lets us generalize the problem as well as the solution: How can we process user–item consumption and choice data and provide recommendations using this information? How can we use this type of data to generate insights? Answering these questions and building algorithms providing smart solutions is crucial to boosting the efficiency and the value of the platform. For example, for a social platform, which posts are engaged with, which accounts are followed by, or which promoted content is interacted with all give useful information about the platform's users. This useful information can be both used to build smarter, personalized products as well as to understand how our users are using the platform.

Processing such data is a relevant question to the fields at the interface of computer science, statistics, mathematics, and signal processing. "Recommendation" in social media platforms is undergoing an explosive growth, mainly due to the usefulness it provides as a result of a massive accumulation of interaction data. The sheer size of these data sets requires large-scale computational (rather than human-powered) data analysis and decision making, and advances in computing resources are a driving force in this growth. However, the scale and high dimensionality of the data are such that powerful present-day computing resources can only partially address the complexity of the problems—they need to be paired with advanced techniques and algorithms.

We elaborate on some of the algorithms here by considering model building, exploratory analysis, visualization, and evaluation. In modern data science, one important problem of the model building phase is how to incorporate data-specific properties to the models. Early machine learning techniques were designed to work on generic data sets, using parameters specified *a priori*. However, as the diversity and complexity of the data sets grew, more advanced approaches were needed, tailored to the specific properties of the type of application under study. Such tailoring can take many different forms. For instance, it may be necessary to learn the model parameters from the data (instead of specifying them from the start); you can incorporate prior information (such as sparsity for special representations, which themselves have to be learned); it may be beneficial to use relational structure within the data, which can be available in many guises.

This chapter visits these approaches, demonstrating the efficiency and accuracy of those models.

Problem Formulation

Now we formulate the problem. Suppose our social media product is out there in use for some period of time and the engagement/interaction data is collected as a list of *<user_id, item_id>* tuples (denoting the interaction of *user_id* with *item_id*), and our goal is to find the possibility of an unobserved interaction of *users* with *items* and later use this as a recommendation to the user in the product. There are several ways of performing this, such as:

- Considering the data as a matrix and "completing" it.
- Applying domain specific algorithms, such as graph link completion for friend recommendation.
- Using similarity sets for item recommendation, clustering, and supervised learning jointly with extensive feature engineering.

This section proceeds with a matrix-based solution; we briefly talk about other techniques later in this chapter.

In a typical popular social media platform, there are millions of users daily visiting the platform with millions of posts/comments generated. Let's suppose there are exactly 1 million (10^6) users and 1 million (10^6) items. In this case, the total possible number of interactions is 10^{12} (the product of the number of users and the number of items). However, in practice the number of such interactions is often significantly fewer than the possible size—for example, on the level of hundreds on average per user, making an approximate total of 10^8. Mathematically speaking, we can view this type of data as a matrix, where rows represent users and columns represent items. For example, for movie recommendations, the rows represent the movie ratings/choices of the users—for each user there is a new row, as shown in Figure 6.4. The type of matrices where the number of entries that are defined or different from zero is much smaller than the total number of entries in the matrix are defined as *sparse matrices*.

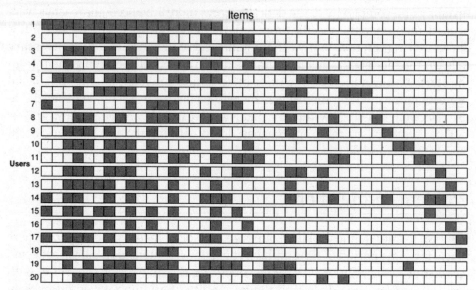

Figure 6.4: Representation of the observation matrix $X \in R^{N \times P}$ (e.g., movie ratings by users, in which rows represent the users and columns represent the items). The image is from "The Indian Buffet Process: An Introduction and Review" by Griffiths, et. al. (`http://jmlr.org/papers/volume12/griffiths11a/griffiths11a.pdf`)

Suppose we denote the data via an observation matrix $\mathbf{X} \in R^{N \times P}$, where rows represent the users and columns represent the items, and the value of interaction is the matrix entry x_{ij} (e.g., the movie ratings example as we referred to above). In binary matrices the value is {0, 1}, in rating data sets generally it's a real value representing the rating of the item by the users: By R we denote the set of real numbers. For example, in Figure 6.4 we assume there are N users and P items and we assume that x_{ij} represents the movie rating of ith user for jth movie.

In real-life scenarios, most of the entries of $\mathbf{X}$ are missing, which makes it a sparse matrix. This is easy to understand because the users watch only a limited number of movies from the entire library in their lifetime based on their taste.

What would be very useful after all is if we could make predictions about matrix element values that are not observed, but in a "parallel universe" could be there if, say, users had more time to watch movies. This corresponds to predicting what users most likely value if they knew about that piece of content. This task is mathematically defined as completing the missing values of the matrix, based on information from given existing entries of the preference matrix we observed.

Learning and Mapping

In all the applications mentioned so far, the fundamental problem is the high dimensionality of the data. This means that the value P corresponding to the number of items (e.g., number of movies in a movie recommendation, number of users in a social media friend recommendation, number of places one can check in at) is extremely high—often on the level of hundreds of thousands or millions. Mathematically speaking, this means that we place every single user in a space of that many dimensions based on what they have done or like. Intuitively, this does not make sense. We know that every human being can be distinct and has her own characteristics. To explain overall behavior, there are a finite and small number of latent possible explanations that fits reality. What we observe as data are just the reflections of those latent dynamics governing reality.

Pure science researchers, such as physicists, chemists, or biologists perform thousands of experiments to try to explain all these observations with simple explanations. For example, Isaac Newton's $F = ma$ formula explains the relation between mass (m), acceleration (a), and force (F). We could find thousands of other things that can be correlated with acceleration. However, the latent reason determining the acceleration of matter can be explained universally with force (F)—though later there were observations this law could not explain, and new theories were proposed. Albert Einstein's $E = mc^2$ formula explains the relation between energy and mass. For hundreds of years scientists thought about this universal problem—the relation of energy and matter—and eventually Einstein reduced all these observations and thoughts into one simple formula explaining these, consistent with all prevailing observations. When you visit a doctor, she listens to all symptoms, records all observations possibly with some tests, and proposes a diagnosis trying to find the underlying cause of all symptoms and test results.

The common theme in all these examples is that they all have quite a significant amount of observations accumulated, and they all try to find a latent reason or factor explaining all these observations. William of Ockham (c. 1287–1347), an influential medieval philosopher, is known for his *Ockham's razor*. In today's language it states that *given two explanations of the data, all other things being equal, the simpler explanation is preferable*. The interpretation of this in machine learning is this: Discover the simplest hypothesis that is consistent with the sample data. This principle is employed in different ways within each area of machine learning. We will not go into each with detail, but we will give some examples. For instance, the simplest hypothesis we seek corresponds to the lowest degree of polynomial when we try to fit the observed data with a different possible family of polynomials. It corresponds to the lowest number of iterations to run a boosting algorithm. Later in this chapter, we discuss what it means in the case of the matrix-based solutions considered in this chapter.

The same applies to the doctor example because doctors diagnose using the exact same principle. Each symptom might be caused by a different illness, but they try to find the simplest solution, preferably a single source for all symptoms. This is also true for scientists like Albert Einstein. He collected information based on observations and tried to explain the energy–mass relationship with the fewest possible causes.

We can apply the same idea to the problem we're exploring in this section. We would like to learn about our stereotype user representation and using what we learn to perform predictions about what to recommend to those users. The issue is that in the raw data, every user is represented in the item space, meaning that each user is denoted via the movies he rated. In this original item space, the data is high dimensional, there are millions of items explaining every user's behavior. This makes the prediction problem difficult. We need to first transform the problem to an easier one. In problem solving this is a common technique in which one first transforms a hard problem into a new one. In this case, this means that instead of representing users in the item space, we need to represent them in a new latent dimension-reduced space. This corresponds to representing every user as a linear combination of the factors that we'll find—we will talk about how to find these factors in the following sections—and the factors are going to have a reduced number of dimensions. Then we need to transform back to the original space. This technique is graphically represented in Figure 6.5.

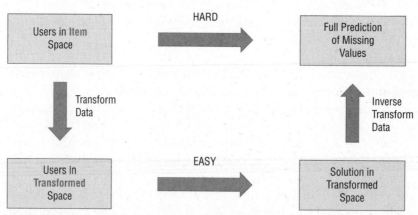

Figure 6.5: A generic problem-solving paradigm explaining why we transform data into different model representations

One way to transform the data is to use linear deterministic transformations. As shown in Equation 6.1, we can transform the observed data X with a linear transformation operator F so that

$$Y = F(X),\qquad(6.1)$$

and F maps the data to the new space in which Y represents the embedding of the data. Genius mathematicians defined deterministic transformations such as the Laplace transform, Fourier transform, and Wavelet transform, in which each carries certain characteristics with beneficial properties. However, in most of these transformations the operator F is a hand-designed operator with rigorous mathematical properties. It does not depend on the data; it is predefined with a given objective: For instance, we either reveal the spectrum, or eigenvectors, and so on, of X. These transformations are out of the scope of this book and not useful in this particular application.

In a modern approach, a new paradigm suggests that you can learn this transformation from the data. The general principle is to define an objective and design an algorithm finding the transformation by optimizing the objective. This objective generally represents how well the current situation of the learned transformation explains the observed data. We will talk about a specific function that realizes these objectives. This new paradigm uses the data and learns both F and Y from the data. The benefits of these new approaches are that you can include your intuitive prior information about the data into learning so that the transformation carries those properties.

The collaborative filtering (CF) approach—predicting the interests of a user by collecting preferences from many users—has dominated the field and made significant progress in recent years. The fundamental idea is to use repeating patterns in both users and items. We know that there are movies similar to each other, and we also know that there are users similar to each other. The question is how to incorporate this information into a predictive model?

Matrix Factorization

A particular technique to extract patterns from data represented as a matrix is to *factorize* it. This means that given an observation matrix, we want to form two matrices out of it. One of the extracted matrices represents the patterns of users; the other represents the patterns for items. You can think of those patterns as hidden distributed similarities between users in the raw data. This technique is widely known as *matrix factorization* (MF). It has become a most important technique in the implementations of collaborative filtering. Depending on what we believe is true for the system we're modeling (the prior assumptions about the data we collect), separate criteria can be used in the factorization. The general principle is to define a quality-checking metric and iteratively change the factorized matrices to converge to high-quality patterns, minimizing the error on the validation set.

Mathematically speaking, we want to factorize a partially observed matrix $X \in R^{N \times P}$ into a product of two other matrices so that, as shown in Equation 6.2,

$$X \approx SD, \tag{6.2}$$

where $S \in R^{N \times K}$ is the learned user score matrix, $D \in R^{K \times P}$ is the learned item matrix. $\widehat{X} = SD$ is called the K-rank approximation of X. Later in this chapter in the "Interpreting the Learned Stereotypes" section we will talk in detail about the meaning of this new K-dimensional space and what the columns and rows correspond to. Moreover, we say that the matrix is partially observed because in many applications, the user was not even exposed to all the content, and it is not fair to consider values for those missing interactions. We do not know if the user would interact with the content if they knew about it. Hence, the data is considered as partially observed.

There are an infinite number of ways to choose S and D, so we could have additional constraints limiting the solution space into a meaningful size that fits the prior assumptions we have. Depending on the data there might be multiple such constraints. For example, conditions on the sparsity of S and D can be one constraint. Also, we might want to have non-negative values in both S and D only. All these constraints depend on the problem, applications, and interpretability of the factorization.

The underlying principle in this approach is to extract recurring patterns and represent the entire user set in this new space of recurring patterns. The observation matrix is generally high dimensional. In other words, there are hundreds of thousands of movies, millions of people to follow, billions of Tweets to engage with. However, we know that there may be only a handful of *stereotypes*. For instance, there are people who like horror movies, comedies, or action movies. For restaurants there are people who like Japanese food, Indian food, or Middle Eastern cuisine. This gives us the idea that although there are millions of dimensions in the item space, indeed we could represent all users by a weighted sum of a set of stereotypes. The learning task includes both extracting those stereotypes (represented by the D matrix) and the weights per-person denoting each person's characteristic (represented by the S matrix).

Here is a simple example: Suppose we want to recommend movies to users. Stereotype movie choices would be horror, action, comedy, drama, and more. Suppose there are K of those stereotypes that should be learned from the data. We can represent each stereotype as a row vector $d_k \in R^P$ where P is the total number of movies. In this notation d_k represents how strongly the kth stereotype would have rated a given movie, and forms the kth row of D. Hence, a stereotype implies a way of movie choices: Each stereotype gives a rating to every movie, but the way they score them (particularly the top weighted movies) defines the characteristic of the stereotype. Suppose we already know all the d_ks. Then the task is to represent every user by weighted combination of these stereotypes. For example, a user can be modeled by a combination of <*Horror: 40%, Comedy: 10%, Classics: 50%*>, but another one can be <*Comedy: 80%, Action: 20%*>, where each of these stereotype movie choices are encoded into the d_k so that the horror movies are highly rated for the "Horror" stereotype and action movies are highly rated for the "Action" stereotype. This opens up the second part of the problem: How do we learn all these scores per person, explaining how each person is represented in the new stereotype space? This information is encapsulated by the **S** matrix so that each row $s_i \in R^K$ encodes the weights for user i, representing her characteristics. In statistics **D** is called the *factor loadings* and **S** is called the *factor scores*. They represent the factorization of the original data matrix **X**.

As mentioned, in data sets **X** has many missing values, and the goal is to learn the user and item matrices from the observed ones and use the *K*-rank approximation as the prediction of user interests. The general principle to learn **D** and **S** is to define a cost function and minimize it iteratively while updating **D** and **S**. Generally, the cost function is a function of the difference between the actual **X** and the reconstruction provided by **SD**. We will talk about specific equations incorporating other constraints later in this chapter.

One way of iteratively minimizing this error is called *coordinate descent*. The name denotes that in every iteration the algorithm takes a step minimizing the cost in the direction of the corresponding variable. This provides a solution with minimum error.

Learning, Training

Learning can be defined as a process of constructing rules from historical observations or data and using them in the future, mostly for making predictions and sometimes for exploratory purposes. Sometimes, the process of specifying the rules, looking at the historical data is called *training*.

Under- and Overfitting

How much one relies on the observation or history during this process is critical. This is related to how complex our rules are going to be as well. If our rules are simple and we do not focus on every single detail in the data, probably we are going to learn very general patterns, and these will not be super useful for predicting challenging future observations. This is called *underfitting* in machine learning. However, if our rules are complex and we want to capture every detail in our observation set, we might learn unnecessary details. This is particularly a big problem when our data set is limited and noisy. In this case, the model parameters tend to focus on noisy samples in the data and tend to be weak at generalization to new samples. This phenomenon is called *overfitting*.

Here's an intuitive example of overfitting. Suppose in a social media platform there is a timeline in which content is presented to the user in a sequence designed by algorithms—the algorithms decide which specific content is shown to the users in what order. One important aspect of such algorithms is measured by the diversity of the content shown to the users. We need to ask questions such as: Is this algorithm designed to show only sports events? Is it biased to showing content only from celebrities?

Another aspect in social media platforms is *user churn*. Any user not coming back or logging in to the platform is considered as churned. The goal of many different features of a social media platform, including the algorithms designing the timelines, is to increase user satisfaction and reduce churn.

Suppose we want to explain the relation between the diversity in an algorithmically curated timeline and user churn rate in a social media platform, and that we have observed data that looks like the data in Figure 6.6. Let's assume for the sake of a concrete example that the x axis is the diversity in the home timeline of a user in terms of content interestingness, and the y axis is the churn rate of the user we would like to model; we assume there is a correlation between how interesting one's timeline is and how likely one comes back to use the service.

Figure 6.6: Intuitive explanations for under- and overfitting of models. Underfitting explains the observed data with a curve with complexity not enough to have a good generalization to new data. Overfitting explains the observed data with a curve with unnecessarily high model complexity. This causes poor generalization as well. The plot is from `http://pingax.com/regularization-implementation-r/`.

In this figure, we observe three polynomials fitted to the observed data: 1) underfitted, 2) fitted with a good balance, and 3) overfitted. The balanced fit, which is in the middle, tells us that if the diversity in the timeline increases too much or decreases too much, the user churn increases. As can be seen in this middle plot, the learned polynomial is about second or third degree, and there is a nonlinearity in the plot. If we underfit as in this example, we try to explain the relation with a very low-dimensional (approximately linear) function, which fails to explain the churn rate particularly when the diversity is low. It should have predicted high churn rate, whereas it predicts low. When overfitting happens, the relation is explained with something that looks like a polynomial of a higher degree. As can be seen in the plot, this is also unnecessary and might cause prediction error.

Practically, how do we detect overfitting? Many learning algorithms have a parameter to control the complexity of the learning algorithm—that is, a parameter tuning how complex we would like the explanation to make to provide a reasoning for complex phenomena. In Figure 6.6, this could be the degree of the polynomials we're fitting. A general framework to detect under- and overfitting is to have a set of those potential parameters and then split the data into parts such as *training* and *test* sets and finally check the *error* of the fits both in the training and test. The optimal fitting is captured when both are minimized. If the training error is minimized but the test is not, this is generally overfitting. If both are not minimized this is underfitting.

Another question we can ask is: Is it possible to assist the learning algorithm during this process? It is obvious that on one side there is an underfitting problem, and on the other side there is an overfitting problem. This is one of the most common trade-offs faced by almost all machine learning algorithms. In general, we should find the optimal point in between. What if we try to do this inside the learning algorithm?

The general solution to this problem in algorithms minimizing a cost function is to add a *regularization term* to the cost. This is a way to enforce the algorithm to have a balance between how much it will *fit* (minimize the vanilla cost function) and how much it will try to have stable model variables. Generally, a parameter governs the trade-off between stabilizing the model variables and fitting according to whatever the data indicates.

Regularizing in Matrix Factorization

In particular, for matrix factorization, we handle this with a regularization parameter η. As shown in Equation 7.3, the full objective function is given as

$$C(\mathbf{S}, \mathbf{D}) = \sum_{i,j} \left(x_{ij} - \sum_{k=1}^{K} s_{ik} d_{kj} \right)^2 + \eta \left(\sum_{i=1}^{N} \|\mathbf{S}_{i.}\|_2^2 + \sum_{j=1}^{P} \|\mathbf{D}_{.j}\|_2^2 \right). \tag{6.3}$$

In this equation the first term corresponds to a squared distance of the current state of the residual (x_{ij} is the observation and $\sum_{k=1}^{K} s_{ik} d_{kj}$ is the approximation with the factorization s_{ik} and d_{kj}). The closer the approximation to the real value, the smaller the residual is and the more we trust the given observations x_{ij}. The latter part is the regularization portion of the cost function controlled by η. $\|\mathbf{S}_{i.}\|_2^2$

is the L_2 norm of the vector $\mathbf{S}_{i,}$ which is simply the squared sums of all items in the ith row of $\mathbf{S}$. When we minimize the entire cost function, the regularization does not let the model variables s_{ik} and d_{kj} overshoot. This simply prevents overfitting. But why? If a learning algorithm overfits, the learner will want to express every single observation in the training data, including a couple of noisy samples. This will make the model parameters significantly affected by just a couple of outlier points. Also, pay attention that the regularization part of the cost function does not include any data related items in it.

The amount of regularization is controlled by the parameter η, which is fed to the algorithm as a fixed constant. A low η tells the algorithm that we want to focus on minimizing the data-related portion of the cost function. Otherwise, we tell the algorithm to try not to overshoot the model variables. If it is too large, the information in the data provided by x_{ij} is simply discarded, which might cause underfitting. The user of those algorithms should be careful while choosing η for this reason. A general framework is to use cross-validation to find an optimal η. Cross-validation is the process of picking a set of candidates for η, trying each, and picking the model that performs better.

Non-Negative Matrix Factorization and Sparsity

This chapter focuses on one particular form of matrix factorization: Non-negative Matrix Factorization (NMF). As mentioned before, the fundamental advantage of learning the transformation from the data is to incorporate intuition and prior information so that the learned transformation is optimal for your application. NMF is a form of matrix factorization in which both the input (interaction data $\mathbf{X}$) and the output (learned factor loadings $\mathbf{D}$ and factor scores $\mathbf{S}$) are subject to the constraint of being non-negative. This makes a lot of sense for recommendation systems because the observed data is almost always non-negative (e.g., click logs, movie ratings, and engagement logs) and we also expect the components of the learned stereotypes to be non-negative.

Regularization is critical to impose prior knowledge or requirements of the variables as well. For example, even though there might be thousands of items or movies, someone might prefer just a handful of them. This is true also for stereotypes $\mathbf{d}_k$ which we extract from the data. In this case, we expect $\mathbf{d}_k$ to be sparse because it represents the choices of the kth stereotype. In this case, we might want to use L_1 regularization, which imposes the L_1 norm to the model variables in the cost function instead of L_2. In Equation 6.3, we used the L_2 norm in the regularization term; the L_1 norm is similar to this, but it would sum over the absolute values of the vector components, instead of their squares. The L_1 norm tends to pick sparse solutions, meaning that only a few components are non-zero in the solution. The reason can be explained in several different rigorous ways such as visualizing the geometric interpretation of the objective function versus constraints, or looking at Bayesian interpretations such as Gaussian and Laplacian priors. We don't go into detail about these, but these can be good directions for the reader for a deeper analysis.

An intuitive explanation for why L_1 suppresses the coefficients more is as follows: The L_2 norm incorporates the sum of the squares of the coefficients. It highly penalizes the big values and favors small values for each coefficient. Any large non-zero value is not preferred. On the other hand, the L_1 norm takes the sum of the absolute values of the coefficients. It is completely fine for one value to be 0. Now look at an example. Suppose you apply the L_1 and L_2 norm to a 3-dimensional coefficient vector. Consider two candidates: (2, 2, 2) and (0, 5, 0). The L_2 norms are $\sqrt{2^2 + 2^2 + 2^2} \approx 3.46$ and $\sqrt{0^2 + 5^2 + 0^2} = 5$, respectively, for the two vectors. The L_1 norms are $|2|+|2|+|2| = 6$ and $|0|+|5|+|0| = 5$. So, the L_2 norm would favor the (2, 2, 2) solution, whereas L_1 would favor the (0, 5, 0) solution.

Demonstration on Movie Ratings

This section demonstrates how NMF works on a movie rating data set called MovieLens (https://grouplens.org/datasets/movielens/). The raw data is the movie ratings {1, 2, 3, 4, 5} of 938 users on 1682 movies. Out of 1.6 M possible combination of user-movie pairs, we observe only 0.1 M ratings. This is only 6% of all possibilities.

Listing 6.1 shows how we fit an NMF model to this data set. Each function is explained in the relevant code comment. The general principle is to load the data and run R's NMF package. Details of the package can be found by typing `help('nmf')` in R after the library is installed and loaded. We specify the rank of the factorization as $K = 20$.

Listing 6.1: Fitting the NMF model on the MovieLens movie ratings data set. (`mf_fit.R`)

```
library(Matrix)
library(NMF)
library(ggplot2)

# Reads data, fits the model, and saves it.
how.i.fit.the.model = function()
{
    x = readMM('data/movielens/ml-100k/u.mm')
    s = as.matrix(x)

    # We know that the number of users is 938.
    number.of.users = 938

    # Get the relevant users only we are interested in.
    s = s[1 : number.of.users,]

    # K, the rank, is set to 20.
    K = 20
```

```
# The model is trained here.
# This is the factorization stage. It takes some time.
# There are several methods/algorithms incorporating different
# regularization techniques. Run help('nmf') in R to see further
# details.
# Here we use the default one incorporating a KL divergence-based
# cost function.
my.nmf.20 = nmf(s, K, .options='v')

# Save the model to disk to be used later. We want to save it to
# disk since it is expensive to re-run it again and again.
save(my.nmf.20, file='data/movielens/fits/nmf20.rda')
}

how.i.fit.the.model()

load('fits/nmf20.rda')

# Give the object a convenient name.
# We will use it later in the following code sections.
m = my.nmf.20

# Look at the structure of the result.
str(m)
```

The choice of K is tricky and there is no single method working for every condition. K represents the number of latent stereotypes we would like to find; in most applications this is unknown. One technique is to try different values of K and check evaluation metrics on hold-out data. We will talk about these evaluation metrics later in the chapter in the "Evaluation" section. Another technique is to use *Bayesian nonparametrics* to learn a posterior distribution of K (see http://www.columbia.edu/~jwp2128/Papers/ZhouWangChenetal2011. pdf). In this case, the model and the algorithm are completely designed for this purpose of using full Bayesian methods. These methods are often more complex than the matrix-based methods discussed here. Finally, one last technique is the *empirical smart guess*. Though the number of stereotypes is hard to know exactly, we can make a guess. For example, we know that this number is not too small (there should be enough diversity), as well as too large (the whole point is to reduce dimensionality). Also, another viewpoint is the level of resolution in the dimension-reduced space. If we pick K high, more detailed stereotypes are going to be learned. For example, if $K = 3$, we are likely to learn only generic stereotypes such as "Action," "Comedy," "Horror," and so on. If we pick $K = 100$, probably we will learn specific horror genres such as "Vintage horror movies," "New horror movies," "Scientific thrillers," and more. Considering all these different angles, we pick $K = 20$ for simplicity: We want to be as simple as possible and we want to capture enough diversity. $K = 20$ means that we will observe 20 different stereotypes.

In Figures 6.7 and 6.8 we show the weights learned for two different latent stereotype movie choices, $\mathbf{d}_k$ where $k = 1$ and $k = 5$. We observe that weights are all positive due to the non-negativity assumption of the model, and they give high weights to different movies, representing their individual characteristics.

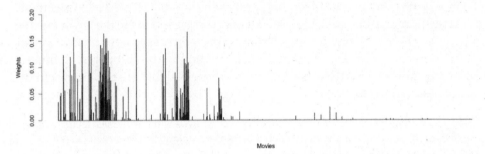

Figure 6.7: Weights for a given latent stereotype movie choice. This is a plot of $\mathbf{d}_k$ where $k = 1$. We observe that weights are all positive due to non-negativity assumption of the model and they give high weights to different movies.

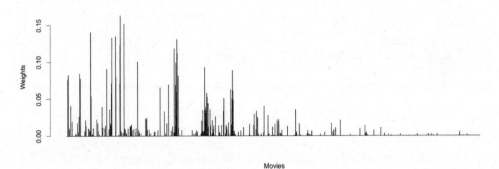

Figure 6.8: This is similar to Figure 6.7, but this plot is for $k = 5$.

In addition to the raw rating data, recommendation systems often have covariate information for both items and users. In this example, for users, this information includes age, gender, occupation, and ZIP code. Covariates are useful to perform exploratory analysis and to extract insights from the user base of the system. For movies, covariates include the date of release, IMDB links, and the genre. We are not using genre in the experiments while fitting the model; however, we do use it to show if the stereotypes found make sense with respect to the homogeneity in genres. This is not necessarily required but we expect some stereotypes to correlate with genres.

Covariates can be useful for prediction as well. There are supervised techniques using such covariate features as those we mention later in this chapter. You can use the NMF as feature extraction, combine the learned factor scores with those covariates, and build a secondary supervised technique to improve the prediction accuracy. The features coming from NMF are simply the factor scores representing the dimension-reduced items. You can simply concatenate those features with other extracted features and use a classifier to predict engagement.

After running Listing 6.1, the `m@fit@H` matrix corresponds to the factor loading matrix **D**. The top 10 movies of each row in this matrix reveal the characteristics of the stereotype. The `print.top.movies` function in the snippet in Listing 6.2 prints the movies for a given stereotype `k` whose weights are the highest in the factor loading matrix.

Listing 6.2: Printing the titles of movies for a given stereotype with the highest factor loading weights; plotting the actual genres of movies that a given stereotype dimension overall describes. (`mf_helpers.R`)

```
# Print the top n movies with names according to what weight they get.
print.top.movies = function(k, fit, items, n=10)
{
    cat((items$title[order(fit@H[k,], decreasing=T)[1 : n]]), sep='\n')
}


# Plot the genre distribution from the downloaded data for a given
# stereotype.
plot.top.genres = function(k, fit, items, n=10)
{
    # In the items data the genres are given in the indexes from 6 : 24.
    # The schema of this is:
    # "id", "title", "date", "video", "imdb",
    # "unknown", "action", "adventure", "animation", "childrens",
    # "comedy", "crime", "documentary", "drama", "fantasy", "film-noir",
    # "horror", "musical", "mystery", "romance", "scifi", "thriller",
    # "war", "western"
    barplot(colSums(items[order(fit@H[k,], decreasing=T)[1 : n], 6 : 24]),
            las=2)
}
```

The `plot.top.genres` function also shown in Listing 6.2 in turn looks at the genres of the top 10 movies for a given stereotype, and plots their overall genre distribution. Note that each movie can have multiple genres, and these genres are part of the ground truth of the MovieLens dataset. Figure 6.9 shows their genre distribution.

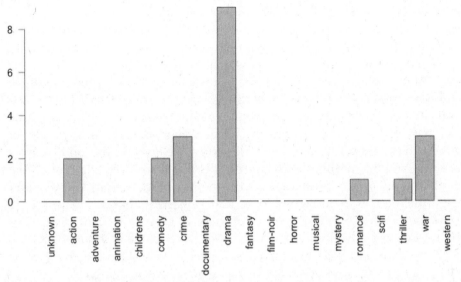

Figure 6.9: The distribution of the actual genres of the top movies for the first latent stereotype we learned from data. This is a plot for $\mathbf{d}_k$ where $k = 1$. We get the top 10 movies with the highest weights in the stereotype. The genre information is part of the MovieLens dataset. Each movie in the top 10 is a binary vector of genres, and one movie can have multiple genres, e.g., drama, fantasy, animation, etc. This data suggests that drama is the most common genre for this stereotype, whereas the others exist with a secondary relevance.

Interpreting the Learned Stereotypes

Each of the k stereotypes is represented in our model with $\mathbf{d}_k \in R^P$. Assuming P movies, each stereotype is a list of movies where their weights are different from stereotype to stereotype. The movies getting high weight in $\mathbf{d}_k$ give us an idea about which stereotype is about what. This section looks at a couple different stereotypes to see if they make sense. While doing this we first look at the top 10 movies according to the magnitude of the weights they get in the corresponding stereotype. We also look at the genres of these top movies in each stereotype: The genre information is a third-party tag we got from the MovieLens data set. Both can give us some idea about what we have learned from the data. We name each stereotype by its corresponding k number. However, be careful: If we rerun these examples, the k values can shuffle around. For example, a stereotype might correspond to $k = 5$ in this chapter, whereas when run again, it might correspond to $k = 12$. This is due to the *identifiability* issue of these types of models. The main reason for this is the randomization in the initialization of the stereotypes while running the matrix factorization. Given the same initialization the algorithm is not randomized. However, different initializations might cause both the change in the order of the stereotypes and a difference in the weights from run to run. This means that, without loss of generality, the columns can be shuffled, and we would get the same quality of learning.

The list following this paragraph shows that the $k = 1$ stereotype consists of well-known movies (based on IMDB ratings) from various dates from the last 30–40 years. This latent dimension presents a hypothetical user who likes these classic movies. Each movie from the third-party genre data is a binary vector of genres, and one movie can have multiple genres. We just take the top 10 movies and count how many times each genre appears. We observe that though the cumulative histogram of the genres of the top 10 movies peak in "drama," and most of the movies are assigned more than one genre. But drama is a more generic genre; the secondary genres of these 10 movies are 3 of "war," 3 of "crime," 2 of "comedy," and 2 of "action." We can conclude that this stereotype is for users who like highly rated movies, not necessarily belonging to a specific genre—there can always be some bias to a specific genre, though.

The movies for stereotype $k = 1$ whose weights are the strongest:

- One Flew Over the Cuckoo's Nest (1975)
- Godfather, The (1972)
- Cool Hand Luke (1967)
- Godfather: Part II, The (1974)
- Shawshank Redemption, The (1994)
- Bridge on the River Kwai, The (1957)
- Sting, The (1973)
- Schindler's List (1993)
- Silence of the Lambs, The (1991)
- Casablanca (1942)

Figure 6.10 shows that the $k = 5$ stereotype consists of horror movies. This latent dimension simply presents a hypothetical user who likes only these kinds of movies. When we look at the genre plot, we observe some difference in the genres compared to the $k = 1$ latent dimension in Figure 6.9. In the $k = 1$ stereotype, the genres were more scattered because the underlying reason for the movies coming together under a stereotype was most likely not genre: We saw that users for $k = 1$ preferred highly-rated classic movies. In this stereotype ($k = 5$), the reason is that all these movies are horror/thriller movies. Genre seems to be the main underlying cause.

The genre information in Figure 6.10 shows that "horror" is the most common genre, and when we look at the top 10 movies, we observe from their names that classical horror movies are being shown. Compare Figure 6.10 with the list following the figure.

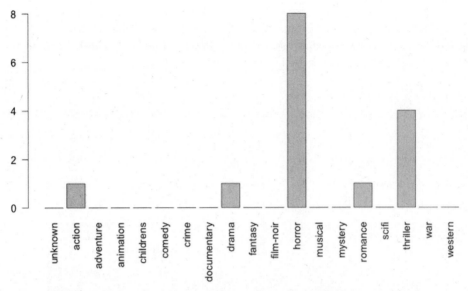

Figure 6.10: The distribution of the actual genres of the top movies for the $k = 5$ latent stereotype we learned from the data. The genre information states that "horror" is the most common genre.

The movies getting the highest weights for the $k = 5$ stereotype:

- Nightmare on Elm Street, A (1984)
- Jaws (1975)
- Silence of the Lambs, The (1991)
- Shining, The (1980)
- Psycho (1960)
- Carrie (1976)
- Cape Fear (1991)
- American Werewolf in London, An (1981)
- Omen, The (1976)
- Scream (1996)

Finally, Figure 6.11 shows that classic top-rated movies belonging to relatively old dates appear again at the stereotype $k = 8$. A closer look shows that they seem to be different than the ones in Figure 6.9. The ones with $k = 1$ are more popular classics, whereas these correspond to an artistic focus, and some can be considered in the independent movies category as well. When we look at the genres, the diversity clearly shows up. In the former the "drama" category peaked, here we have a broader spectrum of movies.

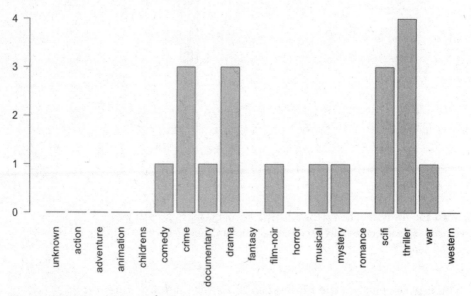

Figure 6.11: This is a plot for d_k where $k = 8$. According to movies seen at the top 10 locations in the stereotype (see the following list), we conclude that this stereotype consists of artistic and independent top-rated classic movies.

The next list shows the movies getting the highest weights for the $k = 8$ stereotype:

- Usual Suspects, The (1995)
- Brazil (1985)
- Blade Runner (1982)
- Taxi Driver (1976)
- Rear Window (1954)
- Crumb (1994)
- Pulp Fiction (1994)
- Dr. Strangelove or: How I Learned to Stop Worrying and Love the Bomb (1963)

- This Is Spinal Tap (1984)
- Reservoir Dogs (1992)

What we have learned so far is that the stereotypes represent hypothetical users with specific tastes. In this movie data set, this is sometimes highly correlated with genre; however, it is often beyond that single feature. For example, the horror movies dominate the $k = 5$ stereotype, whereas $k = 1$ is dominated by overall highly-rated movies. The former is purely about genre, whereas the latter represents users consistently watching high-rated movies all with different genres. User behavior expresses itself in the stereotypes, and it's not always obvious if there's a single axis along which these stereotypes could be delineated. One important aspect is the resolution of the information extracted. The level of detail depends on the number K. For example, at $K = 100$, we would extract more detailed stereotypes and could potentially discover subgenres within genres. This parameter is set by us, depending on the use case, capacity, and more. The higher the number, the harder it is to analyze and interpret the learned stereotypes, besides the added complexity of the model.

Exploratory Analysis

An important use of the model is to perform exploratory analyses of the user base. This is critical for reasons such as optimal product design, growth strategies, and marketing and sales strategies. The social media platform needs to be managed, and critical decisions should be made based on data, particularly user data. For example, in a movie broadcasting system knowing which user type is interested in which movie type can provide a lot of information that may be useful for expanding the movie library. If a certain age and gender is more interested in certain latent stereotypes, marketing can perform better targeting.

For this purpose, we can also analyze third-party covariates of users such as age, gender, and occupation. This is additional data for us to help interpret the model—however, very importantly, keep in mind that we did not use this data while fitting the model. During model fitting we just used the interaction/ rating data in our MovieLens example. The main principle is to split the variables learned within the model to different segments based on the additional covariate data. Specifically, we look at the factor scores **S**. In the code this corresponds to `m@fit@W` in the data structure. The NMF R package we use provides a data structure as output in which `W` represents the factor scores **S**. Recall that $\mathbf{S} \in R^{NxK}$ and $\mathbf{D} \in R^{KxP}$. Rows of **D** correspond to learned stereotypes where each is defined as the weights over the items/movies. Rows of **S** correspond to the characteristics of each user for their weights over the latent stereotypes, which can be interpreted as their representations/preferences in the new stereotype space. So, **D** corresponds to the new space we learned from the data, and **S** corresponds to the representation of this data in this new space **D**.

For each stereotype k, we take the factor scores, representing the weights each user has for the stereotype k, and plot them in the following paragraphs, splitting by gender, age, and occupation, similarly to:

```
qplot(users$gender, m@fit@W[, 5], ylim=c(0, 50))
```

Factor scores represent how much each user is represented using the stereotype. For example, for documentary movies this corresponds to checking each user's weight on documentary movies. This would give us some idea if any segmentation peaks in a certain latent stereotype.

For example, Figure 6.12 shows the factor scores corresponding to $k = 1$ split by gender, age, and by occupations such as engineer, teacher, and so on. In more detail, we plot this figure as follows: Each user i has a weight s_{ik} corresponding to the kth stereotype. The same user also has gender g_i, age a_i, as well as occupation o_i. In each plot we visualize these user weights versus the corresponding user covariates. From Figure 6.9, recall that the first stereotype ($k = 1$) consists of highly-rated classic movies. When we look at the factor scores for this stereotype, we observe that male gender users get slightly higher weights. In terms of age, we observe that generally the adult population is interested in these movies.

Figure 6.13 shows the $k = 5$ stereotype, which prefers to watch movies in the "horror" genre, as shown in Figure 6.10. Similarly to $k = 1$, we observe that the male gender has higher weights than the female gender. An important observation is the age distribution. There is a clear skew toward the young population in horror movies. This is clearly different from the one in Figure 6.12, which corresponds to generic classics of the cinema. This shows that young users tend to have a higher share from the $k = 5$ stereotype. We also observe a non-uniform occupation split. The "student" occupation clearly stands out from the rest, whereas adult jobs such as doctor have minimal share in this stereotype.

In Figure 6.14, which corresponds to independent artistic movies for the 80s and 90s, we observe that there are two bumps in the age distribution. One in young adults who are between 20–30 and the other is between 45–60. This is an interesting observation because we can hypothesize that people between the age 30 and 45 are likely to have kids and have little time to watch their ideal movies—probably movies entertaining their kids is preferable at this time. In terms of occupation, we observe that writers, librarians, educators, and artists seem to have higher weight here.

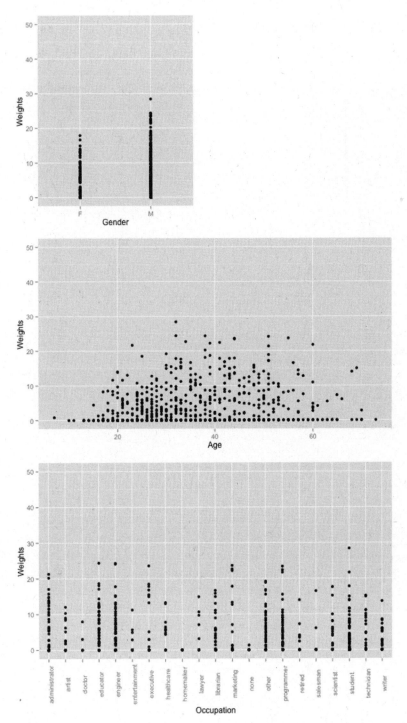

Figure 6.12: Here we plot the factor scores. Every user is represented by a point in the figures, and we mapped users by their ages, genders, and occupations. This is shown for the stereotype $k = 1$. Recall from Figure 6.9 that this stereotype prefers classic movies. We observe a slight bias towards adults and males. We do not observe any specific bias for occupation.

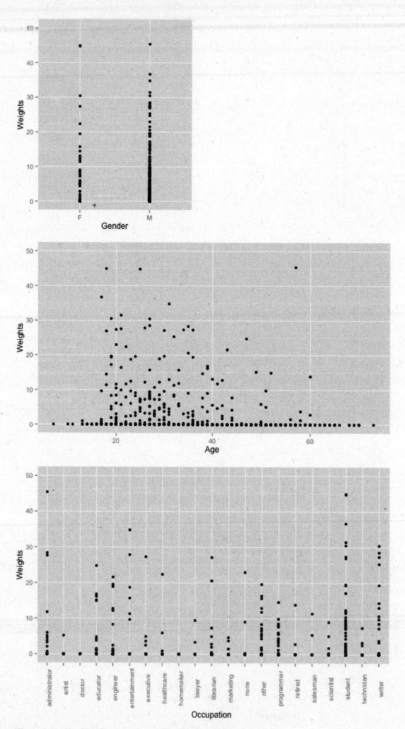

Figure 6.13: The factor scores for the $k = 5$ stereotype

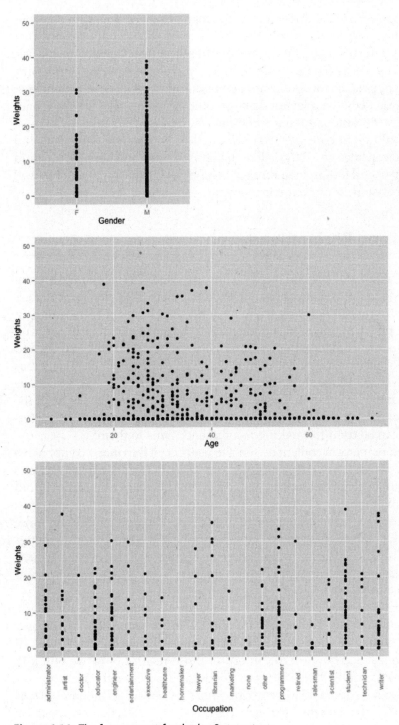

Figure 6.14: The factor scores for the $k = 8$ stereotype

In summary, we looked at three stereotypes for three cases. The main outcome, which might be relevant to not only this movie rating dataset but also to other social media platforms, is that users have different characteristics and tastes, with different use cases. These are often highly correlated with demographics. Sometimes, gender is the most relevant demographic explaining user behavior; sometimes age is the most relevant demographic explaining it; and sometimes it is occupation, and most often a combination of these. The take-away message here should be to consider user satisfaction in different segments and particularly to consider an analysis like the one we provided here. This would be particularly useful for targeted innovation and design for the product as well as content expansion strategy, if it is relevant.

Prediction and Recommendation

In many components of a social media platform, users interact with different kinds of items. Examples as mentioned in this chapter include movie broadcasting, listening to music, shopping for items, and searching for restaurants. In all these examples, a main product problem is to recommend to users new and novel items. In movie broadcasting systems it is to recommend new movies, and in online radio systems it is to recommend playlists, artists, or songs, whereas in shopping systems it is to recommend new items to purchase. The results we used before for exploratory purposes can be also directly incorporated in the product to make it smarter. In this section our goal is to predict users' preferences, which can be used for making recommendations to them.

Surfacing more relevant content or items to users is vital in many components of a social media platform. For example, providing better friend suggestions makes users follow more accounts, and their timelines are almost never out of content, which most probably results in users with higher retention rates. Providing better movie recommendations makes people watch more and more movies and causes users to spend more time on the platform. Providing better shopping items makes users purchase more, resulting in more revenue. Hence, having recommendations that are of high quality is an indispensable part of most any social media platform.

So far, we have studied some topics from the *learning* stage of the paradigm. This corresponded to how we learn the latent stereotypes representing the user behavior and characteristics, given the engagement/interaction history of all users. We also learned how we can interpret those results. Now we will talk about how we recommend new items to existing, as well as new users.

In the scenario we looked at in the previous section, recommending items to existing users is trivial when the matrices $\mathbf{S}$ and $\mathbf{D}$ are learned. Suppose we want to recommend movies to the ith user. The only thing we need to do is to get the *i*th row of **S**, which corresponds to its factor scores, the embedding or mapping of the *i*th user in the new user stereotype space **D**. We then need to multiply it with the matrix **D** to map it back to the original item space. This is shown in the equation below:

$$\hat{\mathbf{x}}_i = \mathbf{s}_i \mathbf{D} \tag{6.4}$$

where the row vector $\hat{\mathbf{x}}_i \in R^{1 \times P}$ and the row vector $\mathbf{s}_i \in R^{1 \times K}$.

Recommending items to a new user is trickier. Suppose a new user joins the platform and watches a movie, for example, "The Terminator." Our *learn, map, recommend* cycle suggests that with this one piece of information we need to map the user to the new space using the *learned* stereotypes **D** and find its corresponding factor scores $\mathbf{s}_i$ and then map back to the movie space—which is the final *recommendation* phase. Listing 6.3 shows an example of this procedure and the top 10 recommendations as the result, and Figure 6.15 shows the estimations for the new user's factor scores.

Listing 6.3: Assuming that a new user watches a particular movie, what other movies can we give as further recommendations? (`movie_prediction.R`)

```
# Generate an empty user
me = numeric(1682)


# The movies 195 and 96 are the items including the search string
# "Terminator".
grep('Terminator', items$title)
195 96


# Here we give the highest possible rating of 5 to movies relevant to
# "Terminator".
# This is just for experimental purposes in this example. One can rate
# any other movie this way with different ratings.
me[195] = 5
me[96] = 5


# Get the factor scores of the user. m is a NMFfit data structure we
# calculated earlier. To reach sub components we need to use @ symbol.
# We find the factor scores for the user who rated Terminators with
# 5 stars.
# This is the mapping stage. fit@H corresponds to matrix D in our
# notation in the book.
# my.factors corresponds to s_i in our notation.
my.factors = me %*% t(m@fit@H)


# Plot the factors according to the stereotypes.
barplot(my.factors)


# With the given factor score, we estimate the entire item scores for
# the user.
```

```
# This is the inverse transform stage. We map back to the movie space
my.prediction = my.factors %*% m@fit@H

# Order the predictions and get the top 10.
items$title[order(my.prediction, decreasing=T)[1 : 10]]
```

```
[1] "Raiders of the Lost Ark (1981)"    "Empire Strikes Back, The (1980)"
[3] "Star Wars (1977)"                   "Terminator 2: Judgment Day (1991)"
[5] "Fugitive, The (1993)"               "Terminator, The (1984)"
[7] "Braveheart (1995)"                  "Return of the Jedi (1983)"
[9] "Pulp Fiction (1994)"                "Indiana Jones and the Last
                                          Crusade (1989)"
```

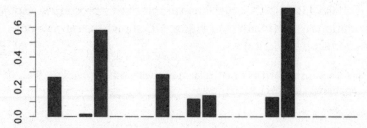

Figure 6.15: Factor scores of a new user after watching and highly rating two movies in the Terminator series. This is a representation of the new user in the latent stereotype space.

Similarly, if we assume that the first two movies that a new user watches are "Psycho" and the "Silence of the Lambs", respectively, Listing 6.4 shows the recommendations as a result. We observe that a similar genre dominates as we had for the first two movies watched. In a real product the movies already watched can be filtered out from the predictions, naturally.

Listing 6.4: The recommendations for a different set of initial movies.

```
# Applying the same principle as above (we gave high ratings to
# movies such as "Psycho" and "Silence of the Lambs"). The
# recommendations based on these choices are given below.
```

```
[1] "Silence of the Lambs, The (1991)"    "Pulp Fiction (1994)"
[3] "Raiders of the Lost Ark (1981)"      "Jaws (1975)"
[5] "Psycho (1960)"                       "Star Wars (1977)"
[7] "One Flew Over the Cuckoo's Nest (1975)"  "Schindler's List (1993)"
[9] "Shawshank Redemption, The (1994)"    "Godfather, The (1972)"
```

This also brings us to an interesting problem: How do we find movies similar to a given movie? In consumer products, this generally appears as "customers who purchased this item also looked at this," "movies similar to this movie," or "users similar to this user." Several methods can be considered, such as nearest neighbor based methods, supervised learning with a lot of feature engineering, and so on. Within the existing framework that we have been using, we can answer this quite easily as follows: We can assume that there is a pseudo user who has just signed up to the platform and just watched this movie. Like we did in the previous example, we can get factor scores of this user, map it back to the original space, and finally pick the top from the list. These movies can be considered as the similar movies based on the user choice—which is the fundamental idea of collaborative filtering. Indeed, the `rec.movies` function in the `mf_helpers.R` file performs these steps, which are analogous to what we saw in Listing 6.3: First, it creates a new empty user, and second, it finds the index of the movie for which we want to find similar items. Third, rating this movie with 5 stars for the pseudo user, it finds factor scores for the pseudo user that are going to determine our recommendations.

Evaluation

In any predictive modeling task we need to have certain evaluation techniques to measure how well we are doing. You can use several different metrics depending on the problem and type of the data.

The most common metric measures the root-mean-square error on hold-out data. This means that we need to hold out some portion of the interactions data—the data matrix **X**—and call the rest as the training data. Sometimes the hold-out portion is uniformly sampled from **X**; sometimes, an entire block of the matrix is used within **X**. We then fit our model based on the training data and try to predict the hold-out interactions. The root-mean-square metric shown in the equation below is often used to quantify the error between the ground truth data and the predictions for continuous variables:

$$RMSE = \sqrt{\frac{\sum_{i \in T_i} \sum_{j \in T_j} \left(x_{ij} - \hat{x}_{ij} \right)^2}{N_{ho}}}, \tag{6.5}$$

where T_i and T_j are the sets of the indexes we held out from **X**. N_{ho} is the cardinality of the hold-out set.

In many recommendation systems, the observation matrix includes real values, such as ratings. In these applications, the RMSE can be a reasonable metric. However, in some applications, the observation matrix includes only binary 1s (with 0s meaning no observations). Missing <*user, item*> values provide uncertainty about the choice of the user regarding the item: It may indicate that a user does not prefer that item, or does not know about it. Regarding the applications we mentioned in this chapter, this means that if the user did not engage with a Tweet yet, for instance, we do not know if the user will not do so later; if a user has not followed another user yet, we cannot assume this is a definite non-link. For evaluation, this makes things more complicated, because we cannot evaluate the algorithm based on how good it is at predicting 0s; 0s in the training set may not be 0 at all given the chance, the user might still be interested in this item with some probability. We can only compare against the 1s. This also means that in this binary case we cannot use the RMSE type of evaluation. (The danger of RMSE is as follows: If we use RMSE, a trivial all-1 output algorithm would give a perfect score because we must compare against only 1s.)

Instead, we should use a metric called *recall*. More specifically, this means that in such scenarios we can output M items sorted by their values in the prediction matrix, and count how many of those were interacted with by that user. Because there are no 0s in the matrix, we cannot talk about how precise our prediction is. However, recall only considers the 1s (interactions) within the top M predictions. A more precise definition of this metric for user i with parameter M is shown by the following equation:

$$R_{i,M} = \frac{\text{the number of items users } i \text{ interacts with in the top } M}{\text{total number of items user } i \text{ interacts with}}. \tag{6.6}$$

The entire system is evaluated based on the mean value of the recall over all users. The beautiful property of this metric is that it has been normalized by the total number of items the user interacts with. We will talk about this metric more in the following section with practical examples.

Overview of Methodologies

The solutions to the recommendation problem can differ from domain to domain and the stage of the problem. After a product reaches a certain maturity, most of these methods use the same principle: Reduce high-dimensional data to find patterns in the user behavior. This section covers some of the most widely used techniques other than matrix factorization, and discusses some domain specific sub-problems and the cold start problem.

Nearest Neighbor-Based Approaches

The K-nearest neighbor is a machine learning algorithm defined as finding the K most similar items to each element in a set. The similarity is based on a distance defined a priori, e.g., Manhattan distance, L_2 distance, and so on.

The way this algorithm is used in recommendation systems can differ based on the application. For example, if the problem is to find the most similar movies to an already watched movie, you can use this algorithm. The first stage includes collecting the *features*. Features are the characteristics of the movies depending on many verticals such as which users interacted with them, text-based features of reviews, signal processing features extracted from video files, etc. After collecting features, you need a similarity metric or a distance metric to compute which movies are similar to each other.

Suppose $\mathbf{f}_i \in R^P$ represents the feature vector for user i, where the components of the vector each describe a particular "property" of that user as mentioned: how frequently they return to the service, how often they use the word "great," when they signed up, and the list can go on. Let's now consider a few different ways of using distance metrics for users' feature vectors. One obvious choice is a distance metric based on the L_2 norm again, defined as

$$d_2\left(\mathbf{f}_i, \mathbf{f}_j\right) = \sqrt{\sum_{t=1}^{P}\left(f_{i,t} - f_{j,t}\right)^2}. \tag{6.7}$$

You need to look at this distance for all possible pairs of feature vectors. Considering that each takes $O(P)$ operations, the complexity of the method is $O(PN^2)$ where N is the number of users or items in the data set. This distance function overweighs the high-magnitude feature values and gives relatively low importance to small values. This is important particularly when the features have different scales. For example, if one feature's range is between 0 and 1, while another one is in between 0 and 10^6, any dissimilarity in the former will be washed out by even small relative differences in the latter. These situations should be carefully handled as explained in the "Common Issues with Features" section later in this chapter.

One important fact to consider is that each problem requires its own optimized distance function. For example, if the features are probability distributions, KL divergence—a way of measuring how dissimilar two distributions are—might be preferred as a distance. If the items are integer valued, *Manhattan distance* (also called L_1 distance) can be used. This is the sum of the absolute differences of their Cartesian coordinates:

$$d_1\left(\mathbf{f}_i, \mathbf{f}_j\right) = \sum_{t=1}^{P}\left|f_{i,t} - f_{j,t}\right|. \tag{6.8}$$

We will not go over every single possible distance metric; however, in a large system, a good strategy is to think about the features as different groups and find a distance metric for each group, and then combine difference distances on a higher level. For instance, we could consider one distance metric for interest topics, one for demographics, one for activity, and so on. If the demographics are real values, using the L_2 norm would be a good choice, if activity is sparse, using L_1 would be wise, and if the interest topics are probability distributions, then using KL divergence would be ideal. Remember that similarity in each domain might mean something else. The final task is to have another metric combining those three different distances.

Approaches Based on Supervised Learning

Supervised learning algorithms are considered in two categories based on the response type we are trying to predict:

- If the response is a real value, the problem is a regression problem.
- If the response is a binary response, it is a classification problem.

In social media applications, we might practice both. For example, friend recommendation is a binary classification problem. Content engagement prediction is also a binary classification problem in which we try to predict whether a user will engage with specific content. However, if we want to predict a movie rating, this is a regression problem because the value of the prediction can be a real value between 0 and 5.

The first step in both a regression and classification problem is feature engineering. The main principle is to collect features from both items and users, and form a large set of feature vectors as we explained in the previous section. Suppose we have a collection of N users and each user i is represented via a d-dimensional feature vector $\mathbf{f}_i \in R^d$. As this is a *supervised* learning problem, we should also collect the *responses* that we would like to learn from and predict. Every observation $\mathbf{f}_i$ should be associated with a response variable, either a real valued (for regression) or a binary variable (for classification). We denote the response variables here with y_i.

Predicting Movie Ratings with Logistic Regression

Next, we focus on how we perform the model fitting if we have a labeled data set $\{\mathbf{f}_i, y_i\}_{i=1}^N$. In this section, we consider a classification problem and work with the very simple *logistic regression* model using the MovieLens data set as an example. We will try to predict which users are likely to watch the "Terminator" movies. We are going to use the user demographic data as features such as age, gender, and occupation.

Logistic regression is a learning algorithm for predicting the probability of a sample having a specific label (say, "1"), given a feature vector $\mathbf{f}_i$. This is denoted via the notation $P(y_i = 1 | \mathbf{f}_i)$. The model, a mathematical function mapping the feature vector to these probabilities, is given via the following equation:

$$P(y_i = 1| \mathbf{f}_i) = \frac{1}{1 + e^{-\mathbf{w}^T \mathbf{f}_i}}, \tag{6.9}$$

where $\mathbf{f}_i$ represents the features and $\mathbf{w}$ represents the weights or coefficients of the model that we'll learn from data. If the features are all in the same range and are comparable, the magnitude of the weights $\mathbf{w}$ can tell us about the importance of the corresponding variable in the classification. If they are not coming from the same family, we cannot easily conclude this and we need to standardize the features first. The type of the standardization would be different for each type of distribution of the features. If we encounter skewness or multimodality among the features, we also need to fix these in a similar way (see the "Common Issues with Features" section next).

The logistic function $h(x) = \dfrac{1}{1+e^{-x}}$ is a special function taking an input $x \in R$ and returning a number between 0 and 1. Considering that we want to model a probability (meaning that we need to return something between 0 and 1) and our input is a real valued $\mathbf{w}^{\mathrm{T}}\mathbf{f}_i$, this transformation function seems to be a perfect fit. Another reason for using the logistic function is that we want to model the log-probability of a class with a linear function, and the logit arises because the probabilities sum to 1.

Model training—fitting to find $\mathbf{w}$ using historical data—is performed by a procedure called maximum likelihood estimation. We will not go into the details of this here; however, model fitting corresponds to iteratively finding $\mathbf{w}$ best explaining the observations $\{y_i\}_{i=1}^{N}$. Regularization is often critical in this procedure as well. Both L_1 and L_2 regularization can be applied. (We explained L_1 and L_2 regularization in the "Regularizing in Matrix Factorization" section earlier in this chapter. These are the same metrics.)

In the R code example shown in Listing 6.5, we use the `glment` package to fit the model. This obviously only shows the last step of the fitting procedure; before that, we have to prepare the feature matrix and the label vectors. Since this is a slightly more lengthy process, the reader is welcome to follow the full code example in `train_model.R`. `glmnet` uses a procedure in which we can decide how much regularization will be performed based on either the L_1 or the L_2 distance metric. This is controlled via a parameter called α, being in the interval [0; 1]. The regularization in this case is defined as

$$(1-\alpha)\| \mathbf{w} \|_2^2 + \alpha \| \mathbf{w} \|_1, \tag{6.10}$$

where $\alpha = 1$ is the L_1 regularization, which is also called the *lasso penalty* in regression, and $\alpha = 0$ is the L_2 regularization, which is also called the *ridge penalty*. Any value in between is a mix of these two penalties. If lasso is given a high weight, then a sparser $\mathbf{w}$ is picked, meaning that only a few items of $\mathbf{w}$ are non-zero.

Listing 6.5: The model fitting part of the logistic regression. We omitted the feature and label preparation part. (`train_model.R`)

```
# We first need to prepare the training features into features_train,
# and the training labels into label_train.

# Here we fit the model. We provide features and labels.
# family='binomial' means that this is a classification problem.
fit = glmnet(as.matrix(features_train), as.matrix(label_train),
        family='binomial', alpha=1)
```

In train_model_R, we first load the user demographics. This data will be used as features. Then we get the user–movie ratings data, find the movies corresponding to the "Terminator," and pick users who watched and rated at least one movie with a 4 or 5 rating. We want to predict users who are likely to be interested in movies with high ratings. Those labels come from the aforementioned user–movie rating data.

The raw demographics data should be modified as features before normalization. Age can be directly used, but the non-numeric gender should be converted to binary labels as 0 and 1 for the two genders. The occupation data has 21 unique elements. This means that we need to generate 21 different binary features, each corresponding to a separate occupation, and only one of them will be non-zero for each user. For example, if a user is a teacher, the "teacher" feature will have value 1, and all the other occupation features will be 0.

Next, we normalize the features. We need to normalize the features to make them comparable (see the next section for more details). For example, ages have values between 10 and 80, while other features are binary. We normalize a feature column by subtracting the mean of that column from all the feature values in that column, and divide by the variance.

During the evaluation, we perform predictions on held-out data. A useful performance metric we often check is the AUC ("area under the curve"). AUC is defined as the probability that a randomly picked positive label is weighted higher than a randomly picked negative label. This explains how well we predict. The maximum value the AUC can take is 1, and the minimum value is 0.5. The higher this value, the stronger the learned classifier is. Depending on the difficulty of predictions and how well the features correlate with the outcomes, the classifier can have AUCs in this range.

Given a sample, there are four possible ways a classifier can predict the label of a new instance:

- **True Positive (TP):** The true label of the sample is positive, and the classifier predicts positive.

- **True Negative (TN):** The true label of the sample is negative, and the classifier predicts negative.

- **False Positive (FP):** The true label of the sample is negative, but the classifier predicts positive. This is an error.

- **False Negative (FN):** The true label of the sample is positive, but the classifier predicts negative. This is an error; the classifier missed the positive label.

For a given data point, the learned classifier outputs a predicted score $P\left(y_i = 1 \mid \mathbf{f}_i\right) = \dfrac{1}{1 + e^{-\mathbf{w}^\mathsf{T}\mathbf{f}_i}}$ between 0 and 1. In some applications getting the probabilities is good enough as an output of the classifier, whereas for others it is important to have a discrete label as the decision. Here, we explain in a typical application of how we use those scores to get a discrete prediction result. The comments apply to most of the problems, but there might be outlier cases that do not fit to these patterns.

By choosing a threshold τ, we can classify an example to be positive if the predicted probability is above the threshold, or to be negative if the score is below the threshold. Then, the question is: How to set this threshold? If the threshold is too high, the classifier is too strict and pessimistic: Only a small portion of true positives can be detected. In this case, the detection process will be probably *precise* (not always, though), but the *recall* rate will be low. Out of two types of error, we will have a low false positive rate but will have a high miss rate. However, if the threshold is low, we can retrieve most of the positive samples with probably many false positives as well. In this case we will not be precise, but we will have a high recall rate. Our FP rate will be high, but the miss rate will be low.

As we can guess based on these two extremes, the optimal value for τ is somewhere between 0 and 1. After a classifier is learned, we should also decide on this operating point—the actual value of the threshold τ. The main criteria for choosing this change from application to application. In mission critical applications where we clearly don't want any miss, we want to have a low threshold. In social media recommendation systems, users with a high engagement rate might be considered for such a choice: Their engagement volume is high generally, and for user satisfaction these types of users should be provided with a high volume of quality content. This means that we should not miss their relevant content. False positives might be tolerable in this case.

In applications where precision is important, we want to have a high threshold. Real-life examples in social media recommendation systems can be content suggestion for new users or for users about to churn. Any content recommendation for them is critical and we want those recommendations to be very precise and highly relevant. Missing content might be okay, but a FP is not tolerable in this scenario. An irrelevant recommendation for these users might result in churn.

In the spectrum of possible values for τ, there is a separate operating point for each use case. At each of these operating points, we have separate *precision–recall values*. These are defined as follows:

$$\text{Precision} = \frac{\text{Number of true positives } (= \text{TP})}{\text{Number of positively redictęd samples } (= \text{TP} + \text{FP})}. \quad (6.11)$$

$$\text{Recall} = \frac{\text{Number of true positives } (= \text{TP})}{\text{Total number of positives } (= \text{TP} + \text{FN})}. \quad (6.12)$$

We also normally plot standard graphs to evaluate the quality of the predictions. One of them is the precision-recall curve, in which precision is shown vs. recall as we continuously change the decision threshold. The other plot is the Receiver Operator Characteristics (ROC) curve. This is one where the true positive rate is plotted against the false positive rate. This curve explains how much we gain in the true positive rate as we start making more false positives. The area under an ROC curve is equal to AUC (that's why it was called as such). In both the precision-recall and the ROC curves, the bigger the area under the curve, the better the prediction power of the classifier is.

Next, we evaluate the classifier we just fit on the MovieLens data set. The procedure is the same for any other type of data. The `glmnet` package by default fits 100 different models with different regularization parameters λ (higher values of λ mean stronger penalties for large coefficients). First, we check the AUC values for those, and we pick one to diagnose further. Visualization is always good to evaluate how our classifier works.

Second, we plot the densities of the predicted probabilities for the held-out data set, as shown in Figure 6.16. Here we split the data into two: The distribution of P over positive examples is painted light gray, and its distribution over negative examples is painted dark gray. A "perfect" classifier would always give $P = 1$ for positives, and would always give $P = 0$ for negatives. The threshold hard-classifying the predictions would be a vertical line in this plot: Any dashed line area to the right of such a vertical line would be a TP, any dashed line on the left would be a FN, any solid line on the right would be a FP, and any solid line on the left would be a TN.

The ROC curve is shown in Figure 6.17 and the precision-recall curve is shown in Figure 6.18. As the precision-recall curve shows, there is always a trade-off between precision and recall. The higher the precision, the lower the recall, and vice versa. The optimal operating point depends on the application as we mentioned. For example, in certain applications we can require certain requirements such as a 0.95 precision and a 0.8 recall. In this case, we locate the appropriate point belonging to these constraints. This might be only precision, only recall, or both. There might be situations in which there is no operating point satisfying both constraints, so to provide a certain precision, it is impossible to provide the requested recall. In that case, the developer needs to either improve the machine learning algorithm, or find better features to boost the predictive power. The higher the predictive power, the less trade-off we have to make between precision and recall.

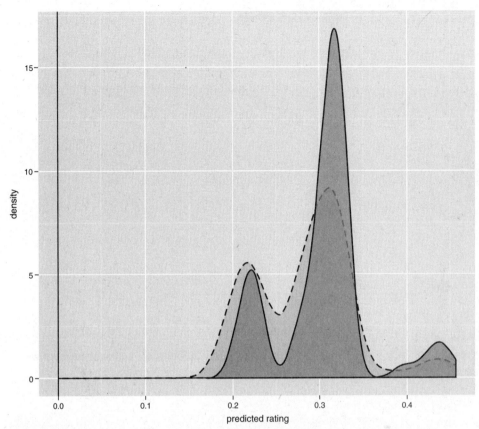

Figure 6.16: The densities of the predicted probabilities P. The held-out data are first split into two: Positive examples, and negative examples. The distribution of the predicted probabilities is plotted here separately for the two groups: For positives (dashed line) and for negatives (solid line). The more separable the two hills, the better.

In this particular example, for clarity, we chose a simple classifier with a small number of features—so it's not too surprising that its performance is on the lower end. An AUC of around 0.6 can certainly be improved by adding more features or considering other models.

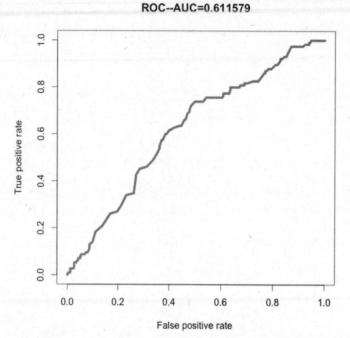

Figure 6.17: Receiver operating characteristics (ROC) curve. This curve explains how much we gain in the true positive rate as we start making more false positive errors.

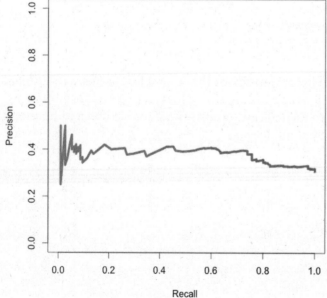

Figure 6.18: Precision-recall curve. This curve explains the trade-off we make between precision and recall and helps determine the classifier threshold, the operating point.

In Listing 6.6, after specifying which model we will use by looking at the AUC values (the one indexed 11), we would like to also interpret the learned model weights. This we print by `fit$beta[, 11]`. As shown in this code, the `gender` and `age` features have negative weights: This means that low age and being male correlates with a preference for the movie "Terminator." When we look at the occupation feature, we see that certain occupations have 0 weights, meaning that there is no bias in any direction for those occupations. However, `occupation.1` (technician) and `occupation.11` (programmer) positively correlate with a preference for the movie, whereas `occupation.8` (educator) correlates very slightly negatively with it.

Listing 6.6: Calculating the performance of the model predictions, and interpreting the model coefficients. (`evaluation.R`)

```
pfit = predict(fit, newx=features_test, type='response')

# Print the AUC values for the 100 different models that glmnet creates.
sample_count = 1000000
for(i in 1 : 100){
    predictions = pfit[, i]
    print(i)
    predicted_values = predictions
    AUC_val = mean(
            sample(predicted_values[which(label_test == 1)],
                        sample_count, replace=TRUE) >
                sample(predicted_values[which(label_test == 0)],
                        sample_count, replace=TRUE))
    print(AUC_val)
}

# Pick one model with a lambda parameter.
predicted_values = pfit[, 11]

# Interpretation of the model weights.
fit$beta[, 11]

# This prints the model coefficients.
#             age           gender  occupation.1   occupation.2  occupation.3
#   -0.085708632   -0.217505006    0.072805243    0.000000000    0.000000000
#
#   occupation.4   occupation.5   occupation.6   occupation.7   occupation.8
#    0.000000000    0.000000000    0.000000000    0.000000000   -0.002271373
#
#   occupation.9  occupation.10  occupation.11  occupation.12  occupation.13
#    0.000000000    0.000000000    0.146183185    0.000000000    0.000000000
#
#   occupation.14 occupation.15  occupation.16  occupation.17  occupation.18
#    0.000000000    0.000000000    0.000000000    0.000000000    0.000000000
#
#   occupation.19 occupation.20
#    0.000000000    0.000000000
```

```
unique_occupation[1]
[1] 'technician'
unique_occupation[8]
[1] 'educator'
unique_occupation[11]
[1] 'programmer'

# Plot the predicted probability densities separated by label values.
qplot(predicted_values, fill=factor(label_test),
               xlab='Predicted label probability', ylab='Density',
               alpha=I(0.5), geom='Density') +
        opts(legend.position='none')

# Plot the precision-recall curve.
pred = prediction(predicted_values, label_test)
perf = performance(pred, 'prec', 'rec')
plot(perf, col='red', xlim=c(0,1), ylim=c(0,1),
        main='Precision-recall', pch=26, lwd=5, cex=10.8)

# Plot the ROC curve.
perf = performance(pred, 'tpr', 'fpr')
plot(perf, col='red', xlim=c(0,1), ylim=c(0,1),
        main="ROC--AUC", pch=26, lwd=5, cex=10.8)
```

Common Issues with Features

This section covers a few common feature problems:

- **Different range problem:** This is the problem mentioned in the example in the previous section. When one feature is in the range $[a; b]$, and another is in $[a; 10^8 \times b]$, for instance, clearly we have an issue with comparability. All items go into the same distance functions and add up to the same common aggregate distance. However, one contributes little, whereas the other contributes significantly more. This works in favor of the latter, and if we continue our algorithm and analysis this way, we will probably find similar users based on the second feature only. Essentially, the first feature will be omitted.

  One solution to this problem is feature standardization. This means that we should map all the features to the same standard distribution, having for instance a 0 mean and unit variance. The way to do this is to simply take the empirical mean and variance, and then subtract the mean from all the features and divide this by the empirical standard deviation. This ensures that the first moments (mean) and the second moments (variance) of the features are the same for all features. However, this is not enough to ensure that the two features have the same population density at feature values as discussed in the next point.

- **Skewness problem:** One of the most common problems in feature extraction is skewness. Suppose we want to use the number of followers of a user or the number of total impressions/engagements a user got in the past month. When we look at the distributions of these types of features, most of the time they follow long-tailed power laws, as we have seen in Chapters 1 and 2, for instance. Practically, this means that a few people are followed by millions of people, so they have a high number of followers, whereas millions of people are followed by only a few people, so they have a low number of followers. In these situations, even standardization will not be enough, because it punishes users with a low number of followers, by making their weights insignificant in comparison to highly-followed users. The solution is *feature transformation*. Particularly in power-law distributions, a simple *log transformation* can help achieve what we want. For example, a feature with log-normal distribution might fall into this category. Log-normal distributions are continuous probability distributions of a variable whose log transformation is normally distributed. This means that we need to take the *logarithm* of the number of followers and then maybe apply the standardization. In this case, the high number and low number of followers will still be distinguished, and neither will be totally discarded.

- **Multimodal features problem:** Often features have a distribution with multiple modes. This means that we can cluster the users according to these features. This causes a lot of problems particularly when supervised techniques are applied. The idea is that the feature can be modeled using discrete buckets. For example, suppose we use the age of the users as a feature. We might want to discretize this value into groups such as teenagers, young adults, mature adults, and senior people.

Domain-Specific Applications

So far, we have explained generic methods applicable to generic data in social media. Several different applications require their own curation or optimization to these generic methods. This section discusses two of these optimizations:

- **Content-based recommendations:** In many applications the content recommended might carry its own raw signals. In a video, this includes a stream of images jointly with voice or music presented to the user. In a music recommendation, this includes the sound signals with different mixtures of instruments. In each of these problems, low-level signal processing can be performed to boost recommendations. Particularly, when the item is new to the system, no users have previously interacted with this yet. In this scenario any recommendation we can perform using just the raw content signal is vital.

For example, if one user likes watching movies including outdoor scenes, probably the matrix factorization-based collaborative filtering will learn this. However, when a new outdoor movie has been added to the library and no user has watched it yet, the only way we can perform a recommendation is by using solely content-based signals as features. Obviously, the same principle may apply to social media services with new content as well—if a new user posts a new Tweet, for instance, we can go by very little but the text of the content, to make recommendations to existing (or the new) users about this content.

- **Crowdsourcing:** As crowdsourcing platforms developed, it became popular to improve recommendation systems using human computation. Examples might include human-curated timelines, music playlists, news digests, and so on. This can be performed in two ways: 1) A set of experts designs those lists/digests; and 2) lists/recommendations are generated by algorithms but voted on by the "crowd" to improve accuracy.

The first approach does not scale, so personalization is almost impossible. However, experts, human editors work on these kinds of systems so that the quality of the most visible content is kept high. Traditional TV, radio broadcasts, and newspapers work based on this principle.

The second approach is more scalable. Generally, crowdsourcing websites or internal crowdsourcing platforms can be used. Another way is to use the platform itself. We can present such lists/recommendations to a proportion of the users (let's say 1% of them), and based on the outcomes of these "experiments," the appropriate content may be chosen to be ranked higher for general consumption. One important thing to do here in particular if crowdsourcing websites are used is to be mindful about the presence of outliers. One typical way to do that is to provide bad or randomly chosen lists/recommendations from time to time to the workers in the crowdsourcing platform. The goal of this is to check the validity of the workers. In these scenarios, we will know the answer beforehand and can eliminate those workers whose quality of work is subpar or who represent an outlier. With crowdsourcing-based recommendations, one significant problem is still the scaling of the majority of the recommendations, but at least it is feasible to evaluate the stereotypes and our learning algorithms.

Summary

In this chapter we considered some selected topics for modeling item selection preferences of users in social media services. Most of the time, users and their interactions with content on the service can be formulated as an assignment or relationship between them; as a result, we could translate the problem to describing users in low-dimensional spaces. This transformation also allowed us to discover latent features about user preferences.

Moreover, these models can also be used to make predictions about what users like, and these in turn can be presented in the form of recommendations. To perform the prediction task, there is a multitude of methods available; we considered an extension of the matrix factorization we used to uncover latent preferences, and logistic regression. These methods operate on known features of the users or items we're working with. If these features are generated from data describing user behavior in social media, we have to be aware that the usual transformations and distance metrics applied to feature vectors have to be carefully chosen so that we properly account for the skewed distributions present in these features.

Conclusions

In the preceding six chapters of the book, you looked at various aspects of social media systems by analyzing data collected from these services. To put it another a way, social media enables you to see how people interact with each other, how they consume and produce content, and what kinds of connections they form with others while doing so. Social media is only the vehicle by which you can observe all these activity patterns. Before the advent of social media, it is likely that people were interacting with each other and their environment in similar ways as they are doing now with the help of an online service. The goal of this chapter is to briefly recap what you have learned about such observations because the commonalities will probably be applicable to any social media system that revolves around human users and relies on their activities.

The Surprising Stability of Human Interaction Patterns

Now review the main characteristics of social media services and human behavior that you have learned in this book.

- **Activity patterns:** In Chapter 1 you learned that the number of times individual users engage in some kind of an activity is usually governed by a long-tailed (power-law) distribution. Many users are active just a few times during a given period, whereas a few of them are active an unexpectedly large number of times. The number of such highly active users is small, but not as small as conventional wisdom might suggest: There are enough users on the far end of the activity spectrum so that they meaningfully influence the average or aggregate metrics that we can generally measure. There is no "average user behavior" as such because if we were to ignore these highly active users, all our expected averages would drop significantly.

- **Periods of observation:** You have also seen that no matter how long you collect data, the distribution of the number of users with a certain number of activities is largely unchanged, except for having larger and larger cutoff values for longer observation windows. This somewhat simplifies how we can reason about our user population: We can assume that there are big variances among their activity levels, but no matter whether we look at daily or monthly periods, for instance, we'll find similar compositions of users in terms of their numbers of engagements. Again, the maximums in the distributions will be dependent on the length of the period, but otherwise we'll see the long-tail behavior on any reasonable time scale.

- **Social networks:** With social media, the social networks that people form to stay in touch and express any kind of a relationship with others are also similar to each other from one service to another. These social networks normally take the shape of *scale-free networks*, which are networks where, in most cases, the number of connections a user has also follows a power-law distribution. Similar to how users who have a surprisingly large number of interactions with either the content on the services or one another, there are people who create a surprisingly large number of connections as well. If you're interested in only exploiting or analyzing this pattern of connection creation, how you can think of the problem is similar to what you have to do with the activity distribution. Most of the connections belong to only a small percentage of the users, and most users have only a small number of connections. Because social networks usually change slower over time than users' engagement patterns, you can take snapshots of the network over time and still observe similar degree distributions.

- **The timing of users' events:** Individual users don't undertake their activities at a uniform rate. You have seen that the way they attend to content is highly bursty; in other words when they do something, they do a lot of it and then go dormant for some amount of time. Of course, over a longer term they can still be characterized by an average interaction rate, but if you consider shorter time windows, users appear to be either active or not active. How we described this bursty phenomenon is that this process has *memory*: When users are active, they stay active for some while, and when they were inactive previously, they have a higher likelihood to stay inactive as well. If you measure the distribution of time between two events a randomly chosen user has, you again see a power-law distribution in the aggregate, which was different from the one you could expect from a memoryless Poisson model. You also observed a similar long tail for the interevent times between activities related to content.

- **Working with social media-generated data:** You face at least two main challenges when you want to process data that originates from social media systems: One is the generally large amount of raw data (attributable to the easy way with which these interactions can be recorded); and the other one is the presence of large variances in the per-user or per-content distributions that characterize these datasets. These call for unique approaches that emphasize execution time while making reasonable compromises for the accuracy of the results, as shown with the large-scale algorithms in Chapter 5. These give good approximations to questions involving the calculations of different metrics when you expect only a "good-enough" answer. This is the case many times with social media as both the data collection process and the human behavior that is captured by the collected data may be noisy to varying degrees.

- **The use cases for social media data:** The application areas of data collected from online services are so numerous that it would be hard to list them all. Chapter 6 gives an example for a particular use case, where we assumed that users come with certain preferences to our service, and our goal was to recommend content to them that they may find appealing. The presence of particular regularities and processing methodologies covered in Chapters 1 to 5, however, hopefully provide some insights into what issues you can anticipate in practice and what pitfalls you can avoid while working with these kinds of datasets. Again, in practice there are many ways in which this kind of data can be used and analyzed further, and the best practices and methodologies of the particular field or industry dictate what tools and techniques are best suited to be used for this process.

It appears, after all, that much of the statistical distributions describing human-induced events and their effects on content creation and consumption can be characterized as *fat tailed*. In other words, they decay more slowly than an exponential distribution for high values. Power laws fit well in many cases (at least the tail ends), and that is the reason we used them as generalizations of social media behavior. In practice, especially in a setting where we have a concrete social media system and we would like to predict future trends accurately, deviations from this simple model matter, but for a general understanding and for developing intuitions about overall online behavior, it's enough to focus on the generalities and to take the simplest most viable model that explains our observations.

The next sections highlight a couple of topics that showcase common issues or explain some of the observations covered throughout this book from a slightly more theoretical perspective; in particular, how to understand the effects of sampling from finite-sized datasets, and how to detect and remove outliers in social media data. We present them here because they should be generally applicable while working with most of the datasets presented in this book, and also other datasets collected from social media services.

Averages, Standard Deviations, and Sampling

A consequence of the long-tailed user activities we uncovered in Chapter 1 is that taking averages over long-tailed distributions gets a little problematic. In most cases, when we study our users or compare the behaviors of two different user segments, we routinely characterize them with the average number of activities per user, for instance. Imagine that we're performing an A/B testing experiment, where we try to decide if version A or version B of a new feature is liked more by the users. In other words, do we see higher activity in version A, or version B? We need to compare the activity levels of the two groups of users to each other. The statistical metric we choose for this is usually most simply the average number of actions that a user took. It is, however, frequently the situation that while performing such a comparison, we find that even the random (or intentional) inclusion of a few active users can bias the averages greatly. This should be no surprise, however, seeing how skewed the activity distribution is and how much only a few users are responsible for most of the actions on the service (see Figure 1.12 in Chapter 1).

How bad is this effect? To illustrate this, Table 7.1 shows the average edit counts for Wikipedia for two cases: for the original dataset (the first row), and with some of the most active users removed. Apparently, by removing only a very small fraction of the users from the top, the value of the mean will change considerably.

Table 7.1: The Average Revision Counts after a Certain Percentage of the Most Active Users Have Been Removed

FRACTION REMOVED (%)	COUNT REMOVED	REVISION MEAN	REVISION MEAN (RELATIVE TO THE FULL DATASET)
0	0	13.67	1
0.001	3	13.13	0.96
0.01	30	10.98	0.80

FRACTION REMOVED (%)	COUNT REMOVED	REVISION MEAN	REVISION MEAN (RELATIVE TO THE FULL DATASET)
0.1	291	8.17	0.60
1	2904	3.58	0.26
5	14516	1.37	0.10

Let's assume that we would like to calculate the average activity of a selected subset of the users. In this case, if the set of users is denoted by $\{U_i\}$, their average activity is

$$\bar{a}(\{U_i\}) = \frac{\sum\limits_{u \in \{U_i\}} a_u}{\sum\limits_{u \in \{U_i\}} 1},$$

(7.1)

where the denominator is obviously the cardinality of the set, or in other words the number of users in this set. a_u is the activity of user u in the observation period. "Activity" can be any kind of user action: For Wikipedia, we considered the edits; for Twitter we took Tweets sent. We can also imagine that we can have many such random sets $\{U_i\}$ drawn from among our users, and naturally, each one of our sample set will yield a slightly different average activity $\bar{a}$ value. But how confident can we be that the $\bar{a}(\{U_i\})$ average that we calculated for one *given* sample set $\{U_i\}$ is close to the "average of the averages" that we would get if we repeated the sampling a large number of times? The reason we're asking this question is exactly because we would usually like to generalize from a small subset of users to the whole population: If the subset yielded a certain average, we'd like to think that under the same conditions the average would be the same for the whole system. We are going to check in the next few paragraphs whether this is a good assumption.

The procedure of taking samples of a finite size from a population is called— not surprisingly—*sampling*. (A *population* in this sense is the set of the subjects that we intend to describe with some aggregate measure.) The point of sampling is that we would like to learn about the value of the population statistic: In the previous example, by drawing a user sample we would like to calculate what the overall mean for the activity would be for a user if we had knowledge about everybody. If we could, we would, of course, take as many users into our sample as possible. But why is it that we intuitively think that a bigger sample size is better?

To answer this question let's assume that the mean of the population distribution is μ, and the distribution's standard deviation is σ. In this case, we can draw samples of size n from this population and calculate the means and standard deviations of these samples (which are called *sample mean* and *sample standard deviation*, respectively). Both the means and standard deviations of the samples should be close enough to those of the population, but we'd like to quantify how close they are.

Because we draw many samples and calculate the mean for each, we can think about how the sample means will follow some kind of a distribution: This is called the *sampling distribution of the sample mean*. (It's called *sampling distribution* because it's the resulting distribution for the means of the individual samples.) We can expect that if the sample size is small, we will frequently be off with the sample mean from the mean of the sampling distribution. Statistics also tells us that the sampling distribution will be a normal distribution if the sample size is large enough and that the mean of the sampling distribution of the sample mean equals the population mean as well. Also, more importantly, it tells us that the *standard deviation* of the sampling distribution of the sample mean will be $\sigma/\sqrt{n}$, where, again, σ denotes the standard deviation of the population distribution (if the samples are uncorrelated). This means that the larger our sample size (n), the more likely it will be that our sample mean is close to the actual population mean because its expected deviation from it ($\sigma/\sqrt{n}$) is going to be close to 0 if n is large.

After this, let's see how this works with an example. For this we will draw samples from a power-law distribution, simulating what would happen if we sampled users whose activities are distributed according to a similar power law. The reasons we chose to work with "simulated" data in this case are the following:

- We can use analytical calculations on exact formulas so that we can anticipate what results we should be getting.

- We're interested in the "generic" behavior of social media systems, and their metrics are most often described by power laws.

The familiar formula for these kinds of distributions is

$$P(x) = Ax^{\gamma}, \tag{7.2}$$

with an appropriate normalizing constant A for a given constant exponent γ. To simplify the example, let's also say that the random variable must be at least $x \geq 1$, therefore the normalizing constant A must be

$$\int_{x=1}^{\infty} Ax^{\gamma}dx = 1$$

$$A = -(\gamma + 1). \tag{7.3}$$

Here we had to assume that $\gamma < -1$ for the integral to be finite. Then the cumulative distribution function of our random variable X will be

$$F(x) = P(X \leq x) = \int_{z=1}^{x} -(\gamma+1)z^{\gamma}dz = -\frac{\gamma+1}{\gamma+1}\left[z^{\gamma+1}\right]_{1}^{x} = 1 - x^{\gamma+1}. \tag{7.4}$$

To draw samples from this distribution, we can utilize the method called *inverse transform sampling*. (And now we can make use of the cumulative distribution function as well that we just derived.) The inverse transform sampling works as its name suggests: If the inverse of the cumulative distribution function F is F^{-1}, and u is a uniform random number generated in the interval $[0, 1]$, then $F^{-1}(u)$ will follow the original F we want to draw examples from. This is a useful algorithm to have if we know the inverse of the cumulative distribution function. First, we need to determine the inverse of F for our power law, Equation 7.4:

$$F(x) = 1 - x^{\gamma+1} = u \Rightarrow F^{-1}(u) = F^{-1}(F(x)) = x$$

$$F^{-1}(u) = x = (1-u)^{\frac{1}{\gamma+1}}. \tag{7.5}$$

Listing 7.1 shows the inverse transform sampling procedure in R.

Listing 7.1: Sampling according to a power-law probability distribution function with exponent gamma. x will be distributed according to this.

```
sample.size = 10000
gamma = -3.5
x = (1 - runif(sample.size)) ^ (1 / (gamma + 1))
```

After running this, x will have a power-law distribution with an exponent gamma that we specified. The reason we created this sample is to see how the sample means will be distributed around the *true* mean of the population, and how disperse the sampling distribution will be. To get a sampling distribution for the sample mean, we naturally have to repeat the sampling many times over; how many times we do this is not relevant, but the more we repeat, the more accurate and smooth the sampling distribution will be.

But before we start the simulations, let's calculate what the population mean is for a power-law distribution so that we can check whether we get this back from the numerical sampling:

$$E(x) = \int_{z=1}^{\infty} z \cdot \left[-(\gamma+1)z^{\gamma} \right] dz = -\frac{\gamma+1}{\gamma+2} \left[z^{\gamma+2} \right]_{1}^{\infty} = \frac{\gamma+1}{\gamma+2}. \tag{7.6}$$

Importantly, we assumed that $\gamma < -2$, otherwise the integral would not have had a finite value. In practice, we can still observe power laws whose exponents this condition apparently does not hold for, however, these power laws always have cutoffs with large effective exponents at the top end of their ranges, so in the end their averages also stay bounded. For now, let's proceed with this condition because we would like to model the "idealized" behavior.

Furthermore, as we mentioned, the standard deviation of the sampling distribution can also be calculated as $\sigma / \sqrt{n}$, so we also need to know what the population standard deviation σ (or equivalently, the variance, σ^2) is:

$$\sigma^2 = E(x^2) - E^2(x) = \int_{z=1}^{\infty} z^2 \cdot \left[-(\gamma+1)z^{\gamma} \right] dz - \left(\frac{\gamma+1}{\gamma+2} \right)^2 = \frac{\gamma+1}{\gamma+3} - \left(\frac{\gamma+1}{\gamma+2} \right)^2. \quad (7.7)$$

Similarly to the population mean, the population variance can stay bounded only if $\gamma < -3$, otherwise the variance would be infinitely large (if we don't have a cutoff for the power law).

Now we have to see whether we can see similar values to the sampling distribution mean and standard deviation in practice from the simulations. Listing 7.2 creates a power-law distribution with $\gamma = -3.5$ (so that both conditions for the finite mean $\gamma < -2$ and finite variance $\gamma < -3$ are satisfied), and samples this distribution by drawing samples of sizes 64, 256, and 1024, respectively. We also repeat the sampling 100,000 times for each sample size so that we can get meaningful statistics for the sample means. Finally, we plot the distributions of the sample means also, which can be seen in Figure 7.1.

Listing 7.2: Creating the sampling distributions of sample means for three different sample sizes, 64, 256, and 1024, respectively. We also calculate the means and standard deviations of the sampling distributions numerically. (check_sampling_distribution.R)

```
gamma = -3.5
samples = data.frame()              # This holds the sample means.
for (sample.size in c(64, 256, 1024)) { # We take 3 different sample
                                    # sizes.
    means = c()                     # The means of the individual
                                    # samples.
    for (i in 1 : 1e5) {            # How many samples we will take.
        # Sampling from a PL distribution with the inverse transform.
        x = (1 - runif(sample.size)) ^ (1 / (gamma + 1))
        mu = mean(x)
        means = c(means, mu)        # Collect the sample means.
    }
    samples = rbind(samples,        # Accumulate all the sample
                                    # means.
            data.frame(sample.mean=means, sample.size=sample.size))
}
# Calculate the means & standard deviations of the sampling
# distributions.
sampling.distribution = ddply(samples, .(sample.size), summarise,
        mean=mean(sample.mean), sd=sd(sample.mean))

# Plot the sampling distributions & their means with vertical lines.
ggplot(samples, aes(x=sample.mean, group=sample.size)) +
        geom_density(alpha=0.3, fill='gray') +
        geom_vline(xintercept=sampling.distribution$mean) +
        xlim(c(1, 2.5)) + xlab('Sample means') + ylab('Density')
```

```
# The population standard deviation, comes from the calculations.
population.sd = sqrt((gamma + 1) / (gamma + 3) - ((gamma + 1) /
(gamma + 2)) ^ 2)

# To compare the measured and theoretical standard deviations.
sampling.distribution = within(sampling.distribution,
        { theor.sd = population.sd / sqrt(sample.size) })
```

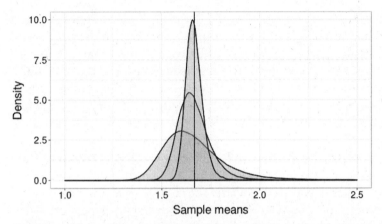

Figure 7.1: The sampling distributions of the sample means for sample size 64, 256, and 1024, respectively. The larger the sample size, the narrower the distribution. Also, the one vertical line at approximately 1.67 is actually three overlapping vertical lines, and these indicate the calculated means of the sampling distributions. According to our expectations, these should be equal to the population mean, 4/3 ≈ 1.67.

We can see from the figure that the means of the sampling distributions overlap with each other and line up with the theoretical expectation well; nevertheless, the numerical values for this and the match between the standard deviations is shown in Table 7.2.

Table 7.2: The measured means and standard deviations of the sampling distributions with varying sample sizes. The expected mean of the sampling distribution is 4/3 = 1.66…. The "SD Expectation" column is calculated using Equation 7.7, divided by the square root of the sample size, as in Listing 7.2. This column should be comparable to the "Measured Standard Deviation" column.

SAMPLE SIZE, N	SAMPLING DISTRIBUTION MEAN	MEASURED STANDARD DEVIATION	SD EXPECTATION
64	1.666955	0.17615611	0.18633900
256	1.667181	0.09047815	0.09316950
1024	1.666818	0.04726784	0.04658475

What does this mean in terms of evaluating averages for user samples? On one side, we saw that the sample means will be different from the population means, but the expected "scatter" (the standard deviation of the mean's distribution) will be smaller as we increase the sample size. However, because the standard deviation is scaled by the *square root* of the sample size only, we need to take 4 times bigger samples to decrease our expected error by one-half.

There is one more important consequence of our thought experiment from the point of view of long-tailed distributions, as commonly occurring in practice. We have seen that for us to take the mean and variance of random variables distributed according to a power law, the exponent γ of this had to be less than −2 and −3, respectively. This is, of course, when we assumed that the power-law relationship holds for *any* value of the activity counts, and that we could observe any arbitrarily large activity counts for a user. This may have been a good working assumption; in reality, our distributions are always bounded due to the finite length of our observation window or because it is humanly impossible to generate an infinitely large number of activities within any measurement period that is finite. For this reason, the power law is not always an accurate model of the underlying random process governing user behavior, and what happens in practice is that—even if the activity distribution's head is well approximated by a power law—the tail gets truncated or tapers off faster than a power law would suggest, as we already mentioned. This results in still *finite* means and variances for the population, and therefore we can measure finite averages for our samples.

There are therefore some particular consequences of the observed power-law distributions on the measured aggregate user statistics:

- As the length of the observation window grows, we expect the power-law cutoff to happen at higher and higher activity values, as Figure 1.14 suggested in Chapter 1. This way both the mean and standard deviation of the distributions will shift to the right: This is a fundamental property of measurements made over time windows with varying lengths, and we must be mindful of this when comparing aggregate statistics that were taken in time windows of different sizes.

- Often, we segment users by activity and would like to answer questions like "How has the average activity changed for users with fewer (or more) number of activities than X? " In Figure 1.14 we could immediately see the dangers and caveats of such an approach: Because the head part of the distribution is mostly unchanged, and the growth of activities happens in the tail, we will see larger relative changes for users segmented at the high end of the activity range than at the low end.

- We have seen that if the power-law exponent for the user activity distribution is approximately what we measure in practice ($\gamma = -1.87$ for

Wikipedia), then we can expect to see large standard deviations both for our samples and our hypothetical population because the $\gamma < -3$ condition does not hold. In theory, for a pure power law, the standard deviation would be infinite, but because truncation always happens, we can work with the assumption that this would still be large, though not infinite. If σ is large, then, we must be aware that the sample means will also be subject to large errors: Even a single "outlier" user in our sample may sway the average tremendously.

Removing Outliers

Assume that you want to track changes in user behavior over time as you make changes to your service, or want to compare different user cohorts to each other. In these cases, you are most often interested in looking at characteristic user activity metrics, for instance, the number of status updates that a user made on the public timeline of your service. The most obvious statistic you usually consider is the average number of activities, and how it has been changing within the scope of your comparison (over time or between user segments).

Outliers in a sample are data points that are unusually far from the "expected" behavior. How you interpret something being "unusually far" is rather subjective and in most cases is up to the analyst to determine. The underlying assumption is generally that the data follows some simple, bounded distribution, and outliers are those points that are indeed present in the data but would be assigned a low probability by this distribution. (Therefore, you wouldn't expect to see them given the sample size and assume that they're there because of some measurement error or the result of some automated mechanism, such as spammers.)

Given that you usually encounter distributions with long tails in users' metrics, you are tempted to think of the high activity users as outliers. Some of them may be outliers (such as the housekeeping robots in Wikipedia), but there can be legitimate users who are just uncannily active but are otherwise within the power-law distribution that describes the particular activity (if you don't pay attention that this may be the case, you may remove them thinking they are outliers). You're right to want to remove outliers in metrics reporting though, as the presence of these individuals will shift your averages to a large extent and therefore possibly taint your conclusions.

It's a general practice therefore to take a fixed percentage, say 5%, and remove all users whose activity metric falls in the top 5% within the full sample. But again, because even normal users may display activities that appear to be "outlying" because of the long-tail distributions that you encounter, you could be removing genuine behavior from the system even though it's exhibited by valid users. But how much do you change your aggregate statistics by removing these high activity individuals, on purpose or accidentally? Read on for the answer.

While you have seen that a lot of metrics stemming from human behavior can be described by long-tailed distributions, as a frame of reference, it will be also instructive for us to consider a more "well-behaved" distribution. The most natural choice for this is the normal distribution. The reason for this is that we're intuitively familiar in real life with this distribution: The heights of people, test scores, and measures of goods produced by machines are usually distributed according to a normal distribution. Because we're exposed to these experiences in the physical world, we're used to them and are somewhat hard-wired to think in terms of this distribution and to assume that it's reasonable to characterize these random phenomena with their (constant) averages and variances. This way of reasoning has its advantages in our everyday life because it makes it easy to simplify our abstractions to expectations of how things should be on average, and what amount of uncertainty (variance) you can anticipate them to have. When you measure actual human behavior through electronic media as you have done, you're confronted that these assumptions about normality will not hold.

Consider what happens to your aggregate metrics when you truncate the samples based on distribution quantiles. Given that the two distributions we focus on are a normal (representing our "everyday" experiences) and an approximate power law (representing human behavior on social media), in Listing 7.3 we first generate random samples with these two distributions. We consider these random samples as something that may have come from an actual measurement: The power law, for instance, would be good to describe our activity distributions (for instance, the number of posts per month per user) on a social media service. The `remove.top.values` R function in lines 21–37 first sorts the random values in ascending order, and then using the values in `thresholds` successively, it calculates both the means and standard deviations of the random samples, *omitting* the top parts of the random variable vector in lines 25–26. What we're interested in from these two examples is by how much the averages and standard deviations of the remaining items have changed, *relative* to the original means and standard deviations, respectively. These ratios are calculated in lines 32–35.

Listing 7.3: Generate two samples with 10 million random draws from a normal distribution and from a power-law distribution, respectively. Then, remove the greatest top fractions of the samples, and check how the means and standard deviations of the remaining sets change. (remove_outliers.R)

```
0 # The number of random numbers to be generated.
1 N = 10e6

2 # Generate pseudorandom numbers with a Gaussian distribution
3 # with a mean of 10, and standard deviation of 1.
4 normal.distribution = rnorm(N, mean=10, sd=1)
```

```
5 # Function to generate random variables according to a power-law
6 # in the [x0, x1] interval, and with a power-law exponent of gamma.
7 # See http://mathworld.wolfram.com/RandomNumber.html
8 generate.powerlaw.distribution = function(sample.size, x0, x1, gamma) {
9     return((((x1 ^ (gamma + 1) - x0 ^ (gamma + 1)) *
10             runif(sample.size) + x0 ^ (gamma + 1)) ^ (1 / (gamma + 1)))
11 }

12 # Generate the random numbers following a power law, between 1 and 100,
13 # and with an exponent of -3.5.
14 powerlaw.distribution = generate.powerlaw.distribution(N, 1, 100, -3.5)

15 # Function to truncate the sample by removing the largest values from
16 # the sample. The list of thresholds (between 0 and 1) is passed to
17 # this function; it then calculates the means and standard deviations
18 # of the samples that remain after removing the largest values
19 # according to these fractions (if the threshold is 0.05, the top 5%
20 # of the sample items will be removed).
21 remove.top.values = function(sample, thresholds) {
22     sample = sample[order(sample)]
23     result = data.frame(top.removed=thresholds)
24     result = ddply(result, .(top.removed), function(df) {
25             remaining = sample[1 : floor(length(sample) *
26                                         (1 - df$top.removed))]
27             return(data.frame(
28                             mean=mean(remaining),
29                             sd=sd(remaining)
30                     ))
31         })
32     result = within(result, {
33             rel.mean = mean / mean[top.removed == 0]
34             rel.sd = sd / sd[top.removed == 0]
35         })
36     return(result)
37 }

38 # Set the thresholds to be between 0 and 0.9 in 0.05 increments.
39 thresholds = seq(0, 0.9, by=0.05)
40 distribs.top.removed = data.frame()

41 # Run the "outlier" removal for the normal distribution.
42 distribs.top.removed = rbind(distribs.top.removed, data.frame(
43                 remove.top.values(normal.distribution, thresholds),
44                 distrib='Normal')
45 )

46 # Run the "outlier" removal for the power-law distribution.
47 distribs.top.removed = rbind(distribs.top.removed, data.frame(
48                 remove.top.values(powerlaw.distribution, thresholds),
49                 distrib='Power law')
50 )
```

When you look at the changes in the means, as Figure 7.2 shows, you can see two things: First, that the mean of the normal distribution is largely robust against the removal of the extreme values, and second, the means of the truncated power law decrease much faster as we keep removing the "outliers." If we did this with actual data coming from a social media system exhibiting long-tail distributions, we could expect that even a small amount of outlier removal (such as the top 5%) would change our measured averages drastically. Table 7.3 shows concisely the actual changes in the means (and standard deviations) of the truncated samples. For instance, if we removed the most active 5% of the users, we would have a measured average that is approximately 12% lower than the original average (cf. the normal distribution, whose mean decreases only by 1.1% after removing the largest 5%). This is a big difference for a small fraction of the users removed; but we have seen earlier that power laws have unstable means that are largely influenced by the top end of the distribution. The fact that the mean decreases by so much after removing the top end can be traced back to these same observations.

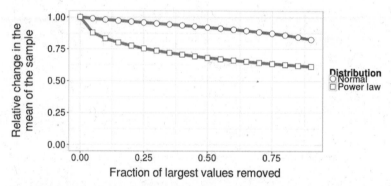

Figure 7.2: The relative change in the means of two samples, drawn from a normal and a power-law distribution, respectively. We removed 0–90% of the largest values in 5% increments. The removed fraction is shown on the x axis.

Table 7.3: The changes in the means and the standard deviations of the remaining samples, after the largest values are removed from the power-law and the normal distribution, respectively. In this example, the power law had an exponent of −3.5, and the normal distribution had a mean of 10 and a standard deviation of 1. The fractions by which the size of the original samples were truncated are shown in the top row of the table.

PERCENT REMOVED		2.5%	5%	7.5%	10%
Change in the mean	Power law	−8.6%	−12%	−15%	−17%
	Normal	−0.5%	−1.1%	−1.5%	−2.0%
Change in the SD	Power law	−54%	−64%	−69%	−73%
	Normal	−6.3%	−10%	−13%	−16%

For the preceding reasons, we must be careful when trying to "clean up" our data by removing outliers: A simple thresholding as we did before may change our important metrics more than we may anticipate. However, how did the standard deviations of the truncated samples decrease after removing the largest values? Again, intuition tells us that the normal distribution probably won't change all that much because even the largest values are not *that* far from the mean given the fast exponential decay of the tail of the distribution. In contrast, we might think that the power law will be more susceptible to changes in the standard deviation and also against the removal of the largest values. Figure 7.3 is a comparison between how much the standard deviations of the distributions change after removing their top ends. In this case, you can see that although the standard deviation of the normal distribution shrinks rather fast (faster than its mean did), the decrease for the power law is the most dramatic. According to Table 7.3, eliminating the top 5% of the distribution has decreased its standard deviation by 64%! It should therefore be obvious that most of the variance in human behavior-induced metrics as we have seen in the social media systems is caused by a few users who are incredibly active.

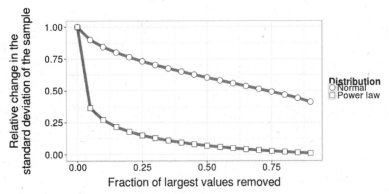

Figure 7.3: The relative change in the standard deviations of two samples, in similar setups to Figure 7.2.

Index